CHERYL L. ERIKSEN

GREYHOUND

*The Remarkable Story of the Legendary Racehorse
Who Inspired a Nation*

FOUR
IN HAND
PRESS

First published in 2025 by

FOUR-IN-HAND PRESS
an imprint of TRAFALGAR SQUARE BOOKS
The Stable Book Group
32 Court Street, Suite 2109
Brooklyn, NY 11201
www.trafalgarbooks.com

Copyright © 2025 *2025 Cheryl L. Eriksen*

All rights reserved. No part of this book may be reproduced, by any means, without written permission of the publisher, except by a reviewer quoting brief excerpts for a review in a magazine, newspaper, or website.

Disclaimer of Liability
The author and publisher shall have neither liability nor responsibility to any person or entity with respect to any loss or damage caused or alleged to be caused directly or indirectly by the information contained in this book. While the book is as accurate as the author can make it, there may be errors, omissions, and inaccuracies.

Trafalgar Square Books certifies that the content in this book was generated by a human expert on the subject, and the content was edited, fact-checked, and proofread by human publishing specialists with a lifetime of equestrian knowledge. TSB does not publish books generated by artificial intelligence (AI).

ISBN: 978-1-64601-305-0
Library of Congress Control Number: 2025013259

Book interior design by *Katarzyna Misiukanis–Celińska (https://misiukanis-artstudio.com)*
Cover design by *Iain Morris and RM Didier*
Index by *Line by Line Indexing*
Typefaces: *Source Serif Pro, Fino Sans, Playfair Display* and *Krul*

Printed in the United States of America
10 9 8 7 6 5 4 3 2 1

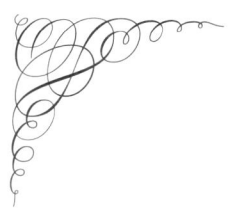
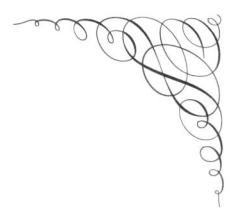

— *for* —
GREYHOUND
who gave much of himself for the joy of others

A N D

— *for* —
FARLETTA
for helping me share Greyhound with the world

This book would not have been possible
without generous backing from the following:

The Hambletonian Society
Alan Ackerman
Jay Farrar and Maggie LeClair
Judy Davis-Wilson
Neil and Shelley Wingfield
Richard G. Stone
Robert Eriksen
Ron and Louise Bower
The Sarah Keesler Family
Tom Charters
USHWA-Delaware Valley
Winbak Farm

To all of you I express my heartfelt gratitude
for your financial support, your encouragement,
and for believing in this project and in me
as the one to tell Greyhound's story.

thank you

Greyhound

Author's Note • V
Foreword by *Neil Wingfield* • IX

PART ONE

Chapter 1: **February 4, 1965** • 3

Chapter 2: **March 4, 1932** • 7

Chapter 3: **Chaos, Change, and the Birth of Almahurst Farm** • 15

Chapter 4: **Ugly Duckling** • 24

Chapter 5: **American Trotter** • 27

Chapter 6: **Hotel Baker Stables** • 37

Chapter 7: **Septer Faith Palin** • 47

PART TWO

Chapter 8: **Underdog** • 55

Chapter 9: **Finding His Stride** • 69

Chapter 10: **Unstoppable** • 81

Chapter 11: **Hambletonian** • 91

Chapter 12: **Champion** • 103

Chapter 13: **In the Shadow of the Trotting King** • 115

Chapter 14: **Gauntlet** • 127

Chapter 15: **Historic Rematch at Goshen** • 133

Chapter 16: **The Race That Never Was** • 139

Chapter 17: **Peter Manning's Crown** • 149

Chapter 18: **Horse of the Year** • 157

Chapter 19: **The King Meets the Queen** • 161

Chapter 20: **Legend** • 173

Chapter 21: **Nothing Left to Prove** • 179

Chapter 22: **Greyhound the Incomparable** • 185

Chapter 23: **The Comeback** • 193

Chapter 24: **Last Call** • 203

Chapter 25: **No Worlds Left to Conquer** • 209

PART III

Chapter 26: **The End of an Era** • 217

Chapter 27: **Dooley and the Grey Ghost** • 225

Chapter 28: **Bakers Acres** • 233

Chapter 29: **Twilight** • 241

Epilogue • 251
Acknowledgments • 261

Appendices • 263
Greyhound's 1933 Sales Catalog Page • 263
Greyhound's Full Race Record • 264
Greyhound's World Records • 267
Greyhound's Two-Minute Miles • 268
Greyhound's Measurements by John Hervey • 269

End Notes • 271
Bibliography • 293
Index • 303

AUTHOR'S NOTE

Telling Greyhound's story with a thoroughness never before attempted has been an adventure and an education. I've done my best to represent Greyhound and his people as accurately as possible. Thousands of hours of scouring old newspapers, harness horse periodicals, books, the amazing Greyhound collection at the Harness Racing Museum in Goshen, New York, materials from the United States Trotting Association in Columbus, Ohio, and from the St. Charles Historical Society in Illinois have gone into bringing this story to you.

That some ninety years have passed since the world saw Greyhound race has made this book a unique challenge as the people directly connected with Greyhound, particularly during his racing career, have long ago passed away and many of the people who knew these people, and were young when they were old, are also gone. The one exception was Jimmie Wingfield's son, Neil—thanks to Jimmie being just 20 when he started working with Greyhound and not having children until he was in his forties.

The facts and direct quotes are delivered as precisely as possible. Quotes attributed to a named person were pulled directly from printed materials used for research and are noted as such in the end notes. Quotes from unnamed persons (such as "a man," "the foaling man," "the foreman," etc.), with a couple exceptions, are from the author's imagination based on research and personal experience. There are a few scenes such as the night Greyhound was born that are constructed from the author's own experience to enable Greyhound's story to be told in a way it has never been before. This gives the reader the rare experience of "being there." These bits of "creative non-fiction" are based in fact, pulling information directly from researched sources, and are noted as such in the end notes section of this book.

Author's Note

Unless otherwise noted, reports on the weather were taken from historical records from the National Weather Service (United States) and the Canadian Weather Service.

I've done my best to bring to you the most complete and accurate biography of Greyhound possible. Through this experience I've often lamented that I came about thirty years late to this project, leaving me only with printed materials and very few people to talk to. Of course, thirty years ago I was a kid, so there's that. And thirty years ago, the release of this book couldn't be part of the 100th Hambletonian Celebration, which is significant and I'm honored to be a part of it.

Greyhound was an amazing horse and I'm grateful to have the opportunity to tell his story. I pray I've done him and his people justice. I've tried my best. I hope you love learning about Greyhound as much as I've loved researching and writing his story.

FOREWORD

At long last, Greyhound's story has been captured, from his foaling through his retirement. At a time when people needed hope in the American Dream, Greyhound's incredible rise to glory revived a sport that had struggled to exist.

Cheryl's exhaustive research weaves a tapestry around his remarkable life and all of the people who cared for and guided him throughout his career. Her writing makes you feel as if you are a part of the action.

Thank you, Cheryl, for bringing to life the story of one of the greatest trotters of all time.

Neil Wingfield
Son of Jimmie Wingfield, Greyhound's longtime groom
December 14, 2024

PART ONE

CHAPTER 1

> "The grey horse is gone and the only winners among us are those old enough to have thrilled to his exploits as he cut an all-conquering path through that otherwise bleak period in harness racing history which bridged the depths of a depression and the flickering dawn of a bright new era."
>
> JIM HARRISON,
> *HOOF BEATS*, MARCH 1965

FEBRUARY 4, 1965

Verner "Dooley" Putnam ran calloused fingers over a worn leather lead shank. Overhead, the February sky yawned crisp and blue. The temperature, a brutally cold zero degrees the morning before, had risen to forty as the afternoon sun warmed the frozen landscape. A beautiful day for early February in Illinois. A gentle breeze touched his cheek and Dooley looked up. His best friend, the greatest trotting harness horse of all time, lay under a mound of freshly turned dirt near a monument placed years before in the great horse's honor. The champion's old racing sulky leaned against the trunk of a gray, winter-dead tree. Wreaths of flowers fluttered in the unusually warm February breeze.

Leone, Dooley's wife of forty years, placed a hand on his shoulder and gave a gentle squeeze. Her tear-streaked face looked into the sorrow-reddened eyes of the man she loved. Her pain was doubly felt as she mourned not only the loss of the horse that she loved like family, but also the pain of loss and inevitable emptiness she could feel within Dooley. For almost twenty-five years he'd dedicated his life to caring for Greyhound, the great trotting champion of the world. Now, the horse was gone, Dooley and Leone left with only an empty stall and a host of memories.

Robert "Doc" Flanery wiped tears from his eyes as he stepped away from the grave and turned to face Dooley and Leone. The three stood together in silence, each knowing how the others felt, and that mere words in this moment would only fall short and flat. Greyhound had lived out his retirement at Flanery Farm. Doc had driven him in front of cheering fans at many exhibitions in the years following the grand horse's retirement from racing. They'd logged many miles together, and Doc had gotten to know and love the great gray horse as only a reinsman can, the intimate connection through the long, leather driving lines conveying a communication unlike any other.

The three turned away from the grave and slowly walked to their cars. Flanery Farm was just a short distance away. Greyhound had been buried alongside champions Volo Song and Winnipeg with a private ceremony at Colonel Baker's Red Gate Farm, just as the colonel had arranged in his will prior to his death six years before. The Putnams arrived back at Flanery Farm to find guests waiting for them. They'd come to see the great champion, not realizing they were a day too late. Dooley showed them Greyhound's stall and the guest lounge in front of it. He answered their questions and accepted their condolences.

The visitors drove away, and Dooley lowered his tall frame into the red-and-white striped cushions of the rattan chair in the viewing area of Greyhound's magnificent stall and guest lounge. Around him, Christmas cards filled with warm holiday and birthday wishes fluttered in the breeze. Knowing 1964 might be his last Christmas, Leone and Dooley hadn't had the heart to take down the birthday and Christmas remembrances as the old horse began to slip away.[1] Racehorses in North America traditionally celebrated their birthdays on January 1, but Greyhound's actual foaling date was just under a month away. On March 4, 1965, the great champion would have been thirty-three.

Dooley eyed the large leather-bound guest book on the table near the door. There were over 30,000 signatures in it. Many more people had come to see Greyhound and neglected to sign. Sometimes on a Sunday as many as two hundred people would arrive by car or bus to visit the Trotting King. Signatures from all fifty states and twenty-seven foreign countries filled the pages of the guest book. Turkey, Denmark, Iran, Australia, Guam, Japan, India, even Tanganyika, West Africa. One man from Holland told Leone he'd heard of Greyhound ever since childhood, saying his trip to America would be a huge disappointment unless he saw the great horse.

Greyhound had that effect on people—they just seemed drawn to him, like they somehow connected with the horse on a deeper, emotional level. Dooley closed his eyes for a moment, bringing up the memory of the first time he'd seen Greyhound in person. It had been in Springfield, Illinois, August 1936. Dooley could still hear the ringing of hooves pounding down the stretch, feel the thunderous applause from the crowd as the four-year-old champion flew under the wire, trotting the mile in 1:57 ¼. Greyhound had set a record that day, the fastest mile ever trotted in a race.

It stood for over fifteen years, until Star's Pride lowered it by the smallest of margins, shaving five one-hundredths of a second off in 1952.[2] Dooley had felt truly lucky to have seen the great horse in person.[3] Things had been so different back then; people consumed sports through the newspaper and over the radio. To see a great racing champion in the flesh was truly a privilege.

The feats that horse had accomplished! Smashing records left and right, defeating all comers; there wasn't a horse that could stay with him. He set twenty-five world records in his career. Upon retirement, eighteen remained intact. Now, some 25 years later, sixteen of Greyhound's records remained unbroken. *Sixteen*! Even with improvements in training and equipment, still, no one had lowered his world record for the mile. Three decades of focused, strategic breeding had not reproduced the likes of Greyhound. Literally tens of thousands of trotters had stepped over the tracks across the country and around the world since Greyhound and none, not one, had touched his record. Dooley shook his head, still in awe. Imagine if he had raced today instead of the Depression era, Dooley thought to himself. Greyhound would have been the sport's first millionaire.

Greyhound's greatest record would one day fall. They always did, eventually. But Dooley was glad it would not happen during the great horse's lifetime. His gaze fell upon the cards hanging along the bottom of the picture window where Greyhound had greeted his guests, and he thought about the stacks of letters they'd received through the years. Most were addressed to Greyhound himself. Grown men telling the horse of a special memory held close to their heart, a glimpse caught of the great champion in a race or setting yet another new record. Over and over the messages were the same, people speaking of a time some decades before when they'd been lucky enough to see him race. How it was their greatest memory, a time they'd never forget.

How had one horse touched so many lives? Dooley ran a hand through his silver-gray hair, remembering carloads of people, children on school buses, governors, media, film companies, photographers—thousands of people had come to see Greyhound in his retirement years. The horse had been the greatest free attraction in the state of Illinois.

Even the Thoroughbred people loved him. Algernon Daingerfield, the secretary of the Jockey Club, cast his vote for 1937 Horse of the Year for Greyhound,[4] saying the champion trotter was "by far the greatest horse before the public."[5] Imagine that, in a year that saw the likes of the champion Seabiscuit and Triple Crown winner War Admiral in their prime, this gent said that about Greyhound.

"You were something else, weren't you, Pappy?" Dooley spoke aloud in the empty room, using the nickname he'd given Greyhound years before, as he and the gelding aged together. How he loved that horse. Fresh tears stung his eyes, but he didn't bother wiping them away. Instead, he let them trickle down his cheeks one by one, each holding a memory of the greatest trotting horse of all time, the great Grey Ghost, the legend, Greyhound.

CHAPTER
—2—

[top]
The foaling barn at Calumet Farm.
• *circa 1962, courtesy of the Keeneland Library Meador Collection*

> *"Don't forget Guy Abbey!*
> *Nobody knows what a great colt he really was.*
> *And he's going to be a great sire.*
> *Remember what I say and don't forget it!"*
>
> —
>
> WILLIAM MONROE WRIGHT,
> FOUNDER OF CALUMET FARM AND OWNER OF GUY ABBEY,
> DECEMBER 1930

MARCH 4, 1932

The early hours of Friday, March 4, 1932 were blustery and cold. With a crisp, clear sky and overnight temperatures dipping into the teens, heavy frost covered the winter-brown grass at William Monroe Wright's Calumet Farm in Lexington, Kentucky. At least it still looked like the elder Wright's farm—for now, anyway. With William Wright's passing the year before, his son Warren had taken over and change could be felt in the air. Uncertainty loomed large, but for now, all remained the same.[1] In the red-roofed, whitewashed foaling barn, stalls were filled with expectant Standardbred broodmares, each holding what would be the last generation of William Wright's legacy as a dominant producer of outstanding Standardbred racehorses.

The gray mare Elizabeth circled in her stall, pawing at the deep straw bedding. Curls of steam rose from her sweat-soaked body. Her nostrils flared and she shook her graceful head, then curled her upper lip, stretching her neck outward as she lifted her nose into the air. In the corner of the large stall, almost completely hidden by shadow, the foaling man watched the mare. Elizabeth stomped her hind foot once, twice, pawed the thick bedding, and then slowly, carefully lowered her big body into the straw.

Outside the stall, the night foreman looked on. The foaling man had delivered hundreds of foals. It was unlikely he'd need the foreman's help, but the man stood by, just in case. Two front hooves presented under Elizabeth's tail, wrapped in the slippery white amniotic sac. The foaling man stepped from the shadows, spoke softly to the gray mare, and knelt quietly in the straw behind her heaving body. He broke the sac and gently pulled it back, exposing long, slender front legs and a tiny black muzzle.

Elizabeth settled into rhythmic pushing. With each effort, more of the foal appeared. The foaling man grasped the foal's front legs but didn't pull. His was more of a steadying presence, applying gentle traction. The mare pushed again, and passed the foal's narrow shoulders, then the torso. With a few more pushes, Elizabeth passed the hips and the foal slid out onto the straw. The mare lay there, her sides heaving, while the foaling man attended to the newborn. He cleared the amniotic sac from the tiny wet body, and ran his fingers down the outside of the foal's nostrils to help clear any fluids. He then rubbed the foal briskly with a clean cloth.

"A colt." The foaling man spoke softly, not taking his eyes from the newborn. The gangly colt lay in the straw, his body trembling as is normal with all newborn foals, regardless of the air temperature. The colt's coat was sleek and dark. It looked nearly black with not a lick of white on him, save a few light hairs sprinkled over his ribs. Emitting a short groan, Elizabeth thrust one foreleg in front of her body, then the other. With great effort, the mare rose to her feet. She turned to her colt and licked him, her throaty nicker carrying through the silent barn as she bonded with her new foal.

The foaling man wiped his hands on a clean cotton cloth and exited the stall, leaving the mare to attend to her colt.

"He's kind of a homely thing," the foreman said, shaking his head. The mare, Elizabeth, was nine years old and had not yet produced a foal of any note. "And that color—hopefully he's not going to be gray like his dam." Racehorse folk were a superstitious lot. Everyone knew gray was an unlucky color for a horse, though no one seemed able to explain why. All had their reasons, running the gamut from poor intestinal fortitude to lack of bone density. Others, like him, just knew them to be unlucky. And slow. The foreman knew if the colt did indeed shed his foal coat and prove to be gray, he would likely be gelded sooner rather than later. There wasn't any market for a gray stallion, especially these days, what with the bad economy and all.

"Too bad." The foreman shook his head, his mouth pulled down at the corners and his brow furrowed as if in deep and knowing thought. The late Mr. Wright had been awfully excited about this colt's sire, Guy Abbey. So far, though, he hadn't produced anything special.

The foaling man nodded, keeping his thoughts to himself. He would care for this colt just as he did all the others, no matter what they looked like or how valuable their dam. He liked this mare, Elizabeth. She was a fine-looking horse—perhaps a little light in her body, but it looked good on her. She was refined, almost like an Arabian, her head long and chiseled. The colt had the same head, his muzzle refined and shapely with a long mouth. The foaling man could see the colt would be intelligent. He had delivered hundreds of foals through the years, watched them grow and seen how they learned. He'd seen the look this colt had about him before. He'd be smart and sensitive, just like his dam. Some would see the sensitivity as "flightiness" or bad behavior, some might even call him mean or ill-tempered, but the foaling man knew better. The intelligent ones could be tricky to figure out, but they'd give everything they had to a handler who treated them with respect.

The foaling man nodded in agreement with his own assessment. He liked the mare's breeding, too. Elizabeth came from the last crop of Peter the Great, an outstanding sire. The colt's sire, Guy Abbey, hadn't shown much on the track; he was fast, for sure, but couldn't stay sound. Of course, it didn't help he'd gone down in that wreck at North Randall back in '28. That had resulted in multiple injuries as a total of six horses were involved. Walter Cox, the driver that caused the accident, had been suspended for thirty days; his horse, Fireglow, had reportedly died from his injuries.[2] A chemist's report later that year would reveal Fireglow had in fact been poisoned, presumably to keep him out of the $66,000 Hambletonian Stake in which he was the heavy favorite.[3]

Guy Abbey seemed to come out of the wreck not too much worse for the experience, and was deemed sound enough to race, winning the Horse Review futurity the following week. In the Hambletonian just a few days later, Guy Abbey had been sent to the post lame. Dick McMahon, his regular driver, was still nursing a fractured collar bone and broken ribs from the wreck just two weeks before, and a substitute driver had driven the chestnut colt in the big race. Guy Abbey had a ton of heart and came in second, racing the final quarter of his winning heat in less than thirty seconds. But he'd aggravated the injury from the North Randall wreck. When Mr. Wright saw Guy Abbey broken down after the Hambletonian, he'd announced the colt's racing career was over.[4]

The foaling man shook his head. A real shame such a nice horse had been pushed like that. Guy Abbey had good breeding, though—a son of the great Guy Axworthy. Time would tell. Maybe Guy Abbey and Elizabeth's new colt wouldn't amount to much, but he'd foaled out a lot of mares in his time, and he knew that one couldn't tell anything about the racing future of a colt so early on. He could have all the brains in the world, but it would do him no good as a racehorse if he didn't also have speed, grit, and heart. The foaling man hoped Elizabeth's colt had all three.

"Well, I suppose ..." The foreman pulled out his pocket watch, leaving the statement unfinished. He nodded to the foaling man, who dipped his head once, slow and deliberate, in return. The foreman went to the barn office and recorded the foaling in the leather-bound ledger:

> *March 4, 1932. Elizabeth foaled a colt by Guy Abbey. Dark bay. No white markings.*

"Sun'll be up soon," he muttered to himself. A light was already on in the office of the farm manager, Mr. McMahon. The foreman made his way toward the yellow light, glowing soft in the pre-dawn darkness. He'd report the new foal to Mr. McMahon, who'd ring the owner, Mr. Knight, and let him know Elizabeth had delivered a colt. The foreman wondered if Mr. Knight was still in town visiting relatives or if he and Mrs. Knight had returned to their home in Chicago. Mr. Knight had just been out a few days ago with the turf reporter, Jesse Shuff, to see his horses. He boarded several at Calumet—broodmares and some yearlings.[5] What would he think of this new colt?

"Shame he's such an ugly thing." The foreman shook his head. His worn leather boots made crisp whooshing sounds as he trudged through the long, frost-covered grass.

Outside Elizabeth's stall, the foaling man turned back to the mare. Her colt pushed his legs into the deep straw, alternating his efforts from one foreleg to the other. Soon he would attempt to rise, his long legs splayed in all directions as he tried to balance himself. The foaling man smiled, relishing the quiet and solitude of the foaling barn and these early moments in the life of a new foal.

Elizabeth's new colt was bred by and belonged to Henry H. Knight of Chicago, Illinois. Knight came by his horse passion naturally; his father and uncle were themselves horse breeders with operations located on the Knight family farm. The farm had been in the family since 1778, when Henry's great-great-grandfather, James, was given the land for his service in the Revolutionary War.[6] Back then, the land had still been part of Virginia. One day it would be known as Almahurst Farm, and Henry Knight would be among the most prolific breeders of both harness and running horses. But when Greyhound was born in 1932, no such name or place existed. A bit of history that would be forgotten over time, along with the then-common knowledge that Calumet Farm got its start as a top producer of harness horses and dominated the Standardbred ranks through the 1920s.

For the first one hundred years or so, the Knight family raised cattle and crops. It wasn't until the latter part of the 19th century that James Knight's three great grandsons began a legacy of the land and family as producers of great racehorses. The two older brothers, William and Dixie Knight, bred and raced Thoroughbreds. Dixie gained early notoriety as breeder of the great Thoroughbred Exterminator, winner of the 1918 Kentucky Derby.[7]

While his brothers were finding success with Thoroughbreds, Henry's father, Joe Knight, took an interest in harness racers. Unlike the jockey-ridden runners his brothers bred, the harness horses competed pulling a two-wheeled sulky and driver around the track. Instead of galloping, the harness horses went at a slower "road gait," competing at a trot or a pace—the challenge being to get the greatest attainable speed from a gait that, by nature, is not the fastest or most efficient for racing.

Joe Knight's first purchase, a yearling filly in 1895 he named Josephine Knight, went on to produce Nervolo Belle, the dam of Peter Volo, by Peter the Great.[8] Peter Volo won every race he entered save one, a match race against Lee Axworthy in 1915. As a breeding stallion, Peter Volo founded many of today's most successful trotting and pacing bloodlines.

Henry H. Knight was born in Nicholasville, Kentucky in 1889. He worked around his family's horses but gained a significant amount of his horse knowledge from his maternal uncle, the harness horse trainer and driver, Scott Hudson.[9] Hudson was legendary in the early part of the 20th century, known as "That Old Red-Headed Burglar" due to his uncanny ability to accurately rate his horse's speed, enabling him to "steal" a race with a well-rated slower horse over a poorly-rated faster one. In 1902, he won nearly $4,000 in a single day by winning all four races on the card at the Glenville track in Cleveland, Ohio.[10] A master reinsman, Hudson also gained notoriety for developing and successfully racing the blind horse Rhythmic.[11]

By 1909, when his son Henry had reached the age of twenty and still hadn't found direction for his life, Joe stepped in and laid down the law.

"That's quite a story." Henry Knight chuckled years later. "Father said I would have to go to school or work. I figured I was too smart to go to school so I told him if I had $100, I'd go someplace. He said 'Son, tomorrow we'll go on down to the bank and I'll give you $200 and you can go twice as far.'"[12]

Henry took that $200 and went to New Hampshire and sold shoes. He soon moved on to Columbus, Ohio, where he sold cars. It was in Ohio that he met and married Miss Alma Horine in 1914. Less than a decade after leaving home with his father's money in his pocket, Henry was a distributor of Pierce Arrow cars and REO Trucks.[13] A great salesman, he made deals and passed around horses, cars, or whatever else he dealt in as quickly and easily as one would pass a dish at a church potluck.

In 1927, Henry gave up his distributorship for a position as special accounts representative for General Motors at the recently acquired Chicago-based Yellow Truck and Coach Manufacturing Company—soon to be rechristened the GMC Truck Company. Two months later, Knight was promoted to assistant to the president, but he soon resigned.

"I couldn't make any money. I was doing things his way. I wanted to sell my way," Knight would say many years later at a dinner honoring him. "So I became a special accounts representative again."[14] This penchant for selling would take Knight far in the horse business. He became known for making million-dollar deals, buying and selling properties and horses throughout his life.[15] But in 1932, when Greyhound was born, his horse operation was still small-scale. At the time, Knight was living and working in Chicago while managing his own small herd of broodmares at Calumet and overseeing the operations of his father's portion of the family farm in Nicholasville, just outside of Lexington, Kentucky. Why he didn't keep his horses at the family farm is unclear. Since he was breeding to Calumet stallions, it may have been a matter of convenience. It may also have been from a desire to make his own way in the horse business, to prove that he could be successful without relying on his family's money.

Knight purchased the gray mare Elizabeth at auction from the Walter Candler (son of Asa Candler—founder of the Coca-Cola company) dispersal in 1930 for $2,250.[16] Candler acquired the mare as a weanling in 1923 when he purchased the entire final foal crop of Peter the Great. Elizabeth's dam, Zombrewer, had produced the useful stallion Peter the Brewer (a full brother to Elizabeth). Zombrewer herself had shown talent in racing as a pacer but suffered a career-ending injury before she could prove herself. Elizabeth was a natural pacer, but Candler only liked trotters. The mare would require such heavy shoes to make her trot, there was no point in racing her, so she was sent to broodmare duties having never made a start.[17]

The most prolific producer of great harness horses in his day, Peter the Great would become one of the founding sires of the modern trotter. But back in 1932, when Elizabeth produced her awkward gray colt, her being the daughter of Peter the Great and a full sister to Peter the Brewer was not enough to excite buyers to take a chance on the colt Henry Knight would eventually christen Greyhound.

Knight bred eight-year-old Elizabeth to the Calumet Farm stallion, Guy Abbey. William Wright, founder of Calumet Farm, had believed strongly in Guy Abbey's potential, breeding many of his own top mares to his unproven young stallion. But he would not live to see whether his predictions would come true. Wright died in 1931, the year before Guy Abbey's greatest son was born.

Elizabeth's colt grew tall and lanky, trotting and galloping by his mother's side in the expansive, lush green fields of Calumet Farm. His dark bay foal coat, now shedding out in patches, revealed his true color underneath to be nearly black, with a spray of white hairs scattered throughout. By late summer, the colt had fully shed his fluffy foal coat and become a sleek steel gray. On a visit to Calumet that summer of 1932, Henry Knight observed the narrow, gangly, long-legged colt and named him Greyhound.

By spring of 1933, Greyhound presented as a tall, narrow, thin yearling, more leg than anything else, with an awkward, disjointed way of going.[18] Shedding patches of winter hair revealed his coat to be a slightly lighter shade of gray than the year before. Such is the nature of gray horses; the colt's coat would lighten every year until he was pure white like Elizabeth.

The big gray colt ran and played with the other Standardbred yearlings at Calumet Farm, napping in the warm sun and growing tall and strong on rich Kentucky bluegrass. Traditionally, Standardbred foals received little handling after weaning, given the freedom to grow and play in huge pastures until their formal training began as yearlings. Whether this was the case at Calumet is unknown, but being that it was traditional and is still practiced by some farms to this day, it is likely this is what Greyhound's life was like in the early part of 1933—a carefree existence with little human intervention.

But change could be felt in the air. Beyond the protective shadow of towering, ancient elm trees and miles of pristine white fences, uncertainty loomed. In less than a year, nothing would be the same.

CHAPTER
—3—

[second from top]
Almahurst Farm, located at the KTHBA Trotting Track.
• *circa 1934, courtesy of the United States Trotting Association*

"The Great Depression cast shadows on the city. The roar of the Twenties had quieted to a soulful cry of the blues."

—

Pamela Hamilton,
Lady Be Good: The Life and Times of Dorothy Hale

CHAOS, CHANGE, AND THE BIRTH OF ALMAHURST FARM

It is difficult to effectively tell Greyhound's story without touching on the chaos he was born into. When Greyhound entered the world early in 1932, the full significance of the stock market crash of 1929 and resulting economic depression had yet to be felt, and the shifting world powers in Europe and Japan had not yet realized their devastating potential. In Kentucky, Calumet Farm was still a top producer of Standardbred racehorses and Henry Knight still had an uncle and a father. Within two years, all of this would change.

Since this is a horse biography and not a history book, a brief glimpse of the world in 1933 will suffice in adding depth and breadth to the story of how the greatest horse Henry Knight ever bred would find his fame under the ownership of someone else. This summary assumes that the reader is familiar with and understands the horror that occurred under the dictatorship of Adolf Hitler and that the world was settling into a decade of devastating economic depression.

In January 1933, Adolf Hitler was sworn in as Chancellor of Germany. Just two months later, the *Reichstag* passed the Enabling Act of 1933, which allowed for the development of Nazi Germany, a single party dictatorship led by Hitler. Within a couple months, construction of the Dachau concentration camp was completed. By the end of March 1933, existing political parties were banned, trade unions had been disempowered, scientific and cultural "cleansing" began, and everything "un-German" was required to disappear. This came to include people as well as ideas and printed material.[1]

Stateside, an assassination attempt on newly elected President Franklin D. Roosevelt was botched, resulting instead in the death of Chicago mayor Anton Cermark. Not everyone was a fan of Roosevelt's plans for pulling America out of her economic tailspin. Many feared government overreach and that Roosevelt would prove to be some kind of socialist dictator. A month later, on March 5, Roosevelt declared a "bank holiday," closing all banks in the country through the Emergency Banking Act and seemingly confirming some of those fearful prognostications. The banks would reopen a few at a time, beginning March 13. Additional "New Deal" acts such as an executive order forbidding the hoarding of gold and the requirement that all securities be registered with the Federal Trade Commission[2] caused further and renewed fears in a country already in dire financial straits. Roosevelt's restructuring eventually helped carry the country through the dark years to come, but in the first half of 1933, things looked bleak.

At the same time, the future of Calumet Farm seemed wrapped in doubt, and by default, the status of Henry Knight's Standardbred holdings. There was talk that Warren Wright planned to disperse his late father's entire stock of Standardbreds and get out of the harness horse business altogether. In these months of uncertainty, Henry Knight announced he would sell his entire crop of yearlings—17 in all—at the Indianapolis Speed Sale that November.

The rumors spoken in hushed tones by unsettled Calumet employees proved to be true. In September 1933, Warren Wright dispersed his late father's entire stock of Standardbred harness horses—everything, including current racers, prospects, and all breeding stock. Every horse at Calumet Farm and at their nearby training barn went under the hammer, aside from a couple pensioners (retired broodmares), including Zombrewer, Elizabeth's dam.

The dispersal of Calumet's Standardbred holdings would usher in a significant era for Calumet and for Henry Knight. Under Warren Wright's stewardship, Calumet Farm would become legendary for breeding and racing Thoroughbreds. Warren made it his goal to put Calumet at the top of the Thoroughbred world, and he succeeded in dramatic fashion, producing two Triple Crown winners, Whirlaway and Citation, within 12 years of the changeover. There were many other champions to come, and Calumet's legendary run as breeder of great Thoroughbred racehorses would last well into the 1970s.[3]

The accomplishments during Warren's tenure would never be matched by any farm, ever. Such was the astronomical rise of Calumet

Farm as a producer of Thoroughbreds that William Wright's legacy and Calumet's history as a top harness horse nursery would be all but forgotten by the 1940s.

Why, after the Calumet dispersal, Henry didn't simply move his horses to the family farm is information lost to history. It may be that Henry kept his horses away from the family farm because he didn't yet own the land and therefore could not make the changes he wanted to the property. It may also be that he wanted to make his own way in the business and not appear to be riding the coat tails of his father and uncle. There were also reports that Knight was considering purchasing the well-appointed Laurel Hall near Indianapolis, Indiana, though ultimately he decided to remain close to his ancestral land.[4]

Regardless of the reason, when Calumet's Standardbred operations ceased, Knight had to either disperse or relocate his horses. He did a little of both. He purchased some of the quality stock from the Calumet dispersal, including Greyhound's sire, Guy Abbey.[5] Later in 1933, Henry rented Calumet's training barn, located at the Kentucky Trotting Horse Breeders Association (KTHBA) track in Lexington. There, he established his new breeding operation, which he called Almahurst Farm, after his wife, Alma.[6] The word "hurst" means "grove" or "wooded hillock." The track, today known formally as the Red Mile, still exists, but the Calumet facility that served as the original Almahurst was long ago razed as the city devoured the land around the historic track.

In 1934, as Greyhound was floundering in his early racing efforts for his new owner, tragedy struck the Knight family when Henry's uncle, "Dixie" Knight, was murdered in his home. His family, bound and helpless in the next room, heard Dixie beg for his life while he opened his office safe. The intruder shot him anyway, then escaped with his accomplice in a stolen car.[7] Although a reward was offered and the police worked the case for years, the identity of the murderer was never discovered. Just nine months later, Henry's father, Grant Lee "Joe" Knight, died of heart failure after an extended illness.[8]

With the three brothers gone (William had passed in 1908), the family land went to Henry, and in 1935, he moved his Almahurst Farm operations to the newly inherited 1,100 acres.[9] By then, Greyhound was well on his way to superstardom for his new owner. Turf magazines and newspapers reported the opening of Almahurst on the Knight family property, printing large spreads showing pictures of the extravagant new stallion barn Henry had built on the site of the old foaling barn, where Exterminator had been born thirty years before. Almahurst would become one of the most prolific Standardbred nurseries in the country and forever be linked to Greyhound as the great horse's birthplace, even though it didn't exist in any form until more than 18 months after the gray champion was born.

The new facility created quite a buzz. A place as large and strikingly beautiful as Calumet Farm, newswriters soon began to report Almahurst Farm as the birthplace of the rising superstar, Greyhound. Possibly because it was easier than explaining how Knight was the breeder, but the horse had actually been born at Calumet—a farm fast becoming a well-known *Thoroughbred* operation. Or possibly to give Knight's new farm a boost before the public, with name recognition by association with the champion trotter. The latter seems likely, as Lexington turf reporter Jesse Shuff, a long-time friend of Knight who had personally seen Elizabeth at Calumet days before she foaled Greyhound,[10] was among the reporters who later described Almahurst as the birthplace of the great trotter. Whether it was in error, intentional for convenience, or even for promotional purposes, soon no one seemed to remember that Greyhound had never in his life set foot on Almahurst Farm.

GREYHOUND

THE REMARKABLE STORY OF THE LEGENDARY RACEHORSE WHO INSPIRED A NATION

An ad for Calumet Farm when it was still a Standardbred nursery. Greyhound's granddam, Zombrewer, is in the center of the top image. Note the typos ("Guy Abba" instead of "Guy Abbey," and "Traux" instead of "Truax").

CIRCA 1929, COURTESY OF THE RICHARD G. STONE COLLECTION

CHAPTER
— 4 —

*"There were even some present at the time
who didn't think he was worth $50."*

—

Colonel E. J. Baker, 1943

UGLY DUCKLING

On March 1, 1933, Greyhound and fourteen of Knight's yearlings went to well-known colt-starter Hunter Moody for preliminary training.[1] Moody worked out of a barn at the KTHBA track in Lexington. He had a knack for working with youngsters and difficult horses and had become known for running a sort of "reform school" for the so-called tough cases, "making gentlemen of the colts," as some of the old-timers put it. Even some of the Thoroughbred people sent their gallopers to Moody's reform school to be worked in harness, a most notable student being 1932 Kentucky Derby and Preakness winner Burgoo King.[2]

Moody never commented on whether Greyhound was a difficult horse, at least not within earshot of a reporter, though there were rumors that aggressive behavior is why he was gelded. But in truth, the colt was gelded due to the poor economic outlook, and his unfortunate color, questionable trotting horse conformation, and unproven breeding.[3]

Back in the early 1930s, a gray colt must have a truly exceptional pedigree and stellar conformation to be left intact as a breeding prospect. Awkward and ugly, Greyhound had neither looks nor pedigree in his favor. Guy Abbey had not yet accomplished anything of note at stud.

Elizabeth had produced two other reportedly unremarkable foals, and herself had no race record. Apparently, Knight thought so little of her prospects, he gave the mare to fellow horseman W. N. Reynolds, brother of tobacco magnate R.J. Reynolds, before her colt, Greyhound, ever made it to the racetrack.[4]

Moody liked Greyhound. He had an impressively long stride and could really move along, once he got his legs sorted out. When he was fully balanced in his gait and in his mouth, Moody suspected he might have some real potential. He liked the way the horse moved and how he handled—he was light and sensitive, the type of horse that could be brilliant if someone didn't ruin him first. Greyhound had a lot of leg and was tall for his age. If he were pushed too hard too soon, his career would be over before it started. Greyhound's future depended on ensuring he found his way into the barn of just the right trainer.

Moody's job was to get the yearlings broken to harness and cart, getting them accustomed to the girth tightening around them, the feel of the bit and bridle, the sensation of the long leather reins running over their backs, and the sound and feel of pulling a two-wheeled jog cart. He just got them started on the basics, allowing them to jog easily, keeping them straight between the cart shafts, without asking for speed. Moody wouldn't focus as much on developing the yearlings' trot in harness; that would be a job for a future trainer. For now, he brought the young horses onto the track with a pony—a catch-all name for a horse ridden alongside a racehorse—to gallop along beside them. This is how they'd show the yearlings' speed and length of stride at the sale in November.

Moody focused on ensuring each yearling had a solid start, a strong foundation on which the next trainer could build. Of utmost importance to Moody was ensuring each horse had a soft, balanced mouth. A balanced mouth was vital, Moody would say in 1940, when training the yearling Grey Fox, a full brother to Greyhound. "When a horse's mouth is properly balanced," he was quoted as saying in a *Lexington Leader* article, "the [driving] lines telegraph to the driver exactly what the horse is going to do. A good driver then can sense before it happens any sudden change in the horse's gait by the feel of the lines ... a well-mouthed horse can be driven faster without breaking [stride] than a horse that has a tough mouth." Once horses learn to hang on and pull the reins, they are very difficult to fix.[5]

By mid-April, turf writer Jesse Shuff reported that Greyhound was the fastest of Knight's yearlings and the second fastest yearling in Moody's training barn.[6] The other, a gray stud colt by the name of Silver King, had what Greyhound didn't—an exceptional pedigree and stunning beauty. Despite the long stride and early speed Greyhound showed, he failed to turn the head of even one prospective buyer. He just didn't look like a trotter. His legs were too long, his body too short, his hocks too straight, and his haunches too low. Back then, harness trainers wanted a horse with the so-called "trotting pitch:" a long-bodied horse with hindquarters higher than his withers. The belief was that this conformation was ideal for a trotter, enabling him to trot faster without striking his hind shin with the toe of his front hoof. For decades, all the best trotters had the trotter's pitch. The most influential sire of the Standardbred breed, Hambletonian 10, had the pitch, and so did many of his best sons and daughters.[7] Greyhound was quite the opposite.

After two months, Hunter Moody turned out the yearlings.[8] Through the summer they would play and grow, soaking up the warm Kentucky sun and devouring acres of calcium-rich bluegrass. Knight had recently leased the Calumet training facility. Located at the top of the stretch at the KTHBA track, it included four barns, five large paddocks, an office, and a blacksmith shop.[9] It is possible the yearlings were turned out there, as would be the case the following year.[10] It's also possible Moody had his own turnout options at the track. Back then, the track we now know as the Red Mile was surrounded by open land, where now it is well ensconced within the urban neighborhoods of Lexington. Regardless, when October came and the edges of the sugar maple leaves turned orange, Henry Knight's manager, Marvin Childs, brought in the yearlings and started preparing them for the November sale in Indianapolis. At the same time, Knight was setting up his breeding operation there with three recently purchased stallions—one of which was Greyhound's sire, Guy Abbey, which he had picked up from the Calumet dispersal for a paltry $1,400.[11]

"Greyhound wasn't so impressive as a yearling," Childs would say in 1939. He had half a dozen yearlings at the KTHBA track one day, preparing them for the Indianapolis sale, when a man approached and asked if any were for sale.

"You can have any one of the bunch for $300," Childs said.

"Well," the prospective buyer exclaimed, "I will take any one of them except that gray thing. I wouldn't have him as a gift."[12]

The man picked a different yearling, handed Childs $300, and went on his way, perhaps never realizing he'd missed the bargain of the century—the greatest trotter of all time for the price of Henry Ford's most economical automobile.

The lore around the sale of Greyhound indicated no one wanted the gray son of Elizabeth. Noted Kentucky turf writer Jesse Shuff wrote in his weekly column in late October of 1933 that Greyhound had shown a lot of speed in his early handling. Shuff went on to speculate that Knight was so impressed with the youngster that it may have influenced his decision to buy Greyhound's sire, Guy Abbey.[13] But Shuff's report about Greyhound's early speed was never printed outside of Kentucky, so all anyone had to go on at the sale in Indiana was the yearling's physical shortcomings, undesirable color, and uninspired pedigree.

Hunter Moody apparently thought enough of the youngster to make an extra effort to get him into the hands of a man with a top trainer and the financial wherewithal to ensure the gray gelding had the best chance at success. Depending on who you asked, once Greyhound proved to be the greatest of all time, there were more than a few people willing to take the credit for being the *one* who noticed Greyhound's potential early on, and encouraged E. J. Baker to buy him for his Hotel Baker Stable—the name under which his Standardbred harness string raced.

Moody teamed up with Dick McMahon, the manager of Calumet and Guy Abbey's former trainer, at the Indianapolis sale to convince E. J. Baker, a wealthy, horse-loving entrepreneur from St. Charles, Illinois, to purchase Greyhound. Marvin Childs and Henry Knight had already pitched the gray youngster to Baker and likely to his trainer, veteran reinsman Sep Palin.

"You may not be strong for gray horses, but that bird sure can trot," Knight said to Baker, *The Harness Horse* later reported.[14]

They knew the highly successful Sep Palin to be a patient and savvy trainer, and that he would be able to guide the gray horse to his best chance at success. Still, Baker wasn't so sure. The gray didn't look like much to him, but Moody and McMahon convinced him to at least come and look at Greyhound.

E. J. Baker was a small man who seemed to swim in the square-shouldered, boxy suit coats that were the style in his day. His ever-present panatela cigar, cane, and seasonally appropriate hat (straw boat hat in the summer, fedora in the cooler months) made him easy to recognize. He stood along the rail at the Indianapolis fairground's racetrack, wrapped in a wool overcoat, collar turned up against the brisk November wind, a crisp, gray fedora placed evenly on his head.

Moody took the gray colt out on a straight stretch of track, leading him while astride a track pony. He made eye contact with Baker, to ensure the older gentleman was watching, then turned his pony and galloped him down the track, with Greyhound between him and Baker. Greyhound trotted easily alongside the pony, taking such long strides he covered the ground without apparent effort, creating the illusion that the gray gelding was moving slowly.

"He doesn't move fast enough to suit me." The slight man leaned over his cane and shook his head slowly.

Moody reined the pony around to face Baker. "That's where you're mistaken," he said. "This time, watch how fast the lead pony is going, and then you'll see that Greyhound moves faster than he seems to."[15]

Moody rode the pony back to the starting point, the gray yearling in tow. He took them down the stretch again, with Greyhound striding out impressively, the pony galloping to keep up.

Baker nodded his head after Greyhound trotted by, but said nothing. When the gray colt, hip number 36, was led into the ring, Baker stood next to Sep Palin, watching Greyhound closely but making no bid.

Henry Knight stood in the auction box alongside the auctioneer, watching the crowd. The auctioneer's chant floated above the crowd and hung in the air over the big gray colt.

"Eight, eight, eight, I've got eight hundred dollars, I need ten, ten, eight-ten." The auctioneer worked the crowd and nods from ringside came slowly, bringing the bid up to $890. "Nine, nine, nine, I need nine!" he chanted. "I got eight-ninety, I need nine, nine, nine." He paused and looked at the crowd. "C'mon, now, who'll go nine for this nice big colt?"

Henry Knight scanned the crowd from his perch in the auction box and found his friend, E. J. Baker. He leaned across the box and said, "Ed, for goodness' sake, put a bid on this colt. You'll never regret it!"[16]

All eyes turned to the small man in the gray fedora. Baker lifted his silver-headed cane and touched the brim of his hat.

"Yeah! I got nine!" the auctioneer shouted. "Now, who'll give me ten, ten, ten, nine-ten, I need nine-ten." The men around the ring fell silent, some shaking their heads and turning away. "Are you all done?" the auctioneer called out. Baker stood, watching the gray. The big colt stood at attention, ears pricked forward and large, dark eyes shining. "Alright, then." The auctioneer brought down his hammer. "Sold to the man from St. Charles!"

The decisive crack of wood on wood added a finality to the auctioneer's words. Sep Palin signed the ticket for Baker, and the awkward gray gelding was his.

CHAPTER 4

CHAPTER
—5—

 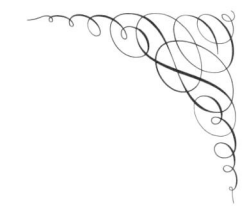

"Horses had been racing in harness for generations, friend against friend, neighbor against neighbor, finding sport where they could amid the hard work of the young country. It has grown alongside the nation of America, through the passage of time and the perspectives of history."

—

NICOLE KRAFT,
100 Years in Harness

AMERICAN TROTTER

It is not logical to talk about Greyhound without a rudimentary understanding of harness racing and its connection to the pioneering spirit that built America. Further, it's impossible to talk about harness racing without also talking about time. And it's impossible to talk about time without understanding the vital role it played in the development of the Standardbred breed. The Standardbred is an American original, the breed developed alongside the sport, and both grew up alongside the young nation.[1]

If Thoroughbred racing—the so-called "runners" raced with a jockey astride—is the sport of kings, then harness racing is the sport of the common man. Horses were once an everyday part of life, a requirement for survival; people depended on them for working fields, transportation of goods, and travel. Everything we do today with cars, trucks, and trains was once the job of the horse. The horse's role as a valuable, contributing member of the family was significant to the history and development of the sport of harness racing and the trotter itself.

While Thoroughbred racing had its beginnings far across the Atlantic Ocean among the aristocracy of Europe, Americans like to claim the modern sport of harness racing as a purely American invention.

And to a point, depending on how you use the terminology, it was. It was the racing of *trotters in harness* as an *organized sport* that most will agree got its start in the United States. Not to say that horses were not raced in harness in other countries or even in earlier times—they certainly were, most notably in Russia, where Orlov-Chesmenskii was organizing road racing* of his Orlov Trotters in harness by the mid-1780s.[2] These races "flourished in Moscow until his death in 1808," when they were quickly forgotten in favor of Thoroughbred runners.[3] The 1840s and 1850s marked the golden age of the Orlov trotter and the emergence of a distinctive racing culture to trial the breed.[4] By then, however, the sport as we understand it today had already developed in America—racing *trotters* in *harness* had moved from the roads to the race track and become an organized sport overseen by governing bodies. But it didn't happen right away. First there was some hair-splitting, law-skirting, and tongue-in-cheek-justifying pioneering spirit. And it didn't hurt when Thoroughbred racing became illegal. Twice.

Some of the earliest contests for money were match races between two rivals for an agreed-upon amount. These impromptu races were held on the streets of Goshen, New York, as early as the Revolutionary War era.[5] After working all day on the farm or perhaps pulling a meat or milk wagon, the horses would then race through the streets of town, sometimes under saddle, sometimes hooked to the same cart or wagon they'd worked with all day. Back then, there were no specialized vehicles for racing in harness. The two-wheeled sulky was still decades away from development.

In colonial times, racing over public roads became illegal, but the trotting horse owners found a way to skirt the law, citing contests between trotters as a *necessity* to improve the quality of the road horse. No such argument could be made for the Thoroughbred runners. These horses were luxury items for the wealthy. Interestingly, it was imported Thoroughbreds from England that were used to replenish the decimated supply of American horses after the Revolutionary War[6] and led to the development of the ideal harness horse. These Thoroughbreds were heavily imported at the end of the eighteenth century and mixed with existing American "native" horses.[7] In 1788, the gray Thoroughbred stallion Messenger was imported to the fledgling country. The stallion had a commanding presence and, upon his exit from the ship after his long voyage, was said to have charged down the gangplank and into the streets, dragging his hapless grooms alongside him.[8]

"On the foundation of [Messenger's] blood, mixed with blood of undistinguished American stock, was reared a great new breed of horses," turf historian Dwight Akers wrote in

---

* *Road* racing was certainly happening simultaneously in multiple countries, and breeds best suited to this were being developed in these areas. It is *organized trotting* races in *harness* on purpose-built *tracks* that is believed to have started in America.

1938. "On it, too, was built a new, and wholly American sport."[9,*]

The new breed Akers referenced was the American Standardbred, the breed synonymous with the sport for which he was developed. It was the blood of Messenger, through his great-grandson Hambletonian 10, from which the future breed was built. But in the beginning, there was no Standardbred. The road horse (or trotter) wasn't a breed so much as an ideal type developed for the purpose of efficiently transporting goods and people. The use of such a horse was a required part of daily life for the citizens of the new country. This fact became the justification that allowed the trotters to flourish when road racing was banned. The Thoroughbred runners were confined to the race track by the anti-road racing laws, but trotters, or road horses, skirted the law and continued to race on the roads in the name of progress.

While competing with trotters was popular and drew many spectators, at the turn of the eighteenth century, it was still considered a pastime, not a sport. Though "gentlemanly wagers" certainly took place, there were no bookies or organized betting as found with the running horse sport. This distinction was among the reasons why trotters were given a pass when reformers began pushing anti-racing legislation. The Thoroughbreds attracted thousands of spectators willing to bet hundreds of thousands of dollars on the outcome of a race. But in 1802, northern states began passing racing prohibition laws and Thoroughbred tracks across the North were closed. These laws, with considerable religious backing, strictly forbade horse racing. The sport was seen as evil and un-gentlemanly due to its link with betting.[10] During this time of racing prohibition, the organized sport of harness racing was born.

The new racing prohibition laws defined racing as a contest between two or more *individuals*. But there was nothing that said a horse couldn't be matched against *time*. Since time was not an individual, trotting against the clock was, by definition, not racing.[11] To further split hairs, the anti-racing laws defined "horse racing" as horses going at a gallop. Therefore, two horses trotting against each other was not technically racing. This same "trotting is not racing" principle protected the rights of citizens to attend trotting contests and served as an acceptable work-around for those who could not attend races or own racehorses based on their religious beliefs.[12] This allowed the upstanding citizen to remain so in the eyes of the law, the church, and his neighbor—so long as he contested trotters and did not engage in the devil's work by racing runners.

"Trotting, as distinct from racing, was regarded tolerantly by worthy citizens on the

---

* It is not this author's intent to claim Americans were the only people developing and racing trotting horses in harness—though, as is evidenced by Akers' 1938 quote, this was a common sentiment often repeated among lovers of the sport.

grounds of public necessity," wrote Akers. Americans needed trotters for transportation of humans and cargo. To serve this vital need and produce a better product, there had to be a way to measure the quality of a horse and their potential value toward improving America's road horses. Trotting against time or against other horses was the best way to do this.

Due to its humble beginnings and image as a working-class or rural-class form of entertainment, the "blue-blooded" Americans who raced Thoroughbreds looked down on the trotters and the people that raced them, considering both "less-than" in quality, class, and substance. But with the loss of Thoroughbred racing to prohibition laws, interest in competition between road horses spread from the country and small towns into the big cities along the northeast coast.[13]

In New York, Third Avenue in Manhattan and the Jamaica turnpike on Long Island became the foundation of the sport of harness racing. Trotting match races and contests against time in harness and under saddle were held in these New York locations, and for decades, before any trotting track existed, these streets were the primary grounds for the American trotting turf.[14] The New York Trotting Club was organized in 1825. Prior to this, no official records were kept and, due to anti-racing legislation, few of these contests garnered any mention in newsprint—to do so would give the appearance of a racing event, which was, of course, illegal.[15]

By the time racing prohibition was repealed in New York, there was healthy interest in trotters in the northern and eastern parts of the United States and Canada—not merely as a pastime but as a regularly practiced sport. The Deep South had ignored the anti-racing legislation and the runners were alive and well in that part of the country.[16] They had little interest in the "Yankee trotter" or anything else the Yanks had to offer, so the sport developed primarily east of the Mississippi River and north of the Mason-Dixon line. It is worth noting, however, that there was briefly a significant hotbed of harness horse production in California toward the end of the nineteenth century, and the first horse to trot a mile in two-minutes was a California-bred.[17]

Trotting as a professional sport made its debut at Union Course on Long Island, May 27, 1823. The crowd had come together to see the famous New York Thoroughbred, Eclipse, run against the top southern contender, Sir Henry, for a $20,000 purse. The Third Avenue trotters saw this as an opportunity to debut their sport on a grander scale. They arranged with the New York Jockey Club to add a race of two-mile heats under saddle for a purse of $1,000.[18]

An estimated sixty thousand spectators saw this first professional trotting race. Six entries went to the post, and the race was won in two straight heats by a trotter from Philadelphia called Topgallant.[19] According to Akers' research, the excitement of the race between Eclipse and Sir Henry completely overshadowed any reporting on how the trotting race was received by the spectators. An inauspicious start, perhaps, but "track trotting, once inaugurated, was not allowed to lapse," Akers wrote. The New York Trotting Club was established soon after, and in 1826, the first official road horse meet was held at the Trotting Club's new course at Centerville, New York. The three-day meet included races for both saddle and harness horses.[20]

Other states followed suit, establishing trotting clubs as associations "for the improvement of the road horse."[21] The purpose of improvement of the breed was an important distinction, as some states still prohibited horse racing (and trotting is not racing). As trotting races over roads and tracks became more popular, the need for a standard a way to measure the ability of the horse—became evident. The ability to trot fast was only part of the equation; the horse also had to carry speed over a distance. In early races, heats of four to five miles each were contested, and a single race could be five or more heats.[22] A race of 15 or more miles—that's testing durability and stamina to an extreme. Such long contests were eventually replaced with heats of one or two miles. By the 1930s, when Greyhound came on the scene, the one-mile heat had become the standard, with, in most instances, a "best two heats of three" configuration.

"Ability to go the [speed] and make the distance, not a fancy pedigree, was the decisive test of a road horse."[23] It was the fast and durable horses who were able to produce fast and durable horses that were selected for breeding. Morgans, Thoroughbreds, and the now-extinct Narragansett trotter were popular choices. In the early days, the common characteristic among the horses selected was not their breed, but their ability to trot. The Third Avenue and Jamaica horseman discovered that the "tops in trotting speed" came from the progeny of a single sire—Messenger.[24]

In 1843, a ten-year-old gray mare named Lady Suffolk, a third-generation descendant of Messenger, became the first horse to trot a mile in two minutes and thirty seconds (2:30). Just less than fifteen years before, in 1829, John Lawrence, authority on the English racehorse, said that "no horse ever did or could" trot a mile in such a short time. "From the excessive rapidity of his trot, his feet would be apt to strike fire and set him ablaze."[25] Whether Lawrence actually believed a horse would catch fire in this manner is left to the imagination of the reader, yet his comment speaks clearly to the beliefs of his time. However, fifty years after his statement, the "impossible" time reached by Lady Suffolk would become the standard by which the speed of the trotter would be measured.[26]

In 1867, John H. Wallace put out his first "American Stud Book," which included a trotting horse registry and established a record of their pedigree. This was followed by "The American Trotting Register."[27] Prior to this, there was no official recording of trotting horse pedigrees, the information being passed on by word-of-mouth and likely at times guessed at or manufactured in order to make a sale or boost a stud fee.

Ability of a horse to trot a mile in a specific amount of time was an early requirement for inclusion in the Trotting Horse Registry. This is where the name "Standardbred" came from—the requirement that a horse be able to meet a specific standard of speed for acceptance into the registry of the developing breed.[28] In 1879, the standard was 2:30, set by "The Old Gray Mare" of Long Island, Lady Suffolk. While there is still an obscure rule about this on the books, which theoretically would allow a non-Standardbred with a fast enough mile to be registered, today horses are bred and registered based on pedigree. However, the measure of time over a mile remains significant.

In the early days of the sport, a trotter was raced with a rider (to saddle), pulling a 250-pound, four-wheeled wagon (to wagon), or pulling a two-wheeled sulky (to harness). As the desire to lower the one-mile speed record became of the utmost importance, racing to saddle and to wagon fell out of favor over use of the 90-pound, "light-weight" high-wheel sulky. Racing horses "to harness" became the standard in trotting horse competition and gave us the term "harness racing."[29]

The use of the sulky had an additional benefit of allowing a more diverse population to compete, wrote Akers. Thoroughbred owners were limited in that they required the services of young, small, wiry jockeys to ride their horses. The owners of trotters could drive their own horses without such strict concerns about height, weight, or age, making the sport more accessible than the aristocratic, highbrow world of Thoroughbred racing, and thus more endearing to the common man.

Another significant difference between harness racing and the racing of Thoroughbreds was the former's fixation on time. In harness racing, the horses raced against each other, but they also raced against the clock. Racing ever faster, the clock became as important to defining greatness as the horse's ability to finish ahead of his rivals. In Thoroughbred racing, the clock no longer held the same significance, though it had at one time, when runners competed in heat races and ability to carry speed over a distance was held in high regard among Thoroughbred breeders. Setting time records was celebrated, but secondary to crossing the finish line ahead of your rivals. Turf historian John Hervey noted in 1938 that the English Thoroughbred races weren't even timed by officials, nor was the time publicly announced.[30] Thoroughbred owners raced each other's horses for prestige and honor; they did not race the clock. In contrast, a harness racer's greatness was never limited to the speed or talent of the horses he competed against. Races against time were held in high regard. This fact would be significant in Greyhound's story.

When the 2:30 mile became the standard, the idea of a horse trotting a two-minute (2:00) mile seemed an unobtainable goal. And with the equipment and tracks of the day, it was certainly out of reach. The high-wheel sulkies were of heavy wood construction, with huge wheels as much as five feet in diameter. The driver sat close behind and slightly above the horse, his outstretched legs near level with the horse's hips. Wind resistance created by the highly perched driver and the heavy weight of the sulky slowed the horse significantly. The turns on the track also presented a speed problem, as the steel-rimmed wooden wheels could not grip the track—the inertia of the speeding horse caused the sulky to slide dangerously sideways on the turns.[31]

When the bicycle craze overtook the country in 1892, the 90-pound high-wheel sulkies were replaced by sulkies with pneumatic tires. These "bikes" were about one-third the weight of the high-wheelers, and had ball bearings to decrease axle friction and rubber tires to grip the track.[32] The driver sat low behind the horse, lessening the wind resistance. High-wheel sulkies had been in use for seventy years, and the first time a pneumatic bike sulky hit the track, the laughter and finger-pointing came from competitors and spectators alike.[33] But when the bike driver's horse set a record for the fastest four heats ever trotted, the laughter fell silent.[34] Soon, everyone clamored for the strange new vehicle. They could not be produced quickly enough to meet demand, so trainers found a way to modify the high-wheel sulky by removing the wheels, and adapting the old sulkies to fit the new, smaller bike wheels.[35]

The bike sulky gave a significant boost to the speeds the horses could attain, which had already been steadily increasing with improved road and track surfaces. Records fell and new world champions were crowned, but even then, at the dawn of the twentieth century, a two-minute mile still seemed to many an impossible goal. Surely the horse had reached peak speed. To trot a mile in under two minutes meant to trot four consecutive quarters in thirty seconds or less—no horse could maintain that speed for that distance, the naysayers argued.[36] But trotters were already going much faster than the 2:30 standard set just a few decades before. With the new bike sulky, the trotting mare Nancy Hanks lowered the world record by almost four seconds, going 2:04 flat in September 1892.[37]

In the first half of the twentieth century, one couldn't talk about harness racing without also talking about the two-minute horse. Many believed the two-minute record was attainable, and eagerly waited for the horse that would come along and prove it. The two were so thoroughly intertwined—harness racing and the ideal of trotting a mile in two minutes or less—one could hardly overstate the significance of achieving what some still deemed to be an impossible goal. When the first two-minute mile was finally recorded in 1897, it was the pacer Star Pointer that broke that supposedly unbreakable barrier, pacing a mile in 1:59 ¼.

It is important to note here that trotting and pacing are regarded separately in the annals of speed. Both the pace and trot are a two-beat gait—the pacing horse moves his legs in lateral pairs, and the trotter in diagonal pairs. But while pacing horses existed in the early days of the sport, they were not popular, considered of lower quality than the trotter, and desirable only as a saddle horse.[38] Back in the late 1700s and into the middle of the next century, some referred to the pacer as the "poor man's trotter," a horse one would only ride or drive until they could afford a "real" road horse.[39]

Star Pointer's accomplishment brought horses of the pacing gait new respect, though many harness racing purists still clung to the trotter as the one true harness horse. Turn-of-the-century slang labeled the pacing horse as a "sidewheeler," due to the lateral stride, or a "wiggler," due to the side-to-side wiggle of the horse when viewed from the front. Despite the historically second-class status of the pacer, the popularity of horses with a pacing gait grew, in part because this lateral gait was generally faster than the trot. However, the trotting gait was more efficient and therefore able to be carried over a longer distance—something that remained significant in a time when races were still five and six one-mile heats in length. Speed and ability to carry it over a distance were equally important.

The first two-minute trotter finally arrived in 1903, when the California-bred mare Lou Dillon trotted a mile in two minutes flat. A few months later, she lowered the record again to 1:58 ½.[40] The two-minute mark had finally been breached by a trotter and it appeared to be the dawning of a new era of super speed and surging popularity for the sport. But a sub-two-minute trotter remained quite rare. In fact, just four horses would lower Lou Dillon's world record over the next sixty-six years.

As the high-wheel sulky gave way to the pneumatic bike, Septer "Sep" Palin entered the world of harness racing. In time, he would become a legend, but back then, he was a young man just getting started in a sport whose golden age had already passed—something harness racing enthusiasts hadn't yet realized. With the lifting of racing prohibition laws, the Thoroughbred industry surged back into prominence. By the early 1900s, this, combined with the dawn of the automobile age, were two major nails in the coffin of the once-thriving sport.

American harness racing publications in the late 1920s and early 1930s carried frequent articles and editorials speculating as to the reasons the sport was failing. Akers noted that harness racing had slowly disappeared from the streets, fairs, and tracks of rural America. Each year, more harness tracks switched to Thoroughbreds or auto races. The horse itself had been forced off the road by the automobile, which some in the sport believed was the primary problem, as it destroyed the earliest and most universal form of harness racing—road racing.[41]

As the machines took over, horses faded into the background, becoming part of the olden days of grandparents and long-dead ancestors. Each year, fewer people owned horses or required them as part of their lives for work and for transportation. The youth of America had no appreciation for the intricacies and details of developing a fine harness horse. The world was rapidly changing. Where once the human connection with horses as part of daily life had kept the sport relevant, now there lingered an ever-widening gap.

During this same time, harness racing remained comparatively healthy in other countries. There were a variety of reasons for this, no small part of it owed to better organization, able to address the concerns of antiquated systems of starting and of contesting the races in heats—both of which were confusing and frustrating to the uninitiated. Many of the old-timers that had grown up in an era when harness racing was significant in America couldn't see any reason to change anything. They couldn't grasp that the sport had to evolve as the world changed, or it would be left behind.

In America, the public no longer understood harness racing as part of the American experience, or as part of their heritage. Attendance dropped, purses fell to all-time lows, and the future of the sport looked bleak. Then the Depression came and everything looked much worse. There was a belief among many that more than change, harness racing needed a superstar to bring back the crowds—another horse that could trot a sub-two-minute mile, a horse that could dethrone the current world record holder Peter Manning. Then they would have something to promote, something to bring the crowds back.

The sport felt ripe for a hero. In the spring of 1934, many thought that superstar horse would be the previous year's $6,800 yearling, the stunning son of Peter Volo—a flashy bay colt named Lawrence Hanover.

CHAPTER 5

CHAPTER
— 6 —

"Few owners in late years have gone on so whole-heartedly and sportsmanlike as he. Baker is well loved. His permanence is an asset to the sport."

— GEORGE M. GAHAGAN, 1933

HOTEL BAKER STABLE

Much lore circulated around the sale of Greyhound, growing ever more grandiose as the horse gained the public's attention. The $900 price Baker paid for Greyhound would be called "bargain basement" as Greyhound catapulted into superstardom. Years later, many writers reported the price as if Baker didn't know what he was getting that November day in Indiana. While it's impossible at this point to know exactly how Baker felt about the gelding when he plunked down $900 for him—roughly $20,000 in today's money—it is worth noting that Greyhound was the highest selling yearling at the November 1933 Indianapolis Speed Sale.* Most yearlings sold at Indianapolis went for between $100 and $200, with some reaching the $400-500 range. [1]

In contrast, however, was the astounding $6,800 paid for the Peter Volo yearling, Lawrence Hanover, later the same month at the Old Glory Sale in New York.[2] The stunning bay colt was a product of the famed Hanover Shoe Farm, a top producer of harness horses in the nation.

---

* Patsy Brewer, a yearling filly by Peter the Brewer (full brother to Greyhound's dam, Elizabeth), also sold for $900.

For perspective, the average annual American salary for those still employed in 1933 was $1,700, and a home cost around $3,300. At the same time, a thousand mortgages were being foreclosed on every day.[3] The amount paid for Lawrence Hanover was inconceivable to the average American. The middling yearling price at the 1933 Old Glory Sale was about $385, according to a lengthy sale report in Hanover, Pennsylvania's *Evening Sun*.

Lawrence Hanover had everything a trotting-bred horse should, and everything that Greyhound did not. He had the look, the conformation, the pedigree, and the incomparable Hanover name behind him. His dam, Miss Bertha Dillon, was the top broodmare of trotting-bred horses in the world. In a time when trotting a mile in two minutes or less had been accomplished by fewer than ten horses out of the hundreds of thousands that had raced over the last century, Lawrence Hanover's dam had produced three of them. For a mare, limited to producing just one foal a year, this was no small feat.

All three of Miss Bertha Dillon's two-minute foals were by Lawrence Hanover's sire, Peter Volo (by Peter the Great and out of Joe Knight's Nervolo Belle). A world-record-holding trotter upon retirement in 1915, Peter Volo was now the top sire of harness horses. However, no colt of Miss Bertha Dillon had ever made it to the track—her three two-minute foals were all fillies. The male foals seemed to be an unlucky sort, unable to stay sound and therefore unable to race. Still, E. J. Kenney, owner of the LaSalle stable of Chicago, readily paid a big price to secure the most promising yearling of 1933. Many felt he'd gotten a great deal on pedigree alone.[4]

With hindsight, Greyhound had obviously been a bargain, especially when compared to Lawrence Hanover. However, Baker wasn't naïve. He had owned and raced harness horses for many years and was well regarded in the sport by 1933, although he'd stepped away from it briefly in recent years. Baker was a horseman, and he knew his way around a good piece of horseflesh. Did he know what he had in Greyhound? It's doubtful anyone suspected the impact Greyhound would have on his sport. Baker wasn't afraid to take a financial risk and he was good at surrounding himself with people who complemented and broadened his knowledge—Palin and Knight were friends of his and he trusted their judgment. At sixty-five years of age, Baker had seen and experienced a lot, but perhaps the best was yet to come.

Edward John Baker was born September 30, 1868 on a farm east of St. Charles, Illinois. His parents, Edward H. and Martha, were successful farmers, but when E. J. was still a small boy, the elder Edward Baker tired of the farming life and moved his family into St. Charles. There he opened a hardware store on Main Street.[5] This seemingly insignificant change of address would have a lasting impact on young E. J.—in part because it would leave the boy with a longing to return to the farm life and animals he loved, and in part because the geographical change would result in his older sister, Dellora, attracting the attention of a particular suitor.

Dellora was known to the local male suitors as "the Belle of St. Charles." She soon caught the eye of John Warne Gates, a farm boy from Turner Junction (West Chicago) who, like the senior Ed Baker, had tired of farm life and instead sought adventure along the banks of the Fox River in St. Charles. Dellora was not impressed with Gates, and neither were her conservative parents. They saw Gates as a nonconformist and a wanderer.[6] To prove them wrong, Gates enrolled in college, earned a degree, and in 1874, married Dellora Baker. Both were just nineteen.[7]

With the help of their families, the young couple established a home and a hardware business in Turner Junction, but Gates wasn't much into settling down for the simple life. He had big dreams. He'd recently learned of a new invention—a type of livestock fencing guaranteed to be impenetrable. Gates believed this invention, barbed wire, could potentially change farming forever by allowing pasture land to effectively be sectioned off into farm fields. Crops could be rotated and stock would be protected from rustlers and Indian raids. But the inventor, Joseph Glidden, was struggling to get his invention patented, let alone convince the farmers his new fencing was as amazing and effective as he claimed.[8]

Gates would bridge the gap for the inventor and convince the skeptical farmers that barbed wire was everything Glidden promised it could be. He became a salesman for Glidden and his partners, and took the invention to Texas to prove its worth. He billed his sales tactic as entertainment, setting up a corral in the town square at San Antonio during a rodeo. He bet the local cattlemen that forty of their Texas Longhorn cattle could not fight their way out of the corral. The poor beasts were herded into the small corral, and by nightfall, the crowded and agitated cattle had not escaped. Gates had proven his product, and sold hundreds of miles of barbed wire at 18 cents a pound—the beginning of his fortune.[9]

In 1901, Gates' fortunes took another incredible turn. While working on a railroad project in Port Arthur, Texas, his drilling crew struck oil on Spindletop Hill near Beaumont. The strike produced 100,000 barrels of oil a day.[10] The Spindletop developers quickly organized and formed the Texas Oil Company. Gates invested heavily and served as director of the new company. With Gates at the helm, Texas Oil rapidly grew and evolved into a multi-billion-dollar company we know as Texaco.[11]

While John Gates was growing his millions in barbed wire and oil, Dellora Gates' younger brother, E. J. Baker, attended business college for a year and then clerked in his father's hardware store.[12] But E. J.'s first love was farming, and during this time, he also developed a keen eye for livestock and an interest in advanced farming practices. Throughout his life, regardless of the success and wealth he achieved in other areas, he always listed his vocation as farmer—not philanthropist or businessman.[13]

At age twenty-one, in 1889, E. J. married Harriet Rockwell, the daughter of a prosperous insurance broker. They lived in a small stone house in St. Charles, where E. J. took a job as a grain tester for the Chicago Board of Trade.[14] Testing the moisture content determines the suitability of the grain for harvest and storage. It is measured whenever grain and seed are traded or sold.

In 1891, Harriet gave birth to the Bakers' only child, Henry Rockwell Baker. Baker was immediately and forever smitten with the boy, who was described as a joy to all who knew him. Henry was adored by his aunt Dellora and uncle John "Bet-a-Million" Gates (the nickname was earned later in life, when Gates became a prolific gambler, once rumored to have bet $1,000,000 on which of two raindrops would slide down a window the fastest).

Gates lavished young Henry with opportunities and experiences he might otherwise not have had, providing him with trips to the theater, and travels across the country and abroad. In 1908, the Gates family took Henry by ship to England. From there, they took their touring car (sent ahead with their chauffeur on a different ship so that all would be ready when they arrived) on a road trip through England, Germany, France, and Switzerland. When Henry returned from his time abroad months later, he had no interest in finishing his education. He sought only adventure, leaving school and setting out in search of it.[15]

Just over a year later, an ailing John Gates grew increasingly worried about his nephew. The young man seemed more interested in having fun and hanging out with his childhood sweetheart Nina Carlson than taking his adult life seriously. In 1910, realizing his death was imminent, Gates quickly got his affairs in order. He left $250,000 (roughly equivalent to $8,000,000 today) to Henry—money Henry would receive only if he first got his act together, finished high school, and held off on any plans to marry the Carlson girl until after he earned a college degree.[16]

"Mr. Gates always wanted Henry to have a good education," Baker told the *Chicago Tribune*. "My son hasn't gone to school for two years, although we have done our best to make him go." Making the gift conditional "is the best arrangement that could have been made."[17]

John W. Gates died in August 1911, leaving the bulk of his $38 million estate to his wife, Dellora, and his son, Charles. Gates' death was only the beginning of seven years of death and devastating loss for E. J. Just four months later, E. J. and Dellora's sister Lavern would suddenly of heart failure at the age of forty-five. The next year, Charles, John Gates' only heir and Henry Baker's favorite cousin, dropped dead from a stroke at only thirty-seven.[18]

To honor his late Uncle John's wishes, Henry finished high school and enrolled in college. But a hard hit in a football game broke several ribs and punctured his lung. Henry Baker soon developed pneumonia from the injury and then tuberculosis.[19] Despite his aunt Dellora promising the Gates' fortune to any doctor that could save Henry,[20] after two years of illness, the young man died of heart failure at the age of twenty-three. E. J. and Harriet were devastated at the loss of their beloved son. The final months of Henry's life had taken an emotional and physical toll on both parents, but particularly Harriet, who was reported near collapse, with her condition serious.[21] Her friends and family feared she would die of a broken heart right along with Henry. The *Chicago Tribune* reported over 5,000 people attended Henry's funeral.[22]

E.J. Baker's sister, Dellora Gates, died in 1918. With both Charles Gates and Henry Baker gone, there was no one to carry on the Gates or Baker names. The remainder of the Gates' fortune and Texaco stock holdings passed to Dellora's only remaining heirs: her brother, E. J. Baker (age 50), and her late sister's only child, Dellora Angell, age 15. Both were suddenly multi-millionaires.

By all accounts, Baker was a kind man and generous with his wealth. His character remained unchanged after inheriting his share of Gates' fortune. The first major gift the Bakers gave to the city of St. Charles came in 1925 with the construction of the $250,000 Henry Rockwell Baker Community Center, built in memory of their son and dedicated to the men and women of St. Charles who served in WWI. The multi-level, mansion-like, English Tudor-style structure boasted fine wood-paneled walls and oak beam ceilings, plus a bowling alley, swimming pool, men's smoking lounge, billiard room, auditorium, and grand lounge featuring an impressive fireplace and a life-sized full-body portrait of Henry Baker in his football uniform. On the upper level were rooms for various club meetings and educational opportunities.[23]

Over the next several years, Baker purchased eight farms in the St. Charles area. He raised crops, cattle, and horses. Baker had a keen eye and ability to select ideal horses for work, carriage, saddle, and later for racing. He was a progressive farmer and an expert stockman. Baker was among the first in his area to use artificial fertilization and hybrid seeds.[24] He managed large acreages (1,500 acres over those eight farms) and many employees. With each piece of land he bought, he made improvements, including nice homes and dairies. He bought the best purebred stock for his dairies, from Texas to the Canadian border, including Holsteins, Guernseys, Jerseys, and Swiss cattle. He also brought purebred feeder cattle to the area from out west.[25]

A generous man, Baker did not hoard his wealth or the quality stock it brought him. Life wasn't a competition for him; he wanted his friends and neighbors to prosper, too. "The sudden good fortune made no change in Mr.

Baker's character, loyalties, or friendships," the *St. Charles Chronicle* wrote on his passing. "He never lost the common touch or forgot his friends of boyhood."[26] He sold some of his stock cheaply to improve the herds of other farmers in St. Charles. Baker also brought in experts in crop science and animal husbandry and held free educational events for anyone who wanted to attend.[27]

Baker loved his town of St. Charles and wanted to see it grow and prosper. Nearly all of his philanthropic efforts were directed to the city and the farming community. "Having friends is more important than anything else," Baker said in his twilight years. "I love this community and have tried to be loyal to it."[28]

In the 1920s, to stimulate business and make easy access to bring people in from Chicago some forty miles to the east, Baker teamed with other community leaders and was instrumental in convincing the governor of Illinois to route the new Highway 64 right down Main Street, providing a main artery out of the larger city directly into St. Charles. He spent $200,000 to build the St. Charles National Bank, an impressive structure of Georgian marble, to anchor the main business district. Baker and his niece continued to lavish gifts on the city of St. Charles through the 1920s and for the rest of their lives.[29]

"Why not?" Baker once said when asked why he gave so much to his city. A whimsical smile brightened his blue eyes. "You see, I never had but one child and he died. I'll never have another. I've lived here all my life. I'll live here the rest of it and die here. Why not these things for the town?" Baker wanted his gifts to leave a legacy of long-term prosperity for residents and businesses by providing employment and income to the people of St. Charles and the surrounding area. He hired only local suppliers and contractors for his building projects.[30]

The grandest gift Baker gave to the city would draw people (and tourist dollars) from all over the country. It would be known as the "Gem of the Fox River Valley"—the luxurious Hotel Baker on the banks of the Fox River. The well-appointed Hotel Baker boasted grand Greek revival architecture, all the modern amenities including air conditioning throughout, stunning gardens, and the exquisite, balconied Rainbow Room, containing a dance floor constructed of three hundred glass tiles with over 2,600 red, green, blue, and yellow lights underneath. The lights were synchronized with the pipe organ music. The hotel served not only as an attraction to bring people to the city, but also a place for Baker to entertain guests and horsemen from the harness racing circuit, a sport that had recently piqued his interest.[31, 32]

Baker bought his first harness horses and, with Iowa-born trainer-driver Chet Kelley at the reins, built a small but formidable stable of trotters and pacers for the 1922 racing season.[33] He had visions of competing at the top of the game—the Grand Circuit, a series of races where the greatest trotters, pacers, and horsemen competed for the largest purses in the sport. This circuit was equivalent to the Major League of baseball—the show, the place where the top horses and drivers came together. The first meet of the Grand Circuit was held in Cleveland, Ohio, in 1873, and it remains the oldest continuing racing series in the United States.

Baker's initial foray into the sport of harness racing met with moderate success. But in 1925, Chet Kelley became ill, and his son took over the training and racing of his father's string, including the Baker stable[34]—a move one might speculate, due to the actions that followed, was not to Baker's liking. By fall of 1925, the gossip around the circuit rumored that Baker was getting out of harness racing altogether and turning his interest to Thoroughbred racing.[35] This rumor seemed confirmed when Baker announced in November that his entire racing stable under Chet Kelley would be dispersed at the December Old Glory sale in New York.[36] The news shocked and saddened the harness racing world, many of whom saw Baker as a major asset to their sport.

But Baker had bigger plans. At the dispersal sale of his racing stable, he met and befriended Sep Palin, an expert trainer-driver and Grand Circuit staple.[37] Together, Baker and Palin built a formidable racing stable. Palin was given free rein to buy whatever horse he thought would give Baker the opportunity to have what he wanted most—a world champion harness horse. Palin found and purchased both unproven youngsters and established racehorses as he sought to fulfill Baker's dream.

In addition to training and racing Baker's stable, Palin partnered with two others to purchase a training and breeding operation in Indiana. Christened The Senator Farm after the stallion of the same name,[38] the farm became a pipeline of sorts, producing horses for Palin to train on behalf of his partners and clients. Baker and Palin both invested in multiple quality broodmares to breed to The Senator and raced sons and daughters of the stallion. They enjoyed much success with horses purchased and produced in the late 1920s, each adding stellar broodmares and excellent racing stock to their separate holdings.[39]

In 1928 and 1929, the Baker-Palin stable won nearly one hundred races, making Baker the winningest owner and Palin the winningest trainer of both years. In 1930, the Hotel Baker Stable was among the largest racing stables in the country, with thirty-five horses in training, a dozen Hambletonian contenders, and two of the fastest pacers on the circuit in Winnipeg and Labrador.[40] The next year, Baker purchased The Senator from Sep Palin and his partners.[41] Rumors spread rapidly that Baker was getting out of racing and into breeding. Some reports, most notably from well-known Illinois turf writer Tom Gahagan, indicated he planned to sell his entire stock of racehorses.[42] Future events during this time of severe economic uncertainty would see the rumor bear some fruit, but for now it appeared that despite the stock market crash of 1929 and the lurking economic depression, Baker was expanding his footprint in the harness horse business. Just two years later, Palin and Baker had a sixty-horse stable occupying three barns at the state fairgrounds in Indianapolis.[43]

The Senator had a substantial book for the 1932 breeding season. Many of these were mares owned by Baker and Palin. The Baker-Palin stable continued to race, having multiple successes, though no results as strong as their stellar seasons of 1928 and 1929. George Gahagan, who penned the "Hoof Beats" column in the *Indianapolis Star*, frequently reported the times set by The Senator's get early in 1932. Gahagan noted in April that the chestnut stallion had sired the fastest two-year-olds thus far that season at Indianapolis.[44] It appeared that Baker and Palin were at the precipice of building a successful breeding program around their star stallion, but the plan would lie in ruins just a couple months later, when The Senator died suddenly in late May of 1932, at the age of twelve. Baker soon after announced the dispersal of all his holdings at the November Indianapolis Speed Sale—his racing string, noted broodmares, and several well-bred yearlings and weanlings—again sparking rumors that he was leaving the sport.[45] Palin also sold off his holdings, including star performers by The Senator.[46]

The newspapers of the day did not speculate as to why Baker and Palin sold everything they had that was related to The Senator, but the reasoning may have been two-fold: Baker and Palin were heavily invested in breeding and racing The Senator's get, with the goal of promoting the stallion and increasing his value. They had much success leading up to the stallion's death, and even in the months after. But with The Senator gone, there was no reason to continue that path, if the sole purpose of the endeavor was to start and promote a homebred breeding and racing program with The Senator at its core.

The second possible reason for the dispersal related to the tanking economy. Just a month prior to liquidating his horse holdings, Baker also sold his entire award-winning dairy herd. With milk prices dropping severely, Baker indicated it no longer made economic sense to own them.[47] Baker was extremely wealthy, but not immune to the concerns of the nation in the grips of the Depression. Liquidating assets gave him disposable income for his philanthropic projects and prevented further loss in a time with an uncertain economic outlook.

By the end of 1932, while a weanling Greyhound romped in the pastures of Calumet Farm, it looked like Baker was out of the harness racing game for good—a move lamented by fans and horsemen alike.

"It is too much to believe such a lover of harness horses will leave," turf writer George M. Gahagan wrote following Baker's dispersal at Indianapolis. "Many moons will come and go before one of greater sentiment and more effective action will enter the equine realm."[48]

Looking back, with almost one hundred years of hindsight to our advantage, one might wonder why Baker would sell everything and then, just over a year later, spend thousands of dollars building a new stable when the economic outlook was so dire. From the newspaper reports of the day, it seems the general but guarded consensus in the harness racing world reflected a feeling that perhaps the worst of the Depression was over. The prices realized at the 1933 harness horse sales were one-third higher than expected. Lexington had a record-breaking year, with top prices ranging from $3,000 to $15,000, though the average price for 233 horses sold was $410.[49]

"Such prices ... make it look as if the harness sport never heard of the depression," said Mr. E. Roland Harriman, president of the Grand Circuit and chairman of the Trotting Horse Club.[50] Elsewhere, similar thoughts were expressed. The intensity of the economic depression seemed to lighten as pieces of Roosevelt's New Deal fell into place. Despite riding waves of renewed hope into the new year, 1934 would show the country that they'd only received a brief breather in a grueling marathon of a decade. For the nation—and the world at large—the worst was yet to come.

Palin continued to successfully train and race horses for other clients through the 1933 season, some of which had been purchased from the Baker dispersal of the previous year. Baker served as secretary of the Indiana state fair board, along with other activities related to his philanthropical projects and his various business endeavors. He attended the Lexington Trots at the famed KTHBA track in late September. While there, he began building a new racing stable at the Lexington sales, picking up some established racehorses and a few young prospects from the Calumet Farm dispersal.[51] In November, Baker purchased more horses of racing age and several yearlings at the Indianapolis Speed Sale, including Henry Knight's gawky gray gelding named Greyhound.

CHAPTER 6

CHAPTER
—7—

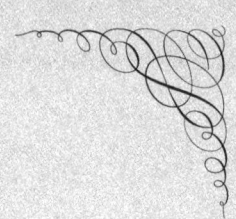

> *"He had a keen mind.
> In the opinion of the men who served with him, he would have been
> equally successful in law with training in that field."*
>
> *"Even though he was one of the coolest individuals to ever board
> a sulky, away from the track he was
> as warm and human as anyone could be."*
>
> —
>
> HOOF BEATS,
> NOVEMBER 1952

SEPTER FAITH PALIN

When E. J. Baker tapped him in 1926 to develop and race his new stable, Sep Palin had been in the harness racing game for nearly thirty years. Together, Baker and Palin would create a racing stable of unmatched quality. A formidable team, they would dominate the sport for the next fourteen years.

Born Septer Faith Palin in Iroquois County, Illinois on April 11, 1878, Sep was the youngest of nine children of Augustus and Nancy Palin. The family hailed from Indiana, and all of Sep's siblings were born in that state. Census records indicate the Palins were in Illinois for a relatively short time, returning to Indiana when Sep was a young boy. Sep would always consider himself a Hoosier, and the Hoosier state would always claim him as their homegrown hero, despite his early years in Illinois.

Young Sep had been around horses "since I was so small, I had to climb into the manger to put a bridle on," the reinsman would reminisce to a reporter in his twilight years.[1] His family had horses, as did most everyone back then. There were farm horses to work the fields and a couple of road horses used for transportation. Sep knew from the start what he wanted to do. As a young boy he'd spend every free moment at the Milford, Illinois track, watching the horses and hoping for an opportunity to help cool one out. Sep also helped his father run the family's butcher shop. He made his rounds driving a gray draft stallion pulling a wooden wagon, delivering meat from the shop. But the young horseman ached to be at the track. In 1896, at the age of eighteen, Sep went to work for Billy Marvin's racing stable in Attica, Indiana.[2]

Sep started as a groom for Marvin,[3] mucking stalls and caring for the racehorses, rubbing their coats to an iridescent shine matched only by the one he worked into the worn leather harnesses. He had a natural talent with the horses, and it's likely Marvin soon had young Sep conditioning trotters and pacers in the early mornings on the training track, as is the typical progression for a capable groom. Marvin, a successful Grand Circuit driver, tutored multiple future top trainer-drivers through the years, but Palin was his most famous pupil.[4] Whether Palin did any race driving for Marvin is information lost to history but after four years with the older trainer, Palin struck out on his own.[5] The young trainer had a quiet way about him, a gentleness that the horses responded to, and an uncanny ability to softly coax the best effort out of each horse. Palin displayed astonishing skill, judgment, and resourcefulness, particularly for a driver so early in his career. It was thought then by others in the sport that Palin would go straight to the top.

Despite his early talent, building a successful racing stable depends heavily on having clients with deep pockets and quality racehorses. The progression of Palin's early career is unclear. The 1900 census shows him living with and working for a relative as a "hand." The 1910 census shows Palin, now married, to be employed as a horse trainer at the race track. Shortly after this, Palin made his Grand Circuit debut with a horse named Stephen A. Palin came fourth overall in a field of five, hardly an auspicious start. Palin drove Stephen A. to a handful of wins in 1911 at lower-level county fair meets, but his showing in Grand Circuit competition was mediocre. The young man's stable, based in Russiaville, Indiana, grew slowly.

Palin first gained notoriety with a pacer named Possibility—a horse that had been a "rather uncertain racing tool," according to turf writer Will Gahagan, before finding his way into Palin's stable in 1914. Previously deemed unreliable by other trainers, Possibility won 14 of his next 16 starts after Palin—"in some mysterious manner," wrote Gahagan, perhaps alluding to Palin's unusually quiet ways—set him on the right path.[6] Palin had a lot of success with Possibility on the half-mile tracks, to the point of gaining small-time celebrity status on the local tracks and county fair circuit. At the end of the 1914 season, Palin, who raced his string in the south after the season ended in the north, was among the top money-earners who raced exclusively on half-mile tracks.[7]

Despite his success with Possibility, Palin

apparently still couldn't make it as a full-time trainer-driver on the small circuit, where purses were less than $100. The Grand Circuit was where the big boys played and where the large purses were. Like a minor league player, he struggled through lean years in the bush leagues. The drivers at this level knew they'd never get rich but kept on because they loved the sport. Naturally Palin's goal was to make it to the Grand Circuit and stay there, but he knew taking horses that weren't ready to win wasn't going to earn him any more business. While Palin built his reputation as a harness horse trainer, he also worked as a horse trader, buying work, road, and racehorses wholesale and selling them at livestock and speed sales.[8]

"A young Indiana teamster that is surely making good at his profession is Sep Palin of Russiaville, who has been racing a large stable of trotters and pacers," *The Indianapolis Star* reported toward the end of 1914. The same article told of Palin's stellar performance the month before at Macon, Georgia, where he drove in nine events during the week, winning six of them and taking second place in two. "The showing made by his string this season reflects great credit on his ability as a trainer and race driver," the article continued.[9]

Thirty-six-year-old Palin wasn't yet making waves, but gaining notice for sure, with ever-widening ripples. He raced mostly on the southern circuit after being suspended by the National Trotting Association until he returned $511 in "unlawful winnings" earned with the horse Dan O. He had been charged with starting out of class—dropping a horse into a slower speed class than he was required to enter—in Ohio.[10] At the time, there were multiple governing bodies overseeing the sport of harness racing, each with different rules and regulations. If you didn't like what one organization did, you could simply race under a different one. Whether this is why Palin raced almost exclusively in the south until the end of the decade or if there was another reason is something this writer could not determine. Nor was any evidence found that he paid his fine or even was guilty of the associated charge.

A few years before, Palin had been among the victims in a cheating scandal where the outcome of each heat in a race was allegedly pre-determined by some drivers and judges at the 1911 Warren County Fair (Indiana). Though he came second overall with his horse, Fiesta Belle, he was placed third by the judges after finishing ahead of the horse that was "supposed" to win second money.[11] Through the 1910s and mid-1920s, cheating in both harness racing and Thoroughbred racing left an indelible black mark. It destroyed public confidence in both sports and led to a prohibition on pari-mutuel betting—an act that reduced the value of betting and therefore the rewards for cheating. Both actions would bring dark days to the sport of harness racing, lean years of poor attendance, and a severe reduction of interest in the sport that had once been more popular than baseball.

"The Grand Circuit meeting ... was all but

called off for lack of attendance," reported the *Dayton Daily News* (Ohio) in a 1925 story about the sale and razing of the Columbus Driving Park. During the closing days of the meet, the price of admission was dropped and then removed altogether, but the desperate act did nothing to improve attendance.[12]

In 1918, it appeared Palin finally had his big horse. He made headlines early in the season with Indianapolis businessman Fred Cline's pacing filly, Esta G.

"Esta G., Indianapolis Owned, Wiggles Around Track in 2:06 ½," read the June 15 headline in *The Indianapolis Star*.[13] Esta G. was a two-year-old pacing filly (or "wiggler," in the parlance of the day) owned by Palin's top client, Fred Cline. In that era, for a two-year-old to go a mile in 2:06 ½ so early in the season was impressive. Many harness horses would never in their lives go that fast. Palin described the filly as "the fastest piece of horse flesh I ever put a line over." Esta G.'s performance generated a lot of excitement for her and for Palin, but she never made it to a race that year. In fact, she disappeared from racing news altogether until Cline finally sold her a couple years later. While Palin never spoke about it to reporters, one could presume perhaps Esta G. taught the young man an important lesson about the merits of slowly developing a harness horse—that pushing too fast too soon wasn't sustainable and often resulted in a horse's career cut short by injury, lameness, or sour attitude. This knowledge would play an important role in the success and longevity of his future champions—especially Greyhound.

By 1921, Palin had twenty-one horses in his training barn and was a Grand Circuit staple. Tall and lanky with blue eyes, light hair, and a kind smile, Palin was described by most as quiet, sometimes gruff, but underneath, a kind man. Due to his rising success, Palin relocated his racing stable from Russiaville to the state fairgrounds at Indianapolis, Indiana—a major stop on the Grand Circuit. This would be his home track for the remainder of his career. Palin had made it to the top—making a name for himself as a top developer of pacing horses and noted around the circuit for his skill.

"No one has anything on Palin as a driver of pacers," reported W. H. Gocher in *The Lexington Herald-Leader*. "When it comes to sifting sand with a pacer on any kind of track, Palin is there with the goods."[14]

Palin "raced his horses into condition" on the fair circuit half-mile tracks early in the season, then moved them on to the Grand Circuit races when they were ready. Palin had great success with this non-traditional approach, building up his horses' strength, stamina, and confidence on the lower level before asking them for more on the "roaring Grand." When Palin brought a horse to the Grand Circuit race, you could be certain that horse was ready to do the job.[15] Palin saw no need to push his horses early; they might not break records early in the season, but they could be relied upon to stay on gait and be top contenders when it counted.

Palin had a knack for working with horses other trainers didn't have the patience for. He preferred a gentle and thoughtful approach, using a soft cleverness and knowledge gained from years of experience. In fact, he was often sent talented horses other trainers could not find success with—horses that likely were strong-minded and sensitive, requiring the touch of a thinking horseman instead of one that relied upon brute force.

One such horse sent to Palin in 1921 was the fast mare Galli Curci, which Cline had pulled from top trainer Tommy Murphy after some reportedly disastrous starts. Palin went on to win several races with the brown mare, and she was among the top trotters of the season.[16] Soon, other horse owners were sending their trotters and "difficult" horses to Palin, and he won with them as well. Known for years as a pacing specialist, Palin had now become a leading trainer of trotters as well. He closed the season among the biggest money earners in the sport.[17]

Palin was ranked the number two winningest driver of 1924 with eighteen winners, in a tie with fellow future hall of famer Ben White.[18] Now forty-eight years old, Palin was still considered quite young in the world of Grand Circuit drivers. A top harness race trainer was created over decades. It was a sport won not just by having a fast horse but by years of experience developing the speed and honing one's craft. Despite his nearly half-century of life and approaching thirty years of experience, the following was reported in *The Indianapolis Star* on December 20, 1925.

"It is several years since Palin discarded short trousers, yet the local reinsman could hardly be called a veteran. [However], what he has accomplished as a trainer and race driver has been equaled by few of the leading veterans," wrote Will Gahagan for his "In the Harness World" column. He went on to note that on multiple occasions, Palin had been sent talented horses that other top trainers could not get along with or were otherwise unable to develop to their fullest potential.[19] Palin's patient and thoughtful style would pay off handsomely when a playful, sensitive, and talented yearling named Greyhound entered the Palin stable in November 1933.

G

Greyhound

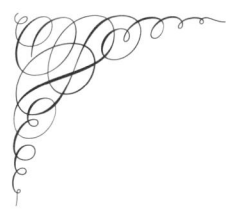

PART TWO

CHAPTER
—8—

> *"Even with all the wealth of high-class juveniles
> that are on parade here, [Lawrence Hanover]
> is one which will be singled out as one far above the ordinary,
> even without knowing that he is a member of the Royal Family."*
>
> —
>
> TOM GAHAGAN,
> NOVEMBER 1933

UNDERDOG

Few people took note of Greyhound as Palin worked him around the mile oval at Indianapolis that winter of 1933-34. Were it not for his unusual color, they might not have noticed him at all. Lots of slow jog miles, five or six a day, six days a week, laid the foundation for the development of Greyhound's trot.

Young Greyhound could certainly be a handful—not mean, but assertive, and anxious to get on with whatever came next. The few bits of motion film that exist today show a horse with a lot of nervous energy and natural curiosity, his mouth and lips constantly searching for something to nip, hold, or play with. Some would mistake this behavior for meanness, and for sure one had to watch their fingers around the gelding, but Greyhound wasn't trying to hurt anyone. He did, however, have his own ideas on how best to work with him, as is often the case with highly intelligent and sensitive horses.

With his decades of experience, Palin knew how to appease Greyhound while simultaneously encouraging him to bring out his best. Some trainers see fidgety, nippy behavior as deliberately obstinate and try to "train" it out of a horse with physical punishment. This most often backfires on a horse like Greyhound, dulling spirit and shutting him down—making him resentful and unwilling or afraid to try.

Since Moody had already broken Greyhound to the jog cart, the early part of Greyhound's training likely went smoothly. Palin probably started the gray from the beginning anyway—not out of disrespect for Moody, but as a wise move on the part of any horse trainer, ensuring he'd learned everything Palin would expect of him while in Moody's barn. During this time, Palin watched Greyhound's way of going very carefully. Developing a trotter's gait for speed was a months-long process that involved building muscle and fitness, careful training, and mindful hoof care. While the trot is a natural gait for the horse, trotting at speed is not. To bring out the most speed at the trot, the horse's hooves need to be meticulously balanced—a game of fractions of inches and ounces. A difference of as little as an eighth of an inch in toe length could cause a horse to switch to a pace, break gait (gallop), or interfere with himself (hit one leg with the hoof of a different leg).

With trotters, interference usually involves striking the shin of the hind leg with the toe of the front hoof on the same side. This interference causes cuts, bruises, and intense pain. It can cause a horse to alter his way of going or resist going faster to prevent a reoccurrence. If interference is allowed to continue, serious injury and lameness will result, which can end a horse's career.

"A proper trotting gait conserves muscle and strength and increases endurance," wrote Johnny Simpson in his 1968 piece on shoeing and balance. The trotting gait is built around an even extension of the legs. At the trot, the hind legs act as pistons and the front legs roll over in a rhythmical manner with a round, fluid stroke and ample forward extension. Uneven extension in one or multiple legs produces a faulty or irregular gait, usually accompanied by interference, and affects both speed and endurance.[1] Pushing a young horse to speed before he is properly balanced will cause him to go lame, said Simpson, further stressing his point by saying trainers who do this often say something like, "Oh, he went lame early and I had to quit with him," when in truth, the horse wouldn't have gone lame at all "if the trainer had taken his time and made sure the colt was balanced properly before [asking for speed]."[2]

Careful use of shoes and weights encourages the horse to move correctly and efficiently without injuring himself. How the hoof is trimmed, plus the shape and weight of the shoe, can significantly influence the horse's way of going. According to Simpson, weight at the toe will balance and steady the action of the leg while aiding in extension—he likens it to the difference between throwing a weighted fishing line or a line with no weight. The weighted line will fly true and plop down into the water with precision, whereas the latter will wiggle around with little control over distance or direction.[3]

"Are you beginning to understand now why horse trainers seem to have a liberal sprinkling of gray in their hair?" Simpson asks, about forty-five pages into his seventy-five-page piece on the theory of shoeing and balancing.[4] It took decades to learn the intricacies of developing a solid trotting gait—something that had to be seen, felt, and experienced over thousands of miles behind hundreds of horses. Perhaps this is why Henry Knight, Hunter Moody, and Dick McMahon were all so interested in getting Greyhound into Palin's hands—he was a master at his craft and had already learned the hard lessons on how easily a brilliant horse could be ruined when pushed too fast too soon.

"The art of gaiting and balancing a harness horse consists of a series of delicate adjustments," Simpson wrote at the close of his piece. "[Including] weight of shoes and length of toe and angle, designed to bring about with the least expenditure of energy, the truest and freest action of gait and, therefore, the greatest speed the horse is capable of producing."[5]

Though he had natural ability and an unusually long stride, Greyhound had a rather awkward and disjointed way of going.[6] Therefore, a significant part of his early training involved trimming and shoeing the big gelding in a way that would make the most of his natural talent, while teaching him to keep his balance and stay on gait at speed. Later in his career, Greyhound would go with a simple six-ounce shoe in front and no added toe weights, with a four-ounce shoe behind.[7] The shoeing record for Greyhound as a two-year-old was long ago tossed in the waste bin, though Palin likely kept an index card on each of his horses, noting hoof care intervals and any changes made, along with notes on how the horse was going. Veteran track blacksmith Art Henrichs shod Palin's horses for a time, and mentioned that early on Greyhound wore square-toed shoes all around.[8] These would aid in easing breakover by moving the breakover point back. Since Palin was opposed to the use of unnatural methods, he likely would have used minimal weight and the most basic shoes possible to achieve a balanced gait, using any specialized shoes for the least amount of time necessary.[9] Though there is no written record, toe weights can be seen in some images from Greyhound's two-year-old season and early in his three-year-old year. The weights are absent from later photos, and this author saw no photographic evidence of them after the 1935 Hambletonian.

As for other equipment, Palin preferred to keep rigging simple. A plain leather harness, open bridle (no blinkers), and protective boots were all Greyhound required—no head pole or gaiting straps or any other claptrap. His head was checked high, but not artificially so, as Greyhound naturally carried his head at a high angle.[10] To the veteran trainer-drivers in Palin's day, developing a trotter was a finely honed skill, one acquired over decades. There were no gadgets or shortcuts to replace skill and careful athletic development. It is the reason why the top trainers in the sport were old men—a top reinsman's career was built over decades. A man with just ten or fifteen years under his belt was still considered a tenderfoot by the grizzled old veterans of the sport.

There is no record of what Greyhound's early training looked like. But by piecing together times reported in newspapers and trade publications, and assuming Palin followed a typical training and conditioning schedule of the era, one can speculate. After about a month of just jogging, Palin would have added in training miles once or twice a week. "Training a mile" or "working a mile" is a term used for taking a horse a mile at a specific timed clip. Early training miles were slower—perhaps a 3:45 clip with a gradual increase in speed[11, 12] as Palin carefully developed Greyhound's fitness, being ever-mindful of the quality of the young horse's trot. Hurrying a horse at any stage of his early training often resulted in a horse that frequently broke gait, interfered, or both. Palin would have been careful to never ask for more than Greyhound could happily give, knowing that a tired youngster was prone to injury and could develop sourness and bad habits that would cause him much trouble down the line.[13]

As Greyhound received his early lessons from Palin, economic depression tightened its grip across America and around the world. Unemployment rates in the United States topped twenty-five percent. People abandoned their homes and traveled west in search of work. Back in St. Charles, Baker employed many extra men on his farms to help the people of his hometown find work. When the need arose, he donated land to the government for use as a camp for President Roosevelt's Civilian Conservation Corps (CCC) program. The camp housed two hundred men and provided much-needed work to citizens of St. Charles.

Baker also donated equipment and supplies for CCC projects and, along with his niece and her husband, helped create more jobs by sponsoring Fox River "beautification" projects. The newly employed workers cleaned up the banks of the Fox River, moving in decorative stone and building walls and walkways along the river. Debris was dredged from the river to improve the flow and the old dam was rebuilt to create an area for swimming and boating.[14] During one of the work days, Baker supplied the men with a banquet lunch and gave each a bonus one-dollar bill, equivalent to a half-day's wages.[15]

Baker further supported his community by selling cheaply or giving away some of his prize stock. He would meet a friend on the street and tell them if they needed a calf, to swing by the farm and tell the manager that he'd said to sell one for $5[16] (roughly one-fifth of its value). One young girl was given a calf as a 4-H project.[17] She showed the calf at the county fair, winning first prize. The calf grew to produce milk for the family and birthed additional calves for the family to sell.

When the town cemetery was at risk of bankruptcy, Baker purchased some of their unneeded land to keep them solvent.

He later donated the land to the city for a park, the creation of which provided more much-needed work for the citizens.[18] Baker made such donations and arrangements throughout his life, with many gifts given in such a way that the individual pride of the receiver could be maintained through their work and societal contributions. Much of Baker's philanthropy went publicly unrecognized, but he was responsible for helping many families during rough times and quietly gifting sums of money to pay college tuition for local youths.[19]

As spring 1934 turned to thoughts of summer, Greyhound prepared to make his racing debut. Palin increased his training miles, going a couple jog miles followed by three or four training miles with times in the three- to three-and-a-half-minute range, brushing the last quarter or eighth of the final mile in a faster clip. These training miles would have a roughly twenty-five or forty-minute break between them where his groom would take Greyhound back to the stable, rub him down with liniment to keep his muscles loose, and cover him in blankets until his next training mile. Horses stood covered and blowing hard while they waited for more training or, if racing, their next heat. The idea back then was to not allow the horse to cool off between heats, as it was believed they would be better prepared for the next if they were still quite warm. After the final heat or training mile, the horse would get bathed in warm water with Tuttle's Elixir,[20] rubbed down, then walked and cooled out slowly, intermittently given a few sips of water, and not returned to their stall until their thirst was slaked and their breathing had returned to normal.[21]

Sep Palin reined Greyhound around the final turn at the Indianapolis training track. The big gelding moved easily between the shafts of the jog cart, his long legs covering ground with smooth efficiency. As he approached the final quarter, Palin moved his hands forward, giving Greyhound a bit more line. The big gelding took it readily and surged forward, Palin's body lurching back slightly as Greyhound changed gears and increased his speed. His stride was like nothing Palin had seen—the roll of his forelegs; the impossibly long reach; the piston-like action of his hind legs' powerful strokes like the coupling rod on the drive wheels of a steam locomotive. Greyhound blazed the final quarter mile in thirty-one seconds.[22] Palin gently took back the reins, slowed the gelding to a walk, then turned and jogged him back to the gap where his groom waited.

"Pretty fast last quarter." John Hogan spoke as much to himself as anyone, unhooking Greyhound's overcheck rein. The gray stretched his neck forward and down, glad to be free of the restrictive leather strap.

Palin, a man of few words, gave a barely perceptible nod and handed the lines to Hogan. Another groom held a young bay colt nearby, ready for the tall reinsman to take his next training mile. Hogan sat sideways on Greyhound's jog cart, his legs hanging off to one side, draped over the arch, and drove Greyhound back toward the stable area to cool him out.[23] Hogan was Greyhound's first groom. The gelding would have three in total during his racing career, but for 1934, the old man and the young horse were a pair.[24]

All around were signs of spring. Delicate buds poked out from the winding branches of the sugar maple trees near the Palin barn at the Indiana state fairgrounds. A robin landed on a branch above Greyhound's head, chirping a merry tune, as the elderly groom worked loose the buckles on the harness and removed the leather straps from the gelding's steel-gray body.

Soon the stable would leave their winter quarters at Indianapolis and travel to Columbus, Ohio. On June 8, the track at the Ohio state fairgrounds would be the stage for the harness racing world's first look at Baker's $900 yearling.

Few took notice of the lanky gray gelding when he stepped onto the track at Columbus, Ohio, for his first training sessions on the road. He wasn't much to look at. "Awkward" and "ugly" were among the most common adjectives used to describe young Greyhound. While he trained well, Greyhound showed nothing sensational in those first weeks in Ohio and failed to raise an eyebrow among the many writers who reported daily on the trotting scene.

In contrast, Lawrence Hanover, the LaSalle Stable's $6,800 purchase of the previous fall, was looking just as a trotting horse should. He was by far the top colt in trainer-driver Doctor Hugh Parshall's stable, already turning in miles much faster than any other two-year-old. "Doc" Parshall, at age thirty-five, was considered youthful among the veteran reinsmen. He'd been training harness horses for just fourteen years; many of the other top drivers had more than twice that time in the sulky. But the veterinarian from Ohio had been the top winning driver for the past five years. Flashy, young, and exciting, Parshall was a popular figure in harness horse news columns and publications, and idolized by many fans and younger horsemen on the circuit.

While Parshall saw much success and would retire a legend in the world of harness racing, his aggressive style resulted in both remarkable wins and spectacular failures. Parshall often got the results owners were looking for, but he, like many horsemen of his era, saw the horse as an animal whose sole purpose was to work and to obey. Where Palin took his time developing Greyhound, Parshall pushed Lawrence Hanover for brilliance early on.

Lawrence Hanover was a beautifully bred individual, oozing with natural talent. But, according to Parshall, the colt was lazy and infuriatingly obstinate. He'd been difficult to break to harness and cart, fighting Doc every step of the way, eventually developing a habit of throwing himself down on the track and refusing to move. Doc solved this problem by hitching the colt tandem with a mule, allowing the beast to drag the colt along the track until he decided to obey.[25] Such techniques were alarmingly common back then, in the days when most people considered the horse to be little more than a reactionary bundle of nervous energy, muscle, and speed.

The harness horse publications and daily newspaper features wrote of Lawrence Hanover frequently. At the end of April, Parshall had the colt go a mile in 2:26, fully four seconds faster than any of his other two-year-olds.[26] A little over a month later, Lawrence Hanover trained a mile in 2:20 and then a second mile in just 2:15,[27] extremely fast consecutive miles for a two-year-old so early in the season. It is likely Parshall was under enormous pressure from Lawrence Hanover's owner and from the press to ensure the colt lived up to the potential expected from his royal breeding and exorbitant price tag. With this display of speed, Parshall got what he needed, a nod from the press that Lawrence Hanover would not "disgrace his illustrious family."[28]

Noticeably absent from the sports writers' frequent reports on the up-and-coming two-year-olds was any mention of Greyhound—until mid-May, when George Gahagan reported Greyhound's thirty-one-second last quarter prior to leaving Indianapolis:

"Palin let the 2-year-old grey trotter, Greyhound, by Guy Abbey ... step a quarter on a slow mile in 31 seconds, which makes it obvious that this one wasn't sailing under false colors last fall when he was sent through the ring at the local sale as one of the best [yearling] prospects."[29]

While sportswriters often commented on the notable accomplishments of horses outside of their area, no one reprinted Gahagan's somewhat defensive-sounding comment on Greyhound. It was Gahagan that had commented on Greyhound's "brilliant speed" prior to the Indianapolis Speed Sale last November, but he seemed to be alone in his admiration. All eyes had been focused then as they were now—on the $6,800 shimmering bay colt, Lawrence Hanover. Parshall had been taking Lawrence Hanover over fast miles, not just brushing a fast quarter at the end of a slow mile—giving the press plenty to talk about.

Palin wasn't worried about the press silence over Greyhound; they would see what he had when the time came. In late May, the gelding went a mile in 2:18, stepping another fast final quarter.[30] Though three seconds slower than Lawrence Hanover's best time, it was a good time for a two-year-old in May. Palin declared his gray youngster ready to race.

Baker arrived at Columbus days before the meet opened. He thoroughly enjoyed being at the track, watching his horses train and race. The love of the horse and the sport ran deep within him—he cared profoundly about the wellbeing of his horses and the promotion of the sport. Baker wanted to help everything and everyone he loved and cared for to thrive. He stood by the rail, watching Palin work Greyhound a moderate mile, going the final quarter in a fast clip. He clicked the stopwatch in his palm, glanced at it, and smiled. Greyhound definitely had speed, but was slow to get going. He just wasn't built for fast starts.

Palin jogged Greyhound back to the gap where Hogan waited. Palin handed off the gray and took the black pacer His Majesty from his groom. Baker looked down at the notes he had on the four-year-old colt he'd recently purchased for $10,800.[31] He puffed his cigar thoughtfully; he and Palin had a strong stable this year. The Gem, Senator Bedell, Lindy Volo[32]—all were good horses, and there were others still back in Indianapolis that would be ready later in the season. He sat down to watch his new colt jog, pleased with his purchase.

Later that afternoon, with his ever-present straw boat hat, cane, and cigar, Baker walked through the stables, stopping at each stall to visit the occupant. With gifts of carrots and sugar cubes, he spoke to them softly and stroked their glistening necks. He greeted each groom by name, even the swipes that bathed and rubbed down the horses after a workout. He knew them all. Palin watched the elderly gent smile and greet each man he encountered and shook his head; he didn't know half these guys by name.[33] Greyhound pushed his head over the stall door at the sound of Baker's voice, ears forward, eyes bright, and lips stretched and seeking. If Baker wasn't fast enough getting to him, Greyhound would stomp his foot or rap it against the stall door. These antics endeared the gelding to Baker even more. Greyhound soon became the stable favorite.[34]

On June 8, 1934, the opening day of the Columbus meet, Baker sat in the stands and watched Greyhound step onto the track for his first career start. The two-year-old jigged a little at the sound of the crowd when he passed the grandstand, but he soon settled. The five-horse field warmed up, the drivers jogging a few loops of the track then brushing a fast quarter or half, depending on the needs of the horse. It had always been this way—the horses trotting sometimes two, three, or more miles before the race ever started, the belief being this work was needed to ensure the horse's muscles were warm and loose before the race.

Baker was pleased. Greyhound was the favorite for this race.[35] Columbus was part of the "Short Ship" circuit—a smaller "minor league" circuit. Palin liked starting the season on the smaller circuit, especially with a new horse making his first start. The fairgrounds at Columbus had a half-mile oval track and lower-level competition. It also was only a two-heat race—an ideal start for two-year-olds. Lawrence Hanover, the high-priced colt everyone was talking about, had shipped to North Randall, Ohio, near Cleveland. His debut would be on the Grand Circuit.

The horses came together to score for the start about a quarter mile from the wire that marked the track's start and finish point. An antiquated and inefficient method of starting a race, "scoring" referred to the process of attempting to bring the horses together to the starting point, on gait, and evenly lined up abreast of each other across the track. The drivers had to arrange their horses without benefit of any sort of a barrier, keeping their horses' noses on the same invisible line as the nose of the pole horse—the horse in first-post position, closest to the inside rail. Since they were sitting behind their horses and couldn't actually see their noses, one can imagine the challenge, particularly when all drivers were anxious to get away fast and first. If the horses were deemed fairly aligned and on gait, the starter yelled, "Go!" and the race was on. If not, a bell was rung, and all the horses had to be stopped, turned, brought back to the three-quarter pole, and started again. It was not uncommon to have the horses score several times, taking twenty or more minutes to get the heat underway.

Five horses scored down for the start of the two-year-old trot.

"C'mon, Palin, get that big gray up here," the starting judge shouted into a megaphone from his perch in front of the grandstand. "That's right—now, Plaxico, get your filly up here. Now, Valentine, get a hold of your filly! I'm not starting this race with you halfway to the first turn! Alright, boys, let's bring them down together, now! And, GO!" The starting judge gave the word, and the horses were off![36, 37]

Greyhound started poorly, struggling to find his balance. His long legs made his gait awkward and ungraceful. Palin steadied the big gelding and didn't rush him—there was no sense in getting him all excited and risking him breaking stride or losing his confidence. Greyhound soon settled into his trot, but due to the tight turns on the smaller track, Palin had to rate him back, and he finished the first half in last place. Coming out of the first turn of the final half, Greyhound slowly moved to the lead, but the fillies Miss Evergreen and Calumet Ferona came right along with him. Coming out of the final turn, Palin touched the lines, asking Greyhound for a bit more speed. The big gray answered, lengthening his stride. He opened a gap between himself and the two fillies, but the pair surged forward, driving Greyhound hard down to the finish as he fought to maintain his lead. The three flashed under the wire with Greyhound in front, setting a maiden race record of 2:17. Miss Evergreen came second.

In the second heat, Miss Evergreen got away fast and went straight to the front. Greyhound got away slowly, again taking some awkward steps as he untangled his long legs and found his stride. He and Calumet Ferona chased the leaders, slowly closing the gap. Coming out of the final turn, Calumet Ferona passed Greyhound and Caharrus Boy, joining Miss Evergreen in the lead. Nearing the finish wire, Greyhound poked a nose in front of Caharrus Boy, but ran out of track before he could catch the front-running fillies, finishing third in the heat and second overall behind Miss Evergreen.[38]

Despite winning the first heat and setting a maiden time record, Greyhound's debut race would be recorded as a loss. Tradition dictated that a good harness horse not only be fast but also able to carry that speed over a distance. The "one and done" dash system embraced by the Thoroughbred runners wasn't seen as a legitimate test for a trotter. Any horse could turn in a single fast mile, but a great horse, the type that over a century of selective breeding had sought to produce, could do it over and over again.

Not long after Greyhound's racing debut, all eyes were on Doc Parshall as he worked Lawrence Hanover two very fast miles (2:12 and 2:13).[39] The pricey star of the Parshall stable had trotted considerably faster than Greyhound had in his racing debut, and unbelievably fast so early in the season, especially for a two-year-old. Even before his first race, Lawrence Hanover drew comparisons with his famous sister, Hambletonian winner Hanover's Bertha. Like her, he "showed lots of power and gait when flat and going," reinsman Tommy Berry would tell reporter Frank Trott after watching Parshall work the colt.[40]

Despite his loss, Greyhound still had the record that mattered most. A 2:17 mile in a maiden race was captured by official timers and therefore entered in the record books, whereas Lawrence Hanover's training times were not clocked by sanctioned officials. Time over a mile in racing conditions was held in higher esteem than that in a trial or in training. Speed was speed, but to produce the fastest speed in racing conditions was more difficult, since the environment could not be controlled. Still, Lawrence Hanover's incredible 2:12 training mile indicated he had plenty of speed, and even if he went slower in racing conditions, he'd still likely smash Greyhound's maiden record. In short, Greyhound was still the underdog—no one was looking for him to be the hero the sport sorely needed. That expectation was heaped solidly on Doc Parshall and Lawrence Hanover.

Lawrence Hanover's first start would be delayed, though. He contracted shipping fever in late June at the North Randall track.[41] Jack Reid reported in the Springfield (Ohio) *News-Sun* that Lawrence Hanover "may not be in shape to race for several weeks," and that proved to be true. The lively filly Belvedere, sired by Peter the Brewer (a full brother to Greyhound's dam, Elizabeth), was the favorite in Lawrence Hanover's absence. But it was Fred Egan with the promising colt Silver King who took first money.[42]

Greyhound's next start came the evening of July 10 under the lights at the Fort Miami Track in Toledo, Ohio, for the Sherwood Trot for two-year-olds. This first start against Grand Circuit horses was a big step up. Trotting a 2:17 mile, which had won him a heat at Columbus the month before, wouldn't do him any good at this level. The horses he would meet that evening had already raced and won at faster speeds than that.

Despite the threat of bad weather, a good turnout of fans watched eight horses go to the post for the Sherwood Trot. The field scored down a few times; then, at the word "Go!" the brown filly Chica got away first, setting the pace for the first heat. Silver King and the flashy bay filly Belvedere followed closely behind, just off the pace. Greyhound started poorly and was mid-pack entering the backstretch. As the horses came around the final turn and into the home stretch, driver Tom Berry brought Belvedere up fast to overtake Chica, and won the heat in 2:09. Greyhound kept up but didn't show up. Never a serious threat, he came in fourth behind Silver King.

In the second heat, Belvedere broke stride in the first turn, causing her to fall well behind the field while her driver struggled to get her back on trot. M'Liss, who'd finished seventh in the first heat, set the early pace while Belvedere, back on gait, slowly worked her way up toward the leader. As they straightened into the final stretch, Belvedere was within striking distance, and Berry let her loose in a burst of speed. She won going away from the field, taking the second heat the same as the first, in 2:09.

Greyhound surged up under a hard drive from Palin, just edging out M'Liss for second. Chica came fourth, and Silver King finished at the back of the pack in seventh. In the final analysis, Belvedere was the clear winner in straight heats with Chica and Greyhound tied, each with one second- and one fourth-place finish.[43]

Greyhound's next start was in Toronto, Ontario for the Canadian National Trotting Stakes for two-year-olds—the feature event for the fourth day of Grand Circuit racing at Thorncliffe Park. The filly Mary Taylor started well and set the pace, but she broke stride after passing the half, at which point Egan, driving the gray colt Silver King, took command. Greyhound came up with Silver King and trotted into second. Coming on strong, Greyhound pushed a nose in front and was in the lead! But Tommy Berry had more horse than Palin that day. He set Belvedere loose and she passed up the two gray leaders, winning the first heat. Greyhound hung on for second, and Silver King was third. Mary Taylor found her gait and came fourth.

The horses scored for the second heat. Mary Taylor got away fastest and set the pace, taking Belvedere with her. She held it through the first half. Silver King stepped swiftly into the stretch, moving in behind Belvedere for a time before Egan moved the stout colt off the rail to pass Belvedere. Silver King came on strong through the stretch and won going away. Mary Taylor came second, and Belvedere a game third. Greyhound came in dead last. Silver King and Belvedere did a third heat run-off with Silver King coming out on top, winning easily by four lengths.[44, 45]

With Lawrence Hanover's absence and Greyhound's inability to win a race, Silver King and Belvedere were easily the top two-year-olds on the circuit. With stellar breeding and striking good looks, Silver King was the exception to the unwritten rule that any gray colt should be gelded. Greyhound had shown some brief flashes of speed, but it seemed he didn't have enough to pull out a win when it counted. It didn't help that he scored poorly and got away slowly. The first part of his race would be a series of awkward strides as he searched for the balance needed to really set down and trot. By then, he had little hope of catching his better coordinated competitors—at least until he matured and developed more speed.

Greyhound and the rest of the Palin stable departed for the next stop on the Grand Circuit—Rockingham Park in Salem, New Hampshire—for the August 3 two-year-old trot. Among them was the current star of the Hotel Baker Stable, a promising two-year-old pacer named The Auctioneer, who'd won his first two starts prior to Baker purchasing him for $10,500.[46] Palin and The Auctioneer won their race, a one-mile dash (no heats) for two-year-old pacers. The roan colt made a mad rush through the stretch and won going away in a blazing 2:08.[47] Undefeated now in three starts, the little roan pacer generated a lot of excitement about his future potential around the Baker-Palin stable. He'd certainly emerged as Baker's top two-year-old.

GREYHOUND

THE REMARKABLE STORY OF THE LEGENDARY RACEHORSE WHO INSPIRED A NATION

Lawrence Hanover with Doc Parshall at Old Orchard Beach, Maine.

AUGUST 1935, GUY KENDALL COLLECTION, COURTESY OF THE UNIVERSITY OF MAINE

CHAPTER
—9—

> "Greyhound was a legend in his own time. And his time came during a period when harness racing needed a legendary figure. The sport's fans were just about to close the door on harness racing when out popped Greyhound."
>
> — Phil Pines,
> Author, Turf Writer, and Director
> of Harness Racing Museum, 1995

FINDING HIS STRIDE

Palin knew Greyhound wasn't a slow horse, just slow to get going. His long legs and awkward stride didn't lend themselves to fast starts—one of the reasons why the gelding's conformation wasn't considered ideal for a trotter, and in fact, his conformation was seen as a detriment. He not only lacked the "trotting pitch," he wasn't even level from front to back. A couple more recent champions, Uhlan and Peter Manning, lacked the trotting pitch, but at least they were even at the withers and hindquarters. Not Greyhound. His withers were nearly two inches higher.

Further, the ideal trotting horse was longer in body than in height—the idea being that a longer body gave the horse more room for a long stride, and he would be less likely to interfere. Greyhound was a full four inches taller than he was long, something trainers of the day believed would make it impossible for a horse to trot fast without injury from interference.[1] At nearly 16 hands and still growing, Greyhound stood three to four inches taller than his competitors. Like his canine namesake, Greyhound was narrow through his body and "tucked up" in his flank. Both features were believed to decrease a horse's lung capacity and stamina—something a horse needed in spades to be competitive in a grueling, multi-heat race.

Despite his presumed physical shortcomings, Palin knew Greyhound had speed. He also knew the big gelding would never score as well at the start as the smaller, quick-footed trotters. However, Greyhound had shown recent improvement in his ability to pick up speed after he found his stride, which would help him overcome any deficit from a poor start. With a little more fitness and maturity, Greyhound might just surprise them all.

After three losses in as many starts,* Palin decided to step Greyhound down in class. He entered him in the $400 one-mile trot at Salem, New Hampshire. A single-mile dash, the race at Salem had no heats. Greyhound had one chance, one mile, to pull out a win. Greyhound's top rivals, Silver King and Belvedere, were absent from the race, competing instead in the $2,700 two-year-old trot, which Silver King won in straight heats with Belvedere finishing second.

In his race on the day's undercard, Greyhound trotted the mile in 2:13 ¼, and finished first in a nine-horse field—the first win of his career, not that anyone was paying much attention. The results were printed in a tiny font near the bottom of the page in a handful of newspapers. But the race itself didn't earn a single mention in the sports columns, or even in the August 3 Rockingham report in *Horseman and Fair World*, filled as they were with the accomplishments of Una Signal and Silver King, the two big stakes winners of the day.[2]

A short paragraph in *American Horse Breeder* noted Greyhound broke stride at the start, got back on gait, then was in contending position at the seven-eighths point. In the stretch, Palin tipped him off the rail, and he "outraced Mary Taylor and Salem with something to spare."[3] A modest win in an insignificant race—but now the big gray had tasted success, and Palin had perhaps found in Greyhound the horse he'd been looking for.

A warm, mid-August summer day greeted the fans at Good Time Park a week later for the August 14, 1934 Good Time stake. The Doc Parshall-trained Prince John, a colt that had recently won a heat in 2:07 ¼ and set a new two-year-old trotter season record, was the favorite. Belvedere was second choice, and Greyhound the third choice among bettors. Silver King sat this one out.

By noon, temperatures were in the mid-eighties with a light southerly wind gently bending the long grass on the infield of the triangle track at Good Time Park. Like several harness tracks of the day, the Good Time track had an unusual shape due to the need for it to fit the

---

* Some sources state Greyhound had three losses in four starts, describing his first race as two separate mile dashes (instead of a two-heat race). For this reason, some sources say Greyhound won his first race, but lost his next three. Most sources, including the comprised record created by the Harness Racing Museum, show the first two heats of Greyhound's career as a single race.

dimensions of the available land. The first turn was the top of the triangle, and while the points were rounded, the tightness of that first turn required a bit of rating back of speed for the drivers to negotiate—something more difficult for a big, long-striding horse like Greyhound.

John Hogan stood with Greyhound in the paddock, ready for Sep Palin, when post time came. The playful gelding nipped at the lead shank. Hogan absently dodged searching teeth as the gray tried to grab his shirt sleeve or nibble his fingers. The man smiled. Greyhound could be a handful for sure, and sometimes an anxious sort, but there wasn't a mean bone in his body. The groom rubbed the toe of his boot in the dirt, observing the clay underneath the thin layer of loose soil. It had rained some the day before, but with the warm sun and slight breeze, the ground had dried well. The old man gave a single, definitive nod in response to his own unasked question. Yes, the track would be fast today.[4]

Palin arrived in his dark green satin jacket, trimmed in white; a matching puffy satin hat crowned his graying head. He took the driving lines and nodded to Hogan, who attached the check rein and then removed the leather shank from the gray's bridle. Anxious to be underway, Greyhound walked forward as Palin lifted a leg over the arch of the sulky. The tall reinsman hopped a couple steps to keep up with the horse, and swung onto the seat.[5]

A field of five two-year-olds scored for the start of the Good Time Stake, the feature race on that day's card. As expected, Prince John scored well and went to the lead. Greyhound had gotten away slowly but now was trotting well within himself at the back of the pack. Prince John led through the back stretch and into the second turn, the bay colt trotting smoothly with Doc Parshall quiet on the lines. Greyhound, trotting mid-pack, had replaced his awkward stride with smooth, powerful strokes.[6] It was the type of trot Palin had been working for, slowly building Greyhound's strength, balance, and confidence over time—now the gray had finally found it.

Stride by stride, Greyhound slowly edged up on Prince John and into second place ahead of Lucre and Salem. The horses surged out of the turn and into the final stretch. Hooves pounding, sulky wheels whirring, drivers shouting—all knew the race would be won or lost in the final quarter. Parshall pushed Prince John for more speed and the colt broke stride. Parshall took hold of the galloping colt, reining him in, trying to get him back on trot before the finish line to avoid disqualification. Greyhound and Palin rushed past the floundering Prince John, taking the lead. The lanky gray flashed under the wire, winning the first heat in 2:09 ½. Prince John, having found his stride too late, finished fourth.[7]

In the second heat, the filly Mary Taylor set the early pace. Greyhound got away slowly but soon settled into a smooth trot near the back of the field. Mary Taylor held the lead all the way around to the three-quarter pole. As the field pounded into the home stretch, Greyhound lengthened his stride, found a new gear, and charged up from behind. He poked a nose ahead of Mary Taylor, winning the heat handily. With a speedy final quarter, Greyhound set a new season record of 2:06 ¾, dethroning Prince John as fastest two-year-old of 1934. Belvedere was second, and Prince John came third.[8] In the press box, the newspaper men hurriedly scribbled down notes and pounded away on typewriters. Greyhound had finally raised a few eyebrows.

With a clean bill of health, Lawrence Hanover had his first start, taking third in the $700 Good Time Consolation trot for two-year-olds[9] a few days after Greyhound's record-breaking trot over the same track. The two would finally meet at Springfield, Illinois, the next week for the Illinois Review Futurity. Though he'd turned in a season-record mile and posted a couple wins, Greyhound did not yet look like a champion—certainly not the caliber of the stunning Lawrence Hanover. The long-legged gelding still got away terribly slowly at the start. At this level, he couldn't afford to give away too much distance to his fleet-footed rivals. Still, the gelding didn't break stride like the other youngsters often did. His spindly legs and gawky body might at times appear uncooperative, but Palin had him well balanced, confident, and strong—the gray kept on trotting, even as the reinsman asked for more speed.

Greyhound had defeated some of the star two-year-olds of the Grand Circuit at Goshen, but many among the fans and press still dismissed him in favor of Lawrence Hanover, or the other speedster in Parshall's stable, Prince John. As the long summer days burned out in the face of approaching autumn, there was no single clearly outstanding juvenile in the two-year-old trotting class. Belvedere, Silver King, Prince John—all had shown some brilliance, and all more consistently than Greyhound.

In Springfield on August 22, five horses went to the post for the $1,600 Illinois Review Futurity. The others in the field needn't have been there, for it was a two-horse race all the way, with Lawrence Hanover pushing hard to best the long-striding Greyhound. The crowd leapt to their feet as the two flashed by and trotted under the wire, Greyhound just holding off Lawrence Hanover to win both heats—the first in 2:07 ¼, and the second in 2:06 flat, a new season record.[10] *American Horse Breeder* noted the gray gelding clearly had speed to spare, likely able to trot 2:05 had it been necessary. Greyhound had shaved nearly a second off the record he'd set the week before. No one could deny him; he was the fastest two-year-old of the season.

From Springfield, the circuit moved on to Syracuse, New York, for the August 31 Two-Year-Old Stake for the Age. Twelve trotters went to the post in the soft yellow sunlight of a beautiful summer afternoon. Temperatures hovered in the upper seventies with a few fluffy white clouds dotting the vast blue sky. In the first heat, Doc Parshall, driving Lawrence Hanover, and Parshall's brother Daryl, driving Prince John, had Greyhound boxed in on the rail. In a crowded twelve-horse field, there was nothing Palin could do to break loose and give his colt room to race. Prince John won the heat in 2:07 with Lawrence Hanover coming second. Trapped on the rail with no escape, Greyhound finished fourth.[11]

In the second heat, Greyhound would not be denied. Whether the Parshall brothers tried to pocket Palin and Greyhound again was not reported. But the gray gelding out-trotted the field, setting yet another season record of 2:05 ½; Silver King was second, and Lawrence Hanover, having broken stride, came eleventh. Prince John and Greyhound had a two-horse run-off for the third and final heat to determine the winner. Daryl Parshall got away fastest with Prince John, taking him to the inside rail, where he'd get the shortest trip. The crowd jumped to their feet and roared as the two colts pounded down the home stretch side-by-side. With each stride, Greyhound took a little more ground from Prince John. As they approached the finish, Palin let Greyhound take a bit more line, and the big horse found another gear. He flew past Prince John and won easily by four lengths, going the last quarter in an impressive :29.[12]

Twenty-nine seconds. The time stood out, significant among the quarters and fractions that made up the time reports for the race. Going a quarter of a mile in less than thirty seconds meant that Greyhound had the potential to trot a two-minute mile. At just two years old, plenty could still go wrong. Producing a two-minute mile meant trotting four consecutive quarters in thirty seconds or less—no small feat. It would take careful handling, stamina, strength and maturity. It wouldn't happen in 1934—no two-year-old could trot a two-minute mile and no trainer in their right mind would try—but the twenty-nine second quarter meant Greyhound had the potential.

Greyhound and Prince John met again a week later in the $3,000 Horsemen Futurity. Lawrence Hanover and Belvedere instead contested the $2,000 Syracuse Hotel Stake. Both races were on the same card, September 5, at the New York State Fairgrounds.

The even-money favorite for The Horseman Futurity, Greyhound sold in the auction pools for $100, or a bettor could pay $100 for the field—a winning bet if *any* horse could beat Baker's gelding. Auction pools were run by bookies and were different from the pari-mutuels today's bettors are familiar with. For an auction pool, a bettor would bid on the horse they thought would win, with the top bidder being the one who "won" the horse. The top bidders would put their money in the pot, but only the one person who won the bid on the heat winner won the pot (minus the bookie's commission).[13] That meant with each heat, only a single bettor won money, unlike pari-mutuels where everyone has a chance at part of the take. However, there could be multiple bookies operating, and therefore more chances to "win" the winner. Still, a relatively small percentage of attendees could bet under this system. Harness racing traditionalists preferred it this way—believing true horsemen came to see the horses, not to bet money.

Six horses contested the September 5 Horseman's Futurity. Greyhound took the first heat easily over Athlone Sally Boy and Prince John. In the second heat, Greyhound again lowered his season record to an astounding 2:04 ¾, clinching his fourth consecutive win and further cementing him as the fastest two-year-old of 1934.[14] Turf writer Tom Gahagan described Greyhound as "the standout junior of the season."

The same day, Lawrence Hanover took the first heat of his race, going a mile in 2:07 ¾, but broke gait in heats two and three, finishing fourth and second respectively. He took second overall to the filly Zillah Hanover.[15]

The fans and reporters had taken notice of Greyhound, and many were calling him the best two-year-old trotter of the year. Except, of course, for those that still favored Lawrence Hanover. Headlines in *The Urbana Daily Citizen* (Ohio), Doc and Daryl Parshall's hometown paper, announced Lawrence Hanover and Prince John took second in their respective races. The actual winners of each race were mentioned only in passing, buried within the printed column.[16] The paper made no mention of Greyhound's record-smashing new season mark of 2:04 ¾. Presumably the unbalanced account was deliberate, to avoid touting the accomplishments of the "low-class" horse from the west over Lawrence Hanover, the blue-blooded product of the east.

Lawrence Hanover and Greyhound would not meet again in 1934. While neither Baker or Palin commented publicly about it, one can imagine both regretted the decision to let Greyhound's eligibility for the prestigious Kentucky Futurity lapse earlier in the season.[17] The big race held at the annual Lexington Trots traditionally determined the top two-year-old trotter of the year. The results gave fans a first look at the top contenders for the next year's Hambletonian Stake—the premier event for three-year-olds. Considered the Kentucky Derby for trotters, the Hambletonian would one day be the first leg of the trotting Triple Crown.

Mid-September, Lawrence Hanover went to Reading, Pennsylvania and took 6th and 7th in the two-heat race.[18] Another uninspired performance. He later worked an impressive training mile in company, going the last half of a moderate mile in 1:01 ½ with the last quarter in :30 ½.[19] The fast works made Lawrence Hanover the favorite in the upcoming two-year-old trot division of the Kentucky Futurity. Fans and reporters lamented that Greyhound had not been kept eligible, wishing Lawrence Hanover would meet the gray gelding in the big race, and perhaps determine once and for all which was the greatest two-year-old.

Silver King won the Kentucky Futurity on September 25. Lawrence Hanover came second, Belvedere third, and Prince John fourth. Lawrence Hanover won the second heat in 2:05 ½, making him the fastest two-year-old *colt* of the season,[20] but still not the top two-year-old trotter of them all. Greyhound held that record of 2:04 ¾. The $6,800 royally bred colt had still not topped Baker's gawky $900 gelding. Crowds booed drivers Parshall and Egan in the third and deciding heat when neither would set the pace. Lawrence Hanover and

Silver King went the first quarter in a snail-like thirty-nine seconds, making the half at about a 2:22 clip. In the final quarter, the pair finally raced, but Lawrence Hanover couldn't stand the pressure, breaking stride at the eighth pole while Silver King trotted home the victor.[21]

"Flashy Greyhound Slated to Race," read a headline in *The Lexington Herald*.[22]

"Brilliant son of Guy Abbey at the top of his division," reported George M. Gahagan in *The Indianapolis Star*. "The lanky gray has proved to be too much for his competition thus far," Gahagan wrote.[23] Now a draw at the tracks, Greyhound's name featured in print and advertising had become a way for promoters to get more people through the gate. And the crowds poured in to see him for his last start of the year—the Lexington Stake.

A lovely fall afternoon greeted guests for "Ladies Day" at the Kentucky Trotting Horse Breeders Association (KTHBA) track at Lexington, October 3, 1934. A deluge of rain in previous days had kept the crowds away, postponing the racing program and even canceling racing altogether one day. But with clear skies, the people turned out in force to see Greyhound trot over Lexington's velvety red mile.[24] Opened in 1875 to replace the track at the old fairgrounds, the famed "red mile" earned its nickname due to the distinctive red clay surface of the one-mile oval track. In time, the track would adopt the moniker as its official name, and it remains in operation under that name today. But in Greyhound's day, the track was still officially known as the KTHBA track, run by the association headed up by Henry Knight, who then ran his recently opened Almahurst Farm from the same location.

Stepping onto the track for the Lexington Stake, Greyhound met rivals Belvedere and Prince John in a six-horse field. In the first heat, Prince John went to the early lead. Some discrepancies in the accounts of the race appear in the printed reports from the event. Lexington turf reporter Jesse Shuff said Greyhound was never in serious trouble, and won easily over Belvedere when Palin tapped him for a bit more speed.[25] Tom Gahagan, on the other hand, reported in *Horseman and Fair World* that Greyhound did not "appear to be as sharp as in some of his previous races and [had to go] all out to beat the filly [Belvedere] in the first heat."[26] It is possible that one of the reporters mixed up the heats, as the Gahagan report sounds more like what happened in the second heat. Regardless, Greyhound won the first heat in 2:06 ¾, Belvedere finished second, and Prince John, third.

In the second heat, Prince John again got away first and took the lead. Greyhound made a slight bobble getting away,[27] taking a couple awkward steps reminiscent of his starts early in the season. But the big gray caught quickly without losing much ground, and surged toward the front, catching Prince John coming out of the final turn. The game filly, Belvedere, came on fast from behind. She caught up to

Greyhound in the stretch, and the pair trotted down to the wire neck-and-neck. At the finish, Greyhound edged the filly by a nose for the win. Prince John again came third.[28]

Greyhound's two-year-old season was over. The gray gelding shipped from Lexington to Sep Palin's home track at the state fairgrounds in Indianapolis, Indiana. The Baker-Palin stable would winter there until January, when the horses moved to Florida for early training in preparation for the next racing season. Baker and Palin had the top two-year-olds of the season in trotter Greyhound and pacer The Auctioneer. The little wiggler had gone undefeated in all starts. The 1935 season would be an exciting one for sure.

Parshall and Lawrence Hanover contested the Paris Trot at Lexington on October 2, where he won, lowering his own record to 2:05 flat—still a couple fractions short of Greyhound's top time. In turf writer Tom Gahagan's column, following his description of the hard-fought three-heat near-victory for Lawrence Hanover in the Kentucky Futurity just a few days before his near-record in the Paris Trot, this paragraph appeared, centered and in bold face so as not to be overlooked:

> *"Such races are killing on the baby trotters. What would a trainer of two-year-old Thoroughbreds say if he was asked to race his youngsters two and sometimes three hard miles one day each week during the season? That is what is asked of these Standardbred youngsters, and it's a wonder so many of them stay up to the end of the season."*[29]

Whether it was a dig at Parshall or meant as a generalized statement was left for the reader to infer for themselves. As recently as the late 1920s, yearlings were asked to trot against the clock, their records held as a badge of honor for their human handlers and stallion owners. A text on training trotters published in 1908 recommended having horses broken to bridle and harness as young as six months.[30] This practice thankfully fell out of favor, but still, many trainers pushed their youngsters up to and often beyond their physical limits.

Just four days after the Paris Trot, Parshall sent the bay colt against the clock, still trying to dethrone Greyhound. Lawrence Hanover lowered the record to 2:03 ¼, finally toppling Greyhound from fastest two-year-old status,[31] the latter now lounging in his stall at Indianapolis. But Parshall wasn't satisfied yet; he felt the colt had more to give. Five days later, he raced the clock again, this time tying the world record for two-year-olds of 2:02 flat.[32]

After Lawrence Hanover's season-record-smashing trot in 2:02—which tied him with his sister Hanover's Bertha for world's champion fastest two-year-old trotter of all-time—the harness world was all abuzz, talking about the stunning young colt. Doc Parshall told reporters he never gave up on the impeccably bred youngster proving he was the best of them all.[33] Chatter among harness fans talked of Parshall taking Lawrence Hanover for another go at the clock the next week, sure that he could lower his record yet again. Sports reporters projected Lawrence Hanover would win the 1935 Hambletonian. Turf writer Jack Reid even went so far as to say Lawrence Hanover would be the one to finally lower Peter Manning's seemingly untouchable world record of 1:56 ¾.[34]

Despite not getting his first start until early August, Lawrence Hanover raced six times over two and a half months, compared to Greyhound's nine starts in just over four months. In October, Lawrence Hanover was asked to trot three race heats and two miles against the clock in the space of nine days—that's five fast miles in just over a week, three of them on the same day. Palin, on the other hand, seemed less concerned with proving anything in particular, at least with a two-year-old. Content to bide his time, he rested up his star two-year-old for slow, easy conditioning in the spring. The three-year-old season would perhaps determine who had the better system, if not the better horse. Indeed, 1935 would reveal how well each would hold up to the intensity of their rivalry.

With Greyhound's outstanding performances, breaking records and going undefeated in the last four races of 1934, the gray gelding was among the early favorites for the 1935 Hambletonian. His accomplishments also brought notoriety to his family. Just two days after Greyhound won the Lexington Stake at the red mile, Henry Knight sold his sire, Guy Abbey, for $20,000.[35] Knight frequently bought and sold horses, never keeping one for any significant length of time. He enjoyed turning a profit and did wonderfully with this transaction, having purchased the stallion for just $1,400 the year before. Rumor had it he also tried to buy back Elizabeth from his friend Walter Candler. Clearly giving the mare away had been a mistake. But Elizabeth wasn't for sale, not at any price.

Later that fall, Baker reportedly turned down an offer of $20,000 for Greyhound,[36] just a year after being scoffed at by some for paying $900 for the gray trotter. Guy Abbey himself, whom few thought much of when Greyhound went through the sales ring as a yearling, now drew a lot of attention among breeders for the upcoming season. Standing stud for his new owner at the famed Kentucky trotting horse nursery, Walnut Hall, Guy Abbey was on the cusp of being among the nation's most valuable Standardbred stallions. He had sired not only Greyhound, the top two-year-old trotter, but also top three-year-old pacer Calumet Evelyn and 10 other winners in 1934. At the end of September, two sons of Guy Abbey brought the top yearling prices at Lexington, selling for $3,750 and $3,000[37]—a significant price increase, though still not at the level of Lawrence Hanover's sire, Peter Volo.

Back in Indianapolis, the still-warm days grew shorter and the nights crisp, as fall drew its temperate arms about the men and horses in Sep Palin's training barn at the state fairgrounds. Greyhound and twenty-one other horses, including some of Baker's stars such as champion pacer His Majesty, the fast trotter Senator Bedell, and undefeated two-year-old pacer The Auctioneer, were housed in the old wooden barn, along with months' worth of feed, hay, and straw.

Pete Wilson had taken over care of Greyhound from John Hogan.[38, 39] Whether the elderly gentleman had retired or otherwise moved on is information lost to history. Pete was a younger man and a good hand. On a cool October night, Wilson rubbed down the gray gelding and carefully wrapped his legs for support and protection, a common practice even still among racehorse people. He covered Greyhound with a light blanket and settled him in his stall for the night. Around him, the other grooms did much the same with their charges, while the swipes threw down hay for the horses and raked the aisle.[40]

Andrew Smiley and Charley Campbell had the night watch. They would sleep in a barebones room in the old barn like the grooms did, staying close to the horses, keeping an ear out for trouble. Night fell and the temperature dropped. After a final late-night check, Charley and Andrew wrapped themselves in blankets and retired to rickety old cots in the dirt-floored room on one end of the old barn.

At the other end of the barn, in the corner of an empty stall, a thin wisp of smoke curled silently in the darkness.

GREYHOUND

THE REMARKABLE STORY OF THE LEGENDARY RACEHORSE WHO INSPIRED A NATION

JULY 13, 1935, *MOUNT CARMEL ITEM*

CHAPTER
— 10 —

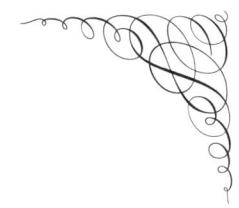

"All year owners and trainers of Hambletonian entries have seen a gray ghost in their sleep, and 'The Hound,' as the stable boys call him, appears ready to make many a nightmare a reality."

—

MAX RIDDLE,
THE LEXINGTON HERALD, AUGUST 11, 1935

UNSTOPPABLE

Andrew Smiley sat up, his legs hanging over the edge of his cot, eyes and ears straining in the darkness. Something had woken him. He could hear the horses in their stalls, shuffling through the deep straw, restless in the dark night. One kicked the heavy oak plank wall. Bang! Bang! The sound carried down the barn aisle as hard hoof connected with solid wood. Not unusual for a horse to kick in their stall, but ... how late was it anyway? Andrew reached for his pocket watch. As he fumbled in the darkness, the smell of smoke reached his nostrils.[1] Fire!

"Charley!" Andrew sprung to his feet. "Charley! Fire!" Andrew ran for the door. "Fire!" he shouted.[2] The word sent a cold chill down Charley's back. He leapt to his feet, donned his boots, and ran out the door to the stable area. Far down the barn row, flames licked the sides of an empty stall. Thick smoke flowed upward. Stopped by the roof, it curled back on itself, searching for escape.

One end of the barn was already completely engulfed. The horses nearest to the flames squealed in terror as the stalls containing feed and supplies burned next to them. The straw and hay in the loft above ignited and burned furiously, flames devouring the dry material.

News reports the next day would read that the space between the rows of stalls acted like a flue, and fanned the fire briskly.[3] Not knowing how the barn was configured, it is difficult to know what was meant, but it is likely the "runway" was the center aisle, and when the men opened the exterior door, the fire sucked air into the barn, spreading flames rapidly toward where Charley and Andrew stood.

The two men ran to the nearest stall, but the horse inside, His Majesty, frightened by the smoke and noise, refused to move.[4] Andrew grabbed a cloth and held it over the terrified horse's eyes while Charley dragged the colt from the burning barn.[5] They turned him loose outside and ran back into the flames and smoke.

The first alarm came in at 11:25 p.m. from a fire box a few blocks away, likely set off by a passing motorist who saw the fire at the fairgrounds and stopped at the first box he found. The alarm would have signaled the nearest station, which was less than a mile away.[6] What we don't know is how long after the fire started the first alarm was sent. Back then, the nearest fire box was at the fairground's administration offices, a considerable distance from the barns on foot. To run there would have taken precious time that could instead be used to save the horses. A second alarm was sent from that box at 11:45 p.m,[7] likely by one of the passersby that stopped to help or a groom from another stable.

One can imagine the scene at the burning barn. Some of the horses screamed as flames engulfed their stalls and burning pieces of timber fell across their backs. They were trapped—nothing could be done for them now. Charley and Andrew kept working as fast as they could, ignoring their own burnt flesh and the thick smoke choking their lungs. People in nearby houses woke to the sound of the fire alarms. They ran to the burning barn, joining the passing motorists who stopped—some to watch, some to help.[8] Charley and Andrew handed off each horse they rescued to one of the many people now milling about.[9] One end of the barn collapsed. The horses that had been trapped in those stalls mercifully fell silent, their suffering over. Charley and Andrew continued their mission. Over and over they ran into the burning barn, and each time they emerged with a terrified horse.

The firemen arrived as the last horse was rescued.* Charley collapsed, overcome with smoke. Andrew had burns on his hands and feet.[10] The scene outside the barn was chaos: some of the horses running loose, others whinnying, trembling, rearing or kicking, still in a panic,[11] trying to escape their handlers and get farther away from the fire. One horse had escaped to the road outside the fairgrounds and now ran back and forth, unable

---

* It is also unknown whether the nearest company was available; they may have already been working on a different fire. Each company would have one truck and four or five men.

to find his way back to the other horses. It would be more than an hour before anyone was able to catch the terrified animal.[12]

The two crews of firemen battled the blaze and had it under control within an hour. An early morning rain shower helped snuff it out completely. Charley was taken to the hospital for smoke inhalation, and Andrew was treated for burns at the scene.[13] Both men were heroes.

In the gray light of morning, Sep Palin's barn lay charred and black. Wisps of smoke rose to meet the rain-soaked dawn. The horses had been captured and led to stalls in other barns. Four yearlings died in the blaze: Djer Kiss, Bobby Belwin, and Eugenia Volo owned by Baker, and an unnamed filly owned by Palin. Four more suffered severely from smoke inhalation and were still coughing many hours later.[14] Miss Almadale, The Gem, Senator Bedell, and The Auctioneer developed pneumonia. After three weeks of struggle, the fire claimed one more life when The Auctioneer, star pacing two-year-old of the Baker-Palin stable, succumbed to his illness and died.[15]

In addition to the loss of life, all feed and equipment were gone, including several recently purchased harnesses and sulkies that had never been used. Bridles, boots, halters, blankets, hay, straw—all were a total loss, as well as the barn.[16] Charley and Andrew survived the fire, but no further information about them could be found after that night. According to news reports, foul play was not suspected, but a cause for the fire was never determined.[17]

Greyhound reportedly remained mostly calm during the whole ordeal, his stall presumably closer to the door and farther from where the fire started. One of the men placed a blindfold on the gelding, wrapped his arm around the big gray's neck, and led the horse to safety.[18] Not yet famous, Greyhound's near loss was sparsely reported. History would soon forget how close we came to losing the star trotter before he had his chance to shine.

The subject of much speculation through the frigid days and long dark nights of January 1935: which three-year-old was the top Hambletonian contender? Named after the most influential sire in the development of the Standardbred breed, the Hambletonian had become the most important race in the sport in the nine years since its conception. Chicago sportsman H. O. Reno had come up with the idea of creating a big race for three-year-old trotters.[19] He believed a trotting race as important as the Kentucky Derby was to the Thoroughbreds would draw attention back to the sport of harness racing.

The first Hambletonian was contested in 1926 with the astounding purse of $75,000 (roughly $1.3 million today). By comparison, the former biggest race for three-year-old trotters, the Kentucky Futurity, had a purse of $14,000 in 1926. Many races had purses of a few hundred dollars or less. That same year, the Kentucky Derby purse was less than

$60,000. The Hambletonian indeed became the premier race for three-year-old trotters, and drew spectators from all over the country and even abroad.

Often, the question of the top Hambletonian contender was satisfactorily answered by the results of the Kentucky Futurity for two-year-olds the previous fall. At least until they started racing in June. But Greyhound, the horse many considered to be the top two-year-old of 1934, hadn't contested the Futurity. Thus, two of the sports fans' favorite off-season pastimes—speculation and argument—were tossed back and forth in the newspapers, sports reports, barrooms, clubs, lounges, and around the dinner table.

"The off-colored youngster won his last four races, each time lowering the season's record for the age," wrote Tom Gahagan, touting his choice in *Collyer's Eye*. Further, "Greyhound defeated Silver King twice at Syracuse," and Silver King's "best time in the [Kentucky] Futurity was a half-second slower than Greyhound's top time at Syracuse."[20]

Determining the two-year-old champion of 1934 was somewhat of a "three-cornered affair," Jesse Shuff reported in his column—Greyhound (2:04 ¾) had won the most races, Silver King (2:06) the most money, and Lawrence Hanover (2:02) had trotted the fastest mile.[21] Such statistics certainly muddied the waters, leaving no clear-cut top two-year-old in 1934 and, in the opinion of many, no obvious top choice for the 1935 Hambletonian.

Winter tightened its grip across the Midwest and along the east coast. Veteran reinsmen and young apprentices bundled up against the cold and jogged horses on the frozen track at the Indiana state fairgrounds. Grizzled old horsemen and young wannabes watched the horses, then sat around the track kitchen, bent over their plates of greasy food and crisp newspapers.

"None can close like Greyhound in the last quarter," one man said to no one in particular, folding his newspaper in disgust.

"But what about the time trials of Lawrence Hanover?" another man scoffed. "He matched the world's record for fastest two-year-old ever."

"Nah," another man grumbled, "we haven't seen the best of Silver King yet!"

"Not a chance," the first man protested. "Greyhound outraced everyone as a two-year-old. Besides, says right here the winter books show Greyhound as the top betting choice!" He stabbed a finger at his newspaper.

"Yeah, right," another man said, smirking, "and right beneath it, George Gahagan says there are still thirty-three trotters eligible. And some nice ones to boot!" He gave a definitive nod and tucked his *Indianapolis Times* under one arm.[22, 23]

Similar conversations were surely had on tracks, in bars, and around living rooms across the country, the stories and heroes modified to fit the geographical location and personal preferences of the speaker.

The Palin stable relocated to another barn following the fire, but remained in

Indianapolis for the winter. Palin and his assistants braved the bitter cold winds and jogged the horses daily, slowly building them back up for the upcoming racing season. As spring approached and the weather warmed some, Greyhound and the others would add training miles along with their jog miles, gradually building to faster times as laid out in Palin's master plan—and, as ever, not pushing the horses too fast too soon.

A new man joined the Palin barn that spring. Just nineteen years old, Jimmie Wingfield had a natural ability with horses and a deep love for the animals and the sport. Jimmie was the second oldest of four siblings, and the oldest of the three boys. His father Marion Wingfield had passed away from pneumonia in 1924, when Jimmie was nine. His mother Mary's cousin was master horseman Sanders Russell. To relieve some pressure on the newly widowed Mrs. Wingfield, the Sanders family invited the three Wingfield boys to live with and work for them on their farm.[24] It was there that Jimmie found he had a real talent with horses. Early in 1935, Russell put in a good word for Jimmie with Palin, and the veteran reinsman decided to give Jimmie a try.[25] He put the young man to work as a groom for His Majesty under the tutelage of an older, more experienced man.

In May, Palin had Greyhound working training miles with stablemates (including The Gem, who had recovered from his smoke inhalation and resulting illness), going in 2:13 and 2:18.[26] The gray gelding "showed his class," George Gahagan wrote, training the last half of a mile in 1:05. The last week of May, Palin moved his string from Indianapolis to Lexington to prepare for the first meet of the season. In the weeks leading up to the first start for the three-year-olds, Lawrence Hanover and Greyhound flipflopped in the ongoing, informal opinion polls gathered among the reporters, horsemen, and railbirds. For some, Lawrence Hanover's 2:02 record made him their top choice. For others, the fact that Greyhound had (eventually) defeated every horse he started against in 1934 made him the obvious choice. Still others noted Lawrence Hanover could be difficult to handle and had been training poorly, while Greyhound had trained beautifully for Palin, making the gray the obvious choice.[27] And so it went, speculation fueling opinion. But none of that really mattered. It all came down to the best horse on the day, and August was still months away.

Turf reporter Jesse Shuff watched the horses train for the opening of the race meet at Lexington from his perch in the tower. Binoculars in hand, he jotted down observations and organized the notes for his "Down in the Bluegrass" column. "The top three colts are working similar times at the KTHBA track," Shuff noted. Lawrence Hanover worked a quarter in :31 ¼, Silver King in :31 ½, and Greyhound in :30 seconds flat.[28]

A week before their first start, Greyhound and Lawrence Hanover each posted brilliant works, with the latter posting a time about a second faster. Baker arrived from St. Charles in time to see Greyhound work.²⁹ The small man stood along the rail. With a silver-tipped cane in one hand and a cigar between the first two fingers of the other, Baker watched while Palin sent Greyhound a fast quarter at the end of his workout. The gelding looked good. He'd matured considerably over the winter. Though he still started slowly, when he hit his stride and really stepped, he seemed to lift on glorious silver wings. He flew around the track like no other horse Baker had ever seen.³⁰

After his workout, Palin handed Greyhound to Wilson and then took his place behind Baker's two-year-old colt The Master. Baker puffed his cigar and leaned into the rail as he watched, pleased to see the dark bay youngster also put in a fine workout. Early opinion touted The Master as the two-year-old to beat this season. Baker and Palin had again built a stable to be reckoned with. Perhaps not as great as '28 and '29, but he had some fine horses for certain. The loss of The Auctioneer in the fire the previous fall still stung as Baker watched his horses work. The precocious pacer would have been a two-minute horse, Baker was certain of that.³¹

Tom Gahagan caught up with Baker later during the Lexington meet, asking him about the horses he'd lost in the fire the previous October. Baker paused thoughtfully. A man looking ever forward, not one to dwell on the tragedies of the past, at least not publicly, Baker waxed philosophical, saying, "Oh, those fires will occur just as long as there are people on this earth, and it just happened that we were the sufferers this time. Naturally, I didn't enjoy being the loser of some splendid prospects, as well as some that had proved themselves, but the matter isn't helped any by mourning oneself to death about it."³²

The words were spoken like a businessman, but in Baker's heart, it was likely a different story. Baker was an animal lover, never coming to the barn without carrots or sugar for his horses. He could often be seen around his farm or at the track, sitting with one of his horses as if visiting with an old friend. In his later years, he would be seen around St. Charles feeding stray cats and dogs, and never failing to save a pancake from breakfast for his Dalmatian, "Fibber," at his Red Gate Farm.³³

Despite heavy rains the day before, favorable weather brought record crowds to the KTHBA track on June 20. All were anxious to see the previous year's top two-year-olds make their three-year-old debut. A six-horse field that included the Palin-owned colt The Saint went to the post for Greyhound's first start of the season. In the end, though, four of the horses needn't have been there at all—it was a two-horse race from the start, all Greyhound and Lawrence Hanover.

Bay and gray, side by side, the two engaged in the stretch, matching strides as they pounded down to the wire. Sulky wheels whirring, men shouting, the two colts moved as one before a breathless crowd. Tom Gahagan wrote in the *Horseman and Fair World* that Parshall's colt had a good race, but Greyhound just had too much trot for

GREYHOUND

THE REMARKABLE STORY
OF THE LEGENDARY RACEHORSE WHO INSPIRED A NATION

gallery

[1]
The Henry Rockwell Baker Community Center.
• *June 2023, courtesy of Cheryl L. Eriksen*

[2]
**Mr. and Mrs. Baker at the dedication
of Henry Rockwell Baker Community Center.**
• *1926, courtesy of the St. Charles Historical Society*

GREYHOUND

THE REMARKABLE STORY
OF THE LEGENDARY RACEHORSE WHO INSPIRED A NATION

gallery

[3]
Guy Abbey,
Sire of Greyhound,
at Calumet Farm.
• *circa 1932, courtesy of the United States Trotting Association*

[4]
The original caption for these images read, "Top: One of the choice mares and foals in the farm pastures. Right: Mr. McElwyn entertained visitors throughout the week at Almahurst stable, K. T. H. B. A. track. Top left: A glimpse of the partially completed stallion barn at Almahurst Farm. Bottom left: The new brood mare barn just finished. Lower right: A section of the cedar post-and-tail fence now being set at Almahurst."
• *circa 1935, courtesy of the United States Trotting Association*

GREYHOUND

**THE REMARKABLE STORY
OF THE LEGENDARY RACEHORSE WHO INSPIRED A NATION**

gallery

[5]
Henry Knight.
• *circa 1937, courtesy of the United States Trotting Association*

[6]
Greyhound's dam Elizabeth and his breeder Henry Knight, with a suckling full brother to Greyhound named Grey Fox.
• *September 1939, courtesy of the Wingfield family*

GREYHOUND

THE REMARKABLE STORY
OF THE LEGENDARY RACEHORSE WHO INSPIRED A NATION

gallery

[7]
Now nearly 100 years old, the colored light dance floor in Hotel Baker's famous Rainbow Room is still in use for special occasions.
• *June 2023, courtesy of Cheryl L. Eriksen*

[8]
Hotel Baker, Gem of the Fox River.
• *June 2023, courtesy of Cheryl L. Eriksen*

GREYHOUND

THE REMARKABLE STORY
OF THE LEGENDARY RACEHORSE WHO INSPIRED A NATION

gallery

[9]
Hotel Baker
promotional booklet.
• circa 1928, courtesy of the
  St. Charles Historical Society

[10]
The original exterior
of Hotel Baker.
• circa 1928, courtesy of the
  St. Charles Historical Society

[11]
A photographic portrait
of E. J. Baker.
• circa 1928, courtesy of the
  St. Charles Historical Society

GREYHOUND

THE REMARKABLE STORY
OF THE LEGENDARY RACEHORSE WHO INSPIRED A NATION

— *gallery* —

[12]
Greyhound winning the second heat of the Illinois Review Futurity, with Lawrence Hanover coming second on the outside, Belvedere (with the white face markings) in the middle of track coming third, and Prince John (on the inside rail) in fourth.
• *August 22, 1934, courtesy of the United States Trotting Association; original photo by P.W. Moser*

[13]
Greyhound warming up prior to the Good Time Trot for two-year-olds at Good Time Park.
• *August 14, 1934, Heitbrink Collection, courtesy of the Harness Racing Museum & Hall of Fame, Goshen, NY*

GREYHOUND

THE REMARKABLE STORY
OF THE LEGENDARY RACEHORSE WHO INSPIRED A NATION

gallery

[14]
Greyhound, age 3, at the Champion Stallion Stake in Syracuse, New York. Note the horse diving platform in the background.
• *August 26, 1935, courtesy of the Harness Racing Museum & Hall of Fame, Goshen, NY*

[15]
In the Hambletonian winner's circle. Left to right: Dellora Norris (Baker's niece and the other heir to Gates' fortune), Sep Palin, W.H. Cane (track owner), and E. J. Baker.
• *August 14, 1935, courtesy of the Hambletonian Society*

GREYHOUND

THE REMARKABLE STORY
OF THE LEGENDARY RACEHORSE WHO INSPIRED A NATION

gallery

[16]
Groom Pete Wilson holds Greyhound after the Hambletonian; Baker and Palin stand nearby.
• *August 14, 1935, Hambletonian Society Collection, courtesy of the Harness Racing Museum & Hall of Fame, Goshen, NY*

[17]
Greyhound admires his Christmas tree at Seminole Park Training Track.
• *December 19, 1935; Hambletonian Society Collection, courtesy of the Harness Racing Museum & Hall of Fame, Goshen, NY*

[18]
Baker holds Greyhound, and Sep Palin holds a flower "horseshoe" in the Hambletonian winner's circle.
• *August 14, 1935, courtesy of the Harness Racing Museum & Hall of Fame, Goshen, NY; original photo by Acme Newspictures*

GREYHOUND

THE REMARKABLE STORY
OF THE LEGENDARY RACEHORSE WHO INSPIRED A NATION

gallery

[19]
Palin drives Greyhound past the grandstand after winning the Hambletonian.
- *August 14, 1935, courtesy of the St. Charles Historical Society*

[20]
A closeup of Palin and Greyhound in the Hambletonian winner's circle. Dellora Norris is visible in the background on the left.
- *August 14, 1935, courtesy of the Harness Racing Museum & Hall of Fame, Goshen, NY*

GREYHOUND

THE REMARKABLE STORY
OF THE LEGENDARY RACEHORSE WHO INSPIRED A NATION

— *gallery* —

[21]
Greyhound winning the first heat of the Hambletonian over Pedro Tipton, charging up on the inside rail.
• *August 14, 1935, courtesy of the United States Trotting Association*

[22]
Artist Jerry Dahl's watercolor rendition of a news photo showing Palin giving Greyhound a kiss in the Hambletonian winner's circle.
• *2014, courtesy of Jerry Dahl*

[23]
Artist Jerry Dahl's watercolor rendition of the famous portrait of Greyhound and Sep Palin in 1935.
• *2014, courtesy of Jerry Dahl*

GREYHOUND

THE REMARKABLE STORY
OF THE LEGENDARY RACEHORSE WHO INSPIRED A NATION

gallery

[24]
Greyhound (middle) just after winning the first heat of the Hambletonian. Pedro Tipton (right) passed him after they went under the wire. Tilly Tonka (left) came third.
• *August 14, 1935, courtesy of the Hambletonian Society*

[25]
Greyhound at the finish of the second heat of the Hambletonian, jogging home some five lengths ahead of Warwell Worthy.
• *August 14, 1935, courtesy of the United States Trotting Association*

GREYHOUND

THE REMARKABLE STORY
OF THE LEGENDARY RACEHORSE WHO INSPIRED A NATION

gallery

[26] A curious Greyhound inspecting his tackbox.
• *circa 1935, courtesy of the Harness Racing Museum & Hall of Fame, Goshen, NY*

[27] Baker's two-minute horses: Sep Palin with Greyhound and Col. Baker with Cardinal Prince.
• *circa 1935, courtesy of the United States Trotting Association*

GREYHOUND

THE REMARKABLE STORY
OF THE LEGENDARY RACEHORSE WHO INSPIRED A NATION

gallery

[28]
A parade of two-minute horses in Reading, Pennsylvania, to celebrate the return of harness racing to the state after a twenty-year absence.
- *September 1936, Hambletonian Society Collection, courtesy of the Harness Racing Museum & Hall of Fame, Goshen, NY*

[29]
Prior to the first heat of the Pine Tree Trot at the Kite Track in Old Orchard, Maine.
- *July 30, 1936, Guy Kendall Collection, courtesy of the University of Maine*

GREYHOUND

THE REMARKABLE STORY
OF THE LEGENDARY RACEHORSE WHO INSPIRED A NATION

gallery

[30]
The first heat of the Pine Tree Trot at the Kite Track.
• *July 30, 1936, Guy Kendall Collection, courtesy of the University of Maine*

[31]
Greyhound warming up for his mile exhibition at Lexington. Note the absence of knee boots. He wore them all of his three-year-old season, except at the KTHBA track in June 1935.
• *June 23, 1936, courtesy of the United States Trotting Association; original photograph by P. W. Moser*

GREYHOUND

THE REMARKABLE STORY
OF THE LEGENDARY RACEHORSE WHO INSPIRED A NATION

gallery

[32]
E. J. Baker with his champion pacer Cardinal Prince.
• *August 6, 1936, courtesy of the United States Trotting Association*

[33]
Greyhound warming up with a jog cart at Good Time Park, probably prior to setting the track record (1:58 ¼).
• *August 1937, courtesy of the United States Trotting Association*

GREYHOUND

THE REMARKABLE STORY
OF THE LEGENDARY RACEHORSE WHO INSPIRED A NATION

gallery

[34]
A conformation shot of Greyhound.
• *circa 1937, courtesy of the Harness Racing Museum & Hall of Fame, Goshen, NY*

[35]
Greyhound setting the mile record of 1:59 ¾ at Historic Half Mile Track in Goshen, NY.
• *July 16, 1937, courtesy of the United States Trotting Association*

Lawrence Hanover. Greyhound won in straight heats, setting a new season record for three-year-olds of 2:04 ¼, trotting the last half in 1:00 ¼.[34]

"Probably the best trotting heat by a three-year-old ever, this early in the season," George Gahagan wrote.[35] Lawrence Hanover came second in both heats. Palin's own colt, The Saint, driven by Fred Eagan, came fourth overall. Notably absent from the race was top filly Belvedere, reported as pulled from training due to "eye troubles" on June 17.[36] The details of Belvedere's eye troubles were not given, but the speedy filly never raced again.

The next stop of the Grand Circuit was Fort Miami Track at Toledo, Ohio. Six three-year-olds would meet for the Matron Stake on July 5. This would be the first look of the season in racing conditions for the top three Hambletonian contenders: Greyhound, Lawrence Hanover, and Silver King. Also in the field was the tough filly Tilly Tonka, who had missed her two-year-old season due to lameness. The black filly was by superb sire Spencer, winner of the Hambletonian in 1928—the same year Greyhound's sire, Guy Abbey, came second in the big race. Tilly Tonka was training well and looked to be a possible contender for the upcoming Hambletonian, having recently worked a half-mile in 1:01, going the last quarter in an impressive :29 ¼.[37] Calumet Finery and Alicea rounded out the field, the latter having won against Belvedere and Lawrence Hanover the previous year.

Greyhound won all three heats, lowering the season's top three-year-old record yet again to a phenomenal 2:03. In his usual style, the gray gelding got away slowly but closed hard and fast, coming from behind in all three heats. Lawrence Hanover, much better at scoring, got away fast and set the early pace, but it wasn't enough to beat Greyhound. The bay colt finished second overall, taking second in heats one and two. Tilly Tonka took second over Lawrence Hanover in the third heat. Silver King was fourth overall.[38]

Greyhound "trounced Lawrence Hanover," sports writer Gene F. Hampson reported, noting Greyhound's fastest heat as being just one-quarter second off from the previous year's fastest Hambletonian heat. "Greyhound's most sensational individual performance in [winning] the Matron Stake was in trotting the last half of the second mile in :59 ¾, last quarter in :28 seconds," Hampson wrote. Those final fractions are significant in their demonstration that Greyhound had sub-two-minute speed. Despite Greyhound's stellar performance, Hampson admitted Lawrence Hanover still looked good for the Hambletonian, as did Tilly Tonka and Silver King.[39] Greyhound may have been edging in as the standalone favorite, but the field was still filled with high-class horses.

From Toledo, the Baker-Palin stable moved to Thorncliffe Park in Toronto, Ontario, Canada, for the Toronto Globe Stakes. The day before his race, the *Indianapolis News* printed a "well authenticated" rumor that a jealous sportsman was "willing to pay $25,000 for the owner's title to [Greyhound], the youngster that appears to be" most likely to win the Hambletonian.[40] One way to get a Hambletonian winner in your stable is to buy one that looks to be a sure thing a few weeks before the big race. Baker, of course, turned the man down.

July 20 dawned warm and humid in Toronto. By mid-afternoon, the temperature approached ninety degrees with a moderate wind.[41] Though there had been significant, crop-damaging rains the week before, the track stood dry and fast for the nine-horse field going to the post. Packed with phenomenal three-year-olds eligible for the Hambletonian, the Toronto Globe Stake was considered by some to be a "dress rehearsal" for the mid-August trotting classic. Crowds gathered in anticipation of seeing the top three Hambletonian contenders meet. Of special interest to the crowd was the chance to see if the sensational Greyhound, undefeated this season, would lower the season's fastest three-year-old record for the third race in a row.

The auction pools had Greyhound the favorite, selling at $25 while the field went for $12. In the first heat, The Viscount, a bay colt by Henry Knight's Mr. McElwyn, got away first with Lawrence Hanover, Prince John, and Tilly Tonka keeping close. Greyhound got away badly and trailed far behind the field on the backstretch. Coming out of the final turn, Lawrence Hanover took the lead. Tilly Tonka followed close behind, and both passed The Viscount in the final strides before the wire. Once he settled into his trot, Greyhound set a blazing pace, picking off five competitors before he ran out of track. His poor start proved too big of a deficit to overcome, and he finished fourth. Lawrence Hanover hung on for the win, taking the first heat in 2:06 ¼.[42] Reporter Evan Shipman wrote that Greyhound's loss was Palin's mistake, saying the reinsman had been overconfident with the gray and let Lawrence Hanover get too far ahead of him.[43] Regardless of what truly happened, Greyhound's perfect season appeared to be in danger. At the betting tent, men crowded around, waving crisp bills in the air. Many that had bet on Greyhound in the first heat now placed their money on Lawrence Hanover.[44]

The horses scored down for the second heat. Volo Arion, a one-eyed colt by Peter Volo, got away first and set the early pace, with Prince John next, then Lawrence Hanover, followed by Tilly Tonka. Greyhound scored a bit better but was still well back of Tilly Tonka, in fifth place going into the first turn. Tilly Tonka and Greyhound moved up together along the back stretch, their pounding hooves gobbling up track and leaving competitors in their wake. Coming out of the final turn and into the home stretch, the two trotted with the field lining out behind them. In the final quarter, Palin lifted the lines, and Greyhound found another gear, trotting a terrific clip. Pulling away from Tilly Tonka, the gelding won the heat by more than a length in 2:02 ¼—a new season record and a new Canadian track record. The gallant gray blazed the final quarter in :28 ¼. Lawrence Hanover was third, and Prince John came fourth.[45]

Though she came in second place in the first two heats, Fred Egan withdrew Tilly Tonka before the final heat. He insisted the filly was sound but wanted to save her for her next big race. By default, she fell to last place in the overall standings for the Toronto Globe Stakes. The hard drive with Greyhound in the second heat likely took a lot out of the filly, and Egan was wise not to push her.

Eight horses scored down for the final heat. Lawrence Hanover and Prince John got away first, setting the early pace. As the field moved into the back stretch, newcomer to the fray Pedro Tipton took command. Greyhound, in his usual far back position, gradually moved up to mid-pack as the horses trotted through the back stretch. The three leaders held their position into the far turn, falling in line along the rail, saving distance. As they came around the third turn, Palin gave the word and Greyhound turned on the speed. Like a big gray freight train, Greyhound's impressive stride devoured the track. He passed horses like fence posts as he closed the gap between him and the leaders. Fleet-footed Warwell Worthy came along with the big gray, trotting in his shadow, until Greyhound's great speed proved too much for her and she fell away.

As the horses trotted into the home stretch, they were spread four-wide across the track—Pedro Tipton, Prince John, Lawrence Hanover, and Greyhound. The crowd leapt to their feet with a deafening roar as the horses approached the grandstand. Pounding hooves, whirring sulky wheels, and shouting drivers moved as one, the four horses straining to put a nose in front before the wire. Palin touched the lines, asking for more speed. The big gray responded with impressive power, passing up the others and snatching the lead from Prince John. They flew past the grandstand and the cheering crowd. Greyhound pulled away and crossed under the wire, winning by a length over Prince John. Lawrence Hanover came third, and Pedro Tipton hung on for fourth. Warwell Worthy faded to sixth behind a lackluster Silver King.[46]

With yet another record-setting win at Toronto, Greyhound cemented himself as the Hambletonian favorite. He had three straight wins, with each one lowering the season's best record—the makings of an undefeated season. It seemed his poor scoring was the only obstacle in his way, but the gray was also really coming into his own. His stride, once so awkward, was now beautiful and flowing, long and ground covering. Deceptively, it appeared he went much slower when you watched the fast, piston-like strides of his competitors. But all you had to do to dispel the mirage was sit back and see the whole picture. The gelding appeared to be floating effortlessly forward, as if sailing on a stronger breeze than his competitors. Greyhound simply cruised along, mane billowing, hooves pounding, his body like a silver comet streaking across a wild blue sky.

CHAPTER
— 11 —

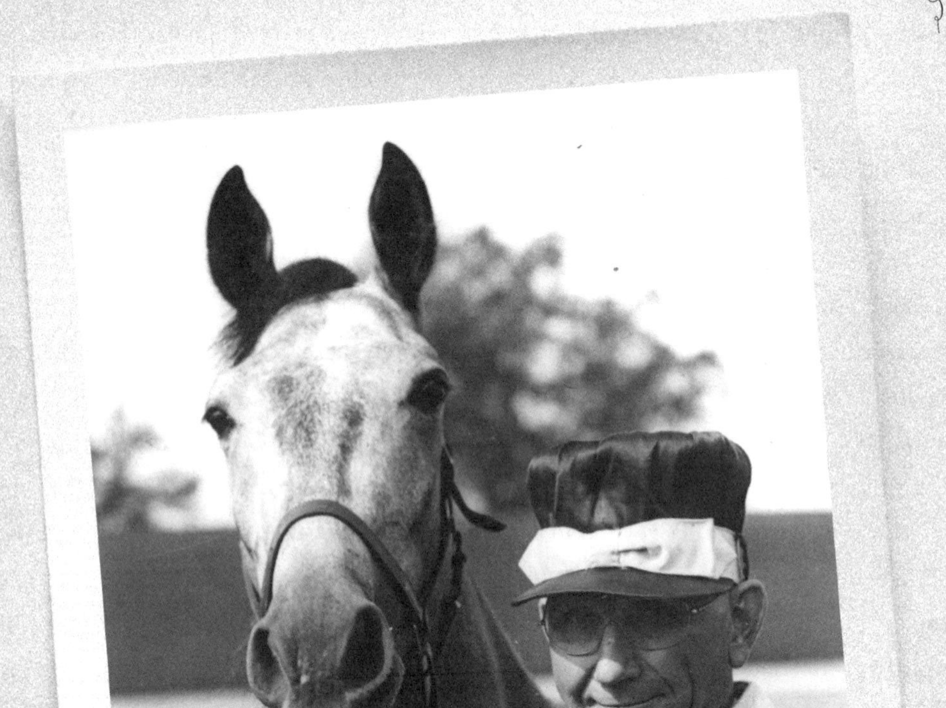

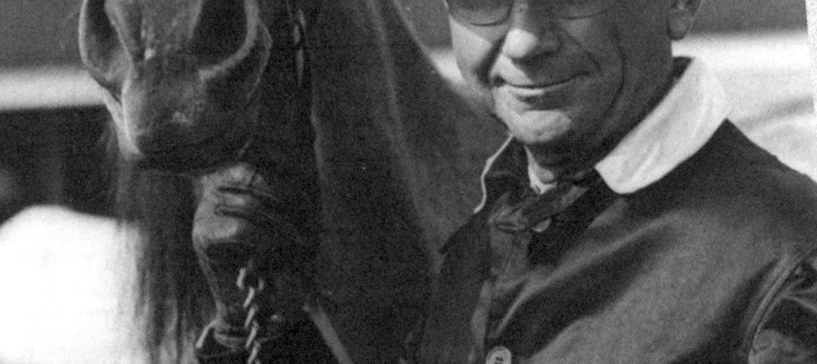

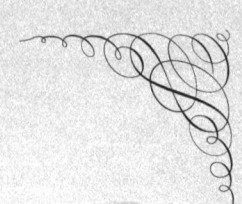

> *"There is no sporting scene in this country exactly like the Hambletonian. There, the upstate farmers mingle with representatives of the big town. Staid professional and business men rub elbows with 'city slickers.' The big town and the small town meet on very common ground."*
>
> —
>
> DAMON RUNYON,
> *BUFFALO EVENING NEWS*, AUGUST 13, 1935.

HAMBLETONIAN

"Greyhound is the greatest three-year-old in training," touted the *Burlington Daily News* on August 3, 1935. Many harness racing fans agreed. Most of the top Hambletonian picks would meet for the American Stake or National Stake at the Rockingham meet on August 3 in Salem, New Hampshire. Greyhound had not been kept eligible for either race;[1] presumably these were among the fees Baker opted not to pay during Greyhound's poor start as a two-year-old. He instead entered the $600 Portland Express three days later at the same meet, for his last start before the Hambletonian.

In the American Stake, Lawrence Hanover dropped the first heat to Tilly Tonka but won the second and third heats handily, taking the win overall. Just five days later, Parshall took Lawrence Hanover into the National Stake. He dropped one heat to Silver King but won impressively in the second and third heats, tacking another win on his resume.[2] Two big wins in less than a week begged the question—did Doc Parshall think he had enough horse in Lawrence Hanover to win the Hambletonian against Greyhound?

"If my horses aren't good enough to win on what they've shown me in training, I never need to look at the opposition to know I'm beaten," Doc Parshall stated in an interview a couple months before the Hambletonian.

Parshall's take was to mind his own business and worry about his own horses. "I've never been able to figure out what difference it makes what the other fellow is doing," said Parshall.

The reporter pressed on, saying Greyhound and Lawrence Hanover were co-favorites. He then pointed out that Parshall worked his own horse on the same track, within arm's reach of Greyhound and the other contenders. Surely, he had an opinion on how they looked compared to his Lawrence Hanover.

Pressed for an answer, Parshall said Greyhound was most likely to win, with Prince John second, and Tilly Tonka third. It seems probable that such an odd answer, dismissing his own horse, was given in frustration. Parshall had already tried to evade the question a few times. The reinsman was no slouch either. Despite—or perhaps because of—Parshall's young age and aggressive horse handling, he'd been the leading driver for the past seven years and had won the Hambletonian the year before with Lord Jim.

The reporter tried again.

"But where do you put Lawrence Hanover, your own entry, the colt you made step a mile in 2:02 to claim the world's record for two-year-olds last year?" The reporter waited silently, pencil poised above his note pad.

"Well, I'll let the other boys rate him as best they can," Parshall replied. "I think I know exactly what Lawrence Hanover will do." Parshall then reminded the reporter again that he preferred to mind his own business and not speculate on what other trainers were doing with their horses. "But since you've asked me, and from what I have heard rather than anything else I know, I think I would rate Greyhound first, and the other two colts second and third."[3]

Parshall again left his own horse out of the top three. Was he playing games with the reporter, had he acquiesced Greyhound's superiority to his own colt, or did he know something no one else did about the condition and readiness of Lawrence Hanover? At this point, some ninety years later, all one can do is speculate. The answers were long ago taken to the grave with Doc Parshall. But a change loomed on the horizon for Doc and for Lawrence Hanover. A tipping point was fast approaching; which way the cards would fall rode on the results of the biggest race of the year.

Intermittent rains greeted horses and fans on August 6 at Salem. The weather made for a miserable day, but it didn't stop the racing or the die-hards who came to see Greyhound and the other Hambletonian hopefuls. Because the track at Rockingham was also used for runners, it was slow for the harness horses. The deeper surface kept for the Thoroughbreds created drag on the sulky wheels. With the rain, the track would be even heavier and slower still. There would be no record-setting mile for Greyhound or any other horse on this day.

A seven-horse field met for the $600 Portland Express three-year-old trot. Pedro Tipton and Countess Zabetta provided the only real competition for Greyhound, but not nearly enough to push the gray gelding to his limit. The horses scored for the start of the first heat. Countess Zabetta set the pace, with Pedro Tipton and Greyhound next. The three horses held their positions into the back stretch, but by the far turn, Countess Zabetta had faded to third. As they passed the three-quarter pole, Palin swung Greyhound around the too-slow Pedro Tipton. The big gray won easily, pulling a length ahead of Pedro Tipton at the wire.

The rain fell harder and the track clung to hooves and sulky wheels. The horses scored down for the second heat. Greyhound jumped and bounced about, unhappy with the heavy footing and the rain pelting his face, threatening to spoil the start.

"C'mon, now, Sep, straighten that big gray out!" the starter shouted, ready to ring the bell and bring the horses back to score again. Palin grumbled something unintelligible and glared at the starter. He spoke softly to Greyhound and the big horse settled. The starter gave the word, and the race was on.

Despite his antics during the score, Greyhound got away first. Palin set a slow pace, going the first three quarters in a dawdling 1:41 and change. At the three-quarter pole, Pedro Tipton charged up on the outside, with his driver Hudson frantically urging him on. Palin, cool and collected, touched the lines and asked Greyhound for a little more speed. The big gray surged ahead, sprinting the last quarter in an impressive :28 seconds, winning easily over Pedro Tipton. Countess Zabetta came third.

Greyhound, still unhappy with the track conditions, scored poorly in the third heat. At the word, the field surged ahead but Greyhound dropped all the way back. He trotted in last place almost to the three-quarter pole. Then, as if realizing he did not want to lose, Greyhound let loose a dazzling demonstration of speed. The gelding rushed to the lead, easily getting ahead of Pedro Tipton, and won going away. Pedro Tipton came second, and Countess Zabetta faded in the stretch to fourth.[4, 5]

After the win at Salem, and the particularly impressive quarter in :28 on a sub-standard track, the press and the fans had Greyhound locked in as favorite to win the Hambletonian. Just two days later, Lawrence Hanover won the August 8 National Stake,[6] another race Greyhound had not been kept eligible for.

Just because Lawrence Hanover won two straight didn't "give him license to beat Greyhound," Walter Moore reported in *Horseman and Fair World*, insisting Parshall's colt would be running for second money in the Hambletonian. This was a strong opinion, considering Lawrence Hanover had met a much stronger field than Greyhound. But Moore was not alone in his thoughts—the other Hambletonian entries were in a race for second place against Baker's astounding gray gelding.

"The Hambletonian?" Baker tapped the turf with the tip of his cane and removed the long cigar from his mouth before answering the question posed by Jerry Nason of the *Boston*

Globe. "Well, we are hoping for the best if Greyhound goes along all right."[7]

There were, of course, some doubters. A few of the old horsemen claimed Greyhound's race at Salem didn't mean much. It was an easier race with lower-class competition, they argued. Others said Palin hadn't done Greyhound any favors taking him in that race, saying he wouldn't be ready for the tough field in the Hambletonian. But the slow miles at Salem didn't worry Palin any; he liked Greyhound's chances in the big race.

"A great horse, that Greyhound," Palin said to Nason after the race at Salem. "Not on a soft track like this, maybe. It makes him mad and he acts up on this track." He puffed his cigar and continued, "A great trotter, but he will be better. I think he will break the world record of Peter Manning as a five-year-old."

A bold statement indeed, especially with Greyhound's best time still nearly six seconds slower than Peter Manning's thirteen-year-old record. A lot could happen to a young racehorse. But "they are bringing him along carefully," Nason wrote, "O so carefully ... he may meet Palin's expectations at that."

From Salem, Greyhound and the other Hambletonian hopefuls traveled to Good Time Park in Goshen, New York. In those days, horses commonly traveled by rail, and many race tracks had abutments of dirt reinforced with wood siding right along the track for easy loading and unloading of horses. Young local boys would mill around, waiting for the train and the chance to make a little pocket change by walking the horses to the stables, allowing the train to be unloaded more quickly. The nearly 240-mile trip from New Hampshire to New York began a grueling travel and racing schedule for Greyhound, one that would see him race five times in four states and travel over 2,600 miles by rail between August 6 and September 4.

As Hambletonian Week approached, Lawrence Hanover was still considered to be the biggest competition for Greyhound. Silver King might still be a contender, but he had yet to show his impressive two-year-old form as a three-year-old, and his fans were losing faith. Tilly Tonka was the top pick of the fillies, but the betting would show few people thought Greyhound could be topped in the big race.

"How can they beat a colt that can trot from fifth place to the lead, coming the last quarter of a 2:02 ¼ mile in :28 ½, over a slow track with too-soft footing?" Walter Moore asked in his Hambletonian Preview, referencing Greyhound's win at Rockingham the week before.[8] He'd gone undefeated in seven starts, having won everything he'd entered since August of the previous year. The big gray freight train looked unstoppable.

Some 40,000 people descended on the town of Goshen, New York, in the second week of August, 1935, for the biggest spectacle in harness racing—the Hambletonian Stake, the most significant race of all for trotting horses.

With the hard economic times, the purse for the 1935 Hambletonian was a modest $33,000, up from the all-time low of $25,000 the previous year. Still a staggering amount, given the economic climate. The winner's share of the purse would be over $18,000—roughly equivalent to $400,000 today.

Goshen, any other week a sleepy town of 3,000, came alive with a fair-like atmosphere when Hambletonian Week came around. Games of chance lined Main Street, with carnival barkers urging people to part with their money in the name of fun. Colorful tents pitched on church lawns served up delectable homemade food selections for the influx of horse lovers and racing fans.[9] *Brooklyn Daily Eagle* columnist Ed Hughes likened the atmosphere to a combination of an "Old Home Week and Visiting Firemen," phrases of the day used to describe a town reunion and the rolling out of the proverbial red carpet for extravagant out-of-town spenders.[10] In short, Hambletonian Week was the biggest party of the year, drawing people from all over the country and abroad—boasting arrivals from Australia, Italy, and even India in years past.

Goshen buzzed with building tension as the town filled with excitement and speculation. Automobiles and special trains brought thousands of spectators from all over the country and beyond, some traveling for days to attend the big event in an era before commercial air travel became common. Add the four hundred trotters and pacers arriving by train and by van to contest the $100,000 five-day race meet at Good Time Park,[11] and the little town was busting at the seams.

Greyhound faced the toughest field in the ten-year history of the sport's richest stake.[12] Lawrence Hanover appeared to be in top form, Tilly Tonka had shown some speed in earlier races, and Silver King, while slow to start this season, appeared to be hitting his stride just in time.

There had never been a gray starter in the Hambletonian, and this year, with Greyhound and Silver King, there were two. Superstitions aside, fans made Greyhound the clear favorite the morning of the race. Lawrence Hanover, having turned some heads in the National Stake the week before, was second choice in betting, with Silver King and Tilly Tonka third and fourth choice respectively.

Reserved seats sold out weeks ahead of the big event. The bleacher seats were expected to fill hours before the start. Track owner W. H. Cane* had a new 35,000-seat grandstand constructed earlier in the year, and had placed 5,000 chairs on the infield to handle the overflow.[13] Men dressed in their summer best with light-colored suits or stylish, muted plaid sport coats and women in light cotton patterned dresses filled the grandstand with a flurry of color and excitement. As post time

---

* The track was named after Cane's Good Time Stable, located at the nearby Historic Half Mile Track. The stable building still stands today and is the home of the Harness Racing Museum and Hall of Fame.

approached, the railbirds, wearing woolen pants hanging from frayed suspenders, worn leather boots, and soft newsboy hats watched the contenders in their warm-up miles.

"I dunno, that Hanover colt looks pretty good," an old railbird tossed out to see who would bite.

"I heard old Silver King worked a bullet the other day. Look how he's muscled up since last year. He's a big, strong colt, that's for sure!" Another man took the bait.

"Nah!" scoffed another. "Greyhound will win from here to China!" Others grunted and nodded in agreement, clutching their race cards and scribbling notes in the margins.[14]

In the big tent, book maker Eli Crutch sold Greyhound for $200 in the auction pools. Lawrence Hanover went for $30, Silver King for $20, Warwell Worthy at $15, Tilly Tonka at $14, and the field at $15.[15] Greyhound, the clear favorite, would pay $294 (minus Eli's fee) to his winning bidder. Other book makers closed off all bidding on Greyhound before the first heat.[16]

Early morning rain threatened on the big day, but the showers had moved on by 6:00 a.m. Instead of a detriment, the light rain served to enhance the speed of the track, once it had been worked with harrows and dried by a warm afternoon sun. The surface stood ready as the three-year-olds prepared to score for the first heat of the big race. Nine horses went to the post, lining up eight wide across the track with Greyhound on the far outside in the eight spot. Tilly Tonka, having drawn the nine post, lined up behind the pole horse, Harper Hanover. Lawrence Hanover had the four post, and Silver King, the six.

After a few false starts, the horses trotted down toward the judges' stand. With all in line across the track and on gait, the starter yelled, "Go!" and the first heat of the 1935 Hambletonian was underway. Harper Hanover got away fast. He went right to the lead, taking Pedro Tipton, Tilly Tonka, and Lawrence Hanover with him. Greyhound, having gotten away slowly, entered the first turn dead last, trailing the leaders by several lengths. Tilly Tonka moved to the front and led at the half. Greyhound trotted into the back stretch in fifth place.[17]

Greyhound straightened out of the turn and Palin gave him a bit more rein. The big horse poured on the speed and a roar went up from the crowd as the gray picked off the leaders one by one. The crowd were on their feet now, shouting and cheering as the horses came out of the far turn of the triangle-shaped track. Black and chestnut legs moved with quick, staccato steps, but Greyhound seemed to float along effortlessly, his stride long and reaching, fluid and powerful, like a great ocean liner cutting smoothly through the open sea. He easily sailed past the others as they approached the final turn.

Coming out of the final turn, Greyhound had them all beaten except the game little filly Tilly Tonka. He eased past her and took the lead in the final stretch. As the gray pulled ahead, Palin took hold of the lines, not wanting to let Greyhound go faster than was necessary. Just then, Pedro Tipton came flying up on the rail with the devil on his tail—but the colt's speed burst only took him to within half a length, nosing up to Greyhound's saddlecloth before the two passed under the finish wire in 2:02 ¼. Greyhound had set another season record, and had trotted the fastest Hambletonian mile of any winner. The last half was clocked in :59 ½, but those in the know figured Greyhound made it in :58 ½, having come from fifth to first in the last half mile. Tilly Tonka came third, and Lawrence Hanover fourth.

The field scored down for the second heat. Tension ran high as each driver fought to get their horse perfectly positioned to grab the lead. They came down to the start but were not lined up to the satisfaction of the starting judge, Steve Philips.* He rang the bell and sent the horses back up the track to try again.

"Now, come on! Bring 'em down together, boys!" Phillips shouted.

The young horses and their drivers were getting irritated, and some lost their tempers, rearing and jumping about.[18] No less than seven times had Phillips sent them back up the track to score again. Greyhound shook his head in frustration, pushing into the bit, trying to get loose from Palin's hold on him. The field turned and scored, trotting eight abreast, the drivers yelling for room to trot as they attempted to bring the horses down to the start evenly.

Whether it was an honest mistake or Phillips didn't want to further delay the race, on this score, he seemed determined the heat would start, no matter what. The horses again approached the start in a jumble of pounding hooves, shouting men, and whirring wheels. Pedro Tipton broke into a run; Tilly Tonka followed suit. Horses were bunched in a fray of flying legs and spinning wheels, some running, some trotting, few in position for a clean start. Inexplicably, Phillips yelled, "Go!" and the race was on.

At the word, Harper Hanover lost his stride and Lawrence Hanover broke into a flat run. All except slow-starting Greyhound and quick-footed Warwell Worthy were in the jumbled mess as they approached the first turn, some on gait, others still running. This time, Greyhound's tendency to get away slowly kept him out of trouble. Seeing an opportunity, Will Caton sent Warwell Worthy to the front, and set a blistering pace. The filly was soon fully ten lengths in front, and easily fifteen lengths ahead of Greyhound, who still trotted at the back of the pack. For a moment, the crowd fell silent in disbelief. Could even the great Greyhound overcome such a disadvantage?

Palin and Greyhound went to work. The gelding soon found his step and was trotting well within himself. The rest of the field sorted themselves out and got to trotting, spreading

---

* Phillips would later invent the mobile starting gate that changed harness racing forever, eliminating the antiquated scoring system. His invention would be featured on the cover of *Popular Mechanics* in September 1946, and is still in use today.

out and looking for racing room. Greyhound stepped effortlessly, his once awkward trot now long and graceful, powerful like a locomotive building steam before an incline. The gelding lengthened his stride, and found another gear. Like a great silver comet, he powered past the others, gobbling up the distance between him and the sprinting Warwell Worthy. Greyhound closed on her as they passed the three-quarter pole, moving effortlessly past the tiring filly and into the lead. At the wire, the big gray was five lengths ahead with Palin holding him back. Warwell Worthy hung on for second, just ahead of Lawrence Hanover in third, with Silver King coming up to take fourth. The rest of the field strung out behind them.[19, 20]

In the winner's circle, Sep Palin stood next to Greyhound, a broad smile on his face. Baker, having removed his jacket in the heat of the day, stood next to them. The people crowded around, trying to get close to the champion. A horseshoe-shaped wreath of flowers on a wire stand was placed near Greyhound. The colt stretched his neck forward, reaching for the flowers. He grasped one in his searching lips, holding it in his mouth for a moment before spitting it out.[21] The people crowding around the winner's circle chuckled at his antics. Palin patted the colt on the neck. Greyhound lifted his muzzle toward the man's weathered face and, in a rare public exhibition of affection, the grizzled old veteran gave the gelding a kiss on his nose.[22] Baker graciously accepted the silver Hambletonian cup and spoke a few words of thanks.

After the brief ceremony, Palin handed Greyhound off to Pete Wilson, who led the gray back to the stable area. The crowd then closed in around Palin, excitedly shoving scraps of paper, race programs, and autograph books at the lanky reinsman.

The press scurried after Greyhound, hurling questions at Pete, who answered as best as he could. He had work to do to care for Greyhound, but he understood the excitement. The "Hound," as Pete and the boys called him, had sure shown them what he was made of. That was a nice field of horses he'd just outclassed. Arriving back at the barn, Pete set about unhooking and untacking the great gelding. The reporters snapped pictures and continued with their questioning.

Back at the track, Palin, usually a man of few words, happily fielded questions from the reporters that hadn't followed Pete and Greyhound.

"How'd it feel to win the biggest race of the year?" one reporter asked.

"Of course I got a kick out of it," Palin said, "any driver would. But the real thrill is climbing into the seat and taking up the reins with the feeling that you have before you one of the greatest trotters of all time." Palin lifted his hands as he spoke, feigning his holding the lines. "Any experienced reinsman would feel the same. The race itself—well, that was just another race I was out to win."

"What about that Warwell Worthy? She sure got ahead of you," another reporter called out.

"I wasn't worried about Warwell Worthy." Palin gave a knowing smile. "I knew Greyhound was capable of trotting a mile faster than the best that filly would be able to turn in, regardless of how she chose to step it. My job was to place Greyhound so that he would step the race he was capable of doing."

When asked why he didn't go after Warwell Worthy sooner, Palin said if he'd panicked and gone after her, he'd have put Greyhound at risk of another horse running him down at the wire. He had to "know how to get the most out of my horse and not worry about a lead that looks dangerous."[23] Palin shifted his cigar in the corner of his mouth; his blue eyes sparkled while he fielded questions. The excitement of his first Hambletonian win colored his responses with unusual enthusiasm.

Back at the barn, Pete washed the sweat from Greyhound's body, then walked him around for a bit and washed him again, slowly cooling the horse down. Greyhound fidgeted in the crossties, twisting his head around to grab hold of the tie ropes with his mouth. He stomped his feet, and shook his head. He had no time for all this nonsense.

"Easy now, Hound. Whoa, now." Pete spoke in a soothing voice. Greyhound flicked an ear toward the groom, sighed, and snorted loudly. Pete scraped the water from the gray's body, placed a cooler over him, then tended to Greyhound's legs, rubbing liniment over them and carefully wrapping each leg with cotton padding.

Pete and his friend, a groom from another stable, walked their horses around in slow circles in front of the barn. He'd sent one of the swipes out to get a couple bottles of beer and smuggle them into the stable area. The beer arrived while Pete and his friend were still walking their horses dry. Pete took one beer and handed the other to his friend.

"He sure earned this today." Pete nodded toward the horse his friend was walking. The groom opened the bottle, took a swig, then gave some to his charge, Pedro Tipton. Pete cracked open his own beer and did the same. Greyhound wrapped his ever-searching lips around the bottle and Pete tipped it, letting some of the liquid roll down Greyhound's throat.[24, 25]

Later that evening, Pete brought a flower from Greyhound's wreath and gave it to Pedro Tipton's groom. The man smiled and tucked it into the colt's halter ring.[26] Pedro Tipton had put up a good fight but had run into some bad luck. Pete knew he had the better horse, but Pedro Tipton's chance at second money had been hurt by the disastrous start in the second heat. Surely Pete understood the deep love a groom develops for his charge, and how each victory and each loss is felt most deeply by the men who live with and care for the horses twenty-four hours a day.

Back in Doc Parshall's barn, Lawrence Hanover's groom rubbed the colt down and cooled him out. He wondered how much longer he'd have care over his colt. Lawrence Hanover had finished fourth overall against horses he should've defeated—on paper, anyway. Maybe not Greyhound, but certainly the others. A few days later, all the LaSalle-owned horses, including Lawrence Hanover, were transferred from Parshall's stable to the Hanover Shoe farm trainer, Henry Thomas.[27]

Greyhound had reached celebrity status. His incredible performance in the Hambletonian was filmed and released in theaters around the country, boosting his fame into the stratosphere. Fairs and Grand Circuit events made a point to mention in ads that Greyhound would be there, significantly increasing the number of attendees on the days he was scheduled to race.

Some reporters penned clever descriptions for Greyhound, like "the gray streak," or "the silver comet." The "great gray ghost," a reference to his ever-lightening coat and his ethereal appearance as he seemed to float rather than trot, was the one that would follow him the rest of his life and is used still to this day. A gray horse always starts dark and gradually turns white over time due to a gene mutation that affects the horse's pigment. As the gelding turned snowy white in later years, the descriptor went from lower case to uppercase, and the Grey Ghost moniker was born.

The day after his Hambletonian win, Greyhound boarded the train for the nearly 1,000-mile trip to Springfield, Illinois. Train travel for horses back then, though a great improvement over the early days, was still far from luxurious. Train trips were long, hot, and noisy. A trip could take twenty-four hours or more depending on the destination, and might involve changing trains on one or more occasions.[28, 29] Early on, horse cars were really just gutted and repurposed baggage cars. Crude stalls were constructed and an open area was used as combination storage and sleeping quarters for the grooms. No efforts were made to improve shock absorption or reduce the noise of train travel.[30] While some railways offered express cars on passenger trains with fewer stops to expedite the horse shipments, this was not always an option.[31] Mile after mile, the car would sway and bounce, clickety-clacking noisily across the country with as many as 16 horses, several men, trunks, tack, equipment, and feed in one car.[32, 33] Many horses arrived exhausted, sore, and cranky or wild-eyed at their next destination—and understandably so.

Greyhound seemed to thrive on the noise and excitement that was the life of a racehorse. Not one to get too worked up about much of anything, Greyhound walked quickly up the wooden ramp and into the train car. Pete settled the big gray into his stall, filling his hay net with soft, green timothy hay and setting a bucket of water where the horse could reach it. Greyhound soon settled in and went to sleep, swaying with the motion of the train as it clicked westward along the silver rails.

GREYHOUND

THE REMARKABLE STORY OF THE LEGENDARY RACEHORSE WHO INSPIRED A NATION

The triangle track at Good Time Park in Goshen, NY, home of the Hambletonian from 1930 to 1956 (except in 1943). Historic Half Mile Track can also be seen here, in the upper right.

 AUGUST 1946, COURTESY OF THE HARNESS RACING MUSEUM & HALL OF FAME, GOSHEN, NY

CHAPTER
— 12 —

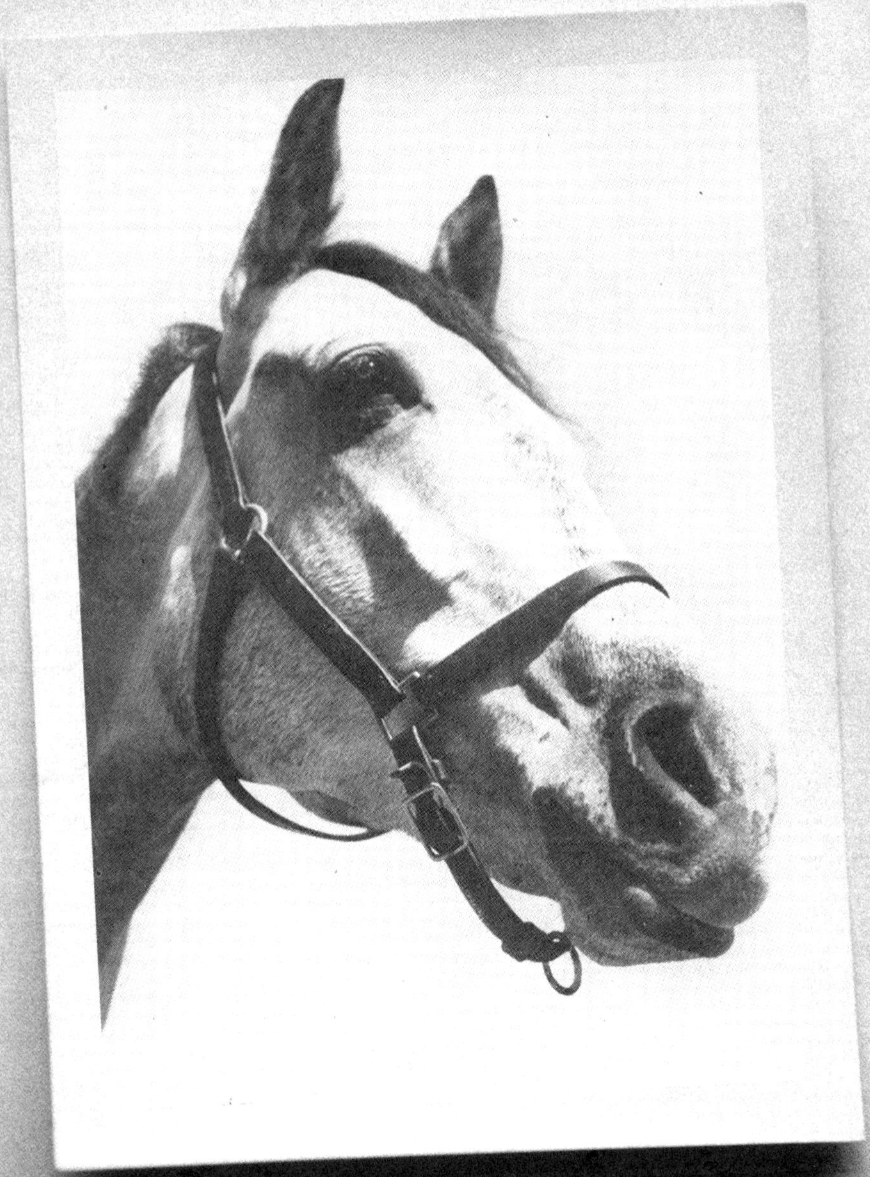

> *"Champions will not come from our midst every year.*
> *Perhaps the coming of Greyhound will mark*
> *the last harness champion to so arise in the lifetime of many of us.*
> *So let's drink in the deep inspiration that should come*
> *from an equine phenomenon that is now with us."*
>
> —
>
> GEORGE M. GAHAGAN, 1935

CHAMPION

Hot, sunny weather greeted fans at Springfield on August 21, 1935. News that Greyhound would be there brought swarms of people and even a film crew to record the event. Baker had intended only to exhibit Greyhound for the Illinois folks—he wanted to help support harness racing in his home state and share his champion with the citizens whenever he could. But upon arrival, he was persuaded to enter him in the Illinois Review Futurity.[1]

Temperatures rose into the 90s that afternoon by the time the field of six stepped onto the track. The horses scored down for the start and at the word, The Saint, a colt owned by Palin and driven by Spec Erskine, set the pace. Greyhound, with an unusually fast start, fell in right behind him and the pair was soon well in the lead. Palin kept Greyhound right behind The Saint, and the gelding followed his stablemate at a moderate pace through the back stretch. At the three-quarter pole, Sep tipped Greyhound off the rail, touched the lines, and asked for a little more speed. The big gray surged ahead and crossed the wire in front, easily the best in 2:05.[2]

In the second heat, The Saint again went to the front with Greyhound in second. By the half, the pair were well ahead of the field and widening the gap. A cameraman followed along in an automobile and filmed the two trotters. A microphone picked up the sound of the pounding hooves, the whir of sulky wheels, and the shouts of the drivers as the two horses came through the stretch. In light of what followed, it seems that Palin and Erskine had differing ideas on what should happen next.

"Get that damn colt out of the way or I'll go over top of him!"[3] Palin shouted to Erskine above the pounding of hooves and roaring wind. Palin had Greyhound trotting so close to Erskine, the gelding could have reached out and grabbed the man's hat as the pair flew down the stretch. The two men yelled back and forth to each other. Though not all the words were clear on the film, the reports of the scene indicated that what was said wasn't fit to print anyway.[4] Finally, with Erskine unwilling to move his slower colt out of the way,* Palin tipped Greyhound off the rail and went around The Saint. The film from this moment is incredible to see. Greyhound lengthened his stride, opening up like the wings of an enormous bird. He surged ahead, flying past The Saint in nine giant strides and still building speed. He crossed under the finish wire several lengths ahead of The Saint, shattering his Hambletonian record by an astonishing 2 ¼ seconds. The rest of the field were strung out far behind, never in contention.[5]

Greyhound not only won the heat, he set a new world record mark for three-year-old geldings of 2:00 flat, going the last half in :59, and joined the elite list of two-minute trotters. The crowd stood stunned when the final time was hung. It hadn't seemed like the gray was going that fast; he wasn't even going all out.[6] Still, he'd annihilated the field of trotters. The spectators soon found their voices and leapt to their feet, erupting in a deafening roar of approval as Palin trotted Greyhound back to the grandstand. Some among them would later state with absolute certainty that Greyhound tipped his head and gave an acknowledging nod in response to his adoring public.

"On this occasion," author M.A. Stoneridge would write some years later, "the same thought flashed through many minds: If the three-year-old gray trotter could already score the [2:00] time that was the target for all ambitious harness racers, could he not, with more experience and under favorable conditions, perhaps be the horse to finally better Peter Manning's world record for the mile in 1:56 ¾, which had stood since 1922?"[7]

The same day, Sep Palin drove Baker's Cardinal Prince to a new pacing record of 1:59 ½, making Palin the only driver in Grand Circuit history to drive two two-minute horses on the same day.[8] Baker had purchased the five-year-old pacer just the week before for $5,000. The stallion had been racing west of the Mississippi on tracks not up to the standards of the Grand Circuit.[9] Over the better surface and in Palin's experienced hands, Cardinal Prince

---

* For Erskine to have "moved his colt out of the way" would have been highly irregular and technically set him up for a fine and/or suspension. This is likely the reason why he refused to move The Saint out of the way.

had shaved four seconds off his best time. Together, Greyhound and Cardinal Prince would keep the Baker-Palin stable at the top of both the trotting and pacing divisions.

Greyhound's next race was just five days away at Syracuse, eight hundred fifty miles northeast in New York. Pete Wilson carefully wrapped Greyhound's legs in white cotton for protection and support over the rough rails. All around him, horses whinnied and bounced around, pulling back on their lead shanks and spooking at the noises of the busy loading area. Loading at the race track wasn't so bad, but sometimes the horses had to switch trains at the train yard, where men shouted, whistles blew, and the roar and smell of powerful locomotives dulled the senses. Greyhound, none too bothered by the excitement, boarded the train with his stablemates and settled in for another long ride.

At Syracuse, six horses went to the post for the August 26 Champion Stallion Stakes. The field, made up of Hambletonian contenders Greyhound had defeated in the big race just 12 days before, had been well-rested, while the gray gelding had traveled some 1,800 miles and set a new world record. To date, Greyhound was the only horse of *any* age to trot a 2:00 mile that season.

The horses scored down for the first heat. Greyhound got away slower than the rest of the field but worked his way to the front, holding the lead when he trotted out of the final turn. It looked like Palin had the win well in hand; Greyhound trotted all alone through the Syracuse track's unusually long home stretch. But then pounding hooves filled Palin's ears. He glanced over his shoulder and there, nostrils flared and legs flying, came a hard-charging Lawrence Hanover! With his new trainer-driver Henry Thomas, the bay colt matched strides with the big gray as the two stepped toward the wire.

"C'mon! Yeah!" Palin shook the lines. Impossible! Lawrence Hanover pushed a nose in front. Palin went to the whip, rapping the powerful gray haunches of a tiring Greyhound.[10] Having seldom felt the sting of a whip, the big horse surged ahead, edging out Lawrence Hanover as they crossed the finish.

Henry Thomas could see Greyhound's daunting schedule had dulled the great gelding's speed. The heat had gone almost as he'd planned. Perhaps today would be the day Lawrence Hanover took down Palin and his big gray freight train—proving Greyhound to be mortal after all.

The horses rested between heats while the first heat of another race was contested by a different field of horses. At the call, Greyhound and the others went to the post for the second heat. Greyhound and Lawrence Hanover lined up in post positions one and two, and the field scored down for the start. At the word, Silver King got away fastest and set the pace. Greyhound trailed the field for the first half; then Palin asked for speed and the gray delivered, surging toward the front behind Silver King, who still held the lead. Thomas sent Lawrence Hanover along with Greyhound, and the two again matched strides, pounding through the stretch. The crowd leapt to their feet, cheering for Greyhound to unleash his power and trot home a winner. But it didn't happen. Lawrence Hanover surged past Greyhound and then nosed ahead of Silver King as they crossed the wire in 2:04. Greyhound came home third, soundly beaten.[11]

Pete Wilson watched from his place near the gap. It was the first time he'd seen Palin ask for speed and Greyhound not give it. He was anxious to get the Hound back to the stable and help him recover before the next heat—the one that would ultimately decide the winner. Pete shook his head. Did Greyhound have enough left to hold off Lawrence Hanover in the third heat? Or would the bay colt hand Greyhound his first defeat of the season? Many in the crowd thought Greyhound was done, and fans rushed to the bookies, laying bets on Lawrence Hanover to win the final heat. Back in the paddock, Pete carefully tended to Greyhound, washing his body with warm water and rubbing liniment into his legs and tired muscles.

About twenty minutes later, the horses stepped onto the track for the final heat. The field scored a couple times, the starter gave the word, and they were off. Greyhound hung back a bit in his usual style, trailing the field until the half. Then Palin lifted the lines and gave them a shake, asking the big gray for speed. The mighty Greyhound delivered, moving in just behind the leader, Lawrence Hanover. Coming out of the final turn, the two engaged in another stretch duel. The bay and the gray, trotting stride-for-stride, muscles gliding smoothly under sleek coats, came down to the wire as one. But Lawrence Hanover could not hold off the gray champion. Greyhound edged a nose in front of the faltering bay colt. With a triumphant surge of power, the gray ghost crossed under the wire in 2:01 ½, winning by a length, much the better of the pair. Lawrence Hanover finished second and Tilly Tonka came third. It was the closest race thus far for the two top trotters, and the most consistent three-heat performance yet by Lawrence Hanover.[12, 13]

"The comeback staged by Greyhound in the final heat was one of the most wonderful ever seen on the harness turf," Tom Gahagan wrote in *The Cincinnati Enquirer*.[14] Greyhound had shown his heart—traveling 1800 miles by rail, setting a world record, and winning a tough race against rested horses, all in the space of a week.

From Syracuse, Greyhound traveled six hundred fifty miles to Indianapolis. The big gray's appearance at Indianapolis had been heavily advertised, and people flocked to the Palin stable to catch a glimpse of the champion. On September 1, they packed the stands to see Greyhound paraded before the crowds on the first day of racing. It was Labor Day weekend, and a celebratory energy flowed through the fair as people gathered for a family outing to take their minds off the troubles of their world.

Greyhound's next start was to be on Labor Day for the $3,000 Indiana Horseman Futurity three-year-old trot. But heavy rains fell that day, postponing the entire race card to the next day. After a straight twenty-four hours of rain, the track was a heavy, muddy mess. In his stall, Greyhound waited with the others for a chance to get out. Used to trotting five or six miles a day, he became restless and agitated. But with the rain, the track was not usable even for exercise, let alone racing.

September 4 dawned gray and dreary, and the rains continued to pour down. When it finally let up by late morning, the horses had been stuck inside for two days. After long but mostly fruitless efforts to dry the track, a few postponed races were contested that afternoon. The track remained a swamp of mud, so wet that the horses had to stay twenty feet off the inside rail to find secure footing. Palin took Cardinal Prince in a classified pace. The mud pulled at the bay stallion's legs and dragged on the sulky tires. He managed a win, but his top time was a slow 2:08. The track remained a muddy mess and, after driver complaints and several horses being scratched by owners and drivers unwilling to race in such conditions, racing was abandoned for the day.[15]

Wilson brought Greyhound out to the track to pose for photos and paraded him in front of the grandstand to appease the disappointed crowd who'd come to see him race. The people clapped and cheered as the big gray walked past the grandstand. Greyhound turned his head toward the throng, both ears pricked forward like two soldiers standing at attention. Pete stopped the horse for the photo op, and Greyhound stood statue-still for a moment. Then he shook his head and pawed the track with one front hoof, then the other. Squirming around at the end of the leather shank held in Pete's hand, Greyhound whinnied. The crowd laughed and clapped.

"You big ham," Pete chided the horse. He walked Greyhound in a large circle, the mud pulling relentlessly at his boots. After another loop, he turned from the crowd, leading the gray back to his stall. Greyhound pranced beside him, fired up from being on the track and anxious to burn off some energy. It was hard on him and the others to be unable to exercise due to the poor track conditions. They were young, finely-tuned athletes; standing around in a twelve-by-twelve-foot box was asking a lot.[16]

After two days stuck inside, the horses were permitted to exercise on a reserved section of dirt road outside the fairgrounds. The crew continued to work on the track, pulling harrows behind noisy tractors. Though it was a less-than-ideal location, exercising on the road got the horses out of their stalls to stretch their legs a bit. The track improved some with help from the afternoon sun, and the men worked on it through the day and into the evening.

The next morning dawned with clear skies and sunlight illuminating the still wet and windswept track. Certainly not the fast, record-making track the race officials hoped for, but suitable enough that a full day of racing would go on as planned. Pete Wilson drove Greyhound to the track early, wanting to give him a few miles at the jog to limber him up for his race later that day. Normally a very calm horse, Greyhound was high-headed and bright-eyed that morning, jigging and dancing on his way to the track.

"Easy now, Hound." Pete spoke softly to the young horse. Greyhound trotted around the track with the intensity of a tightly wound rubber band, one that could snap at any moment. He bucked and kicked out, bouncing Pete in the jog cart. The groom tried to steady him, knowing this behavior was dangerous for both of them, but it was too late. With a playful buck, Greyhound kicked over the shaft of the jog cart, coming down with a hind leg on either side of it. The cart shaft broke where the big horse straddled it and a piece of jagged wood punctured Greyhound's stifle. Pete leapt off the cart and ran to Greyhound's head, quickly unsnapping the overcheck and pulling the horse's nose down between his legs to immobilize him. If the gelding were to panic and bolt in this precarious moment, the results could be devastating. Seeing Wilson's predicament, a track worker rushed to the aid of the horse and handler.

Greyhound remained calm as he was unhooked and disentangled from the jog cart. His hind leg was scratched and scraped, from his hoof to his stifle, and he had abrasions on his inner thigh. The cuts appeared superficial and the puncture not at all deep enough to cause a problem.[17] Back then, the old veterans took care of their own vet work except for the big emergencies. This didn't look serious enough for that, so Palin and Wilson cleaned the gelding up and treated his wounds. Greyhound was stiff that afternoon but moved soundly after jogging a bit to loosen him up.[18] Palin and Baker agreed Greyhound seemed no worse for wear, and would race that afternoon.

Cars lined the roads coming into the fairgrounds. A carnival atmosphere greeted the race goers as they packed the grandstand. People spilled from the overstuffed seating areas and lined up along the inside and outside rails of the mile oval. "The stand was packed, and every point of vantage was occupied," wrote Tom Gahagan in his *Horseman and Fair World* article. Twenty-thousand people, a record crowd for a Wednesday, had come to see Greyhound race.[19]

A small field of four horses, including Hambletonian alumni Silver King, Pedro Tipton, and Warwell Worthy, went to the post for the Indiana Horseman Futurity. Though the others needn't have been there—the day belonged to Greyhound. The big gray out-classed a decidedly high-class field of horses that could have been stars, if not for the misfortune of being born the same year as Greyhound. In the first heat, the gray started slowly at the back of the field before coming on strong, making the last quarter in a blazing :28 ½,[20] a feat made even more impressive given the poor condition of the track.

In the second heat, Greyhound gave the people a real thrill. Palin held him in check on the rail, behind Silver King and Warwell Worthy. The three stayed in line through the first three-quarters. Coming out of the final turn, Palin tipped Greyhound out and around Warwell Worthy in grand fashion. The gelding charged up to Silver King, matching him nearly stride-for-stride. Palin kept a snug hold on Greyhound, keeping him a nose back of Silver King until the final eighth of a mile. At the eighth, he let the gray out a notch. Greyhound grabbed the extra rein, burst forward, and streaked across the finish, winning easily by a half-length.[21, 22]

It was Greyhound's eighth straight win in as many starts—his twelfth if you counted his four wins the previous season. And this at the end of a grueling four weeks of consecutive races while traveling over 2,600 miles by rail. With one final Grand Circuit race before him to end his perfect season, the gallant gray gelding seemed unstoppable.

Following the race, the track officials urged Baker to come forward and say a few words to the crowd of over 20,000 that had come to see his horse. Preferring to stay in the background, Baker reluctantly came forward and accepted the trophy and the adulation.[23] But, like Palin, he gave all the credit to Greyhound. The gelding's impact on the sport had reached enormous proportions. Sports writer George M. Gahagan called Greyhound the "horse of the people."

"The horses themselves, with their human connections" played a great part in drawing in the fair crowds, Gahagan wrote. "A certain lanky gray three-year-old named Greyhound called many persons through the gates ... Thousands of people don't go to races merely to get out and away from their usual surroundings," Gahagan continued. "They go because they love the horses, and because they care for the sport which the horses furnish."[24]

After his winning performance at Indianapolis, the crowds and press followed Pete and Greyhound back to the stable area. Pete wasn't much of a talker when it came to the press. He preferred to work in silence, behind the scenes. The cameras clicked and flashbulbs popped. Pete washed Greyhound with warm water, walked him out, then rubbed him down with liniment, paying close attention to not bother the cuts on the gelding's legs from his exploits earlier in the day. Greyhound was a bit sore in his stifle, but not lame. His attitude was bright and he readily dove into the oats and mash Pete prepared for him.

In lieu of an interview with Greyhound's silent groom, one clever reporter interviewed Greyhound himself instead.[26] The column was a big hit, printed and reprinted in newspapers all over the country. The horse had a personality like none he'd ever seen, Palin had said of Greyhound. People were drawn to him. Quiet, intelligent, and playful, Greyhound endeared himself to his public. In a time well before cell phone technology made everyone a photographer, stacks of pictures were taken of the great horse. His image appeared in newspapers across the country and into Canada. When pictures could not be secured, drawings were made in his likeness. Children and adults alike eagerly snipped photos and articles from newspapers and magazines, filling scrapbooks with stories and images of the great horse. They crowded around his stall at the various tracks, hoping to see or maybe even touch the great champion. Fans brought carrots, apples, and sugar cubes, but feeding treats to Greyhound was a privilege reserved only for Baker.[27] There was something enigmatic about Greyhound, something that drew people to him. Even those that had never seen a harness race before came to see Greyhound. He was truly the people's horse.

Six horses from the Palin stable shipped by truck to Lexington, Kentucky, 10 days after Greyhound's win at Indianapolis.[28] As with his last appearance, Greyhound's name and image were used freely by the Lexington track to promote their race meet, and the upcoming Kentucky Futurity where Greyhound would again meet Lawrence Hanover.

The talk leading up to the Kentucky Futurity said that Lawrence Hanover and maybe Silver King could be a real challenge for Greyhound. Lawrence Hanover worked the second half of a moderate mile in :58 earlier in the month. This led some to believe that the most promising yearling of 1933 might finally hand Greyhound defeat, marring his perfect season record.

Brownie Leach, sports writer for the *Lexington Herald-Leader*, also penned the "Down in Front" column—more of a sports commentary with an editorial slant. He loved a good story and knew it would sell papers. Leading up to the Futurity, he searched for someone among the harness fans that thought Lawrence Hanover would win over Greyhound. He found a few, but largely the consensus was that Greyhound was unbeatable. He'd "won fourteen straight races since he came to his speed last season," Leach wrote. But then he suggested the win against Lawrence Hanover at Syracuse may have been more a matter of Palin outsmarting Lawrence Hanover's driver, Henry Thomas, than the gray being the better horse.[29]

Lawrence Hanover had beaten Greyhound in two heats, Leach wrote, quoting veteran driver Will Dickerson, who suggested that bad luck for Thomas at Syracuse "saved the race for Greyhound."[30] He neglected to mention that the gray had defeated Lawrence Hanover in all five of their meetings. Leach then reminded his readers that Greyhound had been through a tough campaign, and that an Indianapolis horseman said the gray had "lost his bloom" and "will have a tough time of it at Lexington." Leach concluded with his own assessment that Lawrence Hanover was "one of the grandest individuals you've ever gazed upon" and that "few better-looking trotters have been seen on the Grand Circuit in recent years."[31]

In a later edition of "Down in Front," perhaps hoping to increase the drama, Leach continued pushing the Lawrence Hanover vs. Greyhound narrative, opening his September 19 column with, "Henry Thomas won't talk—at least he wouldn't talk the way I'd hoped he would."[32] Leach had asked Thomas if he thought Lawrence Hanover would win the Futurity against Greyhound. But he "wouldn't come out and say [it]. I was hoping he would," Leach admitted. "It would've made a better story." The sportswriter then reminded readers that Lawrence Hanover had trotted a half-mile in :58, the fastest half of the season, suggesting that kind of closing speed might be enough to beat Greyhound. "Moreover," Leach concluded, "they say that Lawrence Hanover is the sort of colt that comes around to his best style in the fall. His recent work apparently justifies that belief."[33]

Despite Leach's niggling jabs, Greyhound remained the odds-on favorite the day before the Futurity. But sometime after the late edition the night before the big race, Baker withdrew Greyhound from the Futurity.[34] The reason was given as illness due to injury. Sports writer Gurney C. Gue suggested that "more than illness was the cause," according to an article in *The Evening Sun*. "Greyhound would have to be at his best to beat [Lawrence Hanover]," said Gue. The late announcement regarding the scratch was so "lacking in details that it caused suspicion in some quarters that [cold feet] might have been the ailment."[35]

The same day, L.G. Duffy wrote in *Horseman and Fair World* that Greyhound was not declared* for the Futurity due to still being quite sore from his mishap in Indianapolis. Greyhound "bruised himself to such an extent that he did not lie down for a week, with the exception of thirty minutes, three days after the accident."[36] On the day of the big race, Greyhound had a fever, his leg was hot and swollen, and the champion gelding was painfully lame.

Lawrence Hanover won the Kentucky Futurity in Greyhound's absence. Many people speculated as to what would have happened in the Kentucky Futurity had Greyhound been sound and contested it. It surely would have been a tough race for both horses and a close finish, provided neither broke gait. Lawrence Hanover won in 2:01 ¾ and 2:00 ¾, taking the second heat by five lengths and trotting the fastest two-heat average of the season[37]—a brilliant performance for sure, but still slower than Greyhound's top time of 2:00 flat. Many of the Hanover colt's fans felt that he would have "given Greyhound the race of his life" and, had the gray been there, he would have pushed Lawrence Hanover to break that elusive two-minute mark in victory.[38]

That afternoon, following the Futurity, Baker, wanting to keep his promise that Greyhound would be seen by his admirers at the Lexington Trots, had the gelding hand-walked in front of the grandstand. A cheering public greeted the clearly lame[39] gelding, who stood and absorbed the adulation before limping back to his stall.

An unnamed reporter for the *Evening Sun* of Hanover, Pennsylvania, cherry-picked Leach's pre-Futurity "Down in Front" columns and tossed in some drama of their own. The "Sports in the Sun" feature in the hometown paper of the famous farm where Lawrence

---

* An eligible horse was declared to start and have final payment made at least twenty-four hours before the race.

Hanover was born led readers to infer that perhaps the gray gelding wasn't lame, but instead his connections were afraid of meeting Lawrence Hanover, who appeared to be better than ever. The writer slyly stated that "according to his trainer," Greyhound was lame and not fit to race,[40] without bothering to relay the information that the gelding was indeed seen to be lame the day of the Futurity.

The anonymous keyboard warrior—or rather typewriter warrior, as it were—continued their assault on the Greyhound camp in their September 30 piece, reporting that Lawrence Hanover was also lame going into the Kentucky Futurity but raced anyway, "despite a leg injury that might have kept many a horse in the stable." Presumably another dig at Greyhound. The same article reported that Lawrence Hanover was now dead lame.[41] With his leg hugely swollen, the colt would remain at Lexington for another week until well enough to travel to his home in Pennsylvania.[42]

Lawrence Hanover never raced again. An attempt was made to bring him back at age four and again at five, but to no avail. With each comeback effort, the colt couldn't stay sound long enough to make it to a race. His best time was 2:00 ¾, made in his final race, the Futurity at Lexington, just shy of the elusive two-minute mile. Lawrence Hanover retired to stud, his lifetime earnings just under $20,000.

Pete Wilson quit in the fall of 1935. The accident and injury to Greyhound had really shaken him. As Greyhound's groom, it was his responsibility to jog the horse daily, saving the fast work for Palin. But Pete never again felt comfortable with the responsibility of sitting behind such a valuable horse, knowing how terribly wrong things could go. Plus, he stated in his resignation, he had bought a farm, and would soon be married.[43]

Upon Wilson's departure, Greyhound became young Jimmie Wingfield's charge. Wingfield's story would intertwine with Greyhound's for the next five years, as Jimmie acted as valet, body guard, and public relations agent for the champion trotter. The two became inseparable friends; their relationship became legendary, like that of Eddie Sweat and the great Thoroughbred Secretariat.

In early November, *Horseman and Fair World* made the astonishing announcement that Guy Abbey's 1936 book was already closed. Walnut Hall, where the chestnut stallion stood, noted a significant influx of breeding requests since early fall.[44] The final tally of the season showed Sep Palin was the top money-winning driver of 1935, though Doc Parshall still came out ahead in number of wins. Greyhound himself was the top money-winning horse of the year with $26,712.52—roughly $605,000 today.[45] He had defeated every horse he came up against, set a new world record, and was the top three-year-old of 1935, hands down.

Greyhound could do no wrong. He was unstoppable—until he wasn't.

GREYHOUND

THE REMARKABLE STORY OF THE LEGENDARY RACEHORSE WHO INSPIRED A NATION

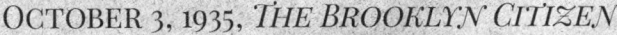

October 3, 1935, *The Brooklyn Citizen*

CHAPTER
— 13 —

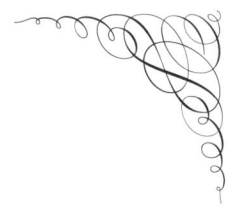

"But a shadow has fallen upon [Peter Manning's] throne. It is that of Greyhound, who stands on the topmost [step] that leads up to it, reaching for the crown."

—

JOHN HERVEY,
HOOF BEATS, 1936

IN THE SHADOW OF THE TROTTING KING

Peter Manning alone had reached the top speed of the trotter, some of the old-timers argued, and no one would top him, ever. Not Greyhound, not any horse. But they'd said that about Uhlan's 1908 record, too. Then Peter Manning came along and lowered it by more than one second in 1922. Still, at age four, Greyhound was awfully young to beat a record like Peter Manning's—he had been six years old when he trotted his top mile. Standardbreds became faster with age and maturity. The athleticism, strength, and fitness required to maintain a trot at speed had to be developed over time. But Greyhound wasn't like any other four-year-old. He didn't trot, he flew. If anyone could take down Peter Manning's record, Greyhound would be the one to do it.

Greyhound started his 1936 season at Lexington for the Spring Trots. Baker traveled from St. Charles to watch his horses train and race. He enjoyed coming to Lexington, a chance to catch up with his old friend Henry Knight and get an early look at the Almahurst yearlings. At Lexington, Greyhound trotted an exhibition mile in front of thousands of fans on June 23. When asked about racing at Lexington, *The Harness Horse* wrote that Palin indicated it might be "unfair" to start the gray in any race, saying that he would "be almost certain to go faster than seemed judicious." A cocky response, for sure, but Greyhound backed him up by zooming through the last half in :58 and the final quarter in :28 ¼[1]—amazing so early in the season, and a clip fast enough to beat Peter Manning's record, if he could maintain it for a mile. The gelding had grown over his nine-month between-season layoff. Now standing 16.1 hands and carrying more flesh, Greyhound was the picture of fitness and looked every inch the champion he was. His coat had whitened considerably with his spring shed, a white base with steel gray dappling laced over the shoulders and haunches. His long mane remained dark, almost black, a stark contrast against his lightening body.

Crowds packed all available spaces at Goshen's Historic Track for the July 22 *Times Herald* free-for-all (FFA) trot, Greyhound's debut race of his four-year-old season. Now, at age four, there were no races for his age group, which meant that for the first time, Greyhound would go against older horses. Some old-timers believed that age four was an off year for a harness horse, an awkward time of growth and development when a horse couldn't be expected to reach the top speeds that an older, stronger horse could obtain. Palin didn't buy into that way of thinking. Greyhound would be better than ever in 1936.

The Historic Track opened in 1838, a half-mile oval situated on the edge of the downtown core of Goshen, in Orange County, New York. An area considered the "cradle of the trotter." Historic had hosted some of the greatest horses in the history of the sport—Goldsmith Maid, Uhlan, and even Hambletonian himself, the father of the modern Standardbred, had been seen there. A half-mile oval was more commonly found on smaller county fair tracks than on the Grand Circuit. Some horses excelled on them, and others struggled. A smaller oval required the driver to rate the horse more aggressively to safely navigate the tight turns. The stretches were also much shorter, which favored a horse that reached top speed quickly—something Greyhound was not built for.

Just four horses went to the post for the FFA trot on July 22. Greyhound went off as the favorite; his main competition was a pair of tough mares, Tara (age 5) and Angel Child (age 7). In addition to the two mares, Greyhound's old rival Silver King, now a muscular and handsome stallion, rounded out the field.

In the first heat, Tara scored out in front and set the pace, trotting the quarter in :31 ¼, with Angel Child next. Tara's driver then quickly shortened his lines, slowing the pace. She made the half in a slow 1:05 ¼ and passed the three-quarter mark in an uninspired 1:38 ¼.[2]

Palin had to rate back hard on the tight turns, and each time a frustrated Greyhound lost ground on the mares, despite the slow fractions. Entering the short home stretch, Palin swung Greyhound out and moved on the leaders with sizzling speed, clipping right along just a neck behind Angel Child as she took the lead from a tiring Tara. The two came down to the wire flying, Greyhound gaining with each stride, but he ran out of track and Angel Child just barely held her lead over the fast-closing gelding. Time for the mile, 2:07. The final quarter in a blazing :28 ¾—"probably the fastest quarter ever raced over a two-lap track," Tom Gahagan later wrote.[3, 4]

In the second heat, Greyhound scored well and took the lead before the first quarter, holding it throughout and finishing ahead of a hard-trotting Tara in 2:05. In the third heat, Greyhound scored poorly, frustrated from fighting Palin's tight hold. Tara and Angel Child both scored well and rushed to the front. Palin put Greyhound on the rail just behind the leaders, biding his time. The reinsman made his move on the back stretch of the second half. Tara moved up at the same time, pushing the gelding out three wide on the far turn[5] as they passed Angel Child. The two raced side-by-side into the home stretch, but Tara edged Greyhound at the end, the extra distance traveled by going wide being too much of a handicap for him.

The three heat winners were called back for a fourth heat race-off to determine the winner. Palin, not wanting to risk Greyhound by pushing him too hard in his first start of the season, withdrew the gelding,[6] thus handing the champion his first defeat since 1934. Tara won the final heat in a hard drive to the wire, and set a new standard of a 2:06 ¼ average over four miles on a half-mile track.[7]

Dejected fans departed Historic Track following Greyhound's first start of 1936. Some wondered if perhaps the old-timers were right. Maybe this would be an off year for four-year-old Greyhound. Or maybe that grand gray ghost had finally met his match in a couple of tough mares.

A week later, Greyhound was at Old Orchard Beach, Maine, to contest the first division of the Pine Tree Trot. Known as the "Kite Track" for its unusual shape, the mile and one-eighth track at Old Orchard Beach was opened in 1892 by horsemen in the high-wheel sulky era who felt that to get a faster time, they needed to build a better track. The track resembled a lopsided figure eight, with a large one-mile loop at one end and a small eighth-of-a-mile loop at the other. Horses scored on the smaller loop, the word "Go" being given at the cross point. The horses then raced on two long stretches and just one sweeping turn. The track had gone idle in 1907, but was resurfaced and reopened some three decades later, becoming a Grand Circuit stop from 1936-49.[8]

The broad, sweeping turn of the kite track suited Greyhound's long stride, much more so than the tight turns of the half-mile oval at Goshen's Historic track. Greyhound again met the small but mighty mare Tara as a field of six scored for the Pine Tree Trot. In the first heat, Greyhound scored poorly, but turned on the speed and made up the deficit with each ground-devouring stride. Neck and neck in the stretch, Greyhound edged Tara by a nose, trotting the final quarter in a blazing twenty-eight seconds flat, which set a world record for fastest four-year-old trotting gelding and broke the state record for trotting horses of any age.[9] The shattered state record had been set just a few days before by Calumet Evelyn, a talented daughter of Guy Abbey, who had been an equally talented pacer before her trainer converted her to trotting. Greyhound again fought a rousing stretch duel with Tara as he captured the next two heats, each time holding the game little trotting mare solidly in second place.[10] The rest of the field were never contenders, spread out behind the two leaders like a scattering of fallen leaves.

"The sight of the gray wonder horse coming from behind," reported Maine's *Biddeford-Saco Journal*, with "head low and stepping at a dizzy speed to overcome the handicap of a slow start, thrilled the big crowd probably more than any other sight of the week at the circuit races."[11] It was the biggest turnout at the Maine track in Grand Circuit history. The newly legalized pari-mutuel machines were a big hit, with the "take" over $26,000. Greyhound went off at 3/5 odds in the first two heats. Both he and Tara were barred from betting in the third heat.[12]

It was an excellent meet for the Baker-Palin stable, with a couple youngsters showing well. Cardinal Prince set a personal best of 1:58 ¾, smashing the forty-year-old record for the fastest pacing mile in the state of Maine by over two seconds.[13]

After leaving Maine, Greyhound returned to the triangle track at Good Time Park amidst the excitement of Hambletonian Week. No one except for Sep Palin had ever driven Greyhound in a race or against the clock. History would be recorded to reflect this as fact, but it's not quite true. On August 8, 1936, Mrs. Gladys Harriman, wife of E. Roland Harriman, a prominent figure in harness racing, drove Greyhound a mile in 2:01 ¾ at Good Time Park. Though just a working mile, it was a new trotting record for a female driver.[14] This gave Mrs. Harriman the top position at both gaits, as she had taken her pacing gelding, Highland Scott, over the mile in 1:59 ¼ in 1929. Mrs. Harriman's record was reported in a handful of papers but never made it into Greyhound's official record, perhaps because at the time, women weren't taken seriously as reinsmen. While there were female-only races staged, they were treated more as a novelty than an event to be taken seriously.

Greyhound's next race was the Progressive Trot on August 13, the day after the Hambletonian. Palin didn't have a horse for the Hambletonian in 1936, Baker's $10,000 colt, The Master, having not panned out as a contender. Palin instead would drive the colt Ed Lasater for Ben White, who had two contenders in his string. Ben would drive his son Gibson's filly, Rosalind.

On August 12, Rosalind won the Hambletonian, lowering Greyhound's record from the previous year by half a second. Palin came third with Ed Lasater. The next day, Greyhound attracted the largest non-Hambletonian day crowd on record at Good Time Park for the one-mile Progressive Trot. Those that couldn't attend crowded around the radio to hear sportscaster Clem McCarthy call the race over the airwaves for NBC.

"Seven of the fastest trotters that ever faced a starting judge were on hand to race ... over a fast track on an atmospherically fast day,"[15] *The Harness Horse* reported in their August 19 issue. The crowd packed the stands, anxious to see Greyhound take on the top mares Angel

Child, who had taken one heat from Greyhound earlier in the year, and Tara and Calumet Evelyn, co-champion aged trotters of 1935. The latter mare was also the 1935 top aged pacer.[16] An outstandingly talented individual, five-year-old Calumet Evelyn held a two-minute record in *both* gaits. In the auction pools, Greyhound and Calumet Evelyn sold for $50 each, Tara for $20, with the field going for $5. At the word, Greyhound got away slowly and the three mares charged past him, with Tara setting the early pace. Out of the final turn, Greyhound gathered himself and stormed down the stretch, seemingly gaining speed with every stride.[17] Closing fast, he easily passed the three talented mares.

In the second heat, Greyhound scored well then dropped to fourth, letting Calumet Evelyn set the pace. At Palin's bidding, Greyhound started that "irresistible brush he is fast becoming noted for." He swept around Angel Child, then Tara, and then Calumet Evelyn. The three mares came on again, coming into the long home stretch, pushing Greyhound, "four perfect trotters" each trying to head the other, *The Harness Horse* later wrote. A man in the crowd shouted, "They have Palin to a drive!" and they did, but Palin let Greyhound out another notch and the gray trotted away from them as if he hadn't already turned in the better part of two fast miles, with three or four quarters at less than thirty seconds![18] He blazed under the wire, winning in 2:00 ¼. Tara finished second.

In the third and final heat, Greyhound took the lead before the half, gaining an incredible six lengths over the field before reaching the three-quarter pole in 1:31. In the final closing stretch run, Greyhound trotted away without urging, going the last quarter in :29.[19]

Greyhound had set three world records in one race. He broke the world record for the fastest third heat, shaving three-quarters of a second off the previous record set by Vanstandt in 1934. With that same mile heat, he also trotted the fastest mile by a four-year-old gelding (2:00 flat), lowering by one second his own record set the previous month at Old Orchard Beach. Finally, he set a new three-heat world record (fastest total of three one-mile heats in a single race), going three miles in just over six minutes, cutting 1 ¾ seconds off the record set by Tara in the same event the year before.[20] Tough little Tara was again Greyhound's main competition, but she just couldn't match the gray ghost's incredible closing power. She took second in all three heats; Angel Child finished third.

At the race judge's request, Palin paraded Greyhound the length of the grandstand, giving the crowd that stayed on an extra day at Goshen a look at the multiple-world-record holder. Baker was presented with a trophy by W. N. Reynolds, who noted in his presentation speech that he owned Greyhound's dam, Elizabeth.[21]

From Goshen, the Baker-Palin stable traveled to Springfield, Illinois for the August 21 FFA Trot. The crowd began cheering the moment Greyhound stepped on the track for his warm-up miles.[22] The only owner willing to put his horse against Greyhound was A. A. Taylor of Maysville, Kentucky, who sent Angel Child to the post for second money. Greyhound won the first heat easily in 2:02, trotting the last half in an impressive :58.

The pair set a blazing pace in the second heat. Angel Child quickly went to the lead and trotted the first half in :59, leading Greyhound by two lengths, passing the three-quarter mark in 1:28 ½. A new wave of thunderous applause and cheering rose from the crowd with each quarter as the clocker hung the time. Greyhound followed Angel Child into the final turn; then Palin tipped the big gelding to the outside and sailed past the mare.[23] Like a shimmering silver whirlwind, Greyhound pounded down the stretch, puffs of dust from his flying hooves rising from the track in his wake. Angel Child hung close but was a length behind when the gray ghost flew under the wire. The crowd of 15,000 stood in stunned silence for a moment, waiting for the official clocker to hang the final time. As the numbers went up, the crowd erupted in thunderous applause, yelling and cheering. The time posted, 1:57 ¼, the fastest mile in a *race* by any horse, of any age, at either gait. Ever.[24, 25]

"Those fortunate enough to be in Springfield today will never forget the Grey Ghost," turf writer P. W. Moser said about Greyhound's record mile. "And he did it on his nerve." Without a prompter, all alone in front, with just a few light taps from Palin, the great gelding displayed speed never before seen in racing conditions.[26] Following this performance, few people doubted that under perfect conditions and with the benefit of prompters to encourage the competitive spirit within him, Greyhound would surely match if not surpass the record of 1:56 ¾ set by Peter Manning in his 1922 time trial. While a fast mile was a fast mile for record-making purposes, extra weight in the way of things as intangible as awe and respect were given to records set in a race, where conditions could not be controlled as they are in a race against time.

In a time trial, a horse is set against the clock in perfect weather and track conditions. The horse can hug the inside rail, traveling the shortest distance the whole way around the track, with no interference from other competitors. In years past, a wind screen was used on a runner in front of the horse, allowing the time-trialing horse to draft behind, making it easier for the horse to reach and maintain top speeds. Approaching the finish, the front runner would move out of the way and allow the horse racing the clock to pass on the inside rail. Front runners and wind screens were no longer permitted in time trials in Peter Manning's era, but still, his record had not been made in racing conditions. Add to the mix the fact that at four years of age, Greyhound was not yet at full maturity, and the possibility of finally dethroning the trotting king seemed within reach. Greyhound would only get stronger and faster.

In the crowd of cheering fans, Dooley Putnam stood along the rail with his friends from work. The young men had snuck away from their employer's barn at the state fairgrounds when they heard Greyhound would be racing that day, knowing it might be their only chance to see the great champion in action.[27] And what a day! One Dooley would never forget. As he watched the gray gelding trot back to the winner's circle for the trophy presentation, Dooley could not have known how their lives would connect in the years to come. If someone had told him then, he most certainly would not have dared believe them.

Greyhound, Cardinal Prince, and others in the Baker-Palin stable boarded the train at Springfield and headed northeast to Syracuse, New York. Jimmie Wingfield accompanied his charge, riding with him in the train car, sleeping in a hammock stretched between the stall walls. He'd grown quite close to the champion in the months he'd been caring for him. The feeling seemed to be mutual between man and horse. Greyhound's eyes softened when he heard Jimmie's voice. Turning away from his hay and pushing his head over the stall gate, Greyhound nickered quietly when Jimmie called to him. He would then nuzzle Jimmie's cheek or gently lip his fingers as they stood close together, a secret conversation passing silently between them.[28]

While Jimmie jogged Greyhound in Syracuse, Palin went to Milwaukee to again take the reins on Ed Lasater, the colt trained by Ben White, in the American Stake at the Wisconsin State Fair. The elder White would drive his son's filly, Rosalind. With each outstanding performance, Rosalind's fame grew. Her story had captured the heart of America. Ben White had gifted Rosalind at birth to his ailing son, Gibson, who was confined to a tuberculosis isolation hospital far from home. Ben White hoped that having the filly to love, think about, and plan her career would help Gibson return to health by giving the boy something to focus on aside from his illness and separation from his family.[29] It had worked, and not only was a now much happier Gibson regaining his health, the young man had the top three-year-old filly of the season.

Rosalind looked unstoppable, winning the American Stake in straight heats over Palin and Ed Lasater. She won going away, White never once having to touch her with the whip. One couldn't help but wonder what would happen if the filly and Greyhound met in a race. But with Rosalind one year younger than the gray champion, it seemed unlikely. Rosalind had many lucrative engagements for her age group, but Greyhound was running out of competition and already people questioned whether there would be any horse for him to race next season.

There were few racing opportunities for an older horse, especially one as fast as Greyhound.[30] Many races for older or lower-level horses were "classified," a handicapping system used by harness racing officials to produce races with evenly matched competition. These races grouped horses based on their best time, money earned, recent past performances, or various combinations thereof. Every year for the better part of a decade brought headlines of an official new classification system from one trotting club or another. Up until the late 1930s, there were multiple governing bodies overseeing harness racing competition. Each larger regional body had several smaller state-level bodies beneath them. All had their own rules that may or may not have been set in stone, which of course led to quite a lot of confusion.

The race meets Greyhound went to early in his career on the Grand Circuit had "undercard" races classified by time. Race officials determined the cutoff for each classification based on the best times of the horses entered. Each classification was marked by a specific time for a mile. For example, a 2:12 trot would be for horses that had never trotted a mile faster than 2:12. A typical race card might have a 2:30, 2:20, 2:15, and 2:08 trot, giving horses of all classes a chance to compete. In 1937, a "money won" classification was embraced by most of the major governing bodies, though they still were to take the "win-race-time into consideration."[31] Clear as mud, right? Regardless, these annual changes made no difference for Greyhound.

The more lucrative races with the higher purses were for the younger horses. The two- and three-year-olds that were fast enough had their pick of large purse engagements, provided their owners paid the fees to keep them eligible. The problem came when you had an older horse like Greyhound, one that had literally outclassed the competition—he was simply too fast to fit into any of the time classifications, which topped out about 2:02. Other races were classed by earnings. There, again, Greyhound was so far ahead of his competition, there was no place for him. The only races open to a horse as fast as Greyhound were a few open free-for-all trots, but the other owners were getting tired of putting their horses up in a race for second money.

Eventually the three main governing bodies—the United Trotting Association, the National Trotting Association, and the American Trotting Association*—absorbed the American Trotting Register (which kept horse registration records and race results), merged, and created the United States Trotting Association (USTA) in 1939.[32] This merger provided more uniformity in the rules and a single harness horse registry. But the fact remained: there were simply very few opportunities for a horse of Greyhound's caliber.

Just three horses met Greyhound in Syracuse for the Empire State FFA trot on September 11. Calumet Evelyn, the bettors second choice, Tara, and the chestnut colt San Bellini, a new contender meeting the champion for the first time, rounded out the field.

In the Empire State trot, Greyhound again demonstrated his superiority, winning easily

---

* The United Trotting Association oversaw Ohio, the National Trotting Association ran things east of Ohio and on the west coast, and the American Trotting Association governed most of the Midwest.[33] Harriman sent out a telegram in 1938 to the leading figures in the sport, inviting them to the "Friends of Trotters" meeting in Indianapolis, IN. Some 300 people showed up and Harriman basically told them to unify "or else," seeing the unification as the only way to preserve the sport. They did and the USTA was born.[34]

in three heats. Greyhound was never really challenged, though the hard-charging Calumet Evelyn came closest. Those who came to see a great display of speed were disappointed. A once-exciting two-minute or sub-2:05 mile was now commonplace whenever Greyhound stepped on the track. Palin made no effort to top his 1:57 ¼ record set in Springfield, only asking enough of the great gelding to win, slowing Greyhound at the end to preserve him.[35] Fans had yet to see how fast the horse could really go.

The next stop on the Grand Circuit was Reading, Pennsylvania. To celebrate the return of Grand Circuit racing to the state for the first time in twenty years, a parade of two-minute horses was presented to the crowd. Led by Greyhound, the parade included seven horses with records of two minutes or faster.[36]

On opening day, Baker's top pacer, Cardinal Prince, set a new three-heat world record. Interestingly, Cardinal Prince was permitted to enter the 2:12 class thanks to one of those odd discrepancies in the rules, which not only differed from location to location, but also between half-mile and full mile tracks. It's also possible that racing out of class was permitted to draw top horses to the small fair, giving the sport an extra boost in the state that had not seen Grand Circuit racing since 1916.[37] Regardless, the handsome bay stallion finished far ahead of his rivals.[38] Greyhound came only for the parade. Whether that was due to the lack of a suitable race for him or because of the half-mile track is unclear. Still, he was the biggest draw of all and Baker was happy to share his champion with the people.

The sport loved Baker as much as he loved it, frequently touting the older gentleman as a great ambassador of harness racing and a true sportsman. He competed for the love of horses and sport, not just for the money. Baker regularly joined both financially and personally in any effort he saw as beneficial to the sport he loved, including by financing the improvement of existing harness parks, exhibiting his great retired pacing champion, Winnipeg, at his own expense to thrill the fans and bring more people to the races, and sponsoring races to build up the sport. Due to his years of dedication to the sport and to the horses, Kentucky governor Ruby Laffoon named him an honorary colonel in 1935. The reporters soon caught on, and the title was often added to his name in print. Years went by and Baker became ever more beloved in the sport. Around his hometown of St. Charles, he would be known as simply "The Colonel."

At the end of September, Greyhound went to the fairgrounds at Allentown, Pennsylvania to attempt to lower the world record for a mile on a half-mile track. The last time he'd been on a half-mile oval was his first start of the season at Goshen's Historic track. He'd lost then, the tight turns costing him much speed when Palin fought to rate him back and navigate them safely. Still, the heat he won in that contest had been the fastest of the three; he'd trotted it in 2:05. The record for a mile over a half-mile track was considerably lower than that at 2:02 ¼, set by Peter Manning in his record-smashing 1922 season.

The crowd roared when Greyhound stepped onto the track. Four official clockers stood in the judges' stand. Palin held his own stopwatch in the palm of his hand, as did several fans in the crowd.[39] A local horseman had a runner hooked to a sulky to serve as a prompter for Greyhound. The prompt horse (often a Thoroughbred) was not restricted in gait and could trot, canter, or gallop—whatever speed was needed to rate and encourage the horse going for the record. They could go along behind or beside the horse racing against time, but not in front. Several trainers kept one or two on hand to work as training mates. Palin had one that traveled with the string, known simply as "The Mare." Despite her uninspired name, she was well-loved in the Palin stable.[40]

Greyhound moved with silky, floating ease, stepping with long and graceful strides. Palin scored the big gray down a couple times, then gave a nod as he passed the judges' stand. He clicked his stopwatch, and sent Greyhound off against the record.

The clockers caught the first half in 1:01. For the second half, the prompter waited at the top of the stretch. When Greyhound came out of the turn, the prompter set off at a gallop to pace the gray down the back stretch, through the final turn, and into the home stretch. Greyhound pounded home ahead of the runner, his legs moving fluidly, his black mane flying, his sleek, gray body moving effortlessly like a marvelous silver machine. Palin tapped the whip a couple times over the powerful gray haunches, asking for a bit more. Greyhound surged forward and flew past the finish. The four official clockers caught him in 2:02 flat, a new world record. Palin's own clock and those of a few of the fans in the crowd had caught the gray in 2:01 ½, but Palin didn't press the issue.[41] Greyhound had lowered his own best time by three seconds and taken down a 14-year-old world record. He had more than proven himself.

After his record trot, Greyhound stayed with Jimmie in Pennsylvania to rest while the other horses in the Palin string traveled more than six hundred miles to Lexington. Two days later, Greyhound also departed by train for Lexington. There, he would contest the Transylvania FFA trot at the closing meet of the 1936 Grand Circuit season.[42]

At Lexington, the morning started with a heavy fog but it burned off by the afternoon. A diverse crowd ranged from society folks to Thoroughbred people, tobacco growers, farmers, and traders—all were represented sipping beer under the canopy, reported the October 7 issue of *The Harness Horse*.

Just three owners dared send their horses to take on the mighty gray trotter on October 1 for the Transylvania. Greyhound was barred from wagering, which left Tara as the "favorite," selling for $25, and the field at $15.[43] Angel Child and Miss Kate B rounded out the field.

The four trotters pranced before the grandstand as the announcer called the name of each horse, owner, and driver. After several scores, the starting judge gave the word with the field surging forward, and the horses were off. As usual, Greyhound got away slowly but nabbed the lead at the quarter pole. The positions remained unchanged, with no "stiff driving" until the three-quarter pole, at which point Berry and Erskine, with Tara and Angel Child respectively, began a bruising stretch. But no one could catch the gray ghost. Angel Child held a length over Tara while Greyhound cruised on home; even with Palin taking back on the reins, they went the last quarter in :28 ¾ and the last half in :59 ¼.[44]

In the second heat, it was Angel Child and Tara fighting it out for second place once more. Palin again held Greyhound back in the final quarter, but he still blazed home in front, coming the last quarter in :28 ¼. In the third heat, Greyhound took the lead easily one more time, and won the heat without visible effort.[45] The champion had won in straight heats, going in 2:02 ¾, 2:01 ¼, and 2:00 flat, while being held back at the end of each mile. Such times, once considered impressive, were now only modest for the likes of Greyhound. Tara and Angel Child swapped back and forth for second place. Miss Kate B came fourth in all three heats.

On October 5 and again on October 14, Palin sent Greyhound against time at Lexington, hoping to lower his 1:57 ¼ mark. His official record would record these attempts as losses, as he "only" managed to match his mark of 1:57 ¼ both times instead of lowering it. In reality, Greyhound had just trotted three sub-two-minute miles in the space of two weeks and trotted the fastest three miles of any horse in a single season, ever. In a time when sub-two-minute miles were a lofty goal never obtained for most trotters, Greyhound seemed to drop them as casually as Bing Crosby crooned number one hits. He'd trotted faster than any other horse in history except one—the great Peter Manning.

Greyhound finished his four-year-old season unquestionably the best trotter of his age group, and by most accounts, the greatest trotter of the decade. Many were already calling him the greatest trotter of all time. But others insisted that, while he was surely a great horse, the 1:56 ¾ record hung up by Peter Manning in 1922 stood between Greyhound and the title of greatest of all time.

"He'll top it if he's sound," Palin told reporters in December, "and there's every indication he will be. I fully expect him to set a new record. He's a great, game horse, he'll come through."[46]

After Greyhound's fantastic Hambletonian win in 1935, Peter Manning's owner, Irving W. Gleason, had this to say: "Well, I'll say this and I'll say it gladly. Greyhound is the best trotter I've seen SINCE Peter Manning." He then conceded his belief that Greyhound *may* be the one to lower the world trotting record,[47] but fell short of stating certain success.

"He's the greatest trotter I have ever handled," Palin told reporters following his Hambletonian win in 1935. "Don't be surprised to hear of him lowering Peter Manning's mark."[48] He later indicated 1937 would be the year. Until then, the world would wait anxiously to see the accuracy of either man's prognostication.

CHAPTER
— 14 —

> *"No cracked earth, no blistering sun,*
> *no burning wind, no grasshoppers, are a permanent match*
> *for the indomitable American farmers and stockmen and their wives*
> *and children who have carried on through desperate days,*
> *and inspire us with their self-reliance,*
> *their tenacity and their courage."*
>
> —
> FRANKLIN DELANO ROOSEVELT, FIRESIDE CHAT 8,
> SEPTEMBER 9, 1936

GAUNTLET

Looking back, those who did not experience the "Dust Bowl" think of it as a single event brought on by a significant drought. In fact, there were four consecutive droughts in the 1930s, each bringing record heat, destroying farm land, and causing thousands of deaths. In 1936, the third such drought devastated the United States, preceded by a record cold winter.

In the newspapers, rain became an event that made headlines. The middle part of the country saw rainfall as much as 50 percent below average for the season;[1] a 15 percent deficit is considered drought conditions.[2] Some months, particularly in the Plains states, had far less. The lowest rainfall occurred during the growing season, which dramatically increased the severity of the drought.[3] The middle of the country became like a desert landscape where nothing could survive.

High temperatures, high winds, insect infestations, and dust storms devastated America's agricultural heartland. In a country already gripped with economic depression, the loss of crops and farm land nearly destroyed the family farm, an American icon of the era. In 1936, one in ten farms changed ownership—the majority of these lost to creditors. People pushed from their homes became migrants, traveling from the Plains states to larger cities, looking for work.[4]

The year 1936 saw some of the hottest temperatures on record. All but three states reported multiple days over 100 degrees, with several states experiencing thirty to sixty days over 100 degrees, and a few with more than twenty days of temperatures above 110 degrees.[5] In the second week of July, the United States census bureau reported more than 12,000 deaths in eighty-six cities so far that year, compared to 8,800 over the same period in 1934.[6] In an eighteen-hour period on July 13, 100 people died from heat in the Twin Cities of Minnesota, while eighty people in Detroit, Michigan, died over the same period. Thousands of Americans suffered from heat exhaustion, and 3,500 drowning deaths were indirectly blamed on the heat as people tried to cool down.[7] By the end of the year, more than 75 percent of the country had been affected by heat and severe drought.[8]

The heat finally broke in September, and people flocked to outdoor activities such as the state fairs in New York and Indiana, returning to the races on the small tracks and at Lexington for the trots. Many harness horse lovers and turf historians credit Greyhound with holding the sport together during this difficult time. In the 1920s, harness racing was in severe decline, but in the 1930s—despite the difficult times, droughts, heat waves, and economic hardships—multiple reports noted harness racing saw increases in spectators each year that Greyhound raced.

Through the long, cold winters, the harness horses remained a topic of conversation as people anxiously waited for the racing season to return. Some popular harness sport-specific publications nearly doubled in size in the late 1930s as renewed interest brought more articles to print.[9] While it did not match the surge of popularity experienced by the Thoroughbreds, 1936 topped 1935 as the best year in harness racing growth. More people came to the track, more horses raced, and more locations were added to the Grand Circuit, which ran 11 weeks in 10 cities in 1936. Further growth was anticipated as the 1937 racing season approached. There was much excitement around the 1936 Hambletonian winner and top three-year-old filly Rosalind. Now that she was a four-year-old, fans anticipated her racing against Greyhound.

Winter of 1936 closed in across the tired and Depression-scarred nation; people huddled around the fire and listened to increasingly alarming news on the radio. Many feared reports coming from Europe, where Hitler was engaged in a series of actions that would ultimately lead to WWII. He had broken the terms of the Treaty of Versailles, tested his army in the Spanish Civil War, and invaded Rhineland. He also formed an alliance with Mussolini, dictator of Italy, and Emperor Hirohito of Japan.[10]

The American people, reeling from the devastating effects of drought and economic depression, drew strength and hope wherever they could find it. From their family, from their friends and neighbors, and from their faith. They found distraction in entertainment and sports news, finding temporary relief in following the actions of their sports heroes. American Jesse Owens won four gold medals in the summer Olympics, humiliating Hitler by defeating his Aryan "super athletes." Upon his return to the United States, Owens was celebrated with a ticker tape parade in New York City.*

As fans of Thoroughbreds waited each season for a new Triple Crown hopeful to emerge, and baseball fans speculated over the next World Series champions, the increasing number of harness racing fans waited through the long off season and wondered. Could Greyhound be the one they'd been waiting for, the one to out-trot Peter Manning and finally dethrone the trotting king?

Greyhound had beaten every horse in his age group and the top older horses as well. So much better than his rivals, he had reached a class that technically did not exist. Low purses for older horses with speed had been a continuing problem in the sport. In 1937, aside from a few cheap free-for-all trots, there were no divisions offered for older horses that had trotted faster than 2:06.[11]

Lack of opportunity for talented older horses and increasing European interest in the American harness horse—the Standardbred—resulted in many top American horses being purchased by European buyers. The fast mare Tara was one such horse. This perceived "loss" of American horses overseas had been an ongoing concern among breeders and fans of harness racing in America. When American champions were sold to Europe, even fewer older horses of any class were left for a horse like Greyhound to go up against.

"When about sixty years ago," reported the August 1937 issue of the sporting journal *Horse and Horseman*, "the sport and the breed began to assume such great success in the United States, the European countries took increasing notice and began importing high-class American stallions and mares for breeding and racing."[13]

Foreign buyers were regularly seen at the speed sales in the fall, buying up yearlings and proven older horses. While Americans tried to keep the potential future top sires and dams in the States, many just didn't have enough money to compete against wealthy foreign buyers. This is likely why Palin partnered with two other men to purchase The Senator back in the 1920s—they wanted to keep the top stallion stateside. Additionally, some foreign buyers negotiated private sales, offering prices that couldn't be refused, even though the horse had not been publicly offered.

By the 1930s, the sport of harness racing was powerfully organized and successful in

---

* Directing such honor toward a black man was shamefully short-lived and Owens continued to battle discrimination and racism in America throughout his life.[12]

numerous European countries and beyond. France, Italy, Germany, Austria, Hungary, Czechoslovakia, Belgium, Denmark, Holland, and the Scandinavian Peninsula all had strong interest in harness racing. In Russia, more records were held by horses descended from American Standardbreds than from pure native Orlov Trotter stock.[14] This was in part by design as in Russia, imported American Standardbreds were not permitted to race* but were crossed with the Orlov Trotters for the development of a new breed, the Russian Trotter.[15]

Of the thousands of horses imported to Europe over the previous half-century, as of 1937, none had been more successful on their new continent than Muscletone.[16] Foaled in 1931 at Coldstream Farm in Lexington, Kentucky, Muscletone was trained by Doc Parshall, who later became the trainer of Greyhound's early nemesis, Lawrence Hanover. Muscletone had a lot of talent but was said to be "difficult"[17] and poorly behaved.[18] His second-place finish in the Hambletonian (driven by Doc's brother, Daryl) was followed by three lackluster performances, making disastrous breaks in almost every heat.[19] Discouraged, Muscletone's owner sold the once-promising stallion to Italian sportsman Giovanni Maiani for just $5,000.

Maiani entrusted Muscletone to Russian reinsman Alessandro Finn. Muscletone improved greatly under Finn's handling. The reinsman eliminated the horse's chronic breaking gait problem and brought out his natural trotting talent. In the two years since he'd left America, the bay stallion dominated European racing,[20] defeating all comers, victorious over any distance and all types of track surfaces. Crowned the European champion, Muscletone won upwards of $100,000. As with Greyhound in America, by 1937, there was no competition remaining for Muscletone in Europe.

Early in 1937, rumors spread that Maiani and Finn were telling anyone who would listen that their Muscletone was the greatest trotter of them all—greater than even Greyhound. Soon, news arrived stateside that a challenge had been printed in *Cavallie*—an Italian trotting horse publication—where Maiani bragged that his horse Muscletone could defeat the U.S. champion, Greyhound.[21]

Baker responded to the challenge, saying Greyhound would race Muscletone for a bet of no less than $10,000, with the sky being the limit. Baker and Palin further stipulated Greyhound would meet Muscletone any time, and at any place with a suitable mile or half-mile track. They'd welcome a race over any distance from one to five miles, with or without heats.[22] In May, *The Lexington Herald-Leader* printed this response from Maiani, which originally appeared in *Cavallie*:

"We accept the challenge for a meeting in

---

* Importations stopped after WWI and began again in the 1950s.[23]

America between your Greyhound and our Muscletone with a minimum wager of $10,000, on the condition that you accept a return match in Italy for $10,000 or more. If you accept, as we hope, Mr. Maiani is at your disposal to meet you either in Europe or the U.S.A. at the earliest convenience to close the deal."[24]

The gauntlet had been thrown. For months, the papers would be all abuzz with the details as negotiations were made between Baker and Maiani. This back-and-forth exchange became the backdrop for Greyhound's 1937 season.

CHAPTER

— 15 —

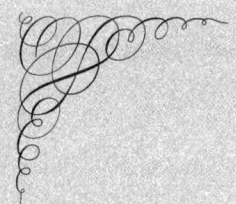

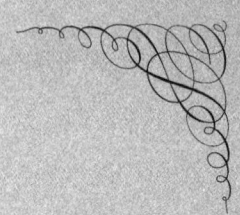

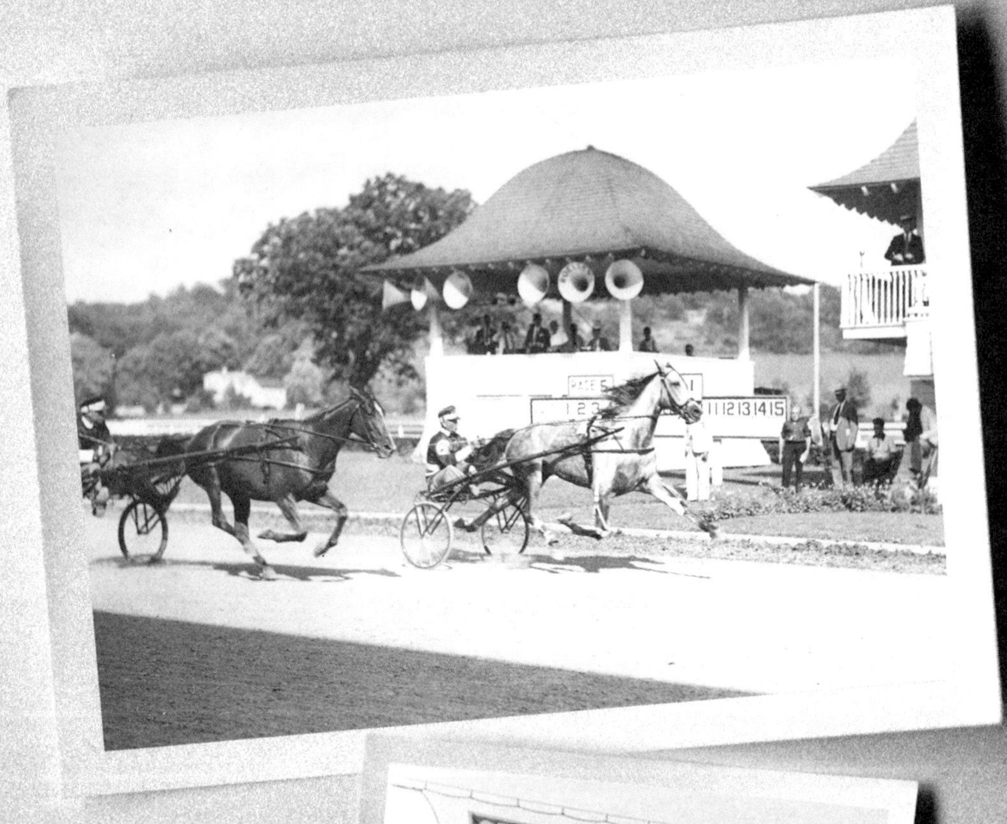
RACE 5
1 2 3
11 12 13 14 15

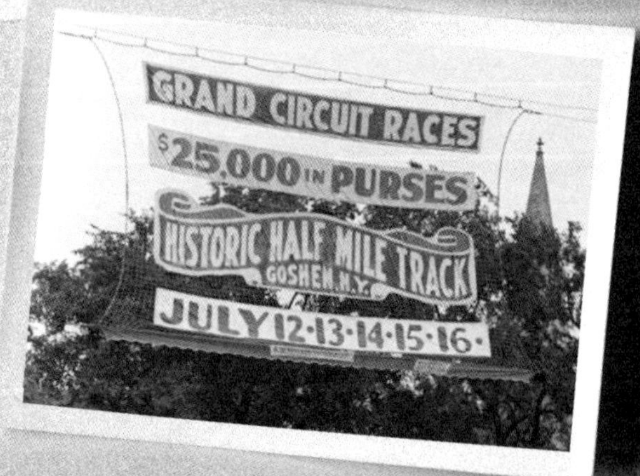
GRAND CIRCUIT RACES
$25,000 IN PURSES
HISTORIC HALF MILE TRACK
GOSHEN, N.Y.
JULY 12·13·14·15·16·

*"But the old saying,
'It is the impossible that happens,'
has once again been made good.
Greyhound has done it!"*

—

JOHN HERVEY,
THE HARNESS HORSE, JULY 21, 1937

HISTORIC REMATCH AT GOSHEN

Five-year-old Greyhound had filled out beautifully over the winter. His steel-gray coat now a matrix of dapples over a snow-white background. His head and neck had turned almost completely white, though his mane remained a striking dark gray in contrast. His legs looked like blue steel with flecks of white hairs mixed among the darker ones. When he trotted, his silver-tipped tail unfurled magnificently behind him.

The "ugly duckling" had lost his gangly, awkward appearance and was now a glorious specimen. His physical features, which had previously been looked upon as deficits for a trotter, were now considered and studied by questioning minds, wondering how these attributes contributed to Greyhound's immense speed. Where once he was considered too tall and too straight-legged behind, his body too short, and his build too uphill, now people wondered if perhaps the perfect harness horse was a new form altogether from what had been considered the ideal for the past century.

During early negotiations, the Muscletone contingent asked for a mile and a half race, to which Palin and Baker readily agreed. In Europe, harness horses raced a variety of distances, but in America, one-mile heats were the standard of the time. This, along with an agreement Palin made with Ben White, and the goal of breaking Peter Manning's record, would shape the way Palin trained and prepared Greyhound for the upcoming season. With few suitable races available for Greyhound, Palin instead turned his focus to preparing the horse for the match race, and for setting more records against time.

Ben White, trainer and driver of Rosalind, the top trotting mare, made a deal with Palin that they would not race their horses for a purse of less than $1,500.[1] Harness racing venues stood to make a lot of money if the two top trotters in the country were to meet in head-to-head competition. Frustrated at the lack of opportunity to race an older horse, and that purses for older horses were not even enough to cover expenses, White and Palin tried to force the trotting association to give them something worth racing for. Apparently, the association tried to call their bluff. Except neither White nor Palin were bluffing. As a result, Greyhound would go to the post for a regular race just once that season.

Greyhound's first effort as a five-year-old would be against his old nemesis, Historic Track in Goshen. The year before, the half-mile oval had handed the champion his only defeat since his first races as an awkward two-year-old. He'd set the world record for a half-mile track the year before, going in 2:02 flat over the fairgrounds track at Allentown, Pennsylvania. The tight turns of the smaller half-mile oval were not ideal for Greyhound's unusually long stride; he couldn't reach top speed before Palin had to rate him back into the turns. In fact, few believed any harness horse could negotiate two circuits of a half-mile track in less than two minutes. Back in 1903, when Lou Dillon made her mile over a one-mile track in 1:58 ½, the record over a half-mile oval stood at 2:09 ¼.[2] But, for this effort, Palin had a new plan.

It rained heavily in Goshen the morning of July 16. Greyhound, Palin, and everyone else waited for the skies to clear and the men to work the track into a dry, fast oval. But by mid-afternoon, the track remained wet and soft along the inside rail.[3] Despite this, hours after his planned start, Palin steered Greyhound onto the track for his warm-up miles. A width of track at least three feet from the inner rail was not in usable condition; this would force Greyhound to travel a so-called "long mile," since the oval size was measured from the innermost track. But this made little difference to Palin's plan.

The people in the stands rumbled with applause as Greyhound stepped onto the track. The flashy gray pulled a new, Faber-brand, twenty-six-pound sulky with pin stripes and "Greyhound" painted on the shaft.[4] The chatter from the crowd rose to a pitch of barely contained anticipation as the champion trotted clockwise around the track, taking his warm-up laps. As is traditional with both harness racers and runners, horses were only asked for racing speed when going the "right" way of the track, or counterclockwise. When he was ready, Palin turned Greyhound and scored him down a few times. The excitement built, the crowd hummed, and the big gray seemed to inflate with coiled power waiting for release. Palin scored Greyhound down once more and, as he passed the judges' stand, gave a nod. The time trial had begun.

Palin had Greyhound keyed up for the start, and the big gelding got away quickly. He entered the first turn a sulky-width or two off the rail.[5] Coming out of the turn at the top of the stretch, Palin swung the gelding wide toward the outside of the track.[6] Greyhound pounded down the back stretch, having lost little speed due to Palin's wide turn. He would cover more ground, but Palin hoped it'd be a good tradeoff, enabling long-legged Greyhound to maintain a faster clip.

"[H]e was trotting with machine-like precision," *The Harness Horse* reported, "and his long, space-devouring strides, seemingly devoid of effort, caused many to think he was not going fast until the Timers announced :29 ½ for the first quarter."[7]

Greyhound flew into the second turn and Palin angled him back toward the inside rail. The move allowed him to save ground on the turn without losing much speed. Palin took up the lines, and Greyhound bowed his neck with his chin tucked.[8] He shook his head in frustration, resenting Palin's rating him on the turn. When he straightened into the stretch, Palin let him out a notch and Greyhound picked up speed, lengthening his glorious stride. He completed the first half in 1:00 flat and the crowd leapt to their feet, cheering and shouting as Greyhound flew by.[9]

"He's got it! He's gonna take down Uhlan's record!" one man shouted.

"C'mon, you gray ghost! Go, go, GO!" another chimed in.

"Send him on, Palin! Let's see him step!" a third fan screamed over the rising din.

Palin sent Greyhound wide at the top of the stretch just as he'd done in the first half-mile, then angled down, rating the gelding back enough to stay tight coming out of the final turn.

"C'mon! Yeah! C'mon!" Palin shouted once Greyhound straightened out of the turn. The gelding burst forward with renewed speed; Palin shook the lines, but never went for the whip. There was no need.

"Yeah! C'mon!" Palin yelled.

Greyhound pounded toward the finish line. The fans cheered him on, their voices rising above the ring of shod hooves over clay track. Greyhound blazed under the wire and the crowd waited, scarcely able to breathe, while the three judges compared their stopwatches. The time went up, metal plates with painted numbers clinked into place on the judges' stand, and the crowd erupted in cheers. Greyhound had done what they said could not be done; he'd made two loops of the half-mile oval in 1:59 ¾. A new track record for Historic, and a new world record for going one mile on a half-mile track by any harness horse at either gait![10, 11]

"The attainment of a mile in two minutes or better by a trotter over a half-mile track," John Hervey wrote days later, "was for generations the dream of the idealist and the goal toward which all breeders and trainers who either believed in or hoped for the realization of that dream, continuously strove for."[12]

Greyhound had smashed the track record set by Uhlan in 1911 by three full seconds, and crushed his own half-mile track record by two and one-quarter seconds.[13]

Roy Miller, the official starter at Historic, said, "I think that's the greatest mile I have ever seen … that big bold stride carrying him on with matchless power." Miller's words seemed to be the consensus among all who had witnessed Greyhound's record that day, the handicap of negotiating a half-mile oval being doubled for a big, long-legged, long-striding horse like Greyhound. One could only guess how far the gray ghost had actually traveled to make that mile record, spending much of the time in the middle of the track or angling toward the outside rail.

Palin steered Greyhound back to the grandstand, and the crowd cheered louder. Trotting past the throng, Greyhound lifted his head and turned it slightly, as if acknowledging the crowd.[14]

"He is the greatest trotter in the history of the game," Palin told reporter William J. Madden. "He took the slack every time I gave it to him. I don't know how fast he can run. I knew he had a new mark so I didn't let him out all the way."[15]

Jimmie waited by the gap, a broad smile on his handsome face. He took hold of Greyhound as Palin exited the sulky. Jimmie spoke softly to the champion and stroked his neck. He then led Greyhound back to the barn, the gray playfully lipping the hand holding the lines. A young Dalmatian followed close behind. How the dog came to be Greyhound's traveling companion is information lost to time. Whether he was purchased or adopted, the Dalmatian was christened Goshen, and became Greyhound's unofficial mascot.*

"Good job, Hound," Jimmie said as he walked the gray, "you showed 'em." A large stone marker stood by the main gate at Historic with Uhlan's name and record engraved on one side. Greyhound's name and record would soon be engraved on the other side, a permanent tribute that would greet fans for generations to come. Nearly three decades would pass before another name would be added.[16]

---

* There is some question regarding the dog's name.
  A couple news articles mention a Dalmatian named Goshen.
  Other sources refer to a Dalmatian named "Fibber"
  belonging to Baker. Jimmie's son, Neil, has pictures
  in his dad's scrapbook of multiple Dalmatians.
  Baker also had multiple Dalmatians.

GREYHOUND

THE REMARKABLE STORY OF THE LEGENDARY RACEHORSE WHO INSPIRED A NATION

CIRCA 1937, COURTESY OF THE UNITED STATES TROTTING ASSOCIATION

CHAPTER
— 16 —

Muscletone to Come to America to Race Greyhound

Sep Palin, trainer for E. J. Baker of St. Charles, Illinois, received the following cablegram on Monday, July 5th, from the owner of Muscletone:

S. F. PALIN,
INDIANAPOLIS, IND.   LUZERNE, SWITZERLAND.
WILL BE THERE AUGUST FIRST MUSCLETONE SEPTEMBER FIFTEENTH AND BE READY TO RACE THE LATTER PART OF SEPTEMBER OR THE FIRST HALF OF OCTOBER.
                                                                GIOVANNI MAIANI.

Thus it looks as though the match race between the star of Europe and the star of America may become a reality.

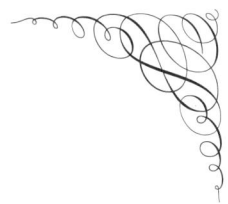

"Greyhound could probably lug a plow behind him and still beat any trotter of this century."

—

WILLIAM J. MADDEN, 1937

THE RACE THAT NEVER WAS

When it came to news about the upcoming match race between Muscletone and Greyhound, half-truths masquerading as facts ran rampant through the newspapers and magazines of the day. Such was not uncommon—a little embellishment could go a long way in stoking the fires of American pride and resilience in the depths of economic depression, severe drought, extreme heat, and a looming war. Excitement rippled through the harness racing community—a match race between the American and European champions had the potential to boost interest in the sport to a level not seen since the dawn of the automobile age. Headlines about the upcoming match were injected with ever-increasing drama with an "America vs. Communism" energy flowing through some of the stories.

In June 1937, sports writer Joe Williams broke the story that Muscletone did not belong to Maiani but was in fact the property of fascist* authoritarian dictator of Italy Benito Mussolini.[1] Williams "wrote

---

* While some Muscletone vs. Greyhound articles of the day implied Mussolini was a communist, he was in fact the founder of Italy's National Fascist Party.

a provocative and assertive sports column," reported the *New York Times* upon his death in 1972.[2] Williams was the first to break the story about Babe Ruth's famous "called shot" during the 1932 World Series.[3] He wrote that "with two outs, Ruth pointed a finger at the center field fence and then hit a home run over that same spot." Ruth originally denied the story but eventually came to accept the legend. Williams himself "later conceded that Ruth was probably holding up the finger as an indication that he had one strike left."[4]

Unnamed "higher authorities" from Italy "whisper smugly that good old Givo is merely the [front man]" and it was Mussolini that paid Muscletone's feed bill, wrote Williams.[5] A few papers picked up and reprinted the unverified rumor and, while it never got as much traction as Babe Ruth's "called shot," its persistence perhaps indicates its effectiveness at cashing in on America's increasing fear of the Hitler-Mussolini alliance. One headline read:

"Mussolini might just as well recall his crack trotter Muscletone; Greyhound unequalled."[6]

What better way to garner excitement and intense feelings of patriotism than to pit the best America had to offer against the threat of communism and fascism from across the sea?

The reports of where and when the match race would occur were confusing, and in some instances spun to sound as if the Muscletone contingent had lost their bravado.

Horseman and Fair World printed a short piece in their July 7, 1937 issue noting that the proposed match race had "advanced a step last week when [Baker] mailed a $1,000 check to the Trotting Club of America to pay [Muscletone's travel] expenses."[7] *The Harness Horse* reprinted the following telegram in their July 7, 1937 issue:

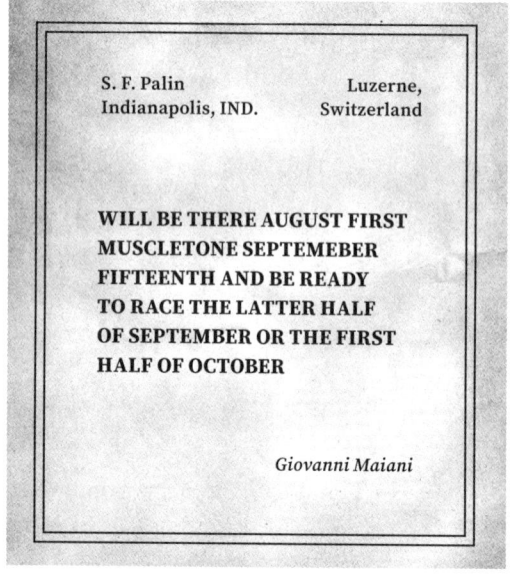

S. F. Palin
Indianapolis, IND.

Luzerne,
Switzerland

WILL BE THERE AUGUST FIRST MUSCLETONE SEPTEMEBER FIFTEENTH AND BE READY TO RACE THE LATTER HALF OF SEPTEMBER OR THE FIRST HALF OF OCTOBER

Giovanni Maiani

Outside of *The Harness Horse*, there was no mention of the telegram. Judging by his writings at the time, even the diligent researcher and turf historian John Hervey did not appear to know about it. It seems likely that some information from the telegram was picked up and then misrepresented in subsequent reports. Early in July, bold headlines spread across the sports pages proclaiming the match race date had been set, and Muscletone would soon depart for the United States. At the end of July, a few papers even reported that Muscletone had boarded a ship[8] and would arrive in America August 1 for a match race at Good Time Park on August 10.[9]

Multiple papers latched onto this misinformation, and excitement grew as August 10 approached. Whether it was overzealous news reporting, intentionally misleading information, or just a slew of reporters falling into the trap of repeating hearsay rather than sussing out the truth is information lost to time. Regardless, when the boat from Italy arrived at the end of July, Muscletone wasn't on it, and some felt that was a sign that Maiani (or Mussolini, depending on which story you followed) was not confident his horse could beat Greyhound. Based on the telegram received by Palin on July 5, it is highly unlikely Maiani ever intended to bring Muscletone to America at the end of that month for an August 10 match race. To do so would have been disastrous for the European champion, who would have had very little time to recover from the voyage and acclimate to his new surroundings before the big race.

Giovanni Maiani and Alessandro Finn did arrive on said ship, reaching port on August 1. They met with Baker and Palin to iron out details and finalize the plans for a match race between the two champions. Nothing much resulted from the meeting aside from Maiani stating that due to his other scheduled engagements, Muscletone would not be available to race until after September 5.

The August 10 match race was quickly rebranded as a race against time, and dozens of papers across the country and in Canada announced on August 9 that Greyhound would go against the clock and attempt to lower Peter Manning's 1922 world record mile. This was also likely a sensationalized headline, as a triangular track like the one at Good Time Park was less than ideal for setting such a world record. After negotiations, the Italians stayed stateside to experience American harness racing. Baker and Palin extended an invitation to Maiani and Finn to join them at Goshen, reportedly to watch Greyhound race against time.[10] What actually happened is open to some interpretation.

The track at Good Time wasn't built for speed. The wicked first turn at the top of the unusual triangle shape required significant rating, especially for a long-striding horse like Greyhound. Not the best choice of location to take down a world record like that of Peter Manning. One might wonder just what Baker and Palin were thinking.

Near 90-degree temperatures and partly cloudy skies greeted fans arriving at Good Time Park on August 10. Alternating American and Italian flags hung from the grandstand,[11] merry and colorful, snapping in the stiff wind. Over 15,000 people, a record crowd for a non-Hambletonian day, flooded the stands at Good Time to see Greyhound—nearly twice as large as the record-setting crowd that had seen Greyhound win the Progressive Trot the year before over the same track.[12] More than a few likely arrived expecting to see a match race between Muscletone and Greyhound; the rebranding of the race as one against time had not been reported until the day before, when some people would have already been en route. Instead, they were told, Greyhound would be going after Peter Manning's 1:56 ¾ mark—a move that horsemen in the know saw as illogical on such a track.

"Do you think Greyhound will lower Peter Manning's record at Goshen?" sportswriter Al Clark asked veteran reinsman Tommy Murphy, who'd driven Peter Manning to his 1922 record.

"Greyhound is no match for him," Murphy replied gruffly, his tone telling Al Clark the interview was over. Clark made note of the response, then sought out Lawrence Sheppard, owner of Hanover Shoe Farm, where champion Peter Manning was living out his retirement years.

"Will Greyhound better Peter Manning's record?"

Mr. Sheppard shook his head. "Not today, son."

Hoping to find an unbiased opinion, Clark put the question to Bowman A. Brown, noted harness horse follower and publisher of *The Harness Horse* magazine.

"Will Peter Manning lose his record to Greyhound?" Clark held his pencil poised above his note pad, his eyes focused on Brown.

"Perhaps," Brown answered. "But not today, not at Goshen."

Clark quickly scribbled down the words on his notepad, then looked back up at Brown before speaking. "But where and when will Greyhound come into the record the harness horse world has been forecasting for him?" Clark looked expectantly at the older gentleman, as if Brown were about to reveal the location of a previously unobtainable treasure.

Mr. Brown smiled. "Not at Goshen," he repeated. "That track wasn't made for record breaking. It's triangular and has three turns. That first turn is bad, very bad, for any speed." Brown smiled again and turned away, leaving the sportswriter swiftly jotting down notes.[13, 14]

The afternoon sun bore down on Good Time Park. Early-arriving fans took shelter under the grandstand roof and under the green-and-white striped canopy erected over the seats near the outer rail. Excess space was standing room only, and people lined up three and four deep in the grass along the outer rail of the first turn. Palin scored Greyhound down a few times, shaking the lines and shouting, trying to stir up the gelding and get him to a faster start. An unusually strong wind blew hot, heavy air over the sunbaked track.[15]

Palin scored down once more with Greyhound pressing at the bit, ready for the word. The reinsman nodded to the judge, touched the lines, and Greyhound sprang forward with a burst of silver speed. His glorious stride lengthened as he approached the line, the starting judge gave the word, and the great gray ghost was off. Entering the first turn, Palin leaned back against the reins, rating the gelding so he could negotiate the tight turn without breaking stride. Greyhound shook his head, resentful of the reins holding him back and forcing him to shorten his step. The clocker posted the time; Greyhound had trotted the first quarter in :31.[16]

"Too slow! Too slow!" a few in the crowd shouted.

"Nah! He closes fast at the end! Just wait!"

"Yeah! Palin will send him on when they're out of that turn!"

Loosened from Palin's hold, Greyhound lengthened his great stride down the back stretch. Turns two and three were not as sharp, but Greyhound still lost speed, making the half in 1:01 ¼. A collective groan whispered through the crowd when the clocker hung the time. The gray straightened into the final stretch and surged forward, pressing against the bit. His powerful stride reached a new level, finding another dimension of speed with each impossible stroke. Electrified, the crowd leapt to their feet, shouting and stomping as Greyhound came charging toward the wire. His body seemed to lift as he flew down the stretch, his feet barely touching the ground. He became a trotting marvel, a floating gray specter, the likes of which no one had seen before.

Greyhound flashed across the finish, a whir of flying legs and spinning wheels. It was difficult to tell for sure, but those closest to the track at the finish felt almost certain Palin had slowed Greyhound in the final eighth, reining the big gray freight train in at the end.[17] All waited in silence for the judges to consult their watches. The wind danced tiny dust whirlwinds across the track. The clocker hung the numbered tiles: 1:58 ¼. A shared sigh of disappointment wandered through the grandstand. Greyhound had failed by a wide margin to lower Peter Manning's record.[18, 19]

The loud speaker crackled and a voice announced that Greyhound had set a new track record,[20] and gone the last half in an astonishing fifty-seven seconds![21] Their disappointment short-lived, the crowd erupted as their hero jogged back to the grandstand. It was the first time any horse had negotiated the triangular mile at Good Time Park in less than two minutes.[22]

The naysayers had been right: not today, indeed. But with a fifty-seven-second last half in less-than-ideal conditions, Peter Manning's record was most certainly in reach. Greyhound had trotted the fastest mile ever seen at Good Time Park. His record would stand for all time, having never been topped when Good Time ceased racing in the late 1950s and closed forever in the early 1970s.

"Due to an unusually heavy wind, coupled with the fact the gelding had not been given any real fast work in practically a month, Palin made no attempt at a record-breaking performance,"[23] reported *The Harness Horse*. The magazine was not alone in their assessment; some papers would also report that Palin had never intended to go for Peter Manning's record. Given that harness racing requires a measure of gamesmanship in addition to speed and stamina, it seems likely the statement was true. Palin, a savvy reinsman, would certainly never tip his hand and let the Italians know just how much horse he had, especially with Muscletone still in Italy. It's not such a stretch to imagine Palin was putting on a show for Maiani and Finn.

By "failing" to break Peter Manning's record in front of Muscletone's owner and trainer, one might suspect that perhaps Maiani and Finn saw exactly what they were supposed to see that day. After all, Baker and Palin believed Greyhound would easily out-trot the European champion. Why not make some money on the side? The Italians appeared quite ready to part with it. The $10,000 side bet plus the winner's share of an equally substantial purse were nothing to sneeze at. But Muscletone's people wouldn't ship him to America unless they thought their horse had a real chance against Greyhound.

Greyhound's fast-closing half had certainly been noted by the Italians. Muscletone's best mile time had been 2:02, set at age three while still stateside. However, one couldn't compare Muscletone's three-year-old form in the U.S. with the current record of the now mature horse. In Europe, most of Muscletone's races were one and a half to three miles. Tracks in Europe were softer and slower than in the U.S., not to mention some of Muscletone's races had been under a European handicapping system. In such a system, the start was staggered—each horse given a specific distance advantage or disadvantage based on their previous race record. Similar to how Thoroughbreds are handicapped by the weight they carry, it's designed to "level the field," bringing the horses to the wire together. Taking those conditions into account, Muscletone's mile time was estimated to be around 1:58 or 1:59.[24] So Greyhound's mile at Good Time in 1:58 ¼ was just about exactly where Palin would want it to be if he was trying to lure the European champion to America.

Maiani was interviewed briefly following the mile at Good Time Park. "It was a great mile, and Greyhound a wonderful trotter, but Muscletone is a worthy opponent," Maiani said through his interpreter.[25] A different source quoted Maiani saying, "I wouldn't be surprised to see your horse win here, but Muscletone should square matters at home, where the tracks are not so hard."[26]

From Goshen, the Baker-Palin stable traveled to the state fair at Springfield, Illinois for the FFA trot, Greyhound's only race of 1937. There he met just four horses, including old rivals Angel Child and Silver King. The Italians also went to Springfield, where a meeting was set with Baker, Palin, and E. E. Irwin, manager of the Springfield fairgrounds and the Illinois State Fair, to discuss holding the big match race there in the fall.

On August 20, Greyhound won the FFA trot easily in straight heats, trotting the first in 2:01 and the second in 1:59 ¼, again making a sub-two-minute mile look like an easy Sunday stroll. Angel Child held the lead until the quarter pole in both heats,[27] at which point Palin casually tipped out from the rail and "came around her like a streak of gray lightning," reporter R. A. Drysdale wrote the next day. Silver King, having never regained the form of his precocious two-year-old season, came last. That same afternoon, Palin also won with Cardinal Prince.

A few days later, Maiani, Finn, Irwin, Baker, and Palin met to discuss the details of the match race. Obviously, with Muscletone still in Europe, a once-discussed September date was out of the question. Besides, Maiani was now saying Muscletone was scheduled to race in Berlin, Germany, on August 29.[28]

"Americans could not comprehend the way the horse was being managed," John Hervey later wrote in *The Harness Horse*. It simply didn't make sense. Maiani's expenses and the horse's expenses were covered. It would cost the Italian sportsman nothing to bring Muscletone to the States. Why, then, did Maiani keep entering Muscletone in races worth much less than the money he could make in America? Even if he lost, Hervey pointed out he would still make more in the match race with Greyhound than he could in Europe.[29] Still, Maiani insisted Muscletone race in Berlin prior to traveling to the States.

The big match race was set tentatively for October. Maiani and Baker agreed on everything but the location. Springfield and Indianapolis were being considered, but both owners agreed they would determine the location later. The first step was to get Muscletone on the right continent. After the race in Berlin, Maiani agreed he would ship Muscletone to the U.S. Then, after the race in the U.S., the two would travel to Europe for a second contest. The minimum $10,000 side bet between Baker and Maiani was eclipsed by the astounding $40,000 purse offered by Irwin if the race were to be contested at Springfield. This offer secured the location. Greyhound and Muscletone would meet in Springfield, Illinois on October 8.[30]

From Springfield, Greyhound returned to his home track in Indianapolis at the state fairgrounds. The state racing board offered a prize of $5,000 if Greyhound could break the track record of 2:00 ¼ set by Angel Child two years before.[31] When the story broke that Greyhound would go for a mile track record, the papers picked it up and fanned the flames of excitement. All year, reporters, horsemen, and fans had been talking about 1937 being the year that Greyhound would dethrone Peter Manning as the fastest trotter of all time. For 14 years, the record had stood with no trotter coming closer than two seconds—except Greyhound.[32]

"Some of the well-informed horsemen expressed the opinion that the limit of trotting speed had been reached in the performance of Peter Manning," *Hoof Beats* reported in January 1937. "Then along came Greyhound and some opinions were hastily revised."[33]

True, Greyhound had smashed multiple records, but to shave over half a second off his 1:57 ¼ record, which was already in the uppermost echelons of speed, was a significant margin to overcome. Still, the *Hoof Beats* article pointed out, Greyhound's top time the previous season at the age of four was over five seconds faster than Peter Manning's best time at that age.[34] By the evening before the September 10 race against time, the *track*-record-breaking attempt had been rebilled in the papers as an attempt to break Peter Manning's record—something it was never intended to be.

Heavy rains and high winds canceled all racing at Indianapolis on the 10th, and the time trial was rescheduled for the 14th. That evening, Maiani announced that Muscletone was ill and the match race would have to be postponed until the next year.[35] Due to the timing, many speculated the postponement had more to do with Greyhound's recent mile-and-a-half workout. There had been no official time for that mile and a half—likely intentional on Palin's part, trying to slip in a workout without getting too much attention from the press or Muscletone's people. One can be certain that Palin carried a watch in the palm of his hand and knew exactly how fast Greyhound had gone. But, according to turf writer P. W. Moser, a reputable horseman stood along the rail that quiet afternoon and recognized that Greyhound was going for speed. He clicked his own watch after the gray had already trotted more than a half mile. With a burst of speed at the end, which Palin unsuccessfully attempted to rein in, the horseman caught Greyhound's final eighth in a blistering :12 ¼—a time that could match a decent Thoroughbred runner over the same distance.[36]

"The foreign news for months past has been full of reports of the close rapprochement between Italy and Germany and the coming visit to Germany of Premier Mussolini—for the purpose of forming an offensive and defensive alliance with that country through its dictator, Der Fuehrer, Adolf Hitler," John Hervey wrote in a lengthy October 6 *Harness Horse* article. Hervey suggested Maiani's waffling on commitment to a date or booking passage for Muscletone might have been more about politics than sport.[37]

Every effort had been made by the Italians to "impress the German public with the might and power" of Italy. Hervey postulated that the Italian government felt part of this display of strength should be in sport, by sending Muscletone to Berlin to show his dominance over the best horses the country could muster. Unfortunately, Muscletone went lame in Berlin and lost the race to the German trotter Probst.[38]

Regardless of the reasoning behind the "race that never was," the Italian contingent left America and went home. Talk of the match race disappeared soon after. Never to be brought up again.

GREYHOUND

THE REMARKABLE STORY OF THE LEGENDARY RACEHORSE WHO INSPIRED A NATION

Like Other Champs, Greyhound Is Stickler For Regular Habits

By GENE MACK

OLD ORCHARD BEACH, Me, July 29—Like so many other champions in different lines of sport, much of the success of the great trotter, Greyhound, is due to his "regular" habits. That is the belief of his faithful young caretaker, the pleasant Jimmy Wingfield of Rome, Ga.

The day for the trotting king starts at 5 a.m. when Jimmy serves breakfast and cleans out the stall. Then if it's work-out day things are pretty busy much of the forenoon, as a harness horse thrives

JULY 29, 1937, THE BOSTON GLOBE

CHAPTER
— 17 —

Peter Manning 1:56¾, held by I. W. Gleason, Williamsport, Pa.

> "Peter Manning rules as the greatest trotter
> of this or any other era."
>
> —
>
> AL CLARK,
> "THE SPORTS SHOP" (COLUMN), AUGUST 10, 1937

> "We have every right to believe that when he is fully matured,
> Greyhound will far surpass everything he has done thus far,
> as well as everything that Peter Manning did."
>
> —
>
> JOHN HERVEY,
> THE HARNESS HORSE, DECEMBER 1936

PETER MANNING'S CROWN

High winds prevailed at the Indianapolis state fairgrounds on September 14, 1937. Track conditions had improved over those on the 10th, but still were not ideal for an attempt to lower Peter Manning's record. Trotting into a head wind would surely add fractions to Greyhound's time. If he were to claim the world record, conditions had to be perfect.

The wind snapped the flags on the track infield. Palin considered his options. He wouldn't waste Greyhound's efforts for the fastest trotting mile when he didn't have every opportunity to succeed. It wasn't worth the risk of dousing Greyhound's indomitable spirit, not even for a $5,000 win-or-lose bonus. The record for a mile and a half, on the other hand—set by Rosalind the week before at Syracuse—was not so daunting, at 3:12 ½. Palin had been training Greyhound over that distance in preparation for the match against Muscletone. Although the mile-and-a-half workout from earlier in the month hadn't been publicly timed, one can be certain Palin knew exactly how fast Greyhound had gone that day, and therefore just what the horse was capable of on this day.

Palin started Greyhound on the back stretch, facing into the wind, for his mile-and-a-half world-record race against time.[1] He scored down a couple times, then gave the starting judge a nod. At the word, the gelding launched into his authoritative trot, lengthening his stride with each piston-like stroke of his powerful hind legs. Greyhound covered the half easily in 1:02.[2] Taking the lines lightly, Palin rated the big gray through the first turn. Then, like a hair-trigger releasing a tightly coiled spring, Palin loosened his hold, and Greyhound burst out of the turn. There, two prompters joined him, one to the side and one to the rear, per trotting association rules.[3] Taking the challenge from the galloping prompters, Greyhound lengthened his stride, each step devouring the track before him. He flew down the backstretch, this time having the benefit of momentum and speed as he again trotted into the wind. Coming around the final turn, the gray ghost pounded down the home stretch. His body seemed to take flight; like a magnificent silver streak, he skimmed along the track surface. The crowd erupted, stomping their feet and shouting.

"Go, Ghost, go!"

"Bring him home, Palin!"

"Yeah! C'mon, Greyhound!"

The gray ghost flashed under the wire, and the people stood in stunned silence. He'd gone the last quarter of his mile-and-a-half effort in an incredible twenty-nine seconds![4] Palin jogged the gallant gray gelding back toward the grandstand. The final time was hung, and the crowd's roar reached a new stratum of excitement.[5]

"The big grey gelding clipped 9 ¾ seconds from the old record set the week before by Rosalind," reported Eau Claire, Wisconsin's *Leader-Telegram*.[6] The final time, 3:02 ½.

The crowds followed Jimmie and Greyhound back to his stall. Mary E. Bostwick of *The Indianapolis Star* stood among the throng.

"Greyhound just stood in his roomy stall and sort of rested his chin on the window sill," she later wrote. "[He] gazed benevolently out at a large group of admirers who stood there just staring at him and not saying anything." Numerous other horses stuck a head over their stall door and watched the people watching Greyhound. No one paid any mind to them. Not even Baker's champion Cardinal Prince, thought by many to be the most handsome pacer in racing, drew the eye of a single admirer.[7]

On the track and in the barn, Greyhound seemed to know the people were there just for him. His personality and presence connected him to them in a way that was difficult to explain. *He's more human than horse—*variations of this statement were frequently heard from those who had seen Greyhound in person. Describing the moments after his world record-breaking mile-and-a-half effort, Bostwick wrote, "As he passed the grandstand [he gave] a sort of equine grin that might well have asked 'How'm I doin'?'"[8]

Palin rescheduled Greyhound's challenge on Peter Manning's record at Indianapolis. But on the intended day, high winds again prevented the attempt.[9] With just one stop left on the 1937 Grand Circuit, Greyhound was running out of time to reach the goal that had eluded thousands of trotters over the past fifteen

GREYHOUND

THE REMARKABLE STORY
OF THE LEGENDARY RACEHORSE WHO INSPIRED A NATION

gallery

[36]
Greyhound warming up prior to setting the track record at Good Time Park in Goshen, NY.
• *August 10, 1937, Tim Bojarski Collection*

[37]
Always curious, Greyhound lips the sponge from a harness cleaning product.
• *March 22, 1937, Tim Bojarski Collection*

GREYHOUND

THE REMARKABLE STORY
OF THE LEGENDARY RACEHORSE WHO INSPIRED A NATION

gallery

[38]
Greyhound, apparently displeased with the smell of said sponge.
• *March 22, 1937, Tim Bojarski Collection*

[39]
Greyhound 1:56 stands above them all.
• *December 8, 1937, Tim Bojarski Collection*

[40]
Col. Baker, Muscletone's owner, Giovani Maiani, and Palin shake hands.
• *August 1937, courtesy of the United States Trotting Association*

GREYHOUND

THE REMARKABLE STORY
OF THE LEGENDARY RACEHORSE WHO INSPIRED A NATION

gallery

[41]
Greyhound takes the first heat of the FFA Trot in Springfield, Illinois.
• *August 20, 1937, courtesy of the United States Trotting Association; original photograph by P.W. Moser*

[42]
Palin rates Greyhound back as he navigates the Historic Half Mile in Goshen, setting the world record of 1:59 ½.
• *July 16, 1937, courtesy of the United States Trotting Association; original photograph by Walter Moore*

[43]
Greyhound coming out of the final turn during his world-record effort at the Historic Half Mile in Goshen, NY.
• *July 16, 1937, courtesy of the United States Trotting Association*

GREYHOUND

THE REMARKABLE STORY
OF THE LEGENDARY RACEHORSE WHO INSPIRED A NATION

gallery

[44]
Jimmie and Greyhound framed by a sulky at Seminole Park, Greyhound's winter training quarters in Longwood, Florida.
• *March 16, 1937, courtesy of the Harness Racing Museum & Hall of Fame, Goshen, NY*

GREYHOUND

THE REMARKABLE STORY
OF THE LEGENDARY RACEHORSE WHO INSPIRED A NATION

gallery

[45]
Greyhound pulling a 90-pound vintage high-wheel sulky at the Historic Half Mile. Palin had considered going for a world record but opted to only do an exhibition.
• *August 1938, courtesy of the Hambletonian Society*

[46]
Jimmie standing with Greyhound.
• *circa 1936, courtesy of the Harness Racing Museum & Hall of Fame, Goshen, NY*

GREYHOUND

THE REMARKABLE STORY
OF THE LEGENDARY RACEHORSE WHO INSPIRED A NATION

gallery

[47]
Greyhound at Seminole Park, Longwood, Florida during the off season.
• *early 1938, courtesy of the Harness Racing Museum & Hall of Fame, Goshen, NY; original photograph by Harold G. Strong*

[48]
Jimmie leads Greyhound near the track at Historic Half Mile, Goshen, NY.
• *July 1938; Peter Stackpole/The LIFE Picture Collection/Shutterstock*

GREYHOUND

THE REMARKABLE STORY
OF THE LEGENDARY RACEHORSE WHO INSPIRED A NATION

gallery

[49]
Jimmie Wingfield—groom, valet, and public relations director for the world's fastest trotter—at the Historic Half Mile, Goshen, NY.
• *July 1938; Peter Stackpole/The LIFE Picture Collection/ Shutterstock*

[50]
Jimmie (left) and another man hooking Greyhound up to the jog cart. Note the kicking strap (not yet secured to the cart shafts) over his rump.
• *July 1938; Peter Stackpole/The LIFE Picture Collection/ Shutterstock*

GREYHOUND

THE REMARKABLE STORY
OF THE LEGENDARY RACEHORSE WHO INSPIRED A NATION

gallery

[51]
Col. Baker peeks into Greyhound's stall at the Historic Half Mile track, Goshen, NY.
• *July 1938; Peter Stackpole/The LIFE Picture Collection/ Shutterstock*

[52]
Jimmie cooling out Greyhound at the Historic Half Mile, Goshen, NY.
• *July 1938; Hansel Mieth/The LIFE Picture Collection/ Shutterstock*

GREYHOUND
THE REMARKABLE STORY
OF THE LEGENDARY RACEHORSE WHO INSPIRED A NATION
— *gallery* —

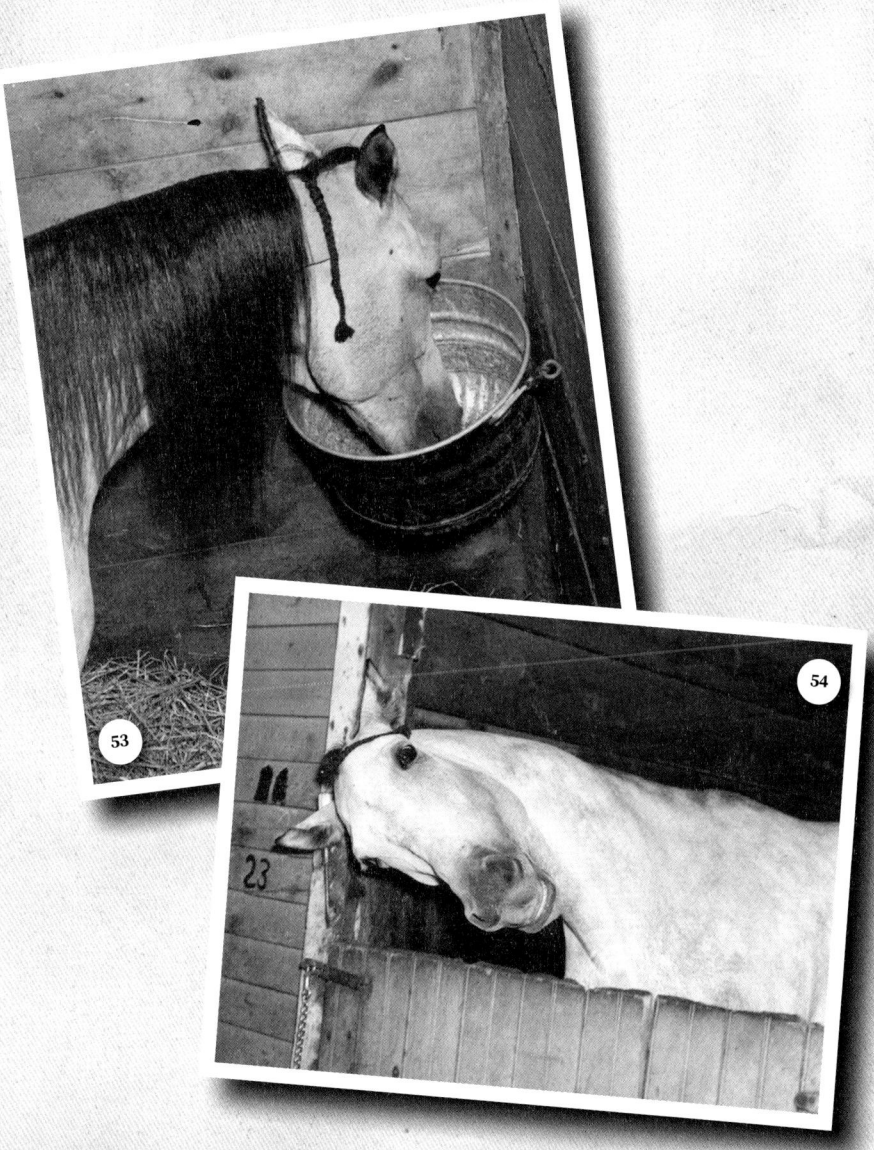

[53]
Greyhound takes a meal at the Historic Half Mile.
• *July 7, 1938; Tim Bojarski Collection*

[54]
Scratching an itch.
• *July 1938; Tim Bojarski Collection*

GREYHOUND

THE REMARKABLE STORY
OF THE LEGENDARY RACEHORSE WHO INSPIRED A NATION

gallery

[55]
Greyhound finishes a 2:01-3/4 mile with a sensational :26 ¾ quarter at North Randall.
• *July 4, 1938, courtesy of the United States Trotting Association*

[56]
Greyhound going to the post at the KTHBA track in Lexington, KY.
• *September 1937, courtesy of the United States Trotting Association*

GREYHOUND

THE REMARKABLE STORY
OF THE LEGENDARY RACEHORSE WHO INSPIRED A NATION

gallery

[57]
Greyhound warming up at Agawam.
• *July/August 1938, courtesy of the Wingfield family*

[58]
Pencil art following Greyhound's record-setting :26 ¾ quarter.
• *July 1938; Dondarski Collection, courtesy of the Hambletonian Society*

GREYHOUND

THE REMARKABLE STORY
OF THE LEGENDARY RACEHORSE WHO INSPIRED A NATION

gallery

[59]
Jimmie and Greyhound.
- *circa 1936, courtesy of the Harness Racing Museum & Hall of Fame, Goshen, NY*

[60]
Jimmie leads Greyhound off a van.
- *circa 1937, courtesy of the Harness Racing Museum & Hall of Fame, Goshen, NY*

GREYHOUND

THE REMARKABLE STORY
OF THE LEGENDARY RACEHORSE WHO INSPIRED A NATION

gallery

[61]
Jimmie walking Greyhound.
- circa 1937, Don Daniels Digital Collection, courtesy of the Harness Racing Museum & Hall of Fame, Goshen, NY

[62]
Sep Palin (left) shakes hands with Col. Baker—possibly at Lexington after the 1:56 record.
- circa 1937, courtesy of the International Museum of the Horse, Lexington, KY

GREYHOUND

THE REMARKABLE STORY
OF THE LEGENDARY RACEHORSE WHO INSPIRED A NATION

———— *gallery* ————

[63]
Greyhound wins the FFA Trot; Angel Child is second, Lee Hanover third, and Silver King, on the far outside, finishes last.
• *August 20, 1937, courtesy of the Harness Racing Museum & Hall of Fame, Goshen, NY*

[64]
Greyhound wins the final heat of the FFA Trot in North Randall. Rosalind is second; Calumet Evelyn is third.
• *July 4, 1938, courtesy of the United States Trotting Association*

GREYHOUND

**THE REMARKABLE STORY
OF THE LEGENDARY RACEHORSE WHO INSPIRED A NATION**

gallery

[65]
Greyhound (Palin), Rosalind (Tom Berry), and Ed Lasater (Ben White) at the start of the Matron Stake in Springfield, IL.
• *August 15, 1938, courtesy of the United States Trotting Association*

[66]
Greyhound from above, likely at Lexington.
• *undated, but probably circa 1936, courtesy of the United States Trotting Association*

GREYHOUND

THE REMARKABLE STORY
OF THE LEGENDARY RACEHORSE WHO INSPIRED A NATION

gallery

[67]
Greyhound taking his last warm up lap prior to his world record mile in 1:55 ¼.
• *September 29, 1938, courtesy of the United States Trotting Association; original photograph by P.W. Moser*

[68]
Greyhound and Sep Palin after breaking their own world record by trotting a mile in 1:55 ¼.
• *September 29, 1938, courtesy of the Hambletonian Society*

years. Peter Manning's record seemed to be just out of reach, not because of lack of talent, but due to lack of opportunity. For such a feat, the stars must align, the track must be fast, and the weather must be absolutely perfect. Palin would've loved to steal Peter Manning's crown on his home track, but it wasn't to be. At the close of the Indianapolis meet, Greyhound and his stablemates boarded the vans and traveled to Lexington, Kentucky, for the fall trots, the final meet of the Grand Circuit season.

The KTHBA track at Lexington, nicknamed the red mile, was considered one of the fastest harness tracks in the country. Despite Palin's desire to break Peter Manning's record on his home turf, historically, the red mile was the ideal setting for such an attempt. Records often fell at the annual trots held there. On September 22, Palin took Greyhound against time to lower his own record of 1:57 ¼, set the previous year. Though not officially branded as a race against Peter Manning's time, the substantial crowd that gathered that day surely hoped they would see history made before their very eyes.

The gray ghost flew around the red clay oval, his ground-covering stride consuming the track before him. Palin urged Greyhound on as he came out of the final turn and into the stretch. His front legs reaching, hind legs firing like a steam locomotive, the gray stormed across the finish line. The crowd waited breathlessly. The judges carefully compared their watches, accuracy being particularly essential with the stakes so high. The track announcer stepped up to the microphone, the apparatus crackled and whined, and the announcement came.

"Ladies and gentlemen." The electronic voice reverberated over the track. "The time for the mile, one minute, fifty-six, and three-quarters seconds!" The crowd drowned out anything else the announcer may have said. Greyhound had matched Peter Manning's record 1:56 ¾![10] Finally, after fifteen years, the long-retired gelding was no longer the sole holder of the record for fastest trotter in the world. A stellar accomplishment indeed! No horse had come close to touching Peter Manning's record. Now, Greyhound was there on the upper-most rung, snatching at Peter Manning's crown. Just one-quarter of a second faster, and Greyhound would stand alone as king of the trotters.

One week later, Palin scored the big gray before another record-setting crowd—more fans than the KTHBA track had seen in the recent memories of those in attendance. On the second score, Palin gave a nod and the starter gave the word. Palin, several spectators, and six official time keepers clicked their respective timepieces. Greyhound burst forward, settling into stride directly, his gait laced with intention as he flew into the first turn. Two prompters came along at the start, one behind and one just off Greyhound's right wheel.[11] Their skilled drivers encouraged Greyhound to go faster, pushing him with the energy of each runner, appealing to the big gelding's competitive spirit.

With ever-increasing speed, Greyhound sailed through the first quarter in :29 ¼. Finding a new gear in the back stretch, he floated effortlessly over the red dirt track. Puffs of dust rose in the wake of flying hooves. The crowd cheered wildly.

"C'mon, Greyhound!"

"Drive him, Sep!"[12]

"Go! Go! Go!" The chant rose from the throng. People pressed against the rail, straining to see the Ghost on the far side of the track. Greyhound passed the half in a blistering :57 ½. The big gray sailed into the far turn, his legs flying, his impossibly long stride devouring the track before him. He made three quarters in 1:27 ½. The people gasped. The prompters kept close but didn't push, not yet. Palin let up on Greyhound, offering him a little breather before the long home stretch.[13] But the gallant champion asked for nothing; his stride remained true, his long legs strong. He powered on.

"C'mon! Yeah! C'mon!" Palin yelled over the eye-stinging rush of wind created by Greyhound's tremendous speed. The runners moved up, one close behind and one coming up beside as Greyhound flew down the stretch.[14] Those looking on wondered if the gray could maintain his speed to the end. But Greyhound never faltered. His stride stayed true. Blue steel mane flying, sulky wheels spinning, the spokes reflecting silver glints of afternoon sun. The mighty trotter sailed under the wire in a blur of gray, white, and silver.[15]

The crowd hummed with excitement. Some stood in stunned silence, the tension palpable as they waited for the official time. The minutes felt like hours[16] as the six judges congregated over their timepieces. Finally, the loudspeaker crackled to life.

"The time for the mile—" An unbearable pause. "—one minute, fifty-six seconds, flat. Ladies and gentlemen, we have a new world record!"

Like the tremendous roar of a locomotive, a cheer carried through the grandstand, spilled over the rail, and rushed across the track. The crowd erupted, clapping their hands and stomping their feet as Palin jogged the newly crowned world champion back to the grandstand. A wide smile stretched across the reinsman's normally demure face.[17] Greyhound lifted his neck and tipped his head toward the crowd. There was no doubt in anyone's mind that the big gray knew the cheering was for him, for now he stood alone, the greatest of all time.

Called up to the judges' stand, Baker stood before the cheering crowds. He smiled broadly, and lifted his silver-tipped cane in salute. Urged to speak, Baker removed his hat and stepped up to the microphone.

"Ladies and gentlemen." The crowd quieted, turning their attention to Baker. "It gives me great pleasure to own a horse like Greyhound, one-fifty-six (1:56)." Baker appended his horse's fastest time to his name, as was the tradition. "And to have a great driver like Sep Palin."[18] The crowd sounded with renewed cheers. The small man stepped back from the microphone. Baker again lifted his cane in salute, immense pride so clearly etched upon his face.

Jimmie jogged onto the track and took a hold of Greyhound. Palin exited the sulky. The veteran reinsman gave the gray a pat on the neck and a quiet word that only Jimmie and Greyhound could hear. Then he turned toward the judges' stand. "Spec" Erskine, another veteran of the sulky, ran up to Palin and shook his hand vigorously. In a moment, other drivers crowded around, eager to shake the reinsman's hand and pat him on the back.[19] The fans surrounded the men, pushing Palin on a wave of gratitude up to the judges' stand.

Palin climbed the stairs, shook hands with Baker and the judges, and then turned to face the crowd as he was pushed toward the microphone.[20] "He appeared visibly affected by the effort he had made with Greyhound, which was not lessened by a heavy cold," the October 6 issue of *The Harness Horse* would later report.[21] The reinsman wiped his brow with a handkerchief, then cleared his throat before speaking.

"Folks." Palin's blue eyes twinkled behind his wire-rimmed spectacles. "It's a pleasure to have the opportunity to drive a horse like Greyhound, and have the horse owned by a liberal sportsman like Mr. E. J. Baker." The crowd applauded and Baker touched the brim of his hat. "He's a great horse, the world's foremost trotter. And he's not done yet."[22] The crowd applauded; some men whooped and hollered, whistled and tossed their hats in the air. Pride colored Palin's features. Not a haughty pride for his own skills, but a humble pride in his own good fortune to be associated with such a grand horse.

Palin left the stand, his face beaming like those of the trotting fans around him. The victory may have belonged to Greyhound, Palin, and Baker, but the celebration belonged to everyone. The harness world had waited a long time for this moment. Henry Knight, president of the KTHBA and Greyhound's breeder, greeted Palin as he exited the track. Knight was the first of many to take the trainer-driver out for a celebratory dinner.[23]

A congratulatory telegram arrived from Thomas Murphy, the trainer that drove Peter Manning to his record in 1922.

> "A wonderful performance by horse, trainer, and owner. My heartiest congratulations to all three of you. Tell Greyhound for me that the crown he will now wear he has earned honestly through his untiring efforts, gameness, speed, and wonderful courage. More power to all three of you from a great admirer of this great performer."
>
> Thos. W. Murphy

Newspapers and horse publications across the country and overseas celebrated the accomplishment of Greyhound.

"The spectacle he presented, coming through the stretch, climaxing the record-breaking achievement with a final quarter in 28 ½ seconds, will be remembered by all privileged to witness it, to the end of their stay on this earth," wrote *The Harness Horse*.[24]

Miss Lena D. Paull was perhaps the most eloquent in stating the effect Greyhound had on the people around him in her October 1937 letter to John Hervey, printed in *The Harness Horse*.

"It is indeed weird the effect he has on one: that of the super-natural, the uncanny. His spell cast upon all who were there. Not a sound—not a breath, a sigh, a cheer, until after the stretch was reached. We sat there in perfect silence, almost until the end." Miss Paull closed the letter with these words: "In all my life here, and perhaps the life to come, I shall never forget Greyhound."[25]

Overlooked in the moment, but pointed out later by writer and KTHBA secretary Jesse Shuff, was the fact that Greyhound had trotted faster than any harness horse of either gait in the open.[26] The fastest time of 1:55 ¼, set by the great pacer Dan Patch in 1905, had been made with a wind screen and a front-runner. Considered an unfair advantage, neither was permissible anymore.

The crowds followed Jimmie and Greyhound back to the stable area, where the young man went about the long cooling-out process. Reporters shouted questions while Jimmie untacked and washed down the great champion. It would be one of many interviews as Greyhound's celebrity status skyrocketed. Suddenly everything the Grey Ghost did was news. From what he ate to how many blankets he had, what type of bedding he slept on, what his work routine was, and what kind of shoes he wore and why. The newspapers and trade magazines across the country and around the world celebrated and reported all things Greyhound, and would continue to do so as his celebrity grew.

Once the crowds had dwindled away and the reporters were gone at last, Jimmie stood with Greyhound in the stillness of the dark night and stroked the gelding's sleek neck. He then pushed his cot up to Greyhound's stall door so he could keep watch even as he slept, and shimmied under the covers. Greyhound pushed his head over the web mesh gate and nuzzled Jimmie's face, stretching his long lips to tousle the young man's hair.

"C'mon, boy." Jimmie patted the blanket beside him, and Goshen the Dalmatian leapt onto the cot, then burrowed down into the dark wool blanket. Greyhound turned a few times in his stall before lowering his great gray body into the knee-deep straw. Jimmie snuffed out the lantern and darkness circled the three—the man, the dog, and the greatest trotter the world had ever known.

GREYHOUND

THE REMARKABLE STORY OF THE LEGENDARY RACEHORSE WHO INSPIRED A NATION

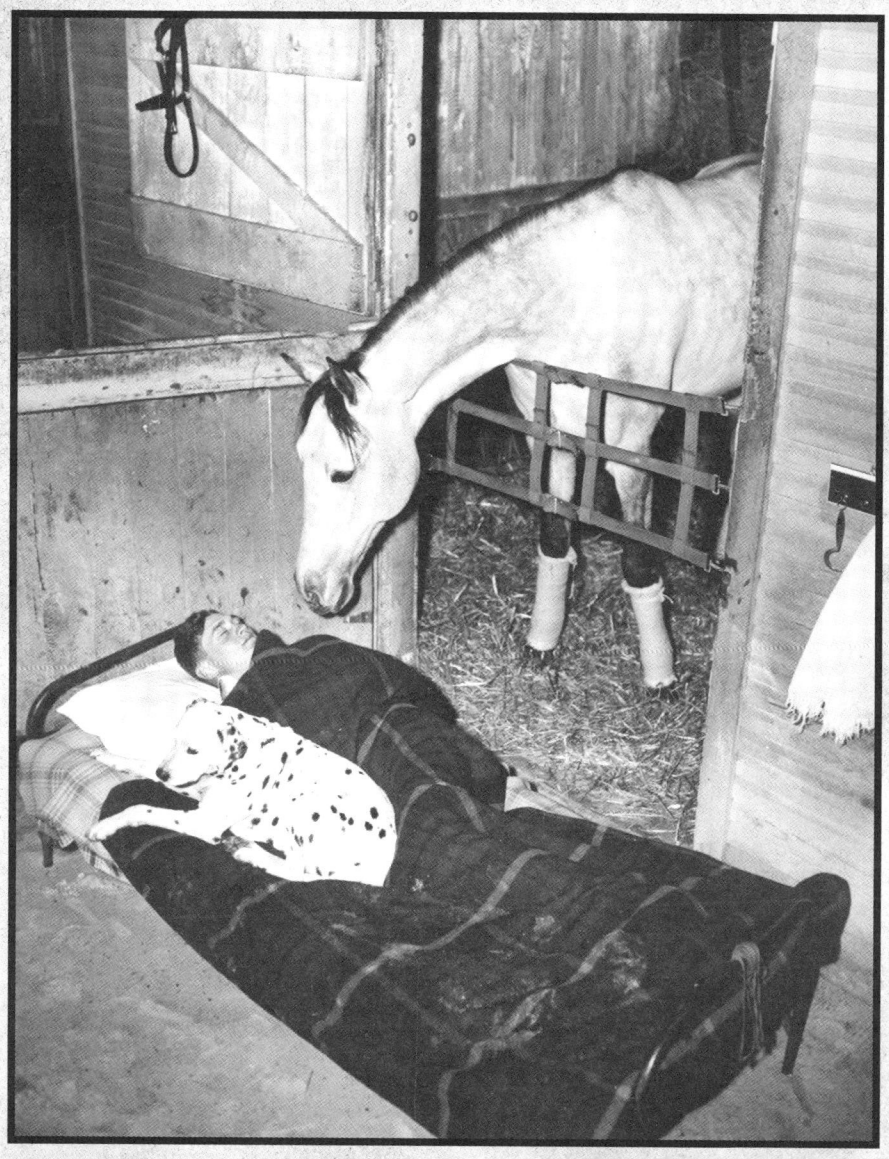

Jimmie and his dog, Goshen, asleep outside Greyhound's stall—likely at Indianapolis, given the date.

JUNE 1, 1938, COURTESY OF THE HARNESS RACING
MUSEUM & HALL OF FAME, GOSHEN, NY

CHAPTER
— 18 —

> "He seemed to gather and poise himself
> when he set sail like some splendid ship with all her canvas spread,
> moving majestically onward, the rhythm of his progress sustained
> from wire to wire in so stately a way that it left the spectator
> with the impression of something invincible."
>
> —
>
> JOHN HERVEY,
> THE AMERICAN TROTTER, 1947

HORSE OF THE YEAR

Pulled along in the wake of a great gray ghost, the sport of harness racing surged in popularity. The 1937 Grand Circuit season saw more venues, more fans, more races, and more money than it had since the Roaring Twenties. Many tracks that had previously been operating in the red showed a profit for the first time in years.

"This year it is evident there is a change in the trend of the sport," reported the *Athol Daily News* (Massachusetts). "More and more people are taking an interest in the rhythmic speed of the animals around the track. Not as stirring as running races, harness races lure many followers because of the grace and form displayed by the animals as they wheel the racing gigs over the dirt tracks."[1]

Greyhound set no less than three world records in 1937 and trotted five sub-two-minute miles, the only outlier being the first heat in the Springfield FFA, which he trotted in 2:01—a time most trotters could never hope to achieve. In the December 1937 issue of *Hoof Beats*, John Hervey celebrated Baker and Palin and how they had handled Greyhound in his career to this point.

"I think we all owe a debt of thanks to Baker and Palin for the careful manner in which Greyhound was developed," wrote Hervey, "which, in my opinion, had much to do with his eventual success in becoming the world champion." Hervey emphasized the significance of Palin not pushing Greyhound too hard at age two and three. He certainly could have gone faster, Hervey observed, but we never saw how fast he could go. Palin only took Greyhound fast enough to win.[3]

Truly, what good was it to have the fastest two- or three-year-old if he was crippled and retired before he reached age four? It must be remembered that harness racing wasn't about the fastest speed the horse could attain by any means possible, but the fastest speed attained while staying on gait. This took careful, slow development over time. The fastest Standardbreds were mature horses, but they had to stay sound to race into maturity and reach their ultimate speed. Many horsemen also credited Jimmie Wingfield for keeping Greyhound in top shape. Palin drove the training miles, but Jimmie drove the jog miles—the slow and careful miles that ensured Greyhound was ready for speed work when Palin called upon him. Jimmie took meticulous care of Greyhound, never leaving the horse's side except to grab a meal.[4]

Also in December 1937, Greyhound was paid a most unique compliment by Algernon Daingerfield, secretary of the Jockey Club—the governing body of Thoroughbred racing. A man deeply involved in the world of Thoroughbred runners, who held a place of prominence and deep respect in that sport, Daingerfield selected Greyhound when he cast his vote for 1937 Horse of the Year.[5] In a year that saw the likes of Triple Crown winner War Admiral and horse hero Seabiscuit, Daingerfield said the following:

"[To choose] between War Admiral and Seabiscuit, I would have to vote for War Admiral. But neither of them, speaking critically, was so great a horse as Greyhound. It is to him the title belongs. He is, emphatically, the one great Horse of the Year."[6]

The honor was even more significant when one considers the negativity the Thoroughbred crowd generally felt toward harness horse people.

"Never before has any trotting champion received so high a compliment," wrote John Hervey (under the name Salvatore[*]) in the December 1937 issue of *The Harness Horse*. "The average Thoroughbred horseman takes no interest whatever in [trotters] and knows nothing about them. He is oftener than not hostile to them, never speaks of them except with derision."[7]

While Daingerfield likely received some good-natured ribbing from his Thoroughbred cohort, he'd also gotten their attention. Twenty-five men cast their votes in the *Horse and*

---

[*] "Salvatore" is the nom de plume John Hervey used in writing for Thoroughbred publications.[8] Why it was used in a harness horse publication is a mystery, though one could speculate that the original piece may have first appeared in a Thoroughbred publication.

Horseman poll. War Admiral ultimately won the honor, but Greyhound had broken through yet another improbable barrier. He'd moved from the relative obscurity of trotting horse columns to his own spreads on the sports page. Even *Time, Newsweek,** and *Life* magazines wrote articles about and featured pictures of the horse that stood alone, crowned the world's fastest trotter.

---

* Greyhound appeared on the cover of the July 25, 1938 issue of *Newsweek*.

CHAPTER
— 19 —

Records Tied By Rosalind

Filly Owned By Gibson White Star Thursday On Trotting Program

Rosalind, Gibson White's winner of the 1936 Kentucky Futurity, continued the assault on world's records at the Lexington Trots when she raced to victory Thursday afternoon in the historic Transylvania for free-for-all trotters.

Driven by young White's father, Ben F. White of Lexington, she

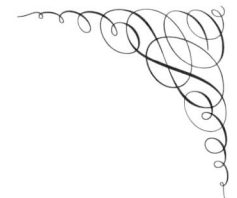

> *"Harness racing fans knew today without a doubt that Greyhound, silver-coated king of trotters, still is king."*
>
> —
>
> Lexington Herald-Leader, July 8, 1938

THE KING MEETS THE QUEEN

"Greyhound, world's champion trotter, after spending 1937 in exhibitions, has returned to racing the field this season in five new all-aged stakes," reported *Rider and Driver* in July 1938.[1] The new races would be held at Cleveland, Goshen, Agawam, and Springfield (Illinois). "With every rival trying to beat him, the 'Grey Ghost' will be busy."

The Trotting Horse Club, headed up by E. Roland Harriman, took notice of Greyhound's nearly complete absence from racing in 1937.[2] Apparently, Palin and White had been serious when they threatened to not race their champions Greyhound and Rosalind for purses less than $1,500. The fans had registered their displeasure and were clamoring to see the two top trotters compete in 1938. In response, the Trotting Club scrambled to attract these top horses, which would draw crowds and give racegoers the thrill they demanded. To do this, five new races were created for older horses, with purse offerings increased dramatically—from a few hundred dollars to amounts between $3,050 and $3,500.

The plan worked. Palin and White were in, as were the only other sub-two-minute trotters currently racing: Calumet Evelyn and Clever Hanover, both with records of 1:59 ½. Additionally, snappy Ed Lasater (2:02 ¼), the colt Palin had driven in Rosalind's Hambletonian, also planned to return for the 1938 season.

The stage was set for a spectacular display of speed, and the people couldn't wait to see Rosalind and Greyhound together. Rosalind was already in the hearts and minds of the public, due not only to her brilliance as a top trotter, but also to the touching story of her owner Gibson White. Having the filly to focus on had proven instrumental in helping Gibson regain his health, due in no small part to the lifting of his spirit through the love he felt for his filly and the enthusiasm he had in planning her future.[3]

Rosalind won the Hambletonian in 1936, bettering Greyhound's 1935 time by nearly one second. In three seasons of racing, she'd won 17 of 22 starts, and lost only one race in her last two seasons. The fastest trotting mare of all time, Rosalind had been christened Queen of the Trotters. Now, at five years old, she would only get better.

A festive energy greeted racegoers on July 4—America's Independence Day—at North Randall near Cleveland, Ohio. The North Randall track heavily advertised Greyhound's appearance against Rosalind, and the pair brought out the largest crowd to attend the track in at least a dozen years.[4] More than 10,000 people packed the grandstand and stood along the rails of the mile oval.[5]

A celebratory atmosphere prevailed. American flags and patriotic red, white, and blue bunting decorated every eave and rail. Women wore white dresses with accents of red and blue ribbons, and dainty white corsages. Men wore straw boat hats with red, white, and blue bands, ties adorned with stars and stripes, and neat little red and white *boutonnières* on their lapels. Children were dressed in fancy costumes decorated with stars and stripes. Some boys in three-cornered hats and brass-buttoned coats, as worn in Revolutionary days, waved miniature American flags while the band played.[6]

Beautiful sunshine and a fast track greeted the afternoon crowds as the horses stepped through the gap. Greyhound was the strong favorite to win the Championship Stallion Stake FFA trot, with Rosalind the second choice.[7] A strong wind prevailed. Gusts upwards of thirty miles per hour[8] would certainly affect the horses in the back stretch when they trotted headfirst into it.

Greyhound stood out in a sea of sleek bay and brown coats, his long, dark mane lifting gently off his arched neck. A riot of colorful satin jackets bedazzled the reinsmen. Raucous cheers arose at the sight of Greyhound and Rosalind. The drivers took their warm-up miles. Potent anticipation hung heavy in the air for the first meeting between the Trotting King and the Trotting Queen.

The horses scored down for the first heat, the starter gave the word, and the race was on! Greyhound, under firm restraint, jumped at the start but quickly regained his composure and settled into his magnificent stride.[9] Vic

Flemming, driving Calumet Evelyn, took the lead and set the early pace, passing the quarter in thirty seconds. Ben White had Rosalind breathing down Flemming's neck before he swung out around the quick black mare and took the lead. The horses trotted through the upper turn; then Palin touched the lines and Greyhound surged ahead, grabbing the lead from Rosalind. With no one ahead of him, the great horse lengthened his stride, moving ever faster. Greyhound crossed under the wire a couple lengths ahead of Rosalind. The latter engaged in an exciting stretch duel with a valiant Calumet Evelyn for second.[10]

Thirty minutes later, the field scored down for the start of the second heat. At the word, Greyhound got away first, holding the lead to the first turn. In a whir of wheels and flying hooves, Ed Lasater snatched the lead from Greyhound.[11] The dark brown stallion held a steady lead to the three-quarter pole, going the distance in an uninspired 1:34. Greyhound dawdled at the back of the pack, trotting easily while Palin waited to make his move. Coming out of the final turn, Palin tipped Greyhound to the center of the track, touched the lines, and the big gray charged up from behind. He moved with such ease, the crowd was unaware of the scope of his dazzling speed until they later consulted their watches.[12] Greyhound's massive shoulders seemed to lift, his hind legs powerful pistons, his front legs rolling along effortlessly as he gobbled up the track before him. Greyhound took the lead easily, passing the other horses like so many fence posts, trotting the last quarter in a blistering :26 ¾ seconds—the fastest quarter in a trotting mile, and the gray gelding's 14th world record.[13] Rosalind held on against Calumet Evelyn for second.

"He put on a performance that thrilled the immense throng to the limit, in fact, never in the history of our sport was such speed in the closing quarter of a race or in an exhibition," raved *Hoof Beats*. "Even the trainers ... marveled at the rare ease displayed by Sep Palin's great pupil ... never appearing to be under a drive at any point."[14]

The accomplishment of trotting a quarter in just over twenty-six seconds in a mile effort was unparalleled in the annals of trotting, at the time. Faster quarters had been recorded, but those had been quarter-mile sprints, not a quarter at the end of a racing mile![15] Greyhound had trotted his quarter at a speed comparable with a Thoroughbred runner—and no slouch of one, either. John Hervey, in his July 13, 1938 piece for *The Harness Horse*, cited several examples of recent Thoroughbred stakes winners galloping a closing quarter in times ranging from twenty-six seconds to twenty-seven and change. While the galloping horse would still come out on top when the full miles were compared, for a trotter to match galloping speed was simply unheard of. Particularly when one considers that the runners often employed a chute at the start of a race, allowing for a long opening straightaway, in some cases as much as a quarter to five-eighths of a mile. In contrast, the trotting horse on a traditional mile oval must navigate "two turns"* before reaching the first quarter.[16]

Writers and historians of harness racing openly stood in awe of Greyhound's accomplishments. John Hervey said of Greyhound: "Behind his speed is the carrying power of not only a motor fabulously geared, but a determination that is invincible, and a mental, as well as physical balance that is as near perfection as anything earthly can hope to be."[17] And all had every confidence the grand Grey Ghost wasn't finished yet.

The next stop on the circuit was Agawam, Massachusetts, for the $3,100 American Stake FFA Trot on July 29. Heavy rains opened the meet at Agawam, drenching Massachusetts in a deluge that would continue off and on for days.[18] The rains threatened to ruin the day as people poured into the grandstand. The opportunity to see the magnificent Greyhound and Rosalind drew them from their homes, despite it being the worst weather of the meet thus far. The track at Agawam was touted as "rain proof" and was in decent condition for the race, despite continued intermittent showers throughout the day. The clay-base track wasn't fast in the rain, but it was safe.[19]

The field of five faced a stout wind mixed with rainfall as they went to the post.[20] Greyhound went in as such a huge favorite, the bookies refused to take bets on him, and pari-mutuel betting, only recently legalized in Massachusetts, was not accepted on the result. Five horses came to the post, with Rosalind the only real competition. The wind and rain had Rosalind and Greyhound a bit jumpy. The mare spoiled a couple scores, but on the third attempt, the field got underway.[21]

Calumet Evelyn got away first; her driver sent the jet-black mare to the front and set the pace. Greyhound did not score well. He took a couple dogged strides—a short choppy step and a long awkward one—before settling into his big trot.[22] The field entered the first turn with Greyhound well back of them. Out in front, Calumet Evelyn trotted the half at a fast clip, but she faltered along the back stretch, slowing before reaching the three-quarter pole. Greyhound, trotting well within himself, moved up into fourth.

Seeing his opportunity, White took Rosalind around Calumet Evelyn, taking the lead on the rail in front of the tiring black mare.

---

* In his original article, Hervey noted that a harness horse trotting a traditional mile oval would have to navigate *four* turns. In harness racing, an oval track is generally considered to have *two* turns, one on each end. In the case of this article, Hervey may have described "four turns" to drive home the point that the harness horse spends about half of their mile turning, and that part of each quarter has the horse in either the top or bottom of a turn, whereas with the use of a chute, a runner can go the same mile distance with the bulk of it being a straight line. This is why Greyhound matching time with a good running quarter was so significant—how much faster could he go if allowed to trot a quarter or more in a straight line?

Greyhound drew along beside Rosalind and the two entered the final stretch together. The game mare could not hold off the assault of speed poured on by Greyhound with his long, powerful stride. He pulled away in the home stretch, finishing the mile well ahead of Rosalind.[23]

In the second heat, White sent Rosalind to the front and Greyhound came along with her. In the first turn, the crowd gasped when Greyhound struck the wheel of Rosalind's sulky, stumbled, and nearly went down.[24] He righted himself and settled back into his gait, but had lost some ground. Rosalind remained in the lead, the pace at the three-quarter pole a dawdling 1:38. Greyhound caught Rosalind coming into the final turn. The two champion trotters hooked up, sprinting through the stretch, matching each other stride-for-stride as they flew down to the wire. Both reinsmen had their horses under hard drive.[25] Rosalind held on gamely, but Palin had a bit more horse. The reinsman asked and Greyhound delivered. He lengthened his stride and pulled away from Rosalind, winning by half a length.[26]

One week later at Agawam, Greyhound went to the post for the National Stake FFA Trot, again meeting the same horses he had raced in previous starts—Rosalind, Calumet Evelyn, Ed Lasater, and Clever Hanover. These horses were fast, quality trotters—three of them had at least one two-minute mile to their credit, but so far, they just couldn't take the measure of the gallant gray.

In the first heat, Palin took Greyhound wide through the first turn. By doing so, he avoided getting caught in a potential first-turn jam,[27] but entered the back stretch dead last. Despite the deep and cuppy track, Greyhound made an incredible last-to-first run, passing the field on the final turn with no apparent urging from Palin. Like a bolt of silver lightning, Greyhound trotted home, winning easily in 1:59 ½. Rosalind trotted a good race, but it was not good enough to push the gray near to his limit.[28] She finished second; Calumet Evelyn, third. It was the fastest mile trotted so far that season by any horse, despite the wet conditions and Agawam being a notoriously slow track.

"He trotted around them as if they were all novices," reported the August 10 issue of *The Harness Horse*. "The class and ability of the mighty son of Guy Abbey makes all wonder at his marvelous speed, manners, and ability to carry it."[29]

In the second heat, Palin sent Greyhound straight to the front and stayed there. He trotted the final quarter in a speedy :28 ¾, finishing strong "with much speed in reserve," reported *The Harness Horse*. Rosalind again came second, and Ed Lasater, third. Calumet Evelyn did not finish. In her valiant drive to wrest second place from Rosalind in the first heat, Evelyn had taken a misstep in the bad footing near the rail and seriously cut the inside quarter of her left front foot.[30] She finished third but was withdrawn from the second heat.

Calumet Evelyn's injury proved quite severe. The amazing daughter of Guy Abbey, record holder at the pace and at the trot, never raced again. She retired to a successful career as a broodmare, though she never produced a foal as spectacular as herself.

August 9, 1938 was Greyhound Day at Good Time Park in Goshen. Large ads adorned the regional papers, touting the celebration of Greyhound's first race at the triangular mile in two years. Adding to the excitement, two Hambletonian winners would meet on the track where each had scored their victory—Greyhound in 1935 and Rosalind in 1936. Articles written at the end of July in anticipation of the big day stated 10 top trotters would meet for the $3,500 FFA Trotting Derby—a new race created to bring the champions together. But on race day, just two owners dared to put their horses up against Greyhound and Rosalind.

In the first heat, for the first time since 1934, Greyhound broke stride, forcing the field to score again. In the second score, Greyhound got away badly.[31] Rosalind went to the lead and the field swept away from the gray as he sorted out his troubles, found his stride, and went after them. Rosalind led the field all the way around to the three-quarter pole,[32] her red-bay coat glistening brilliantly in the afternoon sun.

"Here he comes!" someone shouted. The crowd burst into wild applause and deafening cheers.[33] Greyhound surged forward with his impossible stride, burning up the track and shortening the distance between him and Rosalind with every clap of hard hoof on firm clay. Sulky wheels whirred and hooves pounded as Greyhound whizzed past Ed Lasater, then picked off the speedy gelding Brogan. The crowd leapt to their feet. Greyhound slowly gained on Rosalind in his final push to the wire. For a moment, it looked as if Greyhound would run out of track before he caught her. But, with just twenty-five feet remaining,[34] the gray edged the fleet mare by a head. He again trotted a blistering last quarter, finishing those final two furlongs in a swift :28 ½.

In the second heat, Palin took no chances, sending Greyhound straight to the front and keeping him there. With his unmatched stride, Greyhound soon left the field well behind him, trotting the mile in an easy 1:59 ¼.[35] Rosalind finished a game second. At the time, only twenty-seven trotters* in the world had gone a mile in less than 2:00, and many of them never matched their own top record again.[36, 37] But Greyhound made it look common, as if it were the norm and not the gold standard. He collected sub-two-minute miles like raindrops in a barrel.

"Unlike many pampered champions, Greyhound has no private van in which to tour the

---

* Fifty-six pacers had gone a mile in 2:00 as of July 1938, according to the same article.

country. He goes along just like one of the mob—fourteen horses to a freight car," *Newsweek* reported after his performance at Goshen.[38] The public adored Greyhound and, like the other celebrities of the day, they enjoyed an intimate look into the life of the champion trotter.

"Practically everyone who has visited the silvery-coated horse in his stall roots for him. His personal appeal is magnetic—a face radiating intelligence, quiet, friendly manners," the *Newsweek* article continued. "The only time he forgets his good horse sense is when he sees a cigarette. Given an opportunity, he'll snatch one right out of your hand." One woman, astounded that Greyhound had actually eaten a cigarette, was reassured that the tobacco would fight stomach worms and the great trotter ate cigarettes and chewing tobacco with regularity.[39] Soon the public were sending pouches of tobacco to Greyhound,[40] which he cordially shared with Jimmie.

From Goshen, Greyhound boarded the train for the long trek to Springfield, Illinois, for the Matron All-Age Trot. Only Rosalind and Ed Lasater came to the post to challenge him. Despite threatening clouds and strong winds, thousands of harness horse fans packed the grandstand at the Illinois State Fair on August 15.[41] The crowd stood and gave a rousing ovation when Greyhound paraded onto the track for the Matron Stake. Surely no equally sized group of Thoroughbred fans could hold a candle to the raucous noise made by the devoted fans of the great Grey Ghost, author, photographer, and turf writer P. W. Moser would later write in *The Harness Horse*.[42]

In Springfield were the home crowd fans. While Indiana liked to claim Greyhound due to his connection to their own Sep Palin, the Illinoisians had great love and respect for their home-state hero Colonel Baker. At considerable personal expense, Baker had staged a great show for the home crowd each year since Greyhound gained national celebrity status.[43]

"The crowd was made up of the home folks, Greyhound belongs to them, Ed Baker is one of them," Moser wrote in his 1938 *Harness Horse* article about the event. Springfield had indeed been the site of many of Greyhound's greatest moments. Springfield was where he'd trotted his first two-minute mile, set a world's record for the fastest mile in a race, and "it was here that he received the greatest ovation of his career, that must have been the sweetest music to the ears of his generous owner," Moser wrote.[44]

A significant head wind blew from the northwest on August 15, forcing the horses to trot headfirst into the gusts at the start and finish of each heat. Greyhound won both heats easily. In the second heat, trotting into estimated thirty-mile-per-hour wind gusts,[45] Greyhound still covered the last half in :58 ¼ and the final quarter in :28 ¼. The Matron Stake was Greyhound's fifth consecutive win and his third sub-two-minute mile of the season. But there was more to Greyhound's stellar performances; in these grand efforts he finished strong, never being asked to trot to his limit.

From Springfield, Greyhound made the long trek by rail back to Syracuse for an exhibition trot. There was talk in the papers that Greyhound might go for breaking his own record while at Syracuse, but conditions on the day were unfavorable for such endeavors, with overnight rains making the track slow and heavy. The fans settled for an exhibition trot, and cheered loudly when Greyhound stepped onto the track. Palin, wearing his dark green satin jacket and hat trimmed in white, presented a dark contrast to the nearly white Greyhound. Jimmie had braided a matching green ribbon into the gelding's forelock. A chestnut Thoroughbred prompter followed the champion onto the track, the driver wearing a green jacket and hat to match Palin.[46]

Greyhound got away cleanly on the second score, trotting the first quarter in :30 ½ under restraint. The gelding pulled against the bit, demanding more rein from Palin's firm grip. The reinsman obliged and let him out a notch. Greyhound lengthened his powerful stride, and the prompter galloped along, his head even with Palin's right sulky wheel. Greyhound stepped easily along the back stretch and into the final turn, his stride effortless, powerful, and stunning to see. With barely a wiggle of the rein from Palin, the gallant gray sailed down the home stretch and under the wire.[47] He went the mile in 1:59 ½, making it his fourth sub-two-minute mile of the season. Incredible.[48]

Palin jogged Greyhound back to his cheering fans. Baker met them on the track and stood proudly with his champion as the Fair Queen placed a large wreath of flowers around Greyhound's neck. The gelding, none too impressed with wearing them, nibbled at the white zinnias.[49] He worked the flowers around with flapping lips before dropping them to the ground with a snort. The gray trotter's antics humored the crowd, further enchanting them with their champion.

A week later, Greyhound and the Baker-Palin stable returned to Indianapolis for the Indiana State Fair. There, Greyhound trotted another exhibition mile, turning in an impressive 1:56 ¾ with a single prompt horse and no whip or drive from Palin. He had again matched the world record he had broken the year before—the one just a few years ago many had believed would never fall—and smashed by four full seconds the track record at Indianapolis. Additionally, he trotted the fastest mile by any horse of that season, and made his fifth sub-two-minute mile of 1938.[50] By all accounts, he was ready to take down his own world record. He'd have his chance in less than three weeks when the Grand Circuit returned to Lexington.

The air felt taut with anticipation while Palin drove Greyhound through his warm-up miles on September 23. A crowd of over 2,000 gathered—substantial for an unannounced time trial scheduled one week before the official opening of the trots. The people had come to catch a glimpse of Greyhound, and they would not be disappointed. Everything had to be perfect for any horse going into a time trial—the track, the weather, temperature fluctuations, and even the humidity could slow a horse down, Palin told a reporter earlier in the week, saying excess humidity could cost a horse a full second.[51] Kentucky at the end of September could be hot, dry and sunny, or cold, wet, and blustery.

On this day it was unseasonably warm, the temperature jumping from an overnight low of 48 to a daytime high of 85. A stiff wind assaulted Greyhound as he trotted through the upper turn of the red clay oval. Still, the big gray gelding turned in a brilliant mile, matching his own world record of 1:56. Those watching marveled at the ease with which Greyhound trotted, his stride so efficient he did not appear to be trying at all. Few doubted that the Grey Ghost would set a new world record on his next attempt. Palin himself caught the gelding's time in 1:55 ¾, as did a few other unofficial timers. He argued his point, but the official time of 1:56 stood.[52]

Palin made no announcement as to when he would again send Greyhound after his own world record. Anticipation grew as the days dragged by in the week before the opening of the Lexington trots. Thousands of people descended on Lexington, arriving by car, train, and even by ship. They traveled from all over the country and as far away as Australia to attend the trots and hopefully see Greyhound lower his 1:56 record.

The trots were an annual affair, bringing all classes of people together with just one thing in common—their love of a fast harness horse. Hotels and restaurants filled with people chattering on about which horse was best in the upcoming races, and whether Greyhound would improve upon his own immortal standing as the greatest trotter of all time.

In the stable at the KTHBA track, Jimmie ran a towel over Greyhound's sleek, white body. The gray turned his head to watch him, nipping playfully at the cloth when it came near his mouth. As ever, people wandered into the barn, upwards of one hundred of them each day, hoping to catch a glimpse of the champion. Jimmie greeted them graciously and answered their questions, his pride in his charge ever evident on his young face.

"Yes, ma'am," Jimmie said in his soft Georgian drawl, "he eats three times a day, at five, eleven, and five. He gets four quarts of oats each feeding, but for the evening feed, I mix in four quarts of bran and make a nice, warm mash for him. He gets all the hay and water he wants."[53]

"Oh, my!" The woman placed one hand daintily on her chest. Jimmie smiled.

"Yes, ma'am. He also eats a whole orange every morning. And he gets some tobacco every day." Suspicion etched the woman's face. "To control the parasites," Jimmie added quickly.[54]

"What's his work schedule like?" A reporter held a pencil poised over his notepad.

"He usually gets a work out of about four or six [miles]." Jimmie nodded toward the racing sulky hanging on the wall. "Unless he's got a race. Then he only works about three to five miles."[55]

"Do you take his shoes off at night?" a woman in a fancy hat asked. A few in the crowd snickered impolitely at the woman's lack of horse knowledge.

Jimmie smiled kindly. "No, ma'am, he wears them day and night, but he gets a new set when they're worn down too much."[56]

"Is he always so docile?" a third woman asked.

Jimmie lifted his chin toward the stall where Greyhound now dozed, resting his head against the webbing across the door. "That's just the way he is all the time. He's the nicest horse to handle. Never gives anyone a bit of trouble."[57]

"Does he eat grass?" a young boy asked.

Jimmie crouched down to the youngster's level. "Yes, he does. I take him for a long walk in the evening and he eats grass then."[58]

"Can he have this?" The boy held up his hand, a sugar cube resting on his upturned palm. "I mean, after he eats his dinner, of course," the boy added quickly. The people crowding around the stall chuckled.

"He sure can." Jimmie took the treat and tucked it in his shirt pocket. "Thank you."[59]

"Do you think he'll beat his own record?" The question came from a man in a dark fedora near the back of the crowd.

Jimmie found the man's face and met his eyes. His own, an intense blue, seemed to brighten when he said, "Yes, sir, I believe he will. And soon."[60]

The questions continued as Jimmie went about his work. Greyhound dove into his feed tub when Jimmie filled it, slurping his mash with enthusiasm. Back in the city, the talk continued. How fast could Greyhound go? It wouldn't be long before the great Grey Ghost answered that question in a way no one lucky enough to be there and witness would ever forget.

End of Chapter 19

GREYHOUND

THE REMARKABLE STORY OF THE LEGENDARY RACEHORSE WHO INSPIRED A NATION

JULY 8, 1938, *THE CHRONICLE TRIBUNE*

CHAPTER
— 20 —

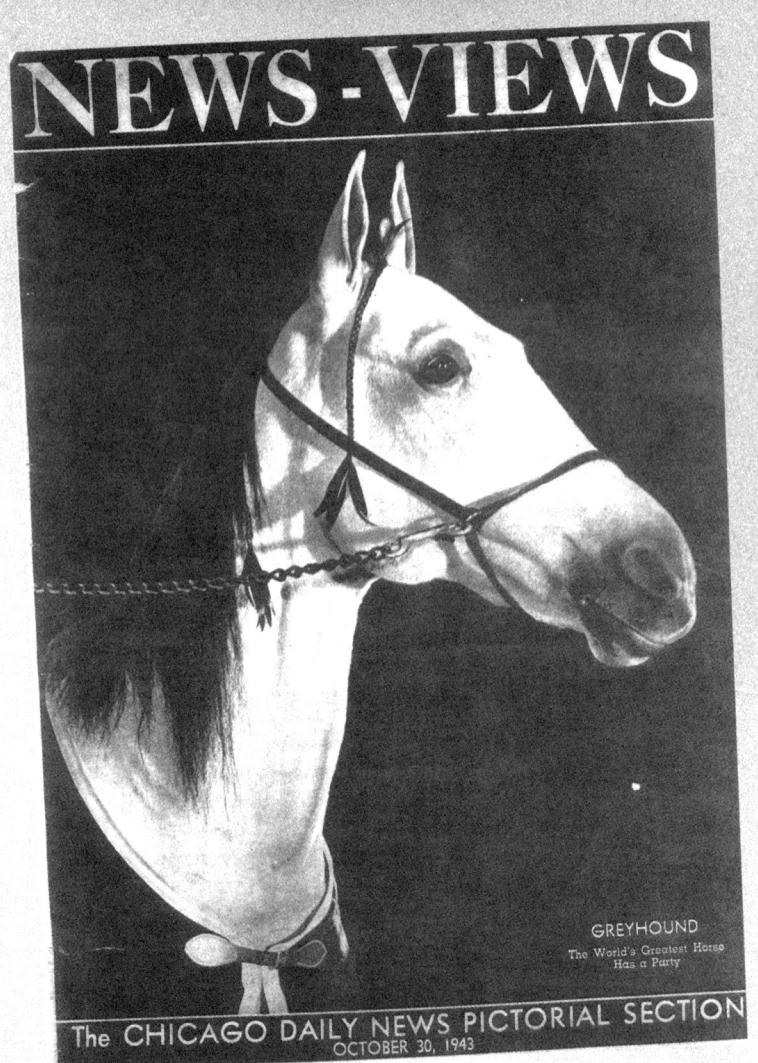

> *"Old-timers talk in fond and wistful ways
> about the fall of 1938, when Greyhound forged a trotting legend
> in the dusk of one September afternoon."*
>
> —
>
> MARYJEAN WALL,
> *LEXINGTON HERALD-LEADER,* SEPTEMBER 27, 1988

LEGEND

Clouds rolled in, winds kicked up, and the temperature began a rapid decline.[1] Palin stood at the rail near the gap, leaning against the great cement gatepost. His wise blue eyes watched Greyhound warm up between heats, gauging the conditions of the track and the weather. The Transylvania stake, the feature race on the Lexington program for September 29, 1938, had been fiercely contested that day, having required four tough heats to determine a winner. It was now approaching 5:00, the sun casting long shadows over the red dirt oval. The temperature had plummeted to the low 50s as the sun departed.* Palin notified the judges he would take Greyhound for an exhibition mile after the final heat. In these conditions, a time trial simply didn't make sense.

---

* In Lexington, Kentucky, September 29, 1938, sunset was at 5:20. It is currently at 7:20, which caused the author some confusion over the idea that dusk would have come two hours earlier on the day in question than on the same date in 2023. Two things account for this discrepancy. The first is that in 1938, all of Kentucky was in the central time zone; and the second is that in 1938, daylight savings time ended earlier in the season, and by September 29, the clocks had already "fallen back."

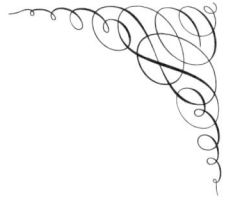

The flags snapped in the wind, and a general feeling of disappointment lingered among the race fans who'd hoped to see a record set that day. But at least they would see the great champion in action. After the final heat of the Transylvania, Jimmie drove Greyhound onto the track and steered him over to where Palin stood. The two men spoke briefly. Palin looked at the sky once more, then walked across the track to notify the judges.[2] Despite the less-than-perfect conditions, Greyhound would go for the record.

Jimmie exited the sulky and Palin took his place. The temperature now hung at fifty-four degrees, colder than is considered ideal for a record attempt.[*] Intermittent clouds chased shadows into the corners on the far side of the track. The sun slipped behind the barns, and dusk settled over the red mile. To go for a record now would be a herculean effort, the horsemen said to one another.[3]

"Drivers, prominent owners, and others hovered about the judges' stand. Others crossed the track to observe from beneath the timer's stand," *Hoof Beats* later reported.[4] They pulled their overcoats around them to block the blustery wind.[5] The high humidity and wind made the temperature feel much colder than the thermometer read—in such conditions, the wind penetrated the body and settled into the bones.

Palin scored Greyhound twice at a moderate pace, then took him down a third time for a longer score.[6] The gelding's great stride lengthened as he approached the starter. Palin nodded, and received the word. The time trial was on!

Greyhound trotted the first quarter in :29 ½, a 1:58 rate, two seconds slower than his current record. Disappointment wafted through many of the onlookers, and some wondered if Palin had made a mistake going against time on an evening such as this. But those in the know murmured, "He's rating alright."[7] The gray trotted to the back stretch, now facing into the wind. The infield flags snapped wildly in the breeze, and dark shadows deepened as the sun dropped below the horizon. Greyhound trotted along the back stretch, his flying gray legs invisible in the dusk and dust. With his effortlessly smooth stride and his ghostly white coat, he appeared as an apparition floating among the shadows. Observers strained their eyes to see him from across the infield in the dimming light. Were it not for his coat, they might not have seen him at all.

---

* There was a strong belief in Greyhound's era that the trotting horse's muscles must stay hot, as during intense work, in order to function at peak performance. During breaks between heats, horses were kept covered and stood in stalls, even while breathing heavily and in warm temperatures, ensuring they were kept out of the wind or a draft. It is likely this way of thinking contributed to the belief that cooler temperatures would negatively impact performance. We now know horses physiologically function better in cooler temperatures, although the sudden temperature drop and blustery wind were less than ideal.

Greyhound trotted the half in :58 ¼, and cheers sounded from the crowd as they realized he had a chance.[8] Roscoe Carlock brought the galloping prompter up to Palin's wheel,[9] nudging the champion's will to win. The gray trotted into the third quarter, where most horses would need a breather—but not Greyhound. He kept up his fight, hooves pounding out a drumbeat of warning to Father Time.

Greyhound sailed through the final turn and into the home stretch. The crowd tore their eyes from the flying gray horse to glance at the time: a staggering 1:26 ½. The fastest three-quarters ever trotted![10] The crowd cheered, sensing a record in the making. Greyhound entered the home stretch straight and true. Palin lifted the lines and leaned forward behind the powerful gray hindquarters, asking his silver-skinned flyer for one final drive.

Greyhound pounded the red clay, trotting into a stout wind.[11] The crowd fell silent, holding their collective breath as the battle intensified. Greyhound propelled himself down the stretch. A low hum rippled through the crowd, their voices ever rising. "Go, go, GO!" they shouted. Not leg-weary as any other horse would have been, the gallant gray trotted full-flight down to the wire, each powerful stride as strong and long as the one before it. He devoured the track one magnificent stroke after another, then flashed under the wire, pulling the roar of the crowd along in his wake.

Palin slowed Greyhound gradually, then turned and jogged the big gelding back to the grandstand. The people bounced on their feet, giving the great horse an ovation with such enthusiasm and passion that no one could recall another so intensely jubilant. Even if Greyhound hadn't beaten his record, they knew they had seen something magnificent—for many, the likes of which would not be seen again in their lifetime.

Anxious eyes shifted between the horse and the blank space on the board where the final time would appear. Palin paraded Greyhound before the grandstand. There, the ovation intensified. "The like and ardor of which has not been seen in modern time," *The Harness Horse* would later report.

One number at a time, the clocker hung the plates to reveal the answer to the question on everyone's mind. Had he done it? The last number fell into place.

For a moment, stunned silence. Then, with whoops and hollers, the crowd surged out onto the track. They cheered, yelled, shook hands, slapped backs, tossed hats, and crowded around the horse and driver.[12] The cool weather, the wind, the darkness, the slight incline of the track coming into the final turn—Greyhound had overcome every handicap the day had imposed upon him. Camera shutters snapped, admiration ran rampant, and the number tiles clinked softly in the wind—1:55 ¼, the fastest mile trotted by any horse, ever.

"Men forgot the time, forgot dinner dates, forgot everything except the fact they had just witnessed the greatest mile of all time. There in the falling darkness they stood reverently before a horse such as none ever expected to see. They were loath to leave him lest the morrow reveal it had all been but a pleasant dream,"[13] wrote P.W. Moser in 1940.

Hundreds followed Greyhound back to his stall. Souvenir hunters asked for shoes, locks of hair, and anything else that was part of or used by the great champion. Greyhound stood and watched his admirers. Head held high, ears pricked forward, eyes liquid and dark, the great horse absorbed his admiration as if he knew he deserved it. And, of course, he did.

"Greyhound looked up and saw the camera," reporter W.F. Fox, Jr. wrote. "Then his ears shot up like two soldiers coming to attention and he didn't even blink his eyes when the flashbulb went off."[14] Greyhound absorbed every ounce of adulation. He posed triumphantly, he bowed gracefully, he drew laughter from the crowd when he curled his upper lip and made silly faces.

Palin signed autographs, and Jimmie fielded questions from fans and reporters. Greyhound grabbed the iron lock on his door with his teeth and shook it.[16]

"Hey, now, that's enough of that." Jimmie spoke softly and stroked Greyhound's silky neck. The crowd chuckled at the horse's antics. "We have to put a lock on the door." Jimmie smiled, his eyes still on Greyhound. "He knows how to open it!" Greyhound snorted loudly and nudged Jimmie's shoulder.

Notably absent from reports that day was Colonel Baker. It is likely he missed the time trial, assuming Palin would not try to lower Greyhound's record on such a day. He attended the sale at the famed Walnut Hall Farm north of Lexington that evening,[17] and probably was there viewing yearlings when his great champion made his record. A decade later, the following quote from Baker appeared in the notes of famed sports historian, author, and reporter Frank G. Menke:

"The time of 1:55 ¼, which gave Greyhound a new world's record for the trotter, was most gratifying," said Baker. "But I've always regretted the gale that blew on that afternoon. If it hadn't been for that, I feel Greyhound would have trotted much faster than 1:55."[18]

It is highly likely Baker's assessment would've proven accurate. Just the day before, on a warm, sunny afternoon without a whisper of wind, the pacer Billy Direct had made a mile in 1:55 flat, lowering the 1905 record of the great Dan Patch. At the three-quarter mark, Greyhound was almost one second faster than Billy Direct's time[19]—an impressive feat, given the conditions and the fact that the pace is naturally a faster gait than the trot. Trotting the last quarter into a strong headwind cost Greyhound precious time.

Palin made an unpublicized attempt a few days later, and Greyhound again matched his incredible time.[20] But the stars did not align as they had on that foreboding, spectral day when Greyhound cemented his legend forever in time as the greatest trotter that ever lived. Veteran horsemen unanimously proclaimed Greyhound's mile in 1:55 ¼ to be the greatest feat of all time.[21] He had not only out-trotted Father Time, he'd done so in incredibly unfavorable conditions and after taking four warm-up miles! Truly, there was not a horse alive that could get close enough to nibble his saddlecloth, let alone put a nose in front of the great Greyhound before the finish line.

"But this I will warrant you," John Hervey would later tell a young fan about that glorious September day. "Namely, that [if you saw him in action] he would take your breath away and you would never, to your dying day, forget him."[22]

The sentiment expressed by Hervey would be echoed by others many times over. The record itself would outlive the horse, Colonel Baker, Sep Palin, and many of the people there that day. Man would set foot upon the moon before another horse trotted faster than Greyhound did on that blustery September day in 1938. The legend, however, would reign for all time.

END of CHAPTER 20

CHAPTER
— 21 —

GREYHOUND
..and the..
HOUGHTON

—*Greyhound Special Sulky,*
"Cushioned in Rubber"—

LEADS THE FIELD

The World's Champion Trotter,
hitched to the World's Champion
Sulky outclasses all horses,
past or present.

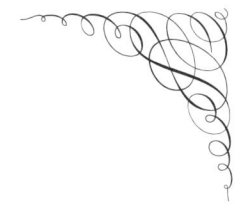

*"He needs do nothing more
to make himself supreme among the turf's immortals."*

—

JOHN HERVEY,
SEPTEMBER 1939

NOTHING LEFT TO PROVE

Baker arrived at the barn to the sound of nickers. Following close behind was a dog, a real racing greyhound named Trego. Baker had acquired Trego in 1936 from a dog track near where the Baker-Palin stable wintered in Longwood, Florida.[1] The dog supposedly held a racing record in New York state.[2] Whether he traveled with the racing stable or with Baker himself is unclear, though he and the Dalmatian, Goshen, had been mentioned separately in newspaper articles.

Baker walked down the hard-packed clay aisle at a leisurely pace, his cane tapping the ground every few steps, more of an accessory than a mobility device.[3] The man paused and greeted each soul he met, be it horse, human, dog, or cat—all received a measure of his time.

"He really loves horses. He comes into the stables and the horses make more of him than they ever do of me," Palin once told a reporter, smiling and shaking his head. "And he knows every groom by first name. Darned if I do."[4] Baker continued down the aisle, patting his horses and offering each a carrot. When he got to Greyhound, the big gelding's eyes softened and he gently nuzzled his friend. Baker offered him a carrot and Greyhound took it carefully, the admiration in the man's eyes clearly mirrored in those of the horse.

Just across the way from Greyhound's stall in Florida stood the grand mare, Rosalind, star of the White stable.⁵ The classy mare had set her own world record at Lexington the previous fall, 1:56 ¾, matching Peter Manning's former world record—a grand accomplishment somewhat dulled by the misfortune of racing in the same era as the great Greyhound. Still, it was a world record for trotting mares, and one that would stand for thirty-six years.

Rosalind was the only horse that had given Greyhound even a measure of competition in 1938—both had far outclassed the few horses with owners brave enough to race against the King and Queen of the trotting turf. But the races set up the previous year as all-age trots with hefty purses to encourage the two stars to compete had been changed back to four-year-old events, and the purses available to older horses were worth thousands less than the year before.⁶ Rosalind essentially was in the same position as Greyhound—nothing left to conquer, nothing left to prove. As of March 1939, neither Rosalind or Greyhound were training for speed.⁷ Instead, they took relaxed jogs on the sun-soaked Florida training track, leaving the press and the fans to guess what their plans were for the upcoming season.

Greyhound went into 1939 in perfect health— "in the pink" and a "good doer," Jimmie Wingfield told reporter Gene Mack. A "good doer" is one that eats well, with enthusiasm, and holds his weight and condition easily, Jimmie explained. "He's just as keen for his workouts as he is for his meals," the young man said with obvious pride.⁸

"Today, after five years of campaigning and a series of extreme miles, in and out of races, dwarfing everything previously known," John Hervey wrote of Greyhound in *The Harness Horse,* "he is not only absolutely sound, but with limbs so smooth, clean, and sinewy in their form and texture [it is] as if he had never seen a race track."⁹

While at Longwood, Palin announced he believed Greyhound had never truly been extended.¹⁰ The world had yet to see how fast the grand horse could go without the inevitable slowing of speed the turns on a track require. Palin felt the firm-packed sand and lack of turns at Daytona Beach would be ideal for a fast, long-striding horse like Greyhound. The reinsman speculated the champion might even make a mile in 1:50.¹¹ If the footing was to his liking, Palin planned to set a trotting record for the mile straightaway. As yet, no such record existed.

Palin took Greyhound to Daytona for some schooling on the beach. At this point, the story takes two different directions. The accounts from days or even years later reported that the gelding wanted no part of it, shying away from the waves as they crashed onto the beach.¹² Palin tried over several days to acclimate the horse to the new environment, but the veteran reinsman, ever mindful of the mental state of his horses, ultimately didn't feel it was worth stressing the champion by pushing him. Conversely, Jimmie Wingfield told trainer-driver Delvin Miller many years later that the weather was to blame for why the record attempt was never made.[13] It is possible both are true, as Palin was reported to have said early in 1939 he would try again after the Grand Circuit season.[14] This never happened—perhaps due to the weather, as Wingfield had recalled. Regardless of the reason, the idea was shelved and never returned to. As a result, the world would never know how fast the grand horse could really trot, limited as he was by the turns on the tracks of the day.

"Greyhound, the world's greatest trotting horse and holder of no less than fifteen all-time world marks ... is in search of new worlds to conquer," *The Noblesville Ledger* proclaimed in an article announcing that Greyhound had returned to Indianapolis from Florida.[15] Around the training track, signs of spring emerged from a winter slumber. Tender young shoots of green grass wafted in warm spring breezes, delicate buds sprung from wandering branches, and spring flowers broke the surface of earth in a state of renewal.

Jimmie jogged Greyhound around the track, watching him closely. Now seven years old, the horse had turned nearly white, with just traces of gray remaining on his legs and shading his haunches. His mane had lightened from near black to a dark gray. Jimmie felt great pride in how well he looked, regal and sure of himself. Greyhound stood nearly 16.2 hands, a full hand higher than the average Standardbred, and weighed 1,080 pounds. The "Grey Ghost" moniker came into more frequent use by the press, as the ever-whitening horse looked more ghost-like with each passing year. But he'd always be Greyhound to Jimmie.

The soft whir of sulky wheels and the tempo of trotting hooves combined to make the music Jimmie loved. The big horse's powerful hindquarters propelled them along, the rhythm hypnotic in the warmth of the afternoon sun. A couple horses jogged past the duo at a faster clip. Greyhound lifted his head, ears pricked forward. He asked for more rein.

"Not yet." Jimmie's words were barely audible, but the big gray softened his tensed body at the young man's gentle touch on the lines. Jimmie smiled to himself at the memory of a news clipping his mother had sent to him. It was a long article. He'd spoken at length with the reporter, Walt Bogart, and talked about everything from his early experiences working for Russell Sanders to Greyhound's world records, to the way the horse's "personality, intelligence, and feeling [were] almost human."[16] The young man felt most fortunate. He loved his work with the horses and he was good at it. Every year, Sep gave him more responsibility. He couldn't be happier; he had a great job, a great horse to look after, and he loved picking up and moving from track to track.[17]

The April 19 issue of *Rider and Driver* had announced that Greyhound and Billy Direct would compete in a match race.[18] *I bet that's news to Mr. Baker and Sep.* Jimmie crinkled his face at the thought. Pacers are supposed to be faster than trotters. But throughout his career, Greyhound had disregarded such "rules." In Lexington the previous fall, he matched the world-record pacing mark set by Dan Patch way back in 1905—a feat few thought would ever be accomplished by a pacer, let alone a trotter. Then along came Billy Direct, and he shaved a quarter off Dan's record. But everyone knew trotters and pacers didn't compete; they were too different. The pacing gait was by nature faster than the trot, and therefore had no relevance in comparison.

The young man shook his head. A match race would never happen; but if it did, he was certain Greyhound would win. He had more heart. Billy Direct had made his record on a perfect weather day without a breath of wind, but Greyhound had made his on a blustery day at dusk. All the horsemen who'd been there that day agreed that Greyhound's record was the greater effort. Another horse jogged by. Greyhound shook his head and tugged at the bit. Jimmie touched the lines, his movement imperceptible but the results obvious as the big gray settled.

"Not yet," he said. The time for speed would come soon enough.[19]

GREYHOUND

THE REMARKABLE STORY
OF THE LEGENDARY RACEHORSE WHO INSPIRED A NATION

gallery

[69]
Probably warming up in Old Orchard, Maine, before setting a track record of 1:57 ½.
• *likely July 27, 1939, courtesy of the Harness Racing Museum & Hall of Fame, Goshen, NY*

[70]
Jimmie leads Greyhound from the barn at Red Gate on Greyhound Day. The (dog) Greyhound is likely Trego; the Dalmatian may be Goshen or Fibber.
• *August 20, 1939, Hambletonian Society Collection, courtesy of the Harness Racing Museum & Hall of Fame, Goshen, NY*

GREYHOUND

THE REMARKABLE STORY
OF THE LEGENDARY RACEHORSE WHO INSPIRED A NATION

— *gallery* —

[71]
Greyhound and Rosalind lower the team to pole record to 1:58 ¼ at Indianapolis.
• *September 5, 1939, courtesy of the Harness Racing Museum & Hall of Fame, Goshen, NY*

[72]
Greyhound warming up before his record-setting exhibition mile in 1:57 ½ at Old Orchard.
• *July 27, 1939, Guy Kendall Collection, courtesy of the University of Maine*

GREYHOUND
THE REMARKABLE STORY
OF THE LEGENDARY RACEHORSE WHO INSPIRED A NATION
gallery

[73]
Greyhound scoring before his record mile at Old Orchard. Jimmie Wingfield is driving the runner.
• *July 27, 1939, Guy Kendall Collection, courtesy of the University of Maine*

[74]
Greyhound finishing his mile in 1:57 ½ at Old Orchard.
• *July 27, 1939, Guy Kendall Collection, courtesy of the University of Maine*

GREYHOUND

THE REMARKABLE STORY
OF THE LEGENDARY RACEHORSE WHO INSPIRED A NATION

gallery

[75]
Left to right: Col. Baker (owner), Henry Knight (breeder), Sep Palin (trainer-driver), and Jimmie Wingfield (groom) pose with Greyhound at Red Gate Farm on Greyhound Day.
• *August 20, 1939, courtesy of the St. Charles Historical Society*

[76]
Mr. and Mrs. Palin in a sleigh pulled by Greyhound in Indianapolis.
• *circa December 1939, courtesy of the United States Trotting Association*

GREYHOUND

THE REMARKABLE STORY
OF THE LEGENDARY RACEHORSE WHO INSPIRED A NATION

gallery

[86]
Jimmie rides Greyhound at Lexington, KY, preparing him for his mile record effort under saddle.
• *September 1940, courtesy of the Hambletonian Society*

[87]
Sep Palin works Greyhound at a winter training track—possibly Aiken, SC.
• *circa 1940, Hambletonian Society Collection, courtesy of the Harness Racing Museum & Hall of Fame, Goshen, NY*

GREYHOUND

THE REMARKABLE STORY
OF THE LEGENDARY RACEHORSE WHO INSPIRED A NATION

gallery

[88]
A portrait of Greyhound.
• *circa 1939, courtesy of the Harness Racing Museum & Hall of Fame, Goshen, NY*

[89]
One of the best-known photos of Jimmie and Greyhound.
• *circa 1939, Hambletonian Society Collection, courtesy of the Harness Racing Museum & Hall of Fame, Goshen, NY*

GREYHOUND

THE REMARKABLE STORY
OF THE LEGENDARY RACEHORSE WHO INSPIRED A NATION

gallery

[90]
Sep Palin and Greyhound.
• *circa 1940, courtesy of the Harness Racing Museum & Hall of Fame, Goshen, NY*

GREYHOUND

**THE REMARKABLE STORY
OF THE LEGENDARY RACEHORSE WHO INSPIRED A NATION**

gallery

[91]
Greyhound and Doc Flanery leading the post parade. An interesting note: an image nearly identical to this one (taken what must have been a couple seconds later) appears in P.W. Moser's 1939 book, but there's no known reason why Doc would have been driving Greyhound around that time.
• *circa 1940, courtesy of the United States Trotting Association; original photograph by P.W. Moser*

GREYHOUND

THE REMARKABLE STORY
OF THE LEGENDARY RACEHORSE WHO INSPIRED A NATION

— gallery —

[92]
Greyhound with an unidentified training mate.
• *circa 1939, courtesy of the United States Trotting Association*

[93]
Greyhound in double harness with a runner. Palin apparently thought about going for the world record, but did not make an official attempt. Lexington, KY.
• *September 1939, courtesy of the United States Trotting Association; original photograph by Walter Moore*

GREYHOUND

THE REMARKABLE STORY
OF THE LEGENDARY RACEHORSE WHO INSPIRED A NATION

gallery

[94]

Robert C. "Doc" Flanery at a show with roadster Senator Crawford, at the Southwestern Exposition and Fat Stock Show in Fort Worth, Texas.
• *March 15, 1937, courtesy of the Fort Worth Star-Telegram Collection, Special Collections, The University of Texas at Arlington Libraries*

[95]

Left to right: Doc Flanery, the president of the Western Rodeo and Horse Show Exposition, Colorado governor Ralph Carr, and Dooley Putnam (holding Greyhound) at the Mid-winter Stock Show in Denver, Colorado.
• *1941, Heitbrink Collection, courtesy of the Harness Racing Museum & Hall of Fame, Goshen, NY*

GREYHOUND

THE REMARKABLE STORY
OF THE LEGENDARY RACEHORSE WHO INSPIRED A NATION

gallery

[96]
Dooley, Doc, and Col. Baker stand with Greyhound as he greets his guests for Greyhound Day.
• October 17, 1943, Hartline Family Collection, courtesy of the Harness Racing Museum & Hall of Fame, Goshen, NY

[97]
Greyhound with Doc Flanery at Santa Anita in California.
• 1946, Heitbrink Collection, courtesy of the Harness Racing Museum & Hall of Fame, Goshen, NY

GREYHOUND

THE REMARKABLE STORY
OF THE LEGENDARY RACEHORSE WHO INSPIRED A NATION

gallery

[98]
Greyhound stands with Dooley outside the barn row at Santa Anita.
• 1946, Heitbrink Collection, courtesy of the Harness Racing Museum & Hall of Fame, Goshen, NY

[99]
Catalog for the Bakers Acres complete dispersal sale.
• 1947, Hartline Family Collection, courtesy of the Harness Racing Museum & Hall of Fame, Goshen, NY

[100]
Greyhound looks out his picture window.
• 1949, courtesy of the United States Trotting Association

GREYHOUND

THE REMARKABLE STORY OF THE LEGENDARY RACEHORSE WHO INSPIRED A NATION

CIRCA 1940, COURTESY OF THE
HAMBLETONIAN SOCIETY

CHAPTER 22

Dick Case
c/o Hoof Beats
Goshen, N. Y.

Aug. 20

Stall Number One
Hotel Baker Stables
St. Charles, Ill.

Just thought I'd drop you a line about my homecoming here at St. Charles. You see I've never been "home" since E. J. bought me and what a grand place Red Gate Farm is, all painted up and grass green as Sep's coat. In the van with me coming from Springfield was Rosalind and Her Ladyship; my what fast company!

Saturday night my Houseman Jimmie Wingfield went to the hotel for the dinner E. J. was throwing the horsemen. When he came back -- I don't say what hour -- he said he'd had a couple Manhattans and seen a great floor show. Among those he mentioned as being present besides The Boss, were Mr. and Mrs. Sep Palin, Pa and Ma Bowser, Mr. and Mrs. Henry Warwick, Mr. and Mrs. Jay Douglass, Mr. and Mrs. Spec Erskine, Frankie Foster, J. J. McIntyre, some local friends and teamsters: White, Parshall, Mahoney, Berry, and Recor.

Then on Sunday I paraded around the driveway circle before some 1,500 enthusiastic spectators that included Dick McMahon of Calumet Butler fame, and my breeder Henry Knight. Then they showed Rosalind, Her Ladyship, Chief Counsel, Peter Astra, Cardinal Prince, Winnipeg, and Labrador. What an array! I'd hate to tackle that field when they were all in their prime.

It's been a great day for me, but I have to go to Milwaukee to tackle Una Signal's 1.59 3/4 track record. (See photo)

GREYHOUND

> "Greyhound accomplishes results not only
> of an unexpected nature, but in such a decisive manner
> and with such evident ease as to cause one and all to marvel at his capacity."
> "He is the horse which never disappoints."
>
> —
>
> THE HARNESS HORSE,
> DEC. 13 AND AUG. 2, 1939

GREYHOUND THE INCOMPARABLE

The track at Old Orchard Beach, Maine, dubbed July 27, 1939, "Greyhound Day." The title would be used by almost every track the grand horse visited. There were races on the card, but none were for Greyhound. Palin planned only an exhibition mile for the horse's admiring fans. The biggest draw and the center of attention wherever he appeared, Greyhound seemed to know his standing as king of all he surveyed. He stepped lightly onto the track at the top of the stretch. Applause greeted him as he jogged past the grandstand. His bearing royal, his gait fluid and free, Greyhound turned his head toward the crowd and seemed to give a nod of appreciation to his public.

Palin took Greyhound through a few warm-up laps while the announcer introduced him as the 1935 Hambletonian winner and listed his other accomplishments.[1] Greyhound's glorious strides were smooth and effortless, his front legs rolling along, almost floating, in contrast to the piston-like action of his powerful hindquarters. Jimmie, wearing Palin's green colors, brought the prompter onto the track. He jogged him over to wait at the top of the stretch. With a stiff wind blowing into the home stretch, no one expected a record that day, but Jimmie would have the prompter ready anyway.[2]

Palin scored down a few times, then gave a nod, and they were off. Greyhound trotted fluidly around the track. His steps effortless, Palin sitting quietly in the sulky, Greyhound brushed through the first half in an easy fifty-nine seconds. He burst into the home stretch and marched "as though propelled by steam, electric power, or some force other than muscular energy," *The Harness Horse* would later report. Jimmie brought the prompter up to Greyhound's sulky wheel for the last quarter, but it wasn't necessary.[3] Greyhound was in his own world of speed. With no prompting from Palin, the great horse finished his mile in 1:57 ½—the fastest mile ever witnessed on any New England track. He'd trotted the mile under mild restraint, lowering his own track record by three-and-a-half seconds and trotting the fastest mile of any horse so far that season.[4] He also beat the track's fastest pacing mile (1:58 ¾), which was set by his now-retired stablemate Cardinal Prince.[5]

"With a long and powerful stride, and yet with motion so frictionless, that it was difficult to believe the speed at which he was moving," reporter Austin Goodwin later wrote.[6] Many horsemen watching felt he could have taken down his own world mark if Palin had just given him his head. But that was not Palin's style. He was easy, calm, not one to rush anything—particularly a great horse. The time for breaking more records would come soon enough.

Following the mile record, Palin was interviewed by a radio commentator. A man known to be of few words, modest and restrained, Palin answered in monosyllables, punctuated with his dry sense of humor.

"You've trained Greyhound for six years, ever since he was a colt..." The radio commentator attempted to lead Sep with an open-ended pause.

"Yes."

"To what do you attribute your success in training racehorses?" the commentator asked.

Palin looked the man dead in the eye, and, without cracking a smile, he replied, "First, you have to have a horse."[7]

Toward the end of August 1939, a letter arrived at the offices of *Hoof Beats* magazine. Addressed to the editor, Dick Case, the letter was penned by Greyhound himself. Or so it would appear. The actual author of the letter is information lost to time. In his letter, Greyhound told of a grand party Colonel Baker had held in his honor at Red Gate Farm in St. Charles, Illinois. Attended by 1,500 people, guests enjoyed a catered luncheon, drinks, live music, and a special parade of champion harness racers. The equine guest list included Rosalind, 1939 Hambletonian winner Peter Astra, and several others, including Baker's champion pacers Her Ladyship, Cardinal Prince, and Winnipeg. Also in attendance, along with Greyhound's human "staff," was his breeder,

Henry Knight. The guests were a mix of famous names in the harness racing scene and residents of St. Charles.[8]

There is color film (silent) of this party, and it is truly a spectacle to see. Baker, Wingfield, Palin, and Knight are all there. The men wore suits, and the women, dresses. The film shows the parade of famous horses, the band, and a man who appears to be giving a speech. Red Gate Farm is beautifully landscaped in the film, with colorful flower beds, white fences, and picturesque barns. Even the greyhound, Trego, and a Dalmatian (probably Goshen or Fibber) make an appearance, both following Jimmie and Greyhound during the parade.

"At all times pleasant and courteous, interested in the success and general welfare of all he meets and always ready to respond liberally to any movement which has the best interest of our sport as its object," reported *The Harness Horse* about Baker, December 16, 1936.[9] The parties would continue annually for many years, as much a gift to the residents of Baker's beloved town as a celebration of his champion trotter and a boon for his favorite sport.

The next Greyhound Day was August 23 at Milwaukee, Wisconsin. Thirteen thousand fans turned out to see the great gray trot a mile in 1:58, without urging from Palin, clipping nearly two seconds off the track record.[10] Greyhound made sub-two-minute miles look easy, to the point where the shiny newness of such spectacular speed dulled in the face of the frequency and ease with which Greyhound trotted them.

A week later, Greyhound was in Syracuse, New York. Rosalind was also there, fresh off her win in the FFA trot in Wisconsin.[11] At Syracuse, White and Palin hatched a plan, one that would thrill the crowds, boost the sport, and potentially add both Greyhound's and Rosalind's names to a new line in the record book. Everyone knew they were the fastest trotters in the world, and they knew how fast each could go separately. But how fast could they go together? At Syracuse, the world would find out. Palin and White announced Greyhound and Rosalind would be hitched together for a "team to pole" race against time. The existing world record had been set in 1912 when Uhlan and Lewis Forrest set the mile mark at 2:03 ¼.

Neither horse had been hitched to another before, but each took to it well, both being good and quiet-minded. On August 31, 1939, the day dawned warm and clear. By late afternoon, conditions seemed right for a race against time. Each horse was warmed up individually, and then the pair were hitched to a specialized "pole cart" that featured a long pole that went between the two horses and attached to a cross bar. Each end of this cross bar was hooked to the front of a yoke at the chest on either horse. The sky was overcast and the evening hour drawing near when the two were hitched and Palin took the lines, ready for the world-record attempt.[12]

Before the pair stepped on the track, the judge requested that the crowd hold their applause until the end, as there was some concern Greyhound might get excited and "act up."[13] The crowd did not heed this warning, applauding with enthusiasm when the two great trotters appeared. However, Greyhound and Rosalind were both calm and "working like a docile old farm team," according to the report in *Hoof Beats*. Palin scored the team a few times with ease. On the next score, he gave the nod and the pair were off![14]

Greyhound and Rosalind trotted as one. They went the first quarter in a worrisome :31 ½, much too slow if there were to be any record smashing that day. The crowd needn't have feared, though. Palin had only taken the first turn slowly out of an abundance of caution, allowing himself and the horses to get a feel for the task at hand.[15] Once out of the turn, Palin sent the pair on and they flew down the back stretch, gaining speed with every stride. They made the half in 1:01. If they could maintain that speed, Greyhound and Rosalind would easily beat the world record.

The crowd rose to their feet, afraid to speak a word, breathless as they waited for the third quarter time to be posted. The numbers went up and the crowd audibly breathed their relief. Greyhound and Rosalind had passed the three-quarter pole well ahead of the world record.

"C'mon, yeah! C'mon!" Palin urged the two champions down the home stretch. The pair moved as one, eye-to-eye, breath-for-breath, stride-for-stride, down to the finish. Greyhound and Rosalind flew under the wire in perfect sync, a beautiful tapestry of bay and gray. All eyes turned to the judges' stand. The clockers compared their watches, the time was posted, and the crowd burst into applause and cheering. They'd gone the mile in 1:59 flat, smashing the twenty-seven-year-old record by more than four seconds![16]

"Those fortunate enough to be present," John Hervey later wrote, "had witnessed a demonstration that marks a milestone in the history of harness speed, and will for all time." Hervey, who had been there when Uhlan and Lewis Forrest set their record twenty-seven years before, had not believed he'd see the day a team broke the two-minute barrier.[17]

Five days later at Indianapolis, Greyhound and Rosalind again went against time as one. The fair board offered Palin $2,000 if he staged an attempt to lower the record at the Indiana state fairgrounds, with a $500 bonus if they succeeded.[18] The horses scored down just twice before Palin gave the nod and the trotting duo pulled away at the start.

Palin again approached the first turn with caution, though they made the quarter pole a bit more quickly than the week before. The team lengthened out of the turn, moving as a single horse, flying down the back stretch. Their hooves beat in rhythm; glints of golden sun shone off the spokes of the wheeled sulky. Palin's green satin jacket puffed out in the rush of air created by the magnificent pair. They rounded the final turn and trotted into a stiff breeze.

"But mere breezes cannot hinder when American trotting marvels are trying," George

M. Gahagan wrote for his column the next day. Despite the wind, Greyhound and Rosalind came through the stretch with increasing speed, pounding toward the finish. Palin waved the whip over their backs but did not strike the horses.[19] The bay and the gray darted under the wire as one magnificent horse. The crowd did not wait for the time to be hung; they broke into wild applause as the pair trotted by, some also yelling the name of Palin, their hometown hero.

The cheers rose in intensity when the official time was posted. The pair had lowered their own record by nearly one second, trotting the mile in 1:58 ¼. In the crowd that day at Indianapolis, Verner "Dooley" Putnam watched the two greatest trotters of all time make history.[20] He felt enormously lucky to have witnessed such a scene and held the memory close in his heart, recalling it with fondness and retelling it with awe. Many decades later, he would tell the story one last time, recorded on tape by his daughter Emma Lou, his love for Greyhound evident as his voice wavered with emotion. Choking back tears, Dooley recalled the moment so many years before, once again expressing the deep gratitude that he and so many others felt for being a part of the momentous day.[21]

Greyhound and Rosalind's team-to-pole record still stands today. A failed attempt to break it was made in 1962 by a pair of fillies, Impish and Sprite Rodney. There was talk of another attempt with a pair of colts around 1980, but it never panned out. More than a century before, racing a team in harness was common, though reserved only for the highly skilled driver. In Greyhound's era, such a thing was seldom seen, though many older fans and horsemen had fond memories of such events from their youth. By the turn of the last century, racing team-to-pole was unheard of. And perhaps that is as it should be—that the king and queen of trotting are forever immortalized in this way, as the first pair to trot a sub-two-minute mile, and the fastest pair of all time.

After her mile record with Greyhound, Rosalind made one final exhibition trot at York. It would be her last appearance in harness before she was retired to the broodmare band at Hanover Shoe Farm in Pennsylvania. Crowds gathered to watch the great mare trot a mile around the track, her powerful legs flying, her mane a whipping sail, her tail like that of an inky black comet. The lovely bay mare stepped lightly around the track, and into the history books—the greatest trotting mare of all time.

Greyhound's final exhibition of 1939 was a race against time for the world record for trotting two miles. On September 19 at Indianapolis, he shaved over four seconds off the record, trotting two miles in 4:06 flat.[22] The previous record had been set by Peter Manning in 1925.

One could no longer make a reasonable comparison between Greyhound and any horse of any era. Greyhound had lowered a world record every season he competed. He had trotted more sub-two-minute miles than any horse in history. In a single season he had trotted three sub-two-minute exhibition miles with ease, two team-to-pole world record miles with Rosalind, and broke the 14-year-old two-mile trotting world record. And once again he'd recorded the fastest trotting mile of the season, going 1:57 ½ at Old Orchard in his first outing of the year, in sub-par conditions. Greyhound had done everything asked of him and he'd done it easily. There were truly no worlds left to conquer.

At the close of the 1939 season, Baker and Palin announced that Greyhound would race no more. He would stay with Palin's string and return in 1940 to do exhibition miles for the fans and possibly a few miles against the clock, but not against competition.[23] There simply were no races left for the likes of Greyhound. But if you listened just right, the words from a December 1939 issue of *The Harness Horse* rang cryptic, and perhaps, fans might allow themselves to believe, even prophetic:

"Just when you think there is nothing left to conquer, he does the impossible."[24]

Winter cloaked the Grand Circuit tracks in icy darkness. Those in the harness racing world wondered if they would ever again see a horse as magnificent as Greyhound. The trotting fans weren't ready to let their great champion go. Not yet. He owed them nothing, but still they dared to ask ... what more could he do? Fans newer to the sport could not appreciate the magnitude of Greyhound's accomplishments. New, younger stars had emerged on the scene. Some dared to wonder if one of them might be able to defeat an aged Greyhound. One can easily imagine the conversations that likely took place among the young and the old:

"Of course not," one man said to another. He adjusted himself on the bar stool to face the stranger next to him.

"Yeah, maybe. But what about that Peter Astra?"

The first man waved a hand in the air dismissively. "Peter Astra hasn't come close to Greyhound's record."

"Maybe not," the other man said, "but Peter Astra was undefeated in nine starts this year. Not a single race lost, his three-year-old season. Just like Greyhound."

"What about Nibble Hanover?" a third man joined in. "He was the top two-year-old, ever. Better than Greyhound at that age!" The man waved his arms, becoming more animated as he continued. "We haven't come close to seeing how good that horse is!"

"Baloney." The first man scoffed. "I bet you think Clever Hanover or Dale Hanover can take Greyhound's measure, too? Nibble Hanover didn't even race last year, he was too *lame*."

Such conversations undoubtedly replayed all over the country that winter of 1939-40.[25] True, some outstanding youngsters had come on the scene in recent years. At the top of the list was the stellar three-year-old Peter Astra, winner of the 1939 Hambletonian. The top four horses of 1939 were Greyhound, Billy Direct (a pacer), Dean Hanover, and Peter Astra.[26] Going into 1940, only two of those remained in training—Peter Astra and Greyhound. In loud drunken discords and hushed hopeful whispers the people wondered: could Greyhound, at eight years old, out-trot the likes of Peter Astra, four years his junior? Did they dare to ask? Did they truly want to know how their great Grey Ghost compared to the next generation?

END of

CHAPTER 22

CHAPTER
— 23 —

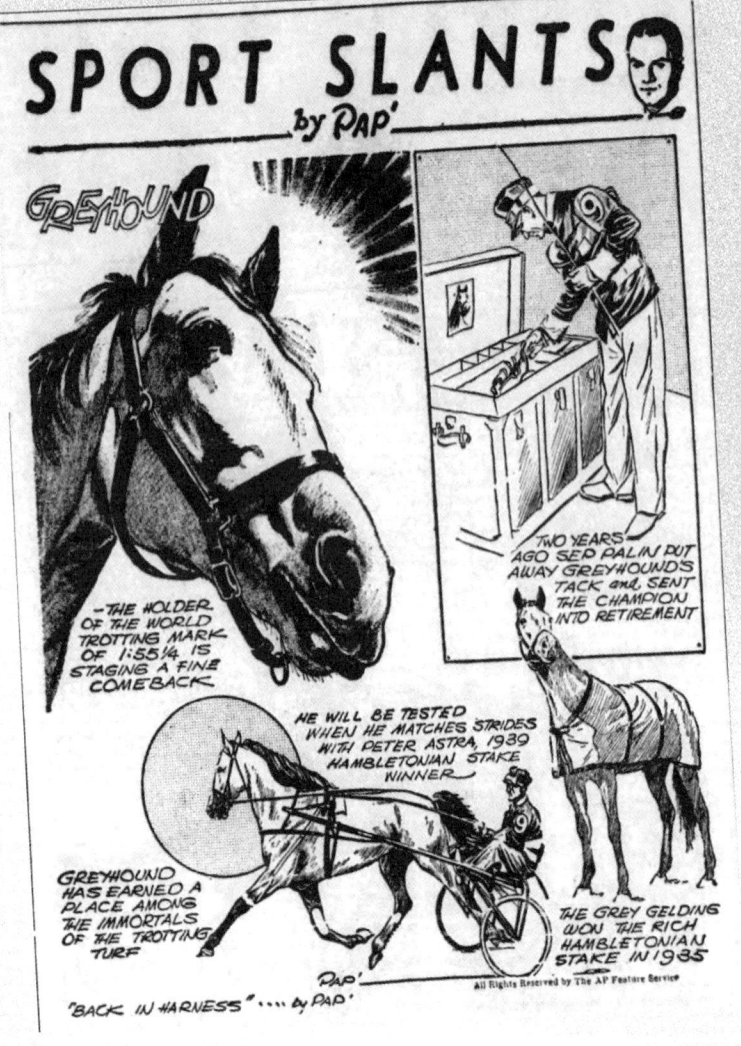

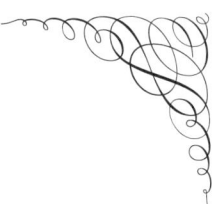

*"They say that youth must be served in sports circles,
and that most comebacks of aged champions end in disaster."*
—
THE MORNING CALL, AUGUST 1940

THE COMEBACK

After a series of attractive races with decent purses were created by E. Roland Harriman's Trotting Horse Club* to lure the gelding out of retirement, Baker and Palin agreed to train Greyhound for another year of racing.[1] But they were adamant they would only do so if he stayed perfectly sound and healthy. They weren't about to risk the gallant horse for any amount of fame or money. As long as he stayed happy and comfortable, they would send the champ to meet any youngster whose owner thought his horse could match strides with the great Greyhound.

The sensational Peter Astra was the horse in the forefront of every conversation. In winning the 1939 Hambletonian, the colt had trounced a nice field in brilliant fashion. He was a son of Peter Volo, the same sire as Greyhound's contemporary rival of 1934-35, Lawrence Hanover. While the flashy bay stallion hadn't touched Greyhound's world record mark, his

---

* Harriman's contributions to the sport were substantial:
he sold the land that would become Good Time Park to Cane,
he oversaw operations at Goshen's Historic Track, and his leadership
was instrumental in creating the United States Trotting Association.
He even went so far as to financially subsidize tracks to keep them solvent
in lean years.[2]

best time being six seconds slower, Peter Astra looked to be in top form as a four-year-old. Now, coming into the 1940 season, he would be stronger, faster, and have more stamina. Four years Greyhound's junior, Peter Astra was trained by Doc Parshall, the top trainer for years running—many saw both as a steep advantage.

Jimmie jogged Greyhound around the Aiken Mile Track. The winter sun hung low, but the weather was warm and pleasant. He'd been at the new training facility in South Carolina for several weeks with twenty-one horses from the Baker-Palin stable.[3] Sep would arrive in a week or so, around the first of February, and start Greyhound's fast work.

"You really are turning into a ghost." Jimmie smiled. "White as a sheet." Aside from his mane and tail, the gelding barely had a speck of gray on him. Greyhound lifted his head, ears standing at attention. Jimmie followed the horse's gaze. A group of men had lined up along the rail. Jimmie nodded to the "railbirds" who'd come to watch the horses train. He understood their passion. There were lots of men on the track who felt the same way. The grooms spent nearly every waking moment with their charges. They knew every intricacy of the horse's mood and behavior. A smart trainer relied on a good groom, knowing he'd be the first to notice the moment something was off—they were the first line of communication with the horse and served a vital role.

On March 23, Greyhound trotted an exhibition mile for 2,500 fans at Aiken. The mile was staged after the Imperial Cup steeple chase. Still early in the season to go for speed; Palin didn't push Greyhound, going the first half in a slow 1:12 ½. Palin then let the big gray out a notch and Greyhound happily took the rein, making the second half in 1:02.[4] Palin felt good about the way Greyhound had trotted—eager and asking to go faster. The gelding was coming along just as he'd hoped. He'd be almost ready to race by the time the stable returned to Indianapolis on May 1.

Greyhound bloomed beautifully in the month prior to his first start of the season. The railbirds and horsemen at Indianapolis watched the nearly white gelding with great interest. Palin trained him carefully, bringing Greyhound into peak physical condition to coincide with the date of his first start. Many commented the grand horse looked better than ever, saying they'd never seen him in such "fine fettle."[5] On June 1, trotting turf writer Merrit Murphy reported Greyhound had worked a mile in 2:03, going the last half in one minute flat—the fastest reported workout of any horse so far that season.[6] Greyhound appeared primed and ready to meet his first field of younger challengers.

Doc Parshall had again been the top money-winning driver in 1939. His best horse, Peter Astra, had won the Hambletonian and gone undefeated in his three-year-old season. Logic dictated he would only get better. Early in June, Parshall was asked if he felt any horse could top Peter Astra. There were only two that could come close to matching his colt,

Parshall said—Spentell, a Parshall trained gelding who'd turned in the fastest racing mile in 1939, and Greyhound.[7]

The $4,000 American Trotting Club Trot at Indianapolis on June 22 was the first race to be contested of the 1940 Grand Circuit season. Five horses met Greyhound at the post for his first race against competition since 1938. The field was made up of Hambletonian contenders of 1936 and 1938, the fastest of which was Clever Hanover, who'd set his top time of 1:59 ½ the year before at the age of six. He was the only two-minute trotter (in competition) of 1939. Others in the field included Ed Lasater and Bagpiper. The latter had finished fourth in the 1939 Hambletonian, but was one of only two horses to take a heat from Peter Astra during his undefeated 1939 season. Dale Hanover and Sister Mary rounded out the field. Though the papers consistently announced Peter Astra as a starter, he did not come to the post.

This would be the first time the new starting barrier designed by Leo C. McNamara would be used in a Grand Circuit race.[8] Though the barrier had been used the year before on some of the smaller circuits, Greyhound had not yet seen it. The barrier, with its 15-second "automatic starter," guaranteed a race would start in a timely manner without endless scoring. Instead, the horses lined up behind a barrier made of a long cord stretched across the track, placed no more than fifty feet before the starting line. A rope hung down every three feet along the cord, ending a few feet above the track surface. Each rope marked a corresponding post position. A pre-recorded phonograph record played a 14-second countdown, after which the barrier sprung up and the race was on, no matter what. Any starting penalties were handed out after the fact.

The new system guaranteed the race would start when it was scheduled. The old scoring system could prolong a start for an indefinite period. Some races went off with 10 or 20 minutes of scoring, as the drivers attempted to bring the horses to the start on gait and all abreast of each other. It was not unheard of for scoring to take forty-five minutes or more. With such a system, it had been impossible to guarantee a set schedule for races—a feature of the sport that had been tolerated for ages by old-timers, but confused and frustrated new fans, many of whom did not return.

Palin vehemently opposed the new system, preferring the old ways, as did many of his generation.[9] Turf writer George M. Gahagan noted the closeness of the McNamara barrier to the starting line as problematic; it would potentially cause slower times overall, as it didn't allow for a "running start" the way scoring did.[10] While inefficient, the scoring system allowed the horses to be nearly in full stride (high speed) before reaching the starting line. But with the barrier system, the horses were essentially starting from a standstill, and wouldn't reach high speed until much closer to the first turn.

Later in the season, the Indiana State Fair (September) would opt to resign from the

Grand Circuit rather than use the new barrier, and the Illinois State Fair (August) would be penalized for setting it aside after one day of use.[11] Lexington turf reporter Jesse Shuff noted that early in the season, the barrier proved to be unpopular with owners and drivers, especially after some heavy starting penalties were handed out after races. But after the introduction of a "recall bell [to bring back the field] when a horse or horses had an unfair advantage" at the start, Shuff wrote, opinions improved. Regardless of conflicting sentiment, in the opinions of the Grand Circuit stewards and many of the fans, the shortcomings of the McNamara barrier were far outweighed by the benefits. The scoring system would soon be a thing of the past.

The field lined up behind the new barrier for the start of the June 22 American Trotting Club stake. A judge dropped the needle on the phonograph record and the countdown began. At the word, the horses lurched toward the barrier. It sprang up, and the race was on. Bagpiper got away fast and went to the lead. Greyhound did not start well, but Palin didn't push him, instead letting him hang back behind the field. The big gray was in last place going into the first turn. At the quarter pole, Ed Lasater took the lead with Dale Hanover coming into second place.[12]

Excitement rippled through the crowd when Palin moved Greyhound to the middle of the track on the back stretch. He was making his move. Greyhound opened up his track-devouring stride. He surged forward like a ship with fresh wind in her sails, passing horses one by one. The big gray easily overtook the leaders, winning by two lengths. The crowd cheered wildly for their champion. Men along the rail slapped one another on the back and shouted, their faces animated, arms rapt in wild gesticulations.

Bagpiper again got away fastest in the second heat, taking the lead and setting a moderate pace. Greyhound, having a better start this heat, was second going into the first turn. At the quarter pole, he easily took the lead from Bagpiper. With long, sweeping strides, Greyhound moved steadily down the back stretch and into the upper turn. It seemed no one could touch him. But then a gasp rippled through the crowd. With a sudden burst of speed, Greyhound's stablemate Sister Mary flew up from the middle of the pack, went around the gray, and took the lead![13]

The field came out of the final turn and into the home stretch with the bay mare still in front, her legs moving rhythmically as she flew toward the wire. Bagpiper found another gear and surged past Greyhound, following close behind Sister Mary. Many in the crowd stood open-mouthed, unable to believe what they were seeing. Just then, Palin moved Greyhound to the middle of the track. Hope colored the faces in the crowd. The reinsman touched the lines, asking for more speed, and Greyhound sailed to the lead. But Bagpiper wasn't done yet; his driver sent him hard after Greyhound, pushing Palin to let the gelding out another notch. The big gray answered the challenge, holding off Bagpiper and crossing the finish line, easily the best.[14] The crowd erupted in enthusiastic celebration. Greyhound jogged back to the grandstand, parading before his fans. A few among them were certain the horse had winked and smiled.*

Meanwhile, Peter Astra had his first start of the season on the Short Ship circuit in Marion, Ohio. There, he won easily, setting the season record for trotting a racing mile—a record that Greyhound subsequently lowered in his first start at Indianapolis. Peter Astra's next start was to be June 20 at Canton, Ohio, but Parshall's license was suspended due to insubordination toward the judges at the Marion meet the week before.[15] There was talk that Peter Astra would meet Greyhound in Toledo on July 9. Fresh off his suspension, Parshall brought Clever Hanover instead.

An unusually large crowd packed the grandstand to watch Greyhound meet a field of six in the Trotting Club FFA at the Fort Miami track in Toledo, Ohio.[16] He won the first heat easily, staving off a late surge by Dale Hanover and finishing the mile in 2:01 ¼, a new speed record for the season.[17] As the horses cleared the track, the skies opened and a deluge poured down, scattering fans in search of cover. The downpour continued, and the track flooded, canceling racing for the rest of the night.

The next day, skies were clear as the field, minus Clever Hanover (withdrawn by Parshall after a poor showing the night before), went to the post for the second heat.[18] Bagpiper led at the start but was soon passed up by Greyhound. The champion held the lead effortlessly, trotting a sub-two-minute clip at the three-quarter mark. Palin slowed him in the final quarter, winning easily by four lengths and matching his season record from the previous day.[19]

Greyhound's next stop was Narragansett Park in Pawtucket, Rhode Island, for two Trotting Club Stakes—July 22 and 29. The Grand Circuit had not been to Pawtucket in thirty-three years, and trotting fans there were anxious to see the great champion. Greyhound did not disappoint the record turnout of East Coast harness horse lovers.

"The same old story, Greyhound first, the rest ..." read the banner above a picture in the *Boston Globe*. The photo showed Greyhound winning the first heat of the Trotting Club stake over Bagpiper, with Sister Mary in third. The accompanying article by Frank G. Trott described both heats as nothing "more than a moderate workout" for the gallant gray, who won easily in a leisurely 2:05 ¾ and 2:05 flat. In the final quarter of both heats, Palin let the gelding out

---

* Multiple editorials on Greyhound made such comments as the horse's fame grew and his personality became a large part of what endeared the horse to people. Did he wink and smile? Probably not. But even turf reporters noted how Greyhound turned his head to look at the crowd and seemed to nod as he trotted by.

a notch or two—giving the crowd a thrilling demonstration of speed. He finished the final quarter of each otherwise slow (by Greyhound's standards) mile heat in :29 ¼, crossing the wire well ahead of his four competitors.[20]

Parshall took Peter Astra in the "Goldsmith Maid" trot for four and five-year-olds the next day. On the surface, it might appear that Parshall was avoiding meeting Greyhound and Palin; however, with a purse of $3,225, the Goldsmith Maid was the highest-value race of the meet, worth $725 more than Greyhound's race. Despite a rousing duel in the second heat, Peter Astra finished fourth overall.[21]

On the 29th, just three horses showed up to challenge Greyhound—Dale Hanover, Bravo, and Sister Mary. All three had trotted 2:01 or better, fast by any standard except the one set by Greyhound. None furnished any real competition. In the first heat, Greyhound went straight to the front and stayed there, winning easily, with Dale Hanover taking second.

The second heat started much the same, with Palin taking the big gray to the front. But at the half, Palin loosened his hold on the champion and gave Greyhound his head.[22] The crowd leapt to their feet and applauded wildly when the gallant gray warrior grabbed the extra rein and lengthened his mighty stride. Greyhound floated over the track, as if gravity itself was no match for the fleet-footed gelding. Raucous fans sent a deafening roar thundering from the stands. Greyhound's bold, ground-covering strides carried him ever farther ahead of the field, increasing his advantage well past the three-quarter pole. With one-eighth of a mile to go, Palin took back the lines, slowing the big gray to avoid "distancing the field" (winning by more than an eighth of a mile), and still set a new track record. He'd given the crowd the thrill they'd come to see—Greyhound was the whole show.[23]

Impressive as his comeback was, Greyhound still hadn't met the one big horse the people wanted to see—Peter Astra. So far, Doc Parshall's champion colt of 1939 had not come forward to meet the older horse. It made sense that Parshall would wait until later in the season, when Peter Astra was in peak form, but the people were getting anxious to see the two meet, and the papers kept fanning the flames of excitement by announcing Peter Astra as confirmed to start (instead of simply eligible to start) each time Greyhound was scheduled to go to the post.

In the weeks leading up to it, the papers touted the August 12 Trotting Derby at Goshen's Good Time Park as *the* meeting between Peter Astra and Greyhound, with as many as 10 other contenders rounding out the field. In the days leading up to the big race, several inches of column space in papers all over the country were devoted to talk of the match-up between the old and the young. Many considered Greyhound, four years older than Peter Astra, to be at a disadvantage compared to the younger horse. Even Peter Astra's driver, Doc Parshall, was twenty years younger than Sep Palin, some pointed out. Others noted

Greyhound held one important record above Peter Astra, the proverbial elephant in the room Peter Astra fans didn't like to mention—Greyhound's mile in 1:55 ¼, the fastest of all time. One was younger, the other was faster, and the only people certain of the outcome were Palin and Parshall.[24] But they couldn't both be right.

Parshall hadn't yet committed Peter Astra to Greyhound's race. The colt was eligible for two events at Goshen—the first division of the Trotting Club Derby against Greyhound, or the second division Trotting Derby for four- and five-year-olds held a few days later.[25] Parshall was apparently considering either or both. If he chose only one, it would likely be the $4,000 Trotting Derby against his contemporaries: Long Key, Nibble Hanover, and Spud Hanover. Although he had beaten these horses in the past, all three had defeated him at Narragansett the previous week. As a *Middletown Times Herald* (New York) writer noted in the August 10 edition, Peter Astra would have to "go a lot faster than he's been going" to triumph over Greyhound or the other three, no matter which race Parshall chose.[26]

The morning of the Trotting Club Stake dawned mild but humid, with temperatures in the mid-fifties over Good Time Park. By afternoon, it had warmed into the eighties and fluffy white clouds dotted the sky over the triangular mile track. Five years before, a steel-gray youngster had trotted to victory in the Hambletonian over this same track. Now, a fully developed veteran trotter with a snow-white coat warmed up around the flat-iron-shaped turf.

Palin and Greyhound knew each other well. Their partnership extended over nearly seven years, back to when the veteran driver signed the ticket for Baker's purchase of the gawky, skinny-legged yearling. It seemed like a lifetime ago. In the intervening years, Palin and Greyhound had developed a subtle, often invisible communication—a combination of soft touches on the driving lines, the way Palin sat and held himself in the sulky, the degree of tension in his arms, the curve of his shoulders—all had become communication within this grand partnership.

When post time for the feature race came around that afternoon, Peter Astra and a few other expected entries had scratched. Just five horses went to the post for the big race. With Peter Astra tucked away in his stall, none were near the same class as Greyhound. It would be the Grey Ghost against the field, the latter battling for second money.

Greyhound was so much the favorite, the betting windows were closed to him.[27] Sister Mary, Bravo, Bagpiper, and new challenger Athlone Flaxey Guy rounded out the field. Starting behind the McNamara barrier, Greyhound got away second. He followed Athlone Flaxey Guy, who took the early lead and carried it through the first tight turn and into the long back stretch.

Then a gasp rose from the crowd. Greyhound had stumbled![28] Hearts thumping, eyes unable to look away, they waited through agonizing moments, seeing nothing but flailing legs and a lurching sulky. Athlone Flaxey Guy whizzed on ahead. Then: an audible sigh of relief. Greyhound recovered quickly, apparently none the worse. He soon regained his stride and powered through the back stretch, trotting on up to the lead and staying there. Sister Mary came up fast in the final stretch; driving hard, she caught Athlone Flaxey Guy to finish second. But Greyhound remained untouchable, with Palin again taking up the reins and slowing the big gray freight train in the final quarter.

In the second heat, Greyhound got away badly but recovered quickly, catching up to the field in the first turn and passing them on the back stretch. Powerful strides drummed the turf. Greyhound sailed easily down the long back stretch. But this time, Sister Mary and Athlone Flaxey Guy hung with him.[29] Greyhound held the lead through the second turn, but couldn't quite shake off the two younger horses. Like unwanted pests buzzing around a prize-winning pie, the mare and the colt nagged Greyhound through the final turn and into the long home stretch. Palin touched the lines, and spoke to the big gray, asking for a bit more speed. Greyhound delivered, lengthening his stride and powering under the finish wire, going the last quarter in a sharp :28 ¼. Sister Mary finished second, and Athlone Flaxey Guy, a soundly-beaten third.

It was Greyhound's last race at Good Time Park, and he lingered on the track afterward. A record-sized crowd, the largest of any opening day, cheered the champion every time he passed the grandstand—be it warming up, racing, or just jogging by to toss his head and say hello. Long after the race was over, "scores" of people still "flocked about [Greyhound's] stall admiring his beauty."[30] Many in the crowd savored the moment, imprinting it on their memories, holding it close to their hearts as a bright and victorious spot in a year filled with uncertainty and impending war.

"The son of Guy Abbey has the popularity of Clark Gable with the ladies and is admired by youths like Babe Ruth," reported the *Middletown Times Herald*, the local paper for the Goshen area. After the race, Greyhound's admirers followed him back to his stall. Reporters snapped pictures and asked questions. Even movie star James Cagney was there, having traveled all the way from California to see what all the fuss was about.[31] He too wanted to get close to Greyhound.

Three days later, Peter Astra met top four- and five-year-olds in the Trotting Derby. There, he was an "also ran," coming in off the board in both heats. He'd yet to regain the previous year's champion form. Greyhound and Peter Astra were slated to meet in the Springfield FFA trot at the Illinois State Fair. But when August 23 arrived, just two horses joined Greyhound at the post in front of the largest crowd ever recorded at Springfield.[32] The race was a cakewalk for Greyhound. He won easily, adding yet another sub-two-minute mile to his growing list—the first one of *any* trotter that season.[33]

The harness world had thrown their top younger horses at Greyhound, and all had come up short. He'd won five consecutive races, all in straight heats. Greyhound trotted home in front with ease, Palin reining him in before he swept under the wire. The one horse he hadn't met was Peter Astra. And time was running out: Greyhound's farewell race was scheduled for August 26, just three days after his win at Springfield, Illinois.

After he had cooled out from the race, Greyhound boarded the train in the sweltering heat for the long trip to Syracuse, New York. Jimmie settled the horse into his stall, then placed his cot right next to him. Technical difficulties would delay the train on multiple occasions, making a long, hot trip even longer.[34] With starts and stops, the train click-clacked over the rails, heading northeast to the last race of Greyhound's illustrious career.

As Greyhound traveled, Peter Astra, the only horse people believed could take Greyhound's measure, slept in his stall at Syracuse and waited. In a couple days' time, he would finally meet the great Grey Ghost in a race over the New York track. Across the country and around the world, people waited and wondered which would prevail—youth or experience?

It would prove to be the toughest race of either horse's career.

END of

CHAPTER 23

CHAPTER
— 24 —

> *"It is not possible for anyone to record the greatness of Greyhound 1:55 ¼. It is not to be measured in words. One must see him to understand how far he is removed from all other trotters, he is one apart, no such have heretofore existed."*
>
> —
>
> P. W. MOSER,
> THE STORY OF GREYHOUND 1:55 ¼, 1940

LAST CALL

A heavy mist hung low above dew-soaked grass at the Syracuse Mile as the sun pushed its way slowly above the horizon. A twinge of nerves roiled in Jimmie Wingfield's belly as he prepared Greyhound's morning feed. The calendar read August 26, 1940. Today would be the last time the great Greyhound would race. Jimmie pulled his jacket collar up around his neck, blocking the brisk morning air. It had been a cold night to spend in the barn, the temperature having dipped down to an unseasonably cool thirty-eight degrees overnight. Jimmie was glad to be up and moving about. He looked forward to a steaming cup of hot coffee once the horses had been fed.

Palin had been pacing the barn row when Jimmie and Greyhound finally detrained at Syracuse Sunday afternoon and walked to the barn, twenty-four hours later than they were scheduled to arrive. The trip had been long and hot. Jimmie worried about the effect on Greyhound; he had not really had any chance to rest since his race on Friday. To Jimmie's surprise, Sep had him jog Greyhound several miles when they finally did arrive, saying he didn't want the big gelding's muscles to stiffen up.[1]

After coffee and a quick breakfast at the track kitchen, Jimmie pulled off Greyhound's stable blanket and ran a brush over his gleaming white coat. Almost no trace of gray hairs remained on the gelding's body, save for a sprinkling of them over his haunches, dotted with soft, more lightly colored dapples. The gelding's shins were still dark, though the steel gray had lightened considerably and an ever-increasing number of white hairs inserted themselves among the darker ones.

Comfortable afternoon temperatures in the low 70s greeted racegoers at the Syracuse Mile for the feature event, the Trotting Club Trot—where Peter Astra and Greyhound would finally match strides. A six-horse field went to the post; among them were Sister Mary, Bravo, Dale Hanover, and, surprisingly, ten-year-old Calumet Dilworthy, a chestnut son of Peter the Brewer. Calumet Dilworthy and Greyhound were certainly among the last of the Calumet-born Standardbreds still on the track in 1940. A half-mile track specialist, the gelding's best time of 2:02 ¼ had been achieved back in 1937. By 1940, he'd been relegated to racing in county fairs and low-level classified trots. One can only speculate as to why the aged gelding, well past his prime, was entered in the big race at all.

In the first heat, Palin's strategy was to control the pace. Greyhound got away last, but Palin quickly moved him to the front. Trotting well within himself through the back stretch, he held a length and a half lead coming out of the final turn.[2] It looked like another cakewalk for the gray champion. But from mid-pack came a fast-closing Peter Astra, looking more his 1939 form than he had all year. Parshall had the bay right where he wanted him. He set his sights on the white-haired veterans. With an eighth of a mile remaining and Peter Astra's nose at his wheel, Palin asked for more speed. But for the first time, Greyhound didn't respond.[3] With fifty yards to go, Peter Astra lunged at the wire, edging out Greyhound by a nostril.[4]

Silence. Disbelief.

Peter Astra had handed Greyhound his first defeat in four years. The time for the mile, 2:01 ½, was a new personal best for Peter Astra—but still not on par with the times Greyhound had trotted earlier in the year. Between heats, a reporter asked Palin about Greyhound's sluggish performance.

"Greyhound raced at Springfield Friday, shipped 1,000 miles to Syracuse, and did not get to the track until [yesterday] afternoon," Palin replied. "He's just a little groggy, that's all."[5] The defensive tone of Palin's comments invites one to speculate on the old reinsman's underlying concerns—had he finally asked too much of the gallant gray champion? Greyhound's perfect season record seemed in doubt.

The horses went to the post for the second heat. Greyhound got away sluggishly in fourth. Palin raised his hands high and shook the lines. "Yeah! Go! C'mon!" he shouted over the pounding hooves and humming wheels. Greyhound responded, getting up to speed before the first turn. But this time, Palin let

Peter Astra and Bravo battle it out for the early lead, allowing Greyhound to hang back in his familiar spot. The frontrunners set a much slower pace, going the half nearly three seconds slower than the pace Palin set in the first heat. Calling on Greyhound to dig deep, Palin touched the lines, shouted encouragement, and made his bid coming out of the final turn. With a burst of renewed energy, Greyhound surged ahead, breezed past the field, and came home a length in front of Peter Astra.[6]

The crowd roared.

Greyhound had won the heat, but it was clear to all watching that he'd lost his usual form. He looked tired. His gait had lost the effortless flow that had been the grand trotter's trademark. Jimmie walked Greyhound around the paddock before the next heat, a plaid wool cooler wrapped around the big gray's body. Palin watched his old friend carefully, looking for any trace of unsoundness, any reason to pull him from the race. Palin was not alone in his concern. Many in the crowd wondered if the Grey Ghost had enough in his tired body left to give.

Those who witnessed the final heat of Greyhound's career said Palin drove him carefully, almost lovingly, around the track. His driving skills honed over four decades, Palin used them all to give Greyhound the best trip possible. The Grey Ghost and Peter Astra had each won one heat. This final heat would decide the winner.

Greyhound got a shaky start, stunning the crowd when he broke gait,[7] something the horse had done only twice in competition in his six-year career. Palin reined him in quickly and got him back on trot without losing too much ground, but Sister Mary rushed to the lead, with Bravo following right after her. The pair set a moderate pace, then swapped places, with Bravo taking the lead. Steady now, Greyhound settled into his long, sweeping stride, and slowly moved up on the leaders. Bravo, trotting well within himself, led the field through the final turn, with Greyhound still mid-pack behind him. Palin leaned forward and raised the lines, asking the champion one last time for more speed.[8] The gallant gray warrior delivered. Like a white locomotive, his mane a plume of silver smoke, the gelding powered through the final turn and into the stretch. In the final eighth, Greyhound caught the hard-driving Bravo and poked a slim nostril in front.

Screams rose from the crowd, and people leapt to their feet, leaning over the rail, waving their hands and shouting encouragement to their hero. Greyhound led the field across the finish line, winning the final race of his glorious career, going the last quarter in :29 seconds. Bravo came second, Sister Mary third, and Peter Astra, soundly beaten, finished last.

Deafening cheers flooded the grandstand and spilled onto the track. Palin jogged Greyhound back to the crowd, giving his fans another look at the great champion. Jimmie met him at the rail. He unclipped the overcheck rein, then rubbed the gelding's face and neck, speaking softly words meant only for Greyhound. Palin swung his legs over the arch of the sulky and stepped onto the track, walking behind the horse. He and Jimmie guided Greyhound to the winner's circle. A new wave of cheers erupted from the crowd when the queen of the fair, Miss Gordyne Sedgwick, presented the Hotel Syracuse trophy to Palin. Baker, having taken ill, was not present.[9]

Palin accepted the trophy and said a few words, but, as ever, directed the glory toward Greyhound. This had truly been the greatest test of the champion's career. He'd been handicapped by age and lack of rest, but had still come out on top, leaving no doubt in anyone's mind that Greyhound was the greatest that had ever been, and for many, the greatest that would ever be.

END of CHAPTER 24

GREYHOUND

THE REMARKABLE STORY OF THE LEGENDARY RACEHORSE WHO INSPIRED A NATION

June 6, 1940, *Deseret News*

CHAPTER
— 25 —

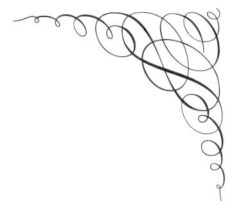

"He drove forward with piston-like thrusts of his long limbs, maintaining such an air of noble dignity that he never seemed to be in a rush. And yet the records continued to fall before the relentless precision of his impeccable trotting gait."

—

M.A. STONERIDGE,
GREAT HORSES OF OUR TIME, 1972

NO WORLDS LEFT TO CONQUER

"I've got something a little different for you, Greyhound." Jimmie lifted a lightweight hunt saddle and rested it over the lower half of the stall door. The gray sniffed the new piece of tack, running his lips over the smooth leather.

"Don't you bite that, now." Jimmie spoke softly, placing his hands firmly on his hips, his body language feigning sternness while his tone carried only pure love for his gray charge. "We're going to try something new today."[1]

After Greyhound's final race, the Baker-Palin stable traveled to Louisville, Kentucky. Riding the wave of renewed interest set in motion by Greyhound, the Grand Circuit was being held at the Kentucky State Fair for the first time in over fifteen years.[2] After a well-earned two-week rest in Lexington, Greyhound and Jimmie had joined the others in Louisville.[3]

On September 11, a record crowd of excited fans packed the grandstand at Louisville to see Greyhound lead a parade of two-minute horses between races.[4] The next afternoon, Palin had Greyhound trot an easy exhibition mile. Despite poor footing over a cuppy, slow track, and air chilly enough for sweaters, Greyhound made the mile in 2:00 ½—a new track record for Louisville's half-mile oval. Doc Parshall and veteran driver Vic Flemming watched the exhibition, and both felt that, given the conditions, Greyhound's effort was on par with his sub-two-minute mile at Historic track.[5] Even at this leisurely pace, he posted a time many harness horses, including two of his toughest rivals, Peter Astra and Lawrence Hanover, would never reach. It was his final appearance in harness while in racing form. Afterward, people crowded around Palin and the reinsman signed autographs for a long time.[6]

"They come from all over just to see you," Jimmie said, entering the stall. He stroked Greyhound's sleek neck, then gently placed the saddle on his back. If all went well, Palin planned to point Greyhound toward the world record for trotting a mile under saddle. Greyhound had never been ridden before. He knew the feel of the harness on his back, and the girth tightening around him, but he'd never felt the weight of a human. Jimmie tightened the girth one hole at a time, allowing Greyhound to adjust gradually to the new sensation of the saddle held snugly on his back.

"He'd never had anyone on his back," Jimmie said many years later. "I just ... got him ready to go out and instead of putting a harness on, I just put a saddle and bridle on him. [He] behaved like a gentleman."[7]

Jimmie led Greyhound out of the barn, placed his foot in the stirrup, and swung on. The big gray lifted his long neck, his ears trained intently toward Jimmie.

"Good boy, Greyhound. Good." Jimmie rubbed the gelding's neck and shifted his weight in the saddle a few times before sliding off again. When he felt the horse was ready, he led Greyhound from the stable area to the fairground's saddle horse ring. There, he again climbed aboard Greyhound. The gelding twitched his ears and lifted his head, uncertain. But Greyhound trusted Jimmie implicitly and remained calm.

The pair walked around the saddle horse ring at the state fairgrounds with Palin watching.[7] The people standing around the ring may have taken note of the long-striding gray among the fancy show horses, and perhaps wondered what his story was. Surely none suspected they were watching the fastest trotter in the world get his first lessons under saddle.

At some point, Jimmie took Greyhound to the track. He walked an eighth of a mile and then asked the gelding to trot.[8]

"When I started posting, he did hump his back up a little," Jimmie told a reporter in 1975, "but that was all."[9] The gelding's gait was smooth and powerful. Pleased with Greyhound's response to being ridden, Palin hatched his plan. The record for trotting a mile under saddle stood at 2:05 ¼, set by Hollyrood Boris in 1936. Palin felt certain Greyhound could break that record. Jimmie wouldn't be the one to ride him in his race against time, though. Palin had seen Mrs. Frances Dodge Johnson, heir of the Dodge auto fortune, show her horse to a championship at the state fair earlier in the week. Johnson, just twenty-five years old, had already made a name for herself in the horse show world. At twenty, in 1935, she owned and operated Dodge Stables at her late father's Meadowbrook estate. Johnson routinely appeared on the cover of national magazines, both in horse sport and as a young socialite in Detroit society. A talented equestrian, Johnson had impressed Palin with how she handled her horses. He believed Johnson, small, strong, and talented, would be an excellent choice to pilot Greyhound to an under-saddle record.

At the close of the fair in Louisville, Greyhound took a van ride to the KTHBA track in Lexington. There, Jimmie continued working with Greyhound under saddle, walking and trotting him around the velvety red racing strip.[10] Mrs. Johnson then rode the big gray under Jimmie's watchful eye. If things continued to go well, Palin planned to aim Greyhound at the under-saddle record the following week.

There is no record of how much time was spent on each phase of getting Greyhound ready to take a rider, though in 1975, Jimmie told a reporter that Frances rode Greyhound just once prior to the record ride.[11] That Greyhound took to the new endeavor easily is evident in that he went for the record just two weeks after his first ride.

The final day of the 1940 Lexington trots doubled as a celebration of Greyhound and his astounding accomplishments in his six-year career. The afternoon began with a parade, and culminated with Greyhound's attempt at setting a new world record for a mile trotted under saddle. On the afternoon of September 26, Jimmie led Greyhound onto the track for the "Parade of Grays."[12] The crowd applauded for their champion, a few whoops and hollers punctuating the celebratory energy as the trotter's accomplishments were announced over the loudspeaker. Following Greyhound onto the track were his sire, Guy Abbey, and his dam, Elizabeth, with her 1940 colt at her side. Several siblings followed, including Whippet, Miss Greyhound, Nathalie Grey, and Grey Fox—all had been or would become good racehorses, but none would come close to the accomplishments of Greyhound.

At the end of the parade, Elizabeth's dam Zombrewer walked gracefully over the red clay track. Zombrewer had made the short van ride from her home at Calumet Farm, where she lived among the Thoroughbreds. Calumet's only remaining representative of William Wright's successful harness horse breeding program, Zombrewer passed away the following year at age thirty-six, the last of an era. Soon no one would remember that Calumet Farm had once been among the premier harness horse nurseries in the nation, or that the greatest trotter of them all took his first breath of life within those famous white board fences that still stand today.

After the final race of the day, Frances Johnson brought Greyhound onto the track for their attempt at the world record for a mile under saddle. She wore her own colors, a deep purple satin jacket and hat accented with white. Light-colored jodhpurs covered her legs, the same type she would wear in the show ring. An elastic strap under each ankle height boot held them in place. She rode with her stirrups long, as she would have if riding one of her Saddlebred show horses. Greyhound wore his protective boots and a simple snaffle bridle. Jimmie braided a green ribbon into his mane and forelock, just as he would for a race.

Johnson and Greyhound jogged a few passes in front of the grandstand, the anticipatory murmurs of thousands of fans rippling along in their wake. After a few scores, Johnson nodded, received the word, and the race against time was on. Driving a prompter, Palin assisted in setting the pace, staying just behind and to the side of the big gray horse.[13] Johnson sat still in the saddle, perfectly balanced, absorbing the rhythmic pounding of Greyhound's powerful stride. She looked small on the big horse. Even with her stirrups long and her legs wrapped around Greyhound's sides, the bottom of each foot was inches above the line of his belly. They rode out of the final turn to the sound of enthusiastic cheers. Greyhound trotted like a machine into the stretch, and the crowd's enthusiasm flowed onto the track in the form of whoops and hollers, cheering and shouts of encouragement.[14] In the final quarter, Greyhound lengthened his stride and surged ahead. The pair flew down toward the finish, and the crowd cheered with renewed enthusiasm. They flashed under the wire in 2:01 ¾, shaving an impressive three and a half seconds off Hollyrood Boris's previous world record.[15]

Palin, Johnson, and Greyhound received the cheers and adulation of the crowd as they jogged back to the grandstand. Jimmie snapped a lead shank onto Greyhound's bridle, and Mrs. Johnson slid off the Grey Ghost, her petite body looking even smaller standing next to the big horse. Excitement rippled through the crowd. All were aware they had witnessed something great.

Greyhound's final world record would stand for more than half a century.

END of

CHAPTER 25

GREYHOUND

THE REMARKABLE STORY OF THE LEGENDARY RACEHORSE WHO INSPIRED A NATION

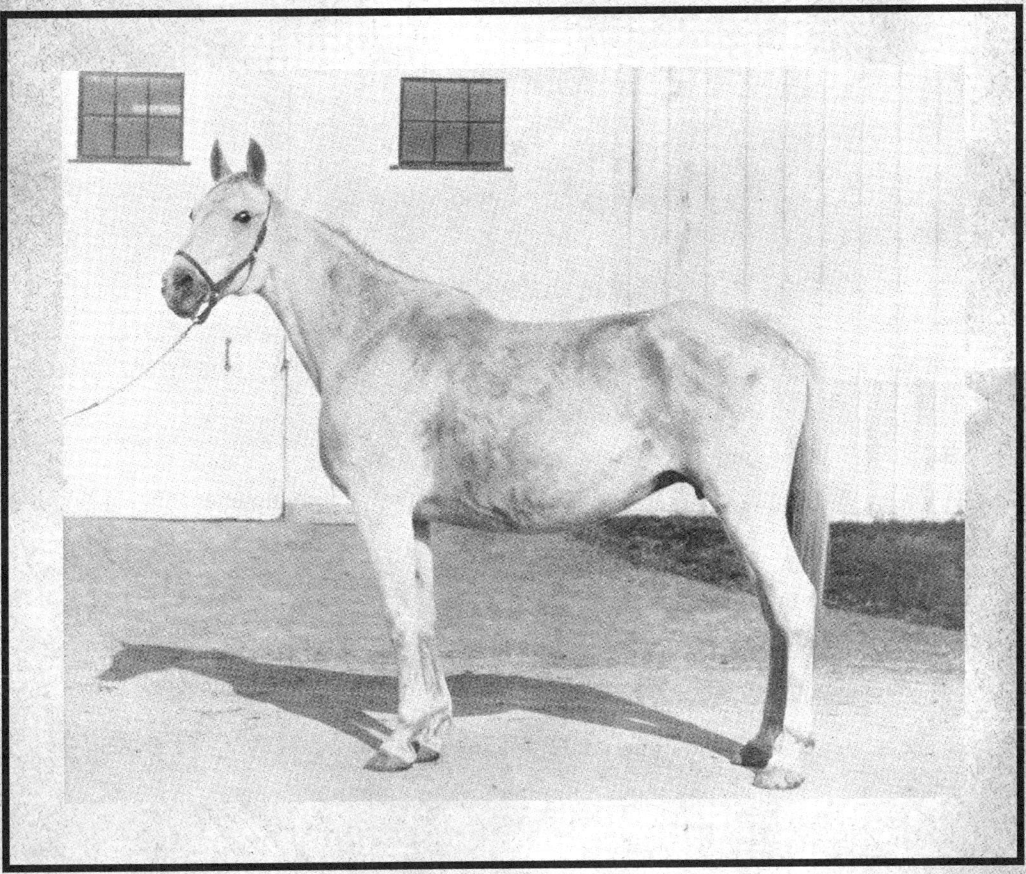

Zombrewer, granddam of Greyhound, at Calumet Farm at age 35.

 CIRCA 1940, COURTESY OF THE HARNESS RACING MUSEUM & HALL OF FAME, GOSHEN, NY

Greyhound

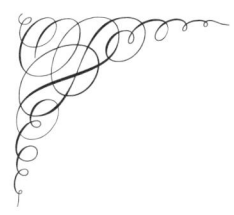

PART THREE

Chapter
— 26 —

Drawing by Jimmie's mother, Mary Wingfield, on Greyhound's retirement.
• *circa 1941, courtesy of the Wingfield family*

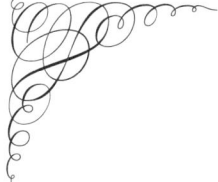
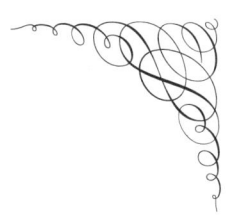

*"Long has your stride enchanted us, propelled by poise serene,
Majestic, calm and undisturbed, as perfect timed machine.
A noble head, with ears afront, alert to catch applause,
From thousands wrapped in ecstasy, that super-action draws."*

—George H. Sweetnam,
Hoof Beats, January 1942
(excerpt from poem)

THE END OF AN ERA

"Greyhound is done racing," Palin had said at Syracuse, following Greyhound's final race. "This season," he'd added cryptically, with a glint in his eye.[1] But soon after Greyhound's under-saddle record at Lexington, Baker announced a total dispersal of all racing stock. Aside from Greyhound, the entirety of Baker's Standardbred holdings would go under the hammer at the Indianapolis Speed Sale in November—effectively dissolving the 14-year Baker-Palin partnership.[2]

His health declining, Baker's doctor had insisted the seventy-three-year-old quit the sport and settle down. In previous years, Baker had traveled frequently to watch his horses race. He visited the racing stable at each track, pockets filled with carrots and sugar cubes. Greyhound seemed to know instantly when Baker was near, pushing his fine head over the stall door and looking down the aisle, nickering softly as soon as Baker came into view. But in 1940, Baker had been sick for most of the year, spending much of that time in the hospital, too ill to travel.[3] During his hospitalization, Harriet, his beloved wife of fifty-one years, had died of a heart attack in their home.[4]

In Baker's absence, Palin had apparently taken it upon himself to send Greyhound after the world record for a mile under saddle. Years later, the wife of the great horse's retirement caretaker would record in her memoirs that Baker hadn't wanted Greyhound to go after the under-saddle record—and that due to Palin's insubordination, Baker had fired him.[5]

This author found no supporting evidence in news or magazine articles from the era; however, there is precedence for this. It wouldn't be the first time Baker had dissolved his racing stable to end a partnership. He'd "left the sport" fifteen years earlier, liquidating his stable under trainer Chet Kelley, only to rebuild a year later with Sep Palin.

Palin had no trouble landing on his feet after losing the Baker horses. In a time when less than 120 horses had recorded a mile in 2:00 or better (pacing or trotting), Sep Palin had driven fifty-eight of them to their record.[6] His patient handling in developing young horses into champion pacers and trotters had brought him great success. While top drivers such as Doc Parshall had larger stables and more overall wins, Palin had accomplished what others had not—consistently producing sound and sane two-minute horses. Palin soon partnered with Frances Dodge Johnson, who, after becoming acquainted with Palin at Louisville and riding Greyhound to his record, became quite interested in harness racing. Much as he'd done with Baker, Palin advised Johnson in purchasing horses. Among her early purchases were Greyhound's yearling full brother, Grey Fox, purchased for $6,100 from Henry Knight, and Sister Mary, undefeated in all races except against Greyhound, purchased for $2,300 from Baker's dispersal.[7]

What is unclear is whether Greyhound returned to Red Gate Farm after his under-saddle mile at Lexington or stayed with the Palin stable. The recollections of his retirement caretaker (recorded over twenty-five years later) diverge from the reported facts at the time and the memories of others. The former states the horse retired to Red Gate in 1940, following his under-saddle record. However, newspapers reported Greyhound was still with the Palin stable in 1941.[8] It is known that Greyhound did not take well to retirement early on, finding life at Red Gate boring compared to the excitement of living at the track, and he proved to be quite a handful for the staff at Red Gate. It's possible he spent a couple months there and did not handle it well. We do know that Palin wasn't ready to retire Greyhound, and that Baker—obviously preoccupied with his poor health, the recent loss of his wife, and the dispersal of his racing stable—made no public comment on whether the great horse would retire.

"If Greyhound trains as well as he did last [season], he should cut a fraction of a second off that 1:55 ¼," Palin told reporters toward the end of December 1940. "I'll take him to Aiken Sunday and slowly work him into shape for next year. We haven't any definite events lined up for him next [season]."[9]

Regardless of where he spent the interim, when the calendar turned from 1940 to 1941,

Greyhound and the rest of the Palin string went to the winter training quarters at the Aiken Mile Track in South Carolina. Jimmie Wingfield, now assistant trainer for Palin, traveled with the training stable a few weeks ahead of Palin, who arrived with his wife toward the end of January.[10] The couple took up residence in their winter home at Aiken and, aside from the lack of Baker horses, things went on as in any other winter season. On the training track among the black and bay horses, the nearly solid white Grey Ghost remained the only lingering remnant of the great partnership that had been the Baker-Palin stable.

The January sports pages carried recaps of the harness racing season. Among the statistics listed, forty-two states held harness races in 1939 and 1940, with purses at just the small fair tracks totaling over $1.5 million, according to the USTA. At the new Roosevelt Raceway in Long Island, New York, the 27-day meet saw a pari-mutuel handle of $1.2 million.[11] Projections for 1941 called for even better attendance and more racing than in 1940. Lovers of the sport filled with hope that harness racing had returned to the glory and popularity it experienced in the days before the automobile.

That Greyhound played a significant role in the resurgence of that popularity cannot be denied. In a time when just thirty-two horses had trotted a mile in 2:00 or better, nearly one quarter of the 108 total two-minute or better miles had been trotted by Greyhound.[12] A feat that seemed impossible just a few decades before had become common for the great champion.

Many journalists and fans already touted Greyhound as the horse that carried the sport through its most difficult decade. Harness racing experienced a surge in popularity, with attendance increasing annually in the last four seasons of Greyhound's career. With his astounding speed and magnificent stride, Greyhound helped bridge the gap between the bygone golden era of harness racing and the huge resurgence brought on by the changes made in the early 1940s. The horses in general were getting faster, and the new McNamara starting system (soon replaced by the mobile starting gate still used today) did away with the endless delays caused by the old scoring system. The adoption of pari-mutuel betting, the construction of large night race courses near big cities, and the eventual turn away from heat races and toward more exciting single-heat dashes were all significant to the resurgence in harness racing that got its start in the late 1930s and grew exponentially into and beyond the 1960s.

Greyhound was not the sole reason for the sport's renaissance, but make no mistake, he was the conduit. He reignited a dying flame. The American people, and by extension the sport of harness racing, had needed a hero, and the Grey Ghost showed up at just the right time. Without a superstar to grab the attention of the public, win their hearts, and draw them back to the races, the improvements that saw harness racing regain a place of prestige would have been irrelevant.

While wintering in Aiken, Greyhound enjoyed leisurely jogs around the track with Jimmie Wingfield holding the lines. The horse was not asked for speed, but slowly and carefully built back up in condition and fitness. At the end of January, Jimmie told reporters Greyhound likely would not race again, but would probably do some exhibition trots locally.[13] Palin told reporters he was bringing Greyhound back into training slowly, planning to build him up over time and see how he went.

That spring, gossip circulated among the harness set that Greyhound had been training for a possible return to racing. Others reported that Greyhound had suffered a career-ending injury during training.[14] Palin scoffed at such reports, insisting the horse was perfectly sound.[15] In July, a paper in Lewiston, Maine, reported that Greyhound had traveled with the Palin string to the track at Old Orchard Beach, saying the horse was in "light training" but it was "doubtful he will ever start again."[16] The next day, a Connecticut paper reported Greyhound had worked a mile in 2:20.[17] The nearly complete silence in the press regarding Greyhound through late spring and summer of 1941 could lead one to speculate that Palin didn't want people to know what was going on with the big gray. At the same time, it seems odd that just a few obscure east-coast newspapers mentioned Greyhound was at Old Orchard, when this would almost certainly have been advertised as a draw to get people through the gate. Over eighty years later, it is a mystery likely to never be unraveled. Regardless of what went on or where Greyhound was through the summer of 1941, come fall, everyone would know all they needed to about Greyhound's future.

In September of 1941, Greyhound traveled with the racing stable to Louisville amid rumors that he would trot an exhibition mile each afternoon that week at the Kentucky State Fair.[18] Instead, he was "presented" to the crowds, but no mention was made, in the few newspapers that picked up the story, of exactly what the "presentation" involved.[19]

As of September 8, Palin was still talking about Greyhound continuing to train for racing. But by the end of the month, he reported the Grey Ghost's future was unclear. Having admitted Greyhound had suffered some "leg troubles" in the spring, Palin said the horse was doing fine now, working back up to a 2:20 trot. But he expected Greyhound would do only the exhibition circuit.[20]

A few weeks later, on October 17, 1941, papers all over the country carried the announcement of Greyhound's retirement. The article stated that a private van had arrived at the Palin barn in Indianapolis, loaded up the champion, and transported him to Baker's Red Gate Farm in St. Charles, Illinois.[21]

"He's done everything there is for him to do, you see," Jimmie told reporters, citing

Greyhound's strangle-hold on the world record book. "He has seventeen* world records and he's in such a class that there are no more places for him. He's in the very pink of condition," Jimmie added. Perhaps in response to questions about the great champion's soundness, the young man reminded the reporters that Greyhound had been jogged daily over the track at Indianapolis.[22]

Two weeks later, Tom Gahagan noted Baker was "back in the game" in his November 2 article in the *Cincinnati Enquirer*. It seems his health had returned, and with it, Baker returned to the trots at Lexington. There, at the annual sale, he purchased two yearlings, and at a later sale, he went $1,900 for a yearling pacer named Noble Hal.[23]

In addition to his new racehorses, Baker also took an interest in the world of fancy show horses. Baker had met and befriended fellow Illinoisan R. C. "Doc" Flanery, a prominent figure and successful trainer in the world of roadsters and high-stepping cart and saddle horses. Baker soon acquired a string of Hackney show ponies and put them in training with Flanery.

Baker's new racehorses were placed in training with Harry Fitzpatrick, who based his stable at the Illinois state fairgrounds in Springfield.[24] This partnership would carry on through 1944, with Baker purchasing horses and Fitzpatrick training and racing them. In 1943, Baker purchased the three-year-old pacer King's Counsel from Doc Parshall for $20,000.[25] The colt would be best known for his intense rivalry with the indomitable Adios. In 1944, King's Counsel won 10 of 12 starts for Baker. In 1946, Baker sold King's Counsel to Gainesway Farm in Lexington, Kentucky.[26] There, he became an outstanding producer, siring twelve 2:00 horses and 118 that went in 2:05 or better.[27]

Baker had returned to racing in a big way, and the sport was thrilled to have him back.

Retirement didn't sit well with Greyhound. He had too much energy, too much passion, and not enough patience. The big gray missed the excitement of life at the track. Instead of the activity of the shed row, the pounding hooves and whir of sulky wheels around the track, and the noise of the crowds, Greyhound had only the old retired roadster Senator Crawford to look at. And Senator Crawford was boring.

One might suspect he also missed the connection he'd had with Jimmie, and, to a degree, Palin himself. The two men had truly loved the horse, devoting years of their lives and endless hours of their energy and concern to the champion. Both Palin and Jimmie

---

* It was challenging to keep track of the number of world records Greyhound held at any one time, especially as he often broke his own record(s) multiple times in the same season. This is why some direct quotes seem to contradict others from the same time frame. A complete list of Greyhound's world records can be found in Appendix 3 (p. 267).

noted upon Greyhound's retirement how attached they'd become to the intelligent horse.[28] Greyhound and Jimmie had been inseparable for five years, the young caretaker seldom leaving the big gray's sight. At Red Gate, Greyhound still saw Baker most every day, but he lost that constant companionship he'd had in Jimmie's care.

The setup at Red Gate was nothing like the race track. No buzz, no excitement, nothing to see. Greyhound was turned out daily in a large paddock adjacent to the one holding old Senator Crawford, and the groom put in charge of him took the big gray for a daily jog—or at least tried to. The young man wasn't used to handling racehorses. Despite his retirement, in his mind, Greyhound was still at the track. Palin had been right when he'd said Greyhound was "too much horse to turn out," just not the type to settle into the life of a retiree.[29]

At 16.1 ½ hands and nearly 1,200 pounds,[30] Greyhound proved to be a bit too much horse for employees who were used to handling ponies at Red Gate. The Ghost was strong, fit, and "on the muscle" when he came off the track, having trotted several miles a day since he was two years old. Additionally, the farm had no training track, so Greyhound was exercised on the dirt road in front of the farm. The wide-open space and long straightaway appealed to Greyhound's sense of adventure. No one had told Greyhound he wasn't a racehorse anymore, and the gallant gray would take off down the road full tilt, with his handler helpless to stop him. One day, a rabbit ran in front of Greyhound and the gelding spooked, then bolted. The driver flipped off the back of the cart, and Greyhound was running free! The horse ran to the next farm and stopped there, where his embarrassed but uninjured handler caught up with him.[31]

Baker saw he had a potentially dangerous situation brewing. Greyhound, while aged for a racehorse, was in the prime of his life. Athletic and full of energy, the big gray needed someone who knew how to handle an active, strong horse. Plus, requests had been coming in from around the country asking that Greyhound make appearances at fairs and race tracks in the upcoming season. Baker wanted to accommodate these requests and share his champion with the fans. Greyhound needed not only a skilled handler but also a manager. The decision was made to move Greyhound to "Doc" Flanery's farm in nearby Maple Park, Illinois.[32]

There, the paths of Verner "Dooley" Putnam and Greyhound would cross once again.

END of CHAPTER 26

GREYHOUND

THE REMARKABLE STORY OF THE LEGENDARY RACEHORSE WHO INSPIRED A NATION

OUTSTANDING ATTRACTION FOR FAIRS
Increase Your Gate and Grandstand Receipts
Draw Patrons from Hundreds of Miles
By securing
GREYHOUND 1:55¼

The greatest trotter of all time

What stall attracts the public? What horse appeals most to the layman? GREYHOUND 1:55¼, World's Champion Trotter. People of all tastes stand before him in his stall in open admiration. Not only has his remarkable record made him the "Horse of the hour," but his great intelligence, regal bearing and his flashing grey color contribute much to his popularity and the desire of everybody to see him, the first World's Champion grey trotter of all time.

Owing to frequent requests, it has been decided to make a limited number of exhibition performances with GREYHOUND 1:55¼, at State and County Fairs. That he will set new high records for paid attendance and provide the most entertainment of any attraction available, has been demonstrated on various occasions at such important expositions as New York State Fair, Illinois State Fair, Indiana State Fair, Wisconsin State Fair, etc., where mammoth crowds turned out to see The Champion of Champions.

Secretaries make plans at once so that YOUR FAIR secures the season's most popular attraction. His appearance at YOUR FAIR means a new record in the way of gate and grandstand receipts, likewise justifies greater returns for your concessions. Get busy at once and address for particulars.

S. F. PALIN, 5450 Washington Blvd., Indianapolis, Ind.

CIRCA 1939, COURTESY OF THE UNITED STATES TROTTING ASSOCIATION

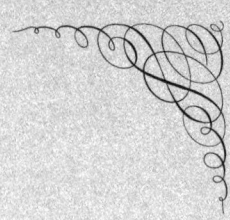

CHAPTER
— 27 —

 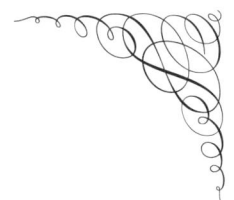

"I looked upon the Champion of Champions—and let the future produce his equal if it can."

—

June VanGundy,
Hoof Beats, January 1942

DOOLEY AND THE GREY GHOST

Everyone had called Verner Putnam "Dooley" since he was four years old. Now, in his early thirties, he was far from a child—but the name, given by an uncle who owned the boy's favorite record, "Mister Dooley," had stuck with him.[1] He'd found his love for horses as a child, living across the street from a farm where Dunk Harris owned and trained harness horses. As a young boy, Dooley stood along the rail and watched Mr. Harris work his horses around the track. One day, Harris asked if Dooley would like to help with the evening chores. Dooley jumped at the opportunity.[2] His horse passion now fully ignited; the flame would never die.

After a short enlistment near the end of WWI, Dooley was discharged from the army. He'd been trained as an auto mechanic prior to his service, but while in the army, he developed a real yearning to return to his first love—horses. He returned to his hometown and found his way out to the harness track at the Brown County fairgrounds.[3] Watching the harness horses trotting and pacing around the track, Dooley was drawn in by their beauty. His heart longed to return to the world of harness horses.

"Once the love of horses gets in your blood," Mr. Harris had told Dooley years before, "it's there forever."

Never a truer statement, Dooley thought to himself as he stood there watching, close to the horses for the first time in years. He imagined working with them again, and his heart bounced and thumped in his chest.

"That's a good-looking horse," Dooley said to the man next to him, motioning to a striking bay colt coming down the track at a brisk trot.

"That's one of Dad Hatch's string," the man said. Dooley watched Hatch work his colt, and when the man reined him toward the gap, Dooley followed them back to the barn. He struck up a conversation with the trainer, introduced himself, and asked if Hatch needed any help.

"It just so happens I do." Hatch smiled. "Have anyone in mind?"

"I'd like the job myself, sir," Dooley said, hope rising in his heart.

Hatch asked about Dooley's horse experience. The young man told him about the time he'd spent working for Mr. Harris while still in school.

"I know Dunk Harris," Hatch said. "He's talked about you. Said you're a good hand and a natural with the horses." Dooley smiled, surprised that Mr. Hatch knew who he was. "You can start Monday," Hatch said, extending his hand.

Dooley grasped the man's hand and gave it a firm shake. A broad smile lightened his face. "Thank you, sir."

Dooley learned a lot working for Mr. Hatch, and got to know the trainers and drivers around the fairgrounds track.[4] One day, one of the trainers, Jack Ewing, asked Dooley if he could deliver a mare to Mason City. Dooley agreed, and the next week, took the mare to John Hubley, who was starting a stable of show horses. The world of high-stepping show horses, totally different from that of Standardbreds, fascinated Dooley, as he walked around Hubley's barn and observed the different types of tack and shoeing used on the Hackney ponies and roadsters.

Mr. Hubley liked the way Dooley handled the mare he'd delivered. The man had a natural, gentle way with a horse. Hubley offered Dooley a job on the spot. After pondering the move for a few days, Dooley accepted Hubley's offer and relocated to Mason City, Illinois.[5] It was in Mason City that Dooley met his future wife, Leone. They were married in 1924 and had a daughter, Emma Lou, in 1927.[6]

Dooley continued to work for Hubley until 1931 when Hubley, a cattle man by trade, realized he needed to focus his efforts on his livelihood and give up his show horses. Hubley dispersed his horse stock, and Dooley, faced with a young wife and daughter and no job, wondered what he would do next. But fate intervened again, and as Dooley contemplated his next steps, he received a call that would change the course of his life in a way he would never have imagined.

"Hello?" Dooley said into the phone receiver.

"Hello, Mr. Putnam, this is Doc Flanery ..."

Robert "Doc" Flanery picked up his nickname at the tender age of four when his dad, hoping

Robert would grow up to be a veterinarian, started calling his son "Doc," just in case. Doc never went to vet school, but he did become an accomplished horseman. Well-known and well-respected in the horse show world, Doc trained and showed light harness horses, saddle horses, and even heavy harness horses on occasion. He had vast experience and knowledge, often serving as a judge at shows in which he was not a competitor. Doc was based in Kansas, Illinois, a small town in the middle third of the state, about forty-five minutes west of Terre Haute, Indiana. He trained and showed horses for multiple customers, in addition to showing his own horses.

By the 1930s, Doc had made a pretty good name for himself on the show circuit, traveling all around the Midwest and down to the big shows in Kentucky. It is likely his path crossed Baker's many times due to Baker's interest in Hackney show ponies. Additionally, the horse shows Doc attended were often part of state and county fairs that also held harness racing meets. At what point Doc Flanery and Colonel Baker became friends is unclear, as is the exact year that Baker became owner of his own string of Hackney show ponies. However, at some point, possibly after Baker dispersed his racing stock due to poor health in 1940 and before he re-entered the harness horse business with the purchase of the two yearlings in late 1941, Doc Flanery became trainer of Baker's show ponies. The friendship would continue for the rest of Baker's life.

One of Doc Flanery's clients was Mrs. Pansy Yount. Doc served as the manager of Mrs. Yount's roadster division of her Spindletop Farm in Lexington, Kentucky. In 1931, Mrs. Yount purchased a Standardbred gelding named Senator Crawford. Illustrating how easily the world of harness racers and the world of light harness show horses touched and sometimes blended, Mrs. Yount's new gelding was a former harness racer, sired by The Senator, a stallion that just so happened to be owned by Palin and later by Baker. Senator Crawford would become Doc Flanery's star roadster—undefeated in eight seasons of competition.[8]

The roadster class is shown to bike (sulky), under saddle, or to wagon. The class's exciting climax occurs when the announcer calls, "Drive on," and the horses trot at full speed around the arena, showing off their gait and manners. Many of the top roadsters were Standardbreds of racing stock. Upon his retirement, Senator Crawford went to Spindletop Farm in Kentucky. But the horse soon became depressed, then agitated, and at times, even dangerous. Mrs. Yount felt certain the horse missed his friend Doc Flanery. Senator Crawford was sent to Flanery, and Mrs. Yount continued to pay for his care throughout his life.[9]

In 1931, while the mare Elizabeth was carrying the foal that would be named Greyhound and the Baker-Palin stable was racing champion pacer Winnipeg around the Grand Circuit, Doc Flanery found himself in need of a new assistant to help with his show stable. He'd likely observed Dooley Putnam at horse shows while the young man worked for John Hubley. He liked what he saw in Dooley: a gentle nature and a natural hand with the horses. When Doc learned Dooley was looking for work, he called and offered him a job.[10]

Dooley traveled with Flanery on the horse show circuit, further developing his skills and becoming an indispensable right-hand man to Doc. While in Flanery's employ, Dooley continued to keep track of his first love, harness racing, taking a special interest in Greyhound's career. While traveling to shows with Flanery, Dooley had been fortunate to see Greyhound set his world record for a racing mile in 1:57 ¼ at Springfield, Illinois in 1936, and again with Rosalind at Indianapolis in 1939—a memory Dooley would recall with tears of emotion decades later.[11]

Around the time Greyhound was making his final appearances, Flanery married Frances Beveridge and relocated his stable to Maple Park, Illinois. Dooley, Leone, and Emma Lou moved into one of the tenant houses at the new farm. The new Flanery Stables were not far from Baker's Red Gate Farm. Dooley perhaps imagined he would be able to visit Greyhound once the great champion retired. The idea filled him with excitement, and his heart swelled with emotion at the thought of seeing the greatest trotter of all time up close.

Never in a million years could he have imagined the turn his life was about to take.

June VanGundy, in a piece he* wrote for the January, 1942 issue of *Hoof Beats*, visited Baker and Greyhound at Red Gate Farm.

"Mr. Baker is a wonderful host," VanGundy wrote, "giving his undivided attention." Baker removed Greyhound's blanket and showed "him with as much pride and gusto as a ten-year-old showing off his pair of red-topped, copper-toed leather boots." VanGundy described Greyhound as Baker's pride and joy. He observed the neatly groomed grounds, the spacious, deeply bedded stall, and the large paddocks filled with lush grass. Impressed, VanGundy expressed to Baker that he'd clearly gone above and beyond in the care of his retired racehorses—Greyhound and his old champion pacer Winnipeg.[12]

"I wasn't doing so much," Baker said to VanGundy, his crisp blue eyes twinkling in the afternoon sun. With deep modesty, Baker added he hadn't done anything "beyond seeing to the matter of making them cozy and comfortable." VanGundy himself saw it as going further—a expression of genuine love for the horses.[13]

"Greyhound stands at attention and absorbs the compliments of his admirers," the article continued. "His stall manners suggest

---

* Harry VanGundy, Jr. was called "Junior" by his family as a child. This was eventually shortened to "June," which is the name he went by and wrote under.

the house manners of a six-month-old puppy. He demands attention and usually gets a lot of it," VanGundy wrote, noting that when he and Baker walked away, Greyhound "pawed at the door and nickered for [them] to come back." Visitors were always welcomed by Greyhound, VanGundy wrote; he seemed to feel he deserved it.[14]

Indeed, the champion trotter loved to be the center of attention. He had been for the past six years and couldn't understand why things were so different now. Where were the people, the horses, and the excitement of the track? After the fiasco with Greyhound ditching his driver and running away, Baker spoke with his friend Doc Flanery, and a plan formed—Doc would take over Greyhound's care at Flanery Stables, ensuring he got plenty of exercise and was handled safely. Additionally, he would manage the horse's exhibitions, training him for and accompanying him to events around the country.

But there was one more thing Greyhound needed. The horse had grown accustomed to a certain level of care and connection with his human friends—he needed more human contact and personal attention than was available at Red Gate. Much like the job Jimmie Wingfield had done on the track, Greyhound needed a personal caretaker. He was disinterested in the other horses and often showed disdain for them, pinning his ears and snapping his teeth whenever another horse walked by.[15] The big horse craved human interaction. He needed a friend like Jimmie had been. Doc knew just the man for the job, too—Dooley Putnam.

"Well, I was just an old country farm boy," Dooley would recall years later, "but I decided I'd do the best I could."[16] Dooley couldn't believe his luck. Had he known what the future held for him back in '36 when he first saw Greyhound race—well, he just wouldn't have believed it. *He's sure a great horse*, Dooley thought to himself. *I just hope he likes me.*[17]

Doc and Dooley were readying the horses for a show in Denver, Colorado. Upon their return, Greyhound would move to Flanery Stables. But word travels fast in the horse world. When the manager of the National Western Horse Show in Denver heard that his old friend Doc Flanery had charge over Greyhound, he had an idea. He quickly placed a call to Colonel Baker and asked if Greyhound could come to Denver with Flanery's show horses and make an appearance.[18]

As the Flanery horses loaded onto the Denver-bound train, a big van from Red Gate backed up to the platform.* Dooley dropped the heavy ramp, and opened the big doors. It was the first time Dooley had seen Greyhound

---

* Dooley's memories of the first time he saw Greyhound up close, which was when the horse arrived at the train platform from Red Gate, are portrayed here. The information is taken from Leone's book and notes. The date given by Leone is January 1941, but since newspaper reports indicate Greyhound was still with Palin in 1941, and specifically with Jimmie in Aiken in January 1941,[19] it is likely January 1942 is the correct date.

up close, and he was surprised at how big he was. The horse stood tall and majestic in the van. His ears pricked up at the sounds of the horses and the train. He stretched his neck forward, pushing hard against the cross ties attached to the side rings of his halter, trying to see outside the door.

Dooley could see Greyhound was curious but not afraid. The horse had done all this many times before. The man rolled out the heavy cactus mat over the wooden ramp for traction, and placed the wood guard rails in the slats on either side of the ramp. Greyhound walked across the ramp to the train car like a gentleman, but his big brown eyes missed nothing. *Eagle eyes.*[20] Dooley settled the big horse into his stall, ensuring Greyhound was comfortable and had plenty of hay and water. The big gray watched the man, as if sizing him up. *Like he can see right through me.*[21] Dooley patted Greyhound on the neck, then found his own cot nearby, and settled in for the long ride.

By the time the train rolled into Denver, Dooley had taken a bit of a liking to Greyhound. The big horse was smart and sensible. But when the other horses began to unload, Greyhound became anxious and pawed the floor of his stall. *Ready to go.* It made sense to Dooley; the horse knew something was up and didn't want to miss a thing. When the cold mountain air filled his lungs for the first time, Greyhound bucked and kicked like a colt. It was all Dooley could do to handle the big horse as Greyhound practically dragged him the three blocks to the coliseum. But once inside, he settled right down.[22]

At Denver, Greyhound made an appearance each night of the show.[23] The fans cheered, hardly believing the champion trotter had come all the way to Denver! It was by far the farthest west Greyhound had ever traveled. People came from all over the area, entering the stables throughout the day to see Greyhound up close. Dooley constantly had to ask them to move so he could go in and out of the horse's stall. Finally, he grabbed some rope and a couple poles, and roped off the area in front of Greyhound's stall—like the velvet ropes that line an entrance at a red-carpet event.[24]

Dooley clipped and trimmed Greyhound up like a show horse, even braiding red ribbon into his mane and forelock. He placed a new bridle on him, with red-and-white checked brow and nose bands that matched Colonel Baker's stable colors.[25] While some people would swear the big horse's hooves were painted bright red—and at a later presentation, one horrified woman would swear the horse's feet were bleeding—it wasn't true. What they actually saw were red protective boots around Greyhound's front hooves,[26] though the "red painted hooves" rumor would persist and become part of the lore surrounding Greyhound well into the next century.

A bugle sounded the "Call to the Post," the signal to take Greyhound to the show ring. The gray's head shot up, his ears pricked forward, his eyes widened, and his nostrils quivered.

He charged forward, pulling Dooley along with him.[27] He knew what that sound meant! Surely he'd returned to the races.

Dooley tried to settle the big gray as the horse half dragged him to the arena. The crowd fell silent as the pair entered the ring, then erupted in applause. Greyhound bucked and kicked out like a colt. The crowd chuckled at his antics. The Grey Ghost strutted about the ring, his head turned to look into the stands—he seemed to know they were all there just for him. The Governor of Colorado and the president of the horse show presented Greyhound with a beautiful trophy.[28]

After returning from Denver, Greyhound settled into his new routine at Flanery's stable. He loved the activity of the show barn; there was so much to see. Dooley hooked him to the cart and jogged him every day to occupy his mind and keep him healthy and happy. The pair soon formed an unbreakable bond, one that would last for nearly twenty-five years.

END of CHAPTER 27

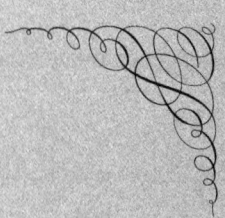

CHAPTER
— 28 —

"The old harness men could control their emotions no longer. They yelled and waved and those who couldn't yell just grinned and shook their heads. At the sight of Greyhound trotting again, some were speechless."

—

JOE ASTON,
THE CINCINNATI POST, OCTOBER 1945

BAKERS ACRES

Early in 1942, the main house at the Flanery farm burned. The weather had been bitterly cold, and a fire broke out when employees attempted to thaw frozen pipes with a blowtorch.[1] Neighbors rallied around and created a bucket brigade to assist the two small area fire departments, but the house could not be saved.[2] However, the diligent work of volunteers and firefighters saved the attached barn and all the horses.[3] Now Doc and Frances had to decide—would they rebuild or relocate?

Baker had an idea of his own. He purchased a farm not far from St. Charles. It had plenty of space, nice facilities, and housing for everyone. He offered Doc a job managing the farm. The Flanerys and the Putnams, along with Greyhound, Senator Crawford, the show horses, and Baker's show ponies soon relocated to the new farm: Bakers Acres* in Northbrook, Illinois.

Bakers Acres sat on three hundred twenty-eight acres, about twenty miles west of Chicago. There were three residences on the property,

---

* Both "Bakers Acres" and "Baker Acres" appear on historical documents. The author has chosen to use the more commonly seen "Bakers Acres." The lack of apostrophe was common for location names in this era.

a forty-stall barn with carriage storage and plenty of useful space, plus a large 90x200 foot indoor arena, with new tanbark footing and a heating system. The barns and homes were painted white with red trim. White, four-board, oak-plank fences surrounded the property and sectioned off paddocks, pastures, a large outdoor track, and a riding ring.[4]

Requests for Greyhound to make an appearance came from all over the country. Baker accommodated as many as he could over the next 14 years. Early on, Greyhound traveled with Doc's show string to the various fairs that also had horse shows, in addition to special appearances at harness racing tracks around the country. Thousands of fans came to see Greyhound's exhibition trots. Doc Flanery, wearing his red and white silks that matched the Hotel Baker Stables colors, and a pure-white Greyhound strutting around the track or the show ring were a magnificent sight. Sometimes Greyhound wore a blanket of red roses like the one placed over the shoulders of the Kentucky Derby winner each year. The people cheered and applauded as the gray trotted for them, the ends of the flower blanket held aloft by the tremendous wind he created as he flew past the grandstand.

Baker loved to share Greyhound with the horse's many fans. He saw it as a privilege to own such a horse, and sharing him was part of his duty as Greyhound's steward. Baker felt he owned Greyhound on paper only, for the horse truly belonged to the people. He sent Greyhound around the country, twice all the way out to California—all at his own expense.[5] He understood how important Greyhound was to the people that loved him. Greyhound had seen them through some of the toughest years of their lives, giving them a reprieve from their worries for at least a few moments while they followed his career in the papers and on the radio. With the Great Depression crushing the nation in the 1930s, many poverty-stricken Americans could not have afforded to travel and see the great horse, but they had been able to read about him and see pictures. And now, as a retiree, he traveled to them, fulfilling the dreams of many who would otherwise not have had an opportunity to see the greatest trotter of them all.

Dooley understood how the people felt. He felt it, too. Sure, some people looked at a horse like Greyhound and thought, *What's the big deal? He's just a horse.* But they'd never felt what Dooley and other horse lovers felt. There was something about a horse that got into the very core of your soul—a passion that coursed through your blood and resided in your heart. Dooley couldn't explain it. In fact, you'd be hard-pressed to find someone who could. But somehow, the sight of a special horse could make a person's heart ache with love while also sending their spirit soaring, lifting them to a place that felt like no other.

Greyhound's birthday parties at Bakers Acres were an annual event for St. Charles residents and anyone else who wanted to come. Formal invitations were sent for these galas, complete with tickets to present at the gate. Baker brought in orchestras and had huge buffet lunches served. People dressed in their Sunday best and viewed the lovely farm, the horses, and the guest of honor, Greyhound. Though Greyhound's actual birthday was in March, these events were often held in August or later in the fall, presumably to take advantage of the much more suitable weather.

In 1943, the *Chicago Daily News* came and did a huge multi-page spread on the affair. The piece featured pictures of Greyhound in his show halter, with red ribbons braided in his mane and forelock. One end of the indoor arena was filled with white folding chairs and tables covered with red-and-white checked linen cloths. Red, white, and blue bunting hung along the rafters and walls.[6] Guests were "wined and dined and treated to a top-notch floor show" on a stage in the center of the arena, reported W. J. Arbuckle in *The Harness Horse*. Even old Senator Crawford made an appearance.[7]

Images of Greyhound being presented to the people, Baker greeting small children and other guests, people viewing Greyhound's sulky on display, and hundreds of people crowding around the outdoor track as Baker's show ponies were presented adorned the three-page spread.

These parties were attended by as many as 3,000 guests, like a huge community picnic that brought horse lovers, family, friends, and neighbors together. Baker paid for it all, never asking for anything in return. A very generous man, he understood how fortunate he was, and had no problem spreading it around. He just enjoyed making and seeing people happy.

Dooley placed a hand on Greyhound's neck. The barn area was quiet now; the crowds of people had finally left for the evening. Dooley enjoyed these quiet times alone with Greyhound. The two had grown quite close. Greyhound had been ill earlier in the year, and Dooley had stayed with him around the clock, applying hot compresses to an abscess on his throat and coaxing the horse to eat by giving him his food a handful at a time. Greyhound had become so sick, Dooley had feared the worst. When the gelding had been in his direst state, he'd nickered weakly at Dooley if the man went to step out of the stall. So Dooley stayed with him, reassuring the big horse, and the two bonded deeply.[8] Tears stung the tall man's eyes as he recalled those long and terrifying nights.[9]

Dooley ran a soft cloth over Greyhound's face. The horse had fully recovered and was now back to his old self, grabbing at the cloth with his lips as Dooley wiped dust from his face and muzzle.

"You were something else today, Grey." Dooley laughed softly. They had returned to Lexington, the site of Greyhound's world-record mile six years before. The track association had arranged for Greyhound to lead a small parade of stars. Elizabeth followed Greyhound with her 1944 colt by Nibble Hanover. Then came Yankee Maid (Elizabeth's daughter by Volomite), winner of the 1944 Hambletonian, and Peter Astra, the only horse to win a heat over Greyhound during his final season of racing.

Greyhound had pranced around on the track with Dooley leading him, bouncing around and kicking out. The crowd loved his antics and cheered louder.[10] Greyhound's popularity seemed to be growing in retirement. He'd always been the "horse of the people," but now, with Greyhound making appearances, he attracted new fans, and even younger fans that hadn't been around to see him when he raced.

April 1946 found Dooley and Greyhound boarding a westbound train. It was an exciting time in harness racing. For the first time ever, a major harness racing event would take place in California. The inaugural California Grand Circuit meeting was staged at Santa Anita. The track normally ran Thoroughbred races, but for twenty-seven days it would be all about the harness racers. The opening day boasted four stakes races, including the Western Harness Grand Trot and the Western Harness Grand Pace—each with a purse of $50,000.[11]

"Can you imagine that?" Dooley spoke softly to Greyhound as he settled him into his stall at Santa Anita. "Fifty thousand dollars—that's more than you made your entire career." Times had certainly changed since the emaciated purses Greyhound raced for during the Depression days.

After the third race on opening day, Doc Flanery drove a pure white Greyhound for an exhibition mile around the Santa Anita oval.[12] Over 35,000 fans stood and cheered for the great champion[13] who, even at the age of fourteen, still possessed the long, ground-covering stride that had made him the greatest trotter of all time. After the exhibition, Greyhound was presented with a silver trophy and a garland of white flowers.

"He's a superb showman," Baker once said of Greyhound, and it was true. In his racing days, he became known for looking into the crowd of cheering fans and nodding his head as if taking a bow. "Greyhound would take to the track, look into the stands, proceed to strut and do his bowing when the audience broke into cheers over his fine exhibitions," sports writer and historian Frank G. Menke wrote of Greyhound's 1946 visit to Santa Anita.[14]

A year later, Baker made local headlines when he arrived in California for the Western Harness Association meet. In addition to Greyhound, he had a 15-horse racing stable at Hollywood Park, the location for the Grand Circuit meet of 1947.[15] Baker didn't settle into retirement any more easily than Greyhound had. He craved the excitement of the track, too. At Hollywood Park, a movie company came to film the great champion. The cameraman followed Dooley and Greyhound through their daily routine. Like so many others who had the opportunity to look more intimately into Greyhound's life, the movie men were surprised by the horse's personality.[16]

"It's like there's a human inside that horse," one man said as he watched Greyhound from outside his stall. "We didn't know until today that a horse could have so much personality," the cameraman said. "He's a magnificent animal." The big gelding shook his head and yawned, his long tongue stretched out briefly over his lower teeth. The men laughed. He was some horse.

Forty-five thousand people came to see Greyhound at Hollywood Park the day the movie was made. He performed an exhibition trot in front of the grandstand with Doc Flanery holding the lines, scoring him down the wrong way of the track, then turning him to trot the last quarter down the stretch. His magnificent stride, still long and powerful, carried him along the quarter mile at a near two-minute clip.[17] Even at the age of fifteen, Greyhound looked like he could still out-trot them all.

"Yup." Dooley placed a hand on Greyhound's sleek, white neck. "They sure love you, Grey." Greyhound turned his head, nuzzling Dooley's shirt pockets with his ever-curious lips. "I used to worry people would forget about you." Dooley placed a hand gently on Greyhound's upper lip, and the big gelding wiggled it back and forth, as if trying to dislodge Dooley's hand. It was a game they played. Dooley shook his head and smiled. "Nope. They'll never forget you, that's for sure."

He turned and pulled a red blanket off the bar by the stall door and placed it over Greyhound's body. The horse fiddled with the buckles at his chest, grabbing the fabric with his teeth and lipping Dooley's hands as the man secured the blanket straps. Baker liked Greyhound to look like a show horse—no small task on a horse with a snow-white coat. The light blanket helped keep the stains from grass, dirt, or hay-slobber off Greyhound's sleek white body.[18, 19]

With his health failing, Colonel Baker's doctor again encouraged him to retire from horses altogether. On October 28, 1947, a total dispersal of all stock and equipment took place at Bakers Acres. The show ponies, all racing stock, carts, harnesses, equipment—everything went under the hammer.[20] Baker had purchased the best horses available through the years, filling his stable with champions and future champions. The auction drew people from all over the country, eager to get a piece of the horse industry icon's valuable stock.

The one horse Baker would never sell was his friend Greyhound. Baker visited the gelding regularly, and Greyhound always seemed to know when the elderly gentleman was nearby. He'd thrust his head over the stall door and nicker as Baker approached. Baker always carried carrots in his pocket, and Greyhound eagerly took them from his owner's hand.

After his horses had all found new homes, the forty-mile drive out to Bakers Acres to see Greyhound was a bittersweet experience. Baker loved to see his friend, but the empty stalls and paddocks where his own horses had been filled him with sadness. Flanery still had his string of horses there, but it wasn't the same. Bakers Acres went up for sale.[21] With tears in his eyes, Baker said goodbye to the farm that had been such a source of joy for so many years.

The Flanerys had maintained ownership of the farm in Maple Park, still running the place as a farm, raising cattle and crops. After the sale of Bakers Acres, the Flanery horses moved back to Maple Park. Since the facility at Maple Park was smaller, there was no extra room for horses not in training. Doc and Frances again considered rebuilding the house that had burned down eight years before, but instead opted to move to town. The Putnams returned to the home they'd lived in previously, a large apartment behind the big barn at Flanery Farm.

Greyhound went to nearby Red Gate Farm, with Doc's old roadster champion, Senator Crawford, for company. As before, Greyhound didn't enjoy life at Red Gate. It wasn't a bad place by any means; he was well cared for and had everything he needed. But Greyhound missed the excitement of the busy training farm.

"I think Greyhound would be happier at your farm, Doc." Baker moved the cigar from one side of his mouth to the other, took a puff, and looked at Flanery.

"I told you, I don't have any empty stalls," Doc said flatly.

Baker wasn't used to hearing "no" and was a bit taken aback. He chewed thoughtfully on his cigar. "What if I build him a stall?"[22]

Doc looked at his old friend for a moment, then nodded his head.

Baker took the cigar from his mouth and smiled warmly. He then returned it and puffed on it thoughtfully, his blue eyes looking toward a future only he could see. Doc looked at his friend—the wheels were already turning. Doc smiled and looked down, rubbing the toe of his boot in the gravel at his feet. He could tell even now—this would be some stall.

GREYHOUND

THE REMARKABLE STORY OF THE LEGENDARY RACEHORSE WHO INSPIRED A NATION

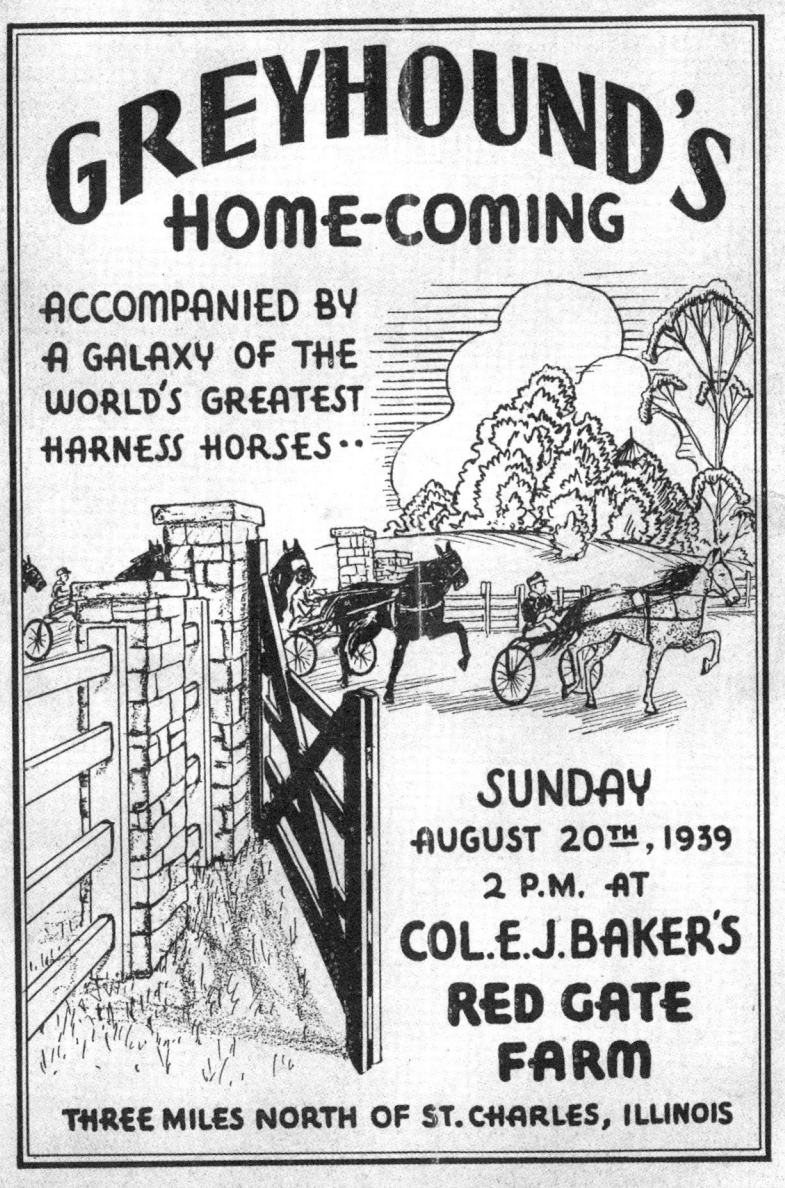

CIRCA 1939, COURTESY OF THE ST. CHARLES HISTORICAL SOCIETY

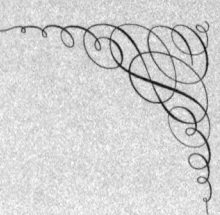

CHAPTER
— 29 —

> "A more fitting finale to such a career as Greyhound's would be unimaginable. With it he passed from the stage 'staggering under the weight of his laurels,' and taking with him fifteen different world's records at all distances from a quarter of a mile to two miles, in single and double harness, under saddle, and over both major and minor tracks."
>
> —
>
> JOHN HERVEY,
> THE AMERICAN TROTTER, 1947

> "Greyhound and I are headed for the easy chair."
>
> —
>
> COL. E. J. BAKER, 1947

TWILIGHT

Two hundred guests—friends and neighbors—came to Greyhound's "house-warming" party on October 11, 1949.[1] The stall Baker had built for Greyhound could be more accurately described as a horse apartment. Guests approaching from the parking area were greeted with what looked like the entrance to a home. The new façade came complete with a large picture window flanked by two smaller windows, and a retractable red-and-white striped awning that ran the length of the windows. Below were flower boxes overflowing with red and white petunias and vines of hanging pothos spilling over the sides. To the right of the partially fenced courtyard, a crushed stone walkway led to the entrance.

Upon crossing the threshold, guests were greeted with a beautifully appointed lounge where Greyhound received his guests. The room featured bleached knotty pine walls, a built-in, glass-fronted trophy case, a custom lamp bearing Greyhound's portrait, and a brass trotting horse desk lamp with marble base, among other fine touches. Hanging on the walls were photos of Greyhound in his racing days, including an image of him and Rosalind setting their record tandem mile. Two large rattan chairs and a rattan couch with custom red-and-white striped cushions offered ample seating.

Directly across from the lounge entrance was Greyhound's "main residence." A second large picture window took up much of the front wall of the horse's stall. This window, by necessity, was made of extremely thick, shatterproof glass—for behind it resided the greatest trotter of all time. It was an unusual feature in a horse stall, but essential, as the stall was fully insulated and air-conditioned. The aging champion had grown intolerant of the at times extreme summer heat. To the left of the large stall window was a traditional stall door made of varnished oak, with red painted steel bars on the upper half. A second door could be closed over this, completely enclosing the stall when the air conditioning was needed.

Greyhound's stall measured 12 feet wide and 21 feet deep. It featured varnished oak panels, brass screened windows looking into the stalls of neighboring horses, recessed lighting, brass tie rings, and an escape door to the rear of the stall. A horse-sized door was added to the lounge so that, if need be, Greyhound could exit through the seating area. Greyhound had lived through two fires in his life and Baker had insisted there should be multiple means of escape from the stall.[2]

The lounge measured about 12 feet deep, and several feet wider than the stall. The door from the stall into the lounge could be opened on top so Greyhound could hang his head out and visit with his guests. There were brass bars mounted on the wall to hang his blankets, a large brass nameplate, and other touches that would rival a fine sitting room in someone's home. On a table near the large picture window, Baker placed a leather-bound guest book. In the years to come, the book would receive thousands of signatures—visitors from every state and 27 different countries.[3]

At the back of the barn was a large apartment for the Putnam family. The barn could be accessed from the Putnams' front yard, or through a door and walkway directly from their kitchen. The latter allowed Dooley to access the barn, Greyhound, and his office without ever going outside. Leone and Dooley would often joke Greyhound's was the only barn with housing added in back for the people, instead of the other way around.[4] From his stall, Greyhound could see other horses through the screened windows, or he could look out a second picture window in the lounge and see the apple orchard and the fields where mares grazed and their foals frolicked or slept in the afternoon sun.

The orchard soon became Greyhound's favorite place to be. There, he'd toss his head like a colt, trotting and galloping about, bucking and playing. Greyhound's favorite tree had a low branch, the perfect height for him to duck under and scratch his back. While outside, the great horse would graze in the shade of the trees, or hold court over the fence with the young horses. It appeared as if the youngsters were gathered around listening, learning from the wisdom and experience of the old man. Greyhound loved to hang out with the foals and yearlings, but had little use for the older horses, pinning his ears and snapping his teeth whenever one came near.

In the winter months, Greyhound enjoyed romping and rolling in the deep, fluffy snow. He'd chase about, tossing his head and trotting through the snow drifts, great puffs of white flakes scattering in his wake. Greyhound never rolled in the grass or dirt, Dooley often said, but he loved to roll in the snow.[5]

On July 1, 1954, thousands of people came to Sportsman's Park near Chicago for Greyhound's twenty-second birthday celebration. A large cake arrived for the people, with a special bag of oats tied with a blue ribbon for Greyhound.[6] A few days after this celebration, the Putnams received a letter from Stanley Bergstein, the track announcer at Sportsman's Park. Mr. Bergstein expressed how thrilling it had been to know Greyhound through his career writing about and calling harness races. "But the highlight of all, I think, came last night as I watched [Dooley] pat [Greyhound] reassuringly on the shoulder ... as the call to the post rang out for the ninth race."[7]

According to Leone's notes, Greyhound's final appearance in harness was on August 19, 1954, on President Eisenhower Day at the Illinois State Fair. Surprisingly, this author found no reports on Greyhound's appearance at the fair. Leone noted that the horse's appearance was overshadowed in the news by the presidential visit, but Dooley felt certain "Greyhound gave Eisenhower a run for his money" when it came to attention-grabbing.[8] Doc and Greyhound had done multiple exhibitions at large race tracks and small county fairs across the country over the past 14 years. Now aged twenty-three, Greyhound, having developed arthritis in his legs that made travel and training too difficult, was finally ready for retirement. He still went for light exercise with Dooley in the jog cart, the movement being good for his arthritic joints. But soon his body began to let him down. His mind and heart still wanted to fly over the ground with lightning speed, legs pumping like the smooth motion of a steam locomotive at full power. But his legs could no longer do what his heart desired, and the big horse resented Dooley asking for a leisurely pace, fighting for his freedom under Dooley's compassionate restraint. Greyhound was hooked to a cart for the last time in 1956.[9]

As Greyhound trotted through the early 1950s on his way to his final retirement, Colonel Baker had started anew once again—he simply could not resist the pull of the sport. Despite completely dispersing his show and racing stable on the advice of his doctor in 1947, he again found his way back to the harness races a few years later. With Doc Flanery as trainer-driver of the racing stable this time, Baker continued to travel and watch Doc race his horses. But in 1955, his health again in decline, Baker's doctor insisted the eighty-six-year-old stop attending the races. Baker reluctantly acquiesced, but continued to visit Greyhound almost every day, his long-time friend and assistant Everett Eastman driving him out to Flanery's farm regularly to see the great champion. Now, they both were relegated to the easy chair.

In the early 1950s, with Greyhound still looking and acting like a much younger horse than his twenty-plus age, Baker realized his friend would likely outlive him. He adjusted his will to ensure Greyhound would be cared for in the manner he was accustomed to throughout the remainder of the grand horse's life. In the will, money was set aside for his care, and specific instructions were left to bury Greyhound at Red Gate Farm.[10] A monument had already been placed there by Baker. It read:

> ***This monument is dedicated in affection and pride to him who needs none. The horse. May neither rain nor wind nor flight of time erase the glory of his memory.***

Beneath the large monument rested the pacer Winnipeg 1:57 ¾, Baker's first champion and the first two-minute horse for both him and Palin. To the right of Winnipeg lay Volo Song 1:57 ¾, another of Baker's beloved champions, winner of the 1943 Hambletonian; the colt had regrettably died the following year in an accident. To the left of Winnipeg, a bronze marker had been placed for Greyhound 1:55 ¼. Flowers were planted each year over the graves, including Greyhound's empty plot. Next to the large monument was the grave of Labrador 2:07, one of Baker's first pacers after teaming up with Palin. Behind the monument were the graves of many of Baker's favorite dogs. Everything looked just exactly as Baker wanted it.

Colonel Baker's health declined steadily from 1955 on, but he still made it out to the farm as often as possible to see Greyhound. Dooley would pull one of the cushioned chairs over to Greyhound's stall and Baker would sit there, gazing up at his friend, with the big gray reaching his long neck over the stall door to touch the man's outstretched hand. Baker's visits became less frequent. One day, Dooley and Leone's daughter, Emma Lou, now grown, saw Baker at the farm, his face looking tired and worn. Concerned, she went to him, speaking gently to the now frail man. His clear blue eyes looked up at her.

"I'll never have to worry about Greyhound as long as Dooley takes care of him," Baker said to Emma Lou through silent tears, "for I believe he loves him as much as I do."[11]

Baker's last visit with his beloved Greyhound was in April 1958.[12] During the last year of his life, Baker was mostly confined to his bed in the top floor apartment of the Hotel Baker. Eastman stayed with him and cared for him along with doctors and nurses. Colonel Edward James Baker died on January 17, 1959. His death was reported in newspapers around the country. Long articles were published in the harness horse magazines, celebrating his life and contributions to the sport. Provisions in his will continued to fund improvements for the city he loved, as well as financial gifts to many friends and employees.

"Churches, city hall, and municipal facilities constructed almost entirely by him for the city of St. Charles attest to his generosity of spirit," Woodford Lawlis wrote for the September 1956 issue of *Hoof Beats*. "But the chief recipient of this generosity is the sport of harness racing, where his name is written as indelibly ... as any other whose contributions have marked milestones."[13]

Greyhound reigned supreme as the king of Flanery Farm. Guests came almost daily to visit him. Sometimes on a Sunday as many as one hundred vehicles drove through the gate, looking for the champion. Greyhound was the most popular free attraction in the state of Illinois. School groups, 4-H groups, Cub Scouts, and many others came. Families and individuals traveled from all over the country and the world. A young man visiting from Holland told Leone he had come to America to see the Grand Canyon, the Statue of Liberty, and Greyhound.[14]

Cards and letters came from around the world, many addressed simply to "Greyhound at Flanery Farm, Maple Park, Illinois." Hundreds of letters were received and answered by Leone and Dooley. Leone made a notation on the envelope of each piece of mail with the date it was responded to. Christmas cards and birthday cards arrived every year. Children who were born many years after the last time Greyhound raced drew pictures of the grand gelding and sent letters, likely learning of him from the stories told as their parents and grandparents shared deeply cherished memories. At least one child, eleven-year-old Charlo Maurer of Yellow Springs, Ohio, learned of Greyhound in 1964 by reading Marguerite Henry's *Born to Trot*, the story of Gibson White's champion mare Rosalind.[15] Almost twenty-five years later, at the same tender age, the author of this book you are reading now would first learn of Greyhound the very same way.

Dooley, Leone, and Greyhound became like a little family, with Greyhound playing the part of the big, overgrown kid. Leone, who worked as the secretary for Flanery Farm, also kept Greyhound's lounge clean and tidy. With a bucket of warm soapy water and a cloth, she'd clean the big picture window in Greyhound's stall. The horse, highly skilled at getting attention, would wait until Leone had finished and was exiting the stall, then wipe his nose on the clean glass.[16] This naturally brought Leone back into the stall for another swipe at the window and a few more neck scratches.

Other times during the cleaning, Greyhound would come up to the stall door and press his face against the bars. This was Greyhound's signal to grab the vacuum, Leone would later record in her notes. She'd walk over to the stall and vacuum the big gray's face and ears with the brush attachment—an activity Greyhound thoroughly enjoyed. Leone's notes were full of wonderful stories about her and Dooley's life with Greyhound, such as the time some photographers came to take pictures of Greyhound in his orchard for a short film. Dooley recommended they stay outside the fence, but the photographers snuck in anyway. Greyhound playfully ran after them, wanting to chase them about, but the frightened photographers didn't see the fun in that and scrambled back over the fence as fast as they could.[17]

After retiring from exhibitions, Greyhound still made one public appearance a year, traveling to nearby Sportsman's Park in Chicago for a birthday celebration. The track sent a private, nine-horse luxury van to haul the champ. The first celebration marked Greyhound's twenty-third birthday in 1955. Dooley led Greyhound out onto the track before 12,000 fans. He was presented with a white blanket with his name and record time in red lettering. A cake large enough to serve five hundred people was made for the occasion.[18]

Greyhound's last public appearance was in June 1962 at Sportsman's Park, in celebration of his thirtieth birthday. Thousands of fans came to see the snow-white horse. His celebrity status had only grown through the years. *It seemed Greyhound was more popular now than ever,* Leone wrote in her notes. The Grey Ghost strutted out onto the track for the last time. Flowers were placed over the champion's shoulders (he'd only allow Dooley to do it) while cameras clicked, light bulbs flashed, and people cheered.

"There wasn't a dry eye in the place," Leone recalled.

In December 1964, a piece was published in newspapers around the United States and in multiple countries around the world. The story recounted Greyhound's tremendous accomplishments and world records, many of which still stood, with the most significant record being that of trotting a mile in 1:55 ¼. It had been twenty-six years and still no trotting horse had touched it.

The article brought a huge influx of letters and cards for Greyhound. The bulk of these were addressed directly to Greyhound, from adult men and women telling the horse of a specific memory they had of him, where they were when they saw him, who they were with, and how special that memory was to them. This author had the opportunity to read these letters, and the emotion in the heartfelt words and remembrances was quite touching. Many people asked for a picture of Greyhound, one of his shoes, or some hair from his brush. Leone and Dooley did their best to respond, but the amount of mail was overwhelming.

"Do take good, good care of him, give him an extra sugar for me and a nice gentle hug, and whisper in his ear that I wish him many more healthy birthdays."—Mrs. C M Bonner, Dayton, OH, 12/28/64[20]

"Seeing a great horse as Greyhound is an experience I am grateful for and will always remember."—Marianne Weyker, December 1964[21]

"To Greyhound, Happy Birthday to you and hope you may have many more."—Art Morris, December 1964.[22]

Mr. Morris noted in his three-page letter to Greyhound that he had cared for his granddam Zombrewer as a filly back in 1906.

GREYHOUND

THE REMARKABLE STORY
OF THE LEGENDARY RACEHORSE WHO INSPIRED A NATION

gallery

[101]
Col. Baker and Greyhound.
- *1949, courtesy of the United States Trotting Association*

[102]
Greyhound looks over his stall door into his visitors' lounge.
- *1949, courtesy of the United States Trotting Association*

[103]
Dooley taking Greyhound for exercise at Flanery Farm.
- *1953, courtesy of the United States Trotting Association*

GREYHOUND

THE REMARKABLE STORY
OF THE LEGENDARY RACEHORSE WHO INSPIRED A NATION

gallery

[104]
Dooley leads Greyhound before the crowd at Sportsman's Park, Chicago.
• *1954, Heitbrink Collection, courtesy of the Harness Racing Museum & Hall of Fame, Goshen, NY*

[105]
Dooley and Greyhound outside Doc's horse trailer.
• *1955, Heitbrink Collection, courtesy of the Harness Racing Museum & Hall of Fame, Goshen, NY*

GREYHOUND

THE REMARKABLE STORY
OF THE LEGENDARY RACEHORSE WHO INSPIRED A NATION

gallery

[106]
Greyhound and Dooley check out Greyhound's 24th birthday card.
• *1956, courtesy of the Harness Racing Museum & Hall of Fame, Goshen, NY*

[107]
The original caption for this photo read: "KARROTS FOR A KING. Greyhound, most famous trotter of them all, gets a huge birthday present as he celebrates his No. 24 at Sportsman's Park. Left to right are Bud Zigler of St. Charles, [IL], President Don Burnett of Chicago Downs, Doc Flanery, last to drive the Grey Ghost to victory in a race, and [Verner] Putnam, caretaker of the fabulous trotter. Bouquet includes 24 bunches of carrots." The caption was wrong about Doc Flanery, who never drove Greyhound in a race, only after his retirement.
• *1956, courtesy of the United States Trotting Association*

GREYHOUND
THE REMARKABLE STORY
OF THE LEGENDARY RACEHORSE WHO INSPIRED A NATION
gallery

[108]
Dooley and Greyhound.
• *summer 1957, Heitbrink Collection, courtesy of the Harness Racing Museum & Hall of Fame, Goshen, NY*

[109]
Cemetery at Red Gate Farm; Dooley is standing by the monument.
• *1957, Heitbrink Collection, courtesy of the Harness Racing Museum & Hall of Fame, Goshen, NY*

[110]
Baker and Greyhound's last picture together.
• *1958, Heitbrink Collection, courtesy of the Harness Racing Museum & Hall of Fame, Goshen, NY*

GREYHOUND

THE REMARKABLE STORY
OF THE LEGENDARY RACEHORSE WHO INSPIRED A NATION

gallery

[111]
Greyhound in his stall.
- *October 1960, Heitbrink Collection, courtesy of the Harness Racing Museum & Hall of Fame, Goshen, NY*

[112]
Greyhound at age 29.
- *August 1961, Heitbrink Collection, courtesy of the Harness Racing Museum & Hall of Fame, Goshen, NY*

[113]
Celebrating Greyhound's 30th birthday.
- *March 1962, Heitbrink Collection, courtesy of the Harness Racing Museum & Hall of Fame, Goshen, NY*

GREYHOUND

THE REMARKABLE STORY
OF THE LEGENDARY RACEHORSE WHO INSPIRED A NATION

gallery

[114]
Greyhound with his Hambletonian Trophy.
• *June 1962, Heitbrink Collection, courtesy of the Harness Racing Museum & Hall of Fame, Goshen, NY*

[115]
Leone and Dooley Putnam with Greyhound.
• *July 1962, Heitbrink Collection, courtesy of the Harness Racing Museum & Hall of Fame, Goshen, NY*

[116]
Greyhound sleeps after his last exhibition at Sportsman's Park.
• *June 14, 1962, Heitbrink Collection, courtesy of the Harness Racing Museum & Hall of Fame, Goshen, NY*

GREYHOUND

THE REMARKABLE STORY
OF THE LEGENDARY RACEHORSE WHO INSPIRED A NATION

gallery

[117]
Flowers and remembrances for Greyhound were sent to Flanery Farm from all over.
• *March 1965, Heitbrink Collection, courtesy of the Harness Racing Museum & Hall of Fame, Goshen, NY*

[118]
Dooley and Greyhound.
• *October 1964, Heitbrink Collection, courtesy of the Harness Racing Museum & Hall of Fame, Goshen, NY*

GREYHOUND

THE REMARKABLE STORY
OF THE LEGENDARY RACEHORSE WHO INSPIRED A NATION

gallery

[119]
Playing cards gifted to friends by Col. Baker; reception committee ribbon and pin from Greyhound Day, October 13, 1946.
• *2023, items courtesy of the Harness Racing Museum & Hall of Fame, Goshen, NY, photo courtesy of Cheryl L. Eriksen*

[120]
Greyhound's grave marker.
• *June 2023, courtesy of Cheryl L. Eriksen*

GREYHOUND

THE REMARKABLE STORY
OF THE LEGENDARY RACEHORSE WHO INSPIRED A NATION

gallery

[121]
The monument erected by Col. Baker at Red Gate Farm Cemetery in 1959.
• *June 2023, courtesy of Cheryl L. Eriksen*

GREYHOUND

THE REMARKABLE STORY
OF THE LEGENDARY RACEHORSE WHO INSPIRED A NATION

gallery

[122]
Col. Baker with Greyhound at Flanery Farm.
• circa 1948, courtesy of the St. Charles Historical Society

[123]
Greyhound shortly after retirement.
• circa 1942, courtesy of the Hambletonian Society

[124]
Greyhound's final appearance at Good Time Park with Doc Flanery, on Hambletonian Day.
• 1947, courtesy of the Harness Racing Museum & Hall of Fame, Goshen, NY

GREYHOUND

THE REMARKABLE STORY
OF THE LEGENDARY RACEHORSE WHO INSPIRED A NATION

gallery

[125]
Greyhound poses among the apple blossoms.
• *circa 1960, Heitbrink Collection, courtesy of the Harness Racing Museum & Hall of Fame, Goshen, NY*

[126]
Greyhound scratches his back on his favorite apple tree.
• *circa 1960, Heitbrink Collection, courtesy of the Harness Racing Museum & Hall of Fame, Goshen, NY*

GREYHOUND

THE REMARKABLE STORY
OF THE LEGENDARY RACEHORSE WHO INSPIRED A NATION

gallery

[127]
Dooley standing with Greyhound. Note the photo of Greyhound and Rosalind on the wall, and a Santa Claus decoration on the mirror.
• *circa 1961, Heitbrink Collection, courtesy of the Harness Racing Museum & Hall of Fame, Goshen, NY*

[128]
A portion of Greyhound's lounge, reconstructed at the Harness Racing Museum & Hall of Fame in Goshen, NY.
• *2014, courtesy of the United States Trotting Association*

GREYHOUND

THE REMARKABLE STORY
OF THE LEGENDARY RACEHORSE WHO INSPIRED A NATION

gallery

[129]
Col. Baker at Hotel Baker.
• *circa 1950s, courtesy of the St. Charles Historical Society*

[130]
Dooley and Greyhound in the courtyard outside his deluxe stall.
• *circa 1950s, courtesy of the Hambletonian Society*

[131]
Dooley and Greyhound.
• *circa 1950s, Heitbrink Collection, courtesy of the Harness Racing Museum & Hall of Fame, Goshen, NY*

GREYHOUND

THE REMARKABLE STORY
OF THE LEGENDARY RACEHORSE WHO INSPIRED A NATION

gallery

[132]
Greyhound at age 32 with Dooley Putnam.
• October 13, 1964, Heitbrink Collection, courtesy of the Harness Racing Museum & Hall of Fame, Goshen, NY

[133]
Undated portrait of Greyhound.
• circa 1940s, courtesy of the Harness Racing Museum & Hall of Fame, Goshen, NY; original photograph by Harold G. Strong

[134]
Undated photo of Dooley with Greyhound at Sportsman's Park.
• circa 1950s, courtesy of the United States Trotting Association

GREYHOUND

THE REMARKABLE STORY
OF THE LEGENDARY RACEHORSE WHO INSPIRED A NATION

gallery

[135]
Invitation and ticket to Greyhound Day.
• 1946, courtesy of the St. Charles Historical Society

GREYHOUND

THE REMARKABLE STORY
OF THE LEGENDARY RACEHORSE WHO INSPIRED A NATION

gallery

[136]
Christmas card from Colonel Baker.
• *circa 1940s, courtesy of the St. Charles Historical Society*

[137]
A coaster from the Hotel Baker cocktail lounge. It's noteworthy that Baker was not interested in making money off of Greyhound; he could have used Greyhound's image to sell products and paid endorsements, as was common with famous horses at the time. But Baker evidently didn't want to exploit Greyhound in that way. The few items made with Greyhound's image were given as gifts, or had a practical use, such as the coasters and placemats used in the hotel.
• *circa 1940s, courtesy of the St. Charles Historical Society*

Young Kathy Fletcher of Selma, Indiana, wrote the Putnams asking for information about Greyhound. Though he had retired from racing many years before she was born, Kathy, out of "personal respect to this great gelding," planned to write her next school research paper on the life of Greyhound.[23] She included a pencil drawing she had made of the great horse trotting in harness. These letters, cards, and drawings today remain safely stored in the Harness Racing Museum in Goshen, New York.

And so it was with Greyhound, his fame growing as the years went by. Stacks of mail, including correspondence with a writer from Sweden who had published several articles about Greyhound, a letter from a young girl in Holland, cards with hand-drawn pictures from children, oversized birthday cards, and letters from around the country arrived at Flanery Farm. Even in the fifties and sixties, his fans were anxious to hear about him, and the harness racing publications like *Hoof Beats* and *The Harness Horse*, as well as other non-industry publications such as *Illinois Sportsman* and *Look* magazine, did articles on Greyhound in his retirement years. These and other publications also did big spreads on Greyhound's luxury apartment. Film footage of Greyhound playing in the orchard at Flanery Farm was used at the beginning and end of a 15-minute clip made to promote international racing at Roosevelt Raceway—citing the story of the first international harness racing meet that almost happened: the match between Greyhound and Muscletone.

"Hey there, Pappy." Greyhound nickered at the sound of Dooley's voice. The man and horse had been together for nearly twenty-five years. Dooley ran a hand over Greyhound's winter-wooly neck. The old horse wore a thick, red blanket that covered his large shoulders and protruding ribs. He had lost weight that year, and was down a couple hundred pounds under his ideal weight. He ate well, especially when Dooley stayed by his side to encourage him to consume his specially prepared mash, but the weight still came off—a common occurrence with elderly horses. Greyhound nuzzled the man's shirt, and then touched his cheek. Soft whiskers brushed Dooley's neck and a tear stung the man's eye. Greyhound was almost thirty-three years old—very old for a horse. Dooley wondered how much time remained.

"They still love you, Pappy." Dooley motioned to the cards hanging around Greyhound's stall. Greyhound touched the man's arm and looked at his friend. *Sometimes it feels as if he can see right through me*, Dooley thought to himself.[18]

"We get mail for you 'most every day." Dooley smiled and scratched the old gelding behind his ear. "Imagine, I used to worry they'd forget about you." Dooley chuckled softly and shook his head. Greyhound was genuinely loved, perhaps more than any other horse in the public eye, because he truly belonged to the people. Colonel Baker had made sure of that.

Dooley gazed at Greyhound. The gelding stood with his lower lip drooping and his eyes half-closed. Dooley understood now it would never happen. Greyhound would never be forgotten. There was something about the horse that extended beyond the story of a great trotter, beyond the records set, beyond the awards and acclaim over his grand talent. Greyhound was loved for more than his tremendous speed—people loved *him*. His personality, human-like antics, and sense of humor endeared him to them. But more than that, the horse had touched lives across generations, connecting horse lovers both young and old with a single gray thread.

Dooley knew great horses would come and go, but there would never be another like Greyhound. He shook his head slowly.

"Not like you, Pappy." The gelding twitched an ear at the sound of Dooley's voice and nickered softly. A long-ago memory crept to the surface—Greyhound as Dooley had seen him that first time in 1936, steel-gray body glistening in the hot summer sun, black legs flying, gray hooves pounding a rhythm matched only by Dooley's racing heart as he came under the wire in world-record time. The roar of the crowd echoed in the old man's mind. Greyhound rested his chin on Dooley's arm; the man placed a hand on the grand horse's forehead, closed his eyes, and remembered.

END of

CHAPTER 29

GREYHOUND

THE REMARKABLE STORY OF THE LEGENDARY RACEHORSE WHO INSPIRED A NATION

FEBRUARY 2, 1965, *SUN POST NEWS*

EPILOGUE
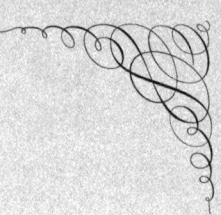

 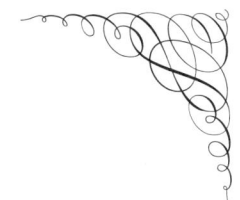

"If there is anything Greyhound didn't do in his time, it is only because he was never asked."

— MARYJEAN WALL,
LEXINGTON HERALD, JUNE 13, 1975

EPILOGUE

Dooley stood outside of Greyhound's stall, just wanting to be near him. The gray had been struggling that fall, his once-powerful legs now weak and at times uncooperative. Greyhound had been off his feed for a couple days. That day, the big horse had been unable to get to his feet without help, and Dooley feared the end was near. Outside, a brisk wind blew ahead of a storm; a loud crack split the night. Dawn would reveal Greyhound's favorite apple tree, the one with the low-hanging branch perfect for back scratching, had fallen.[1] It felt like an omen.

But Greyhound had looked beaten before and then rebounded. And that's just what he did. The vet had been called, but instead of finding a horse unable to rise and unwilling to eat, Dr. Foley saw Greyhound standing and clamoring for attention.[2] The champion earned a reprieve, and everyone breathed a sigh of relief. Greyhound still had plenty of light and fire within him.

Fall turned to winter, Christmas came and went, and Greyhound remained. Outside, a cold February wind blew as winter held Flanery Farm in her icy grip. Dooley and Leone stood together and watched Greyhound resting in the deep wheat straw. The old horse was slipping away.

Dooley entered the stall; Greyhound lifted his tired head and nickered.

"We've been through a lot together, haven't we?" Dooley spoke to his friend, his voice cracking. He patted Greyhound on the neck. "I've been nursemaid to you for a quarter century." Dooley smiled. "I wouldn't have it any other way."

The calendar read February 4, 1965. Outside, the wind howled. Inside, with Dooley and Leone by his side, the gallant gray champion closed his eyes and died peacefully in his sleep.

After the burial, Dooley and Leone stood together in the lounge, outside Greyhound's empty stall. They gazed out the window toward the apple orchard. Fog hovered low above the ground and swirled around the trunks of the winter-bare trees. A familiar nicker seemed to float above the fog, emanating from where Greyhound's favorite apple tree once stood.[3] Dooley and Leone looked at each other, each wondering if the other had heard, and finding the answer in the wonder and emotion that colored the other's face. The two turned their gazes back to the orchard, each lost in their own memories of America's trotting legend, the great Grey Ghost: the incomparable Greyhound.

Greyhound's Impact and Legacy

The press came from all over, even Europe, to report on Greyhound's passing and burial, said Jim Cooke, current owner of Red Gate Farm, in a 1998 interview. Cooke was a young boy in 1965; his family had purchased the farm from the Baker estate in 1959. He remembers that day clearly. For many years, busloads of people came to see Greyhound's grave, said Cooke.[4]

Four and a half years after Greyhound's passing, a stallion named Nevele Pride, with trainer-driver Stanley Dancer, shaved the slimmest fraction of a second off Greyhound's mile record. With a time of 1:54 4/5, the four-year-old bay stallion became the new world champion trotter. He was a worthy champion—winner of fifty-seven races, including the 1968 trotting Triple Crown—and a producer of many great harness horses.

The current world trotting record of 1:48.4, set by Homicide Hunter in 2018, is faster than anyone in Greyhound's era could have conceived of. But today's horses benefit from equipment and technology not yet imagined when Greyhound dominated his sport. Harnesses with elastic gussets to allow for lung expansion, lighter and more aerodynamic racing bikes, better shoeing materials, faster track surfaces, and improved understanding of nutrition and sports medicine have all contributed to faster speeds. Horses travel in vans with rubber mats and high-tech shock absorbers instead of modified baggage cars with steel wheels and wooden floors. And almost all races are single-heat dashes. Gone are the days of trotting four or five warm-up miles before competing in three heats to win one race.

Greyhound won just over $38,000 in purse money during his racing career. Upon his retirement, some papers reported his winnings to be over $55,000. The latter amount would be more accurately termed his career *earnings,* as that amount includes bonuses given for exhibitions. Multiple turf writers and historians have suggested that, had Greyhound raced in the post-Depression years, he easily would have been the sport's first millionaire.

Harness racing experienced a huge resurgence in popularity beginning in the late 1930s, which continued into the 1980s. Night racing at big city tracks drew young people to the sport. The introduction of mobile starting gates and the elimination of multi-heat racing streamlined the sport and made it easier for newcomers to understand. The advent of television introduced harness racing to more people, which in turn brought them to the track. The purses grew and the horses got faster. The rush of popularity in the decades following Greyhound enhanced his legend as the one who started the climb.

Did Greyhound truly save his sport from extinction? Speaking as a researcher, there is not enough evidence to provide a definitive answer. As a horse lover and one whose life has been intertwined with Greyhound's story for thousands of hours over the past few years, I question whether it matters. I think the greatness and contribution of a horse goes beyond the facts of what he accomplished and into the realm of the intangible. People who never saw Greyhound in life spoke of him as if they were there and experienced every great moment, every smashed record, every outstanding victory.

Greyhound has been lifted to a level far beyond that of mere horse, beyond legend, to something words cannot adequately describe. He was a hero that people clung to in their most difficult times. When the Depression robbed them of their security and impending war threatened their freedom, people turned their attention to what gave them relief, hope, and something else to focus on—something that made a world in upheaval feel normal, if only for the two minutes when Greyhound flew around the track.

As a gelding, Greyhound's legacy could never be in his contributions to the gene pool. But Greyhound somehow transcends such simplistic comparisons. His outstanding speed and incomparable achievements made him great. But to many, he was far more than a great trotting horse. Like an infallible glue, he cobbled together old-time horsemen, youth, newcomers, rich, poor, downtrodden, and upper class with the pieces of a once-great but failing sport. Greyhound connected people to him, to his sport, and to each other—and he continues to do this today. Just whisper the name "Greyhound" among fans of harness racing and lovers of the Standardbred breed, and you will feel hearts warm, see eyes soften, and watch smiles spread triumphantly, each individual carrying their own piece of Greyhound: the champion, the hero, the legend.

WHAT HAPPENED TO...?

Sep Palin's contributions to harness racing were immense. He participated in the founding of the United States Trotting Association

(USTA) and served on the organization's board from 1939 to 1950. Palin was deeply respected for his expertise as a horseman and his excellent judgment as a representative of the USTA's Rules Committee. At the time of his passing, Palin was credited with twenty-nine world records, eight more than his nearest rival. Palin drove a total of sixty-four two-minute miles in his career. He contested 14 Hambletonian stakes with two winners: Greyhound in 1935 and Hoot Mon in 1947.

Palin drove his last Hambletonian horse, Hardy Hanover, in 1952, at the age of seventy-four. That fall, while attending the Lexington Trots, Palin suffered a cerebral hemorrhage, fell backward off the wall on which he'd been sitting, and struck his head on the cement, fracturing his skull. He died five days later on October 3 in a Lexington hospital, having never fully regained consciousness.[5]

Flags were flown half-mast at Lexington's Red Mile (formerly the KTHBA track), the site of many of Palin's greatest moments, the day he died. He was among the last of the great trainer-drivers who came up in the golden era of the sport with a true understanding and appreciation of the intricacies of developing a great trotter—and a deep respect for the time and patience required to do it right, while also doing right by the horse.

Shortly after his seventieth birthday, Palin was asked why he'd had so much success in his career. "Well, it helps to have strong wrists and sensitive hands," he said. "But most of all, you have to have the best horses."

Jimmie Wingfield, when asked about Greyhound in 1975, said, "I remember him very vividly. I remember him as being the smartest and probably the kindest horse I've ever known. One with great feeling."[6]

Jimmie went on to a successful career and was among the most respected and beloved trainer-drivers in the sport. In 1940, he was promoted to Palin's second (assistant) trainer. He stayed in that position until he joined the army in 1942, where he served first in the mounted cavalry, then as a second lieutenant in the armored cavalry (tanks) in Italy. When the ground proved to be too rugged for the tanks, Jimmie was charged with requisitioning mules from area farms to bring much needed supplies to the front lines. Jimmie served until the war ended and was honorably discharged in 1945. After the war, he resumed his position as Palin's second-in-command until 1947. In 1948, Wingfield struck out on his own and operated a public stable, and later was a private trainer for H. C. Wilson before partnering with a semi-retired Palin in 1952.[7]

Leone Putnam's notes showed Jimmie came out to visit Greyhound at Flanery's on at least two occasions—1952 and 1960.

Wingfield found his greatest success in the 1950s when he had heat victories in the Hambletonian and the Little Brown Jug (the top race for three-year-old pacers). In later years, he partnered with his son, Neil. He won over 350 races and $750,000 in his fifty-year career. Wingfield was well-respected among his peers for his ability to start youngsters,

EPILOGUE

and continued to do so even after closing his public stable in the 1980s. In 1973, Jimmie and Neil developed a business raising cattle and growing their own hay to feed their stock and to sell locally. This continued into the late 1980s. Jim Kyle Wingfield passed away on June 8, 1987, after a long illness. He was 71.[8]

"He was a gentleman's gentleman," said longtime friend and USTA official Walter Russell (son of Jimmie's mother's cousin, Sanders Russell). "He stood for all the best things in this sport, and he had friends from Maine to California."[9]

Dooley Putnam retired as farm manager of Flanery Farm in 1971, six years after Greyhound's passing. In the years after Greyhound's death, Dooley would recall the horse with great emotion. His daughter, Emma Lou, had the foresight to record Dooley talking about Greyhound, and the depth of love he had for the horse is evident in his voice. A portion of this recording can be heard in the Greyhound exhibit at the Harness Racing Museum and Hall of Fame in Goshen, New York. Verner "Dooley" Putnam passed away November 29, 1979, in Mountain Home, Alabama. He was 80 years old.

Leone Putnam worked as secretary at Flanery Farm and presumably retired when her husband did. After Greyhound's death in 1965, Leone gathered articles and information about Greyhound and began outlining a manuscript for a book called *Dooley and the Grey Ghost*. With a nearly completed manuscript, she queried many publishers in the late 1960s and the 1970s, but none bought the idea. After her death in December 1995, at the age of 87, Leone's manuscript, notes, and everything she saved were donated by Emma Lou (Putnam) Heitbrink to the Harness Racing Museum and Hall of Fame in Goshen, New York. Staff there finished the manuscript using Leone's notes, and it was published in 2018.

The completed book has many color and grayscale photographs and tells Greyhound's story through Dooley's experiences. It is a lovely book, and has further details of the twenty-five years Dooley and Greyhound spent together beyond what is shared here. It is available from www.harnessmuseum.com.

R. C. "Doc" Flanery was regarded as one of the greatest trainers and drivers in show horse history, but his contributions to harness racing are lesser known or celebrated. The exhibitions that allowed Greyhound's public to see him and celebrate the sport of harness racing would not have been possible without Doc's management, training, and handling of the great champion's engagements. A horse like Greyhound with high energy, major talent, and extreme intelligence required a special level of skill and patience.

Doc owned and bred Standardbred harness horses through the mid-1960s. He stood the 1956 Little Brown Jug winner Noble Adios at stud, though by that time he had retired from race driving years earlier. An article in the

December 4, 1966 issue of the *Lexington Herald-Leader* announced that Flanery was dispersing his stock at the Tattersalls winter sale. Doc Flanery was hospitalized in June 1974 after suffering a stroke. He died on October 31 at the age of 73.

Dooley, Leone, and Doc were honored at the 1965 Illinois State Fair for their contributions to the sport and the state of Illinois as caretakers of Greyhound. The award was given before the $25,000 two-year-old trot race named in Greyhound's honor. The race would continue under that name through the mid-1990s.

Henry H. Knight, when asked in 1958 about his outstanding success as a commercial horse breeder, had this to say: "Take the best stock you have to the right market where there are smart buyers. Don't kid yourself about the value of your horses. Take the public's judgment and let the horses go to the highest bidder."[10]

Knight was a world-renowned breeder of Standardbreds, and later of Thoroughbreds, on his famed Almahurst Farm. In 1935, he purchased his first Thoroughbreds, including the mare Possible, whose son Bold Venture won the Kentucky Derby the following year. Knight bred both Standardbreds and Thoroughbreds until 1950, when he sold his Standardbred holdings—over eighty horses—to the Van Lenneps (the former Frances Dodge Johnson) of Castleton Farm.[11]

Despite "retiring" in 1955, Knight was the leading breeder in money earners and races won in 1955, '56, and '57.[12] As of December 1958, horses bred by Knight had won over $7.1 million, according to an Almahurst Farm stallion ad. In January 1959, at a dinner celebrating his contributions to the horse industry, Knight mentioned that he planned to buy some Standardbred mares and re-enter the world of harness horses again.[13] However, he suffered a stroke in late February and died on March 7, at the age of sixty-nine,[14] less than two months after his friend E. J. Baker passed away.

Frances Dodge Johnson Van Lennep fell in love with the Bluegrass Region and purchased the once-grand, but at the time run-down, Castleton Farm in Lexington. After divorcing her first husband, she married Frederick Van Lennep. Together, she and her husband restored Castleton to its former glory and, with Sep Palin as trainer, became a dominant force in harness racing in the 1940s and 1950s.[15] She continued her success in the show ring as well, breeding and campaigning the top American Saddlebred Wing Commander, among others.

As with show horses, Frances Dodge Van Lennep became known in the Standardbred world for her excellent eye for horse flesh. She purchased eventual Hambletonian winner Hoot Mon for $50,000 as a two-year-old, won $74,500 with him, then sold him to Hanover Shoe Farm, where he sired four Hambletonian winners. In 1966, Castleton purchased a 50 percent interest in Bret Hanover, a top pacing stallion who became one of the greatest sires in the sport, for a record $2 million.[16]

EPILOGUE

Almahurst Farm still exists today, though under a new name and new ownership. From the 1960s into the 1990s, P J Baugh owned the property and raised Standardbreds there. In 1994, Kenneth and Sarah Ramsey purchased the farm and renamed it Ramsey Farm. The Ramseys are well-loved in the world of Thoroughbreds. Their top stallion was Kitten's Joy. Now in their eighties, the Ramseys have downsized considerably, but Ramsey Farm and many of Henry Knight's original barns, including the stunning stallion barn, are still there today. Also still standing is a state historical marker incorrectly identifying Almahurst as the location of Greyhound's birth.

Red Gate Farm is among the last of Baker's eight farms still intact today. The current owners, Jim and Lori Cooke, are dedicated to preserving it, and much of it looks just as it did in Baker's day. The Cooke family purchased the farm from the Baker estate in 1959, when Jim was just six, and has cared for it ever since. Greyhound's grave and the cemetery it is part of are maintained by the Cookes and can still be seen. The Cookes welcome visitors during the daytime.

Elizabeth, Greyhound's dam, was given away to W. N. Reynolds, but a few years later, Henry Knight managed to get her back for an undisclosed amount of money. In 1941, she produced her second Hambletonian winner, Yankee Maid, by Volomite. Elizabeth had 15 named foals, six of them by Guy Abbey. She lived out her retirement years at Almahurst, and her final years in a large paddock with the mare Possible, making Almahurst the only farm to house both the dam of a Hambletonian winner and a Kentucky Derby winner.

Guy Abbey had a successful breeding career, producing 187 trotters and 113 pacers. More than fifty of his foals had records of 2:05 or better. Guy Abbey lived out his retirement years at Walnut Hall in Lexington, Kentucky. He died on April 24, 1957, at the age of 32 and is buried at Walnut Hall near a statue of his sire, Guy Axworthy.

St. Charles, Illinois: Evidence of Baker's love for and dedication to St. Charles can still be seen and felt all over the town. The buildings he built still stand, including the bank, a Methodist church, and the municipal building. Fittingly, the old Texaco station on Main Street now houses the historical society and museum—a fine throwback, as part of the millions that built St. Charles came from Texaco oil money.

Baker's niece Dellora Angell, the other beneficiary of the Gates fortune, was equally generous with her wealth. She married Lester J. Norris in 1923 and together they funded multiple civic projects to benefit St. Charles, including the Arcada Theatre, Delnor Hospital, St. Charles East High School, and the Dellora A. Norris Cultural Arts Center, among others. The Norrises also did much for the community of Naples, Florida, the location of their vacation home. Upon Baker's death, Dellora inherited the bulk of his estate and continued her philanthropy until her death in 1979.[17]

Hotel Baker was donated to Lutheran Social Services in 1968, and turned into a senior care home in 1976. Regrettably, the upkeep was too expensive for the non-profit organization, and the hotel had fallen into disrepair by the late 1990s and been vacated. Purchased in 1996, the hotel underwent a $9 million renovation and reopened in 1997. Restored to its original glory, it stands as the beacon Baker created it to be, the "Crown Jewel of the Fox River Valley."[18]

The community center, built and named in Henry Baker's honor, remains today, externally looking much as it did when dedicated in 1926. Internally, it has been reconfigured for the modern needs of the community, but is still reminiscent of its original design. The swimming pool was filled in and the bowling alley removed in the 1960s to repurpose the area to a teen center, and other modifications have been made, but the grand lounge still looks much as it did a century ago. The life-sized oil portrait of Henry still hangs along with portraits of Colonel Baker with one of his dogs, and a large portrait of Harriet Baker over the fireplace.

St. Charles is a beautiful place and I thoroughly enjoyed my time there researching this book. I believe Colonel Baker would be thrilled to see the thriving place it is, big and bustling, while still retaining its small-town charm.

Flanery Farm and Greyhound's magnificent stall were almost lost entirely. A few years before his death, Flanery donated some of Greyhound's items such as the guest book, a patent leather harness, and a whip to the Harness Racing Museum in Goshen. Other items such as photos and trophies went to the Hotel Baker, and were displayed there after Greyhound's death.

Unfortunately, no single person kept track of Greyhound's things, and while well-meaning people saved them from the farm, due to relatives not knowing their significance as time went by, many items were lost. One such item is Greyhound's Hambletonian trophy. Some items were discovered in storage at the Hotel Baker; other items were found in odd places. One painting was found in the store room of a building slated for demolition.

In 1974, veterinarian Dr. Ken Walker leased Flanery Farm and raised Standardbred racehorses there, as did other Standardbred people through the years. During the 1980s, friends Nancy Brejc and Jan Heine worked for Walker, and both recalled that the Walkers took meticulous care of the stall and lounge. After Walker left, the two friends kept tabs on Greyhound's stall, which Heine reported in 2014 had been cared for by all tenants.[19]

In 2014, the two friends learned that all the buildings at Flanery Farm were to be razed. It would still be a farm, but not a horse farm. The buildings were not needed and were taxed heavily. Nancy and Jan set to work and saved Greyhound's stall, which was still intact. They took it apart, board by board, carefully numbering each piece so it could be reassembled at a later date. The stall was donated to the

Harness Racing Museum in Goshen, New York, where Executive Director Janet Terhune and her staff worked to raise the substantial funds necessary to rebuild the stall as a permanent exhibit.[20] Everything was preserved, right down to the chewed wood and the scratches on the window from Greyhound's teeth. The harness racing world owes a great debt of gratitude to Nancy, Jan, Janet, and numerous others who made this wonderful exhibit possible.

A FINAL NOTE

I cannot adequately explain it, but since I decided to write Greyhound's story late in 2022, I have felt an intense urgency to complete it—that for some reason the story needed to be told *now*. I felt this so strongly that I dropped everything else in my life and devoted myself and my savings to bringing this book to press as quickly as possible, while still giving it the thoroughness and accuracy it deserves.

Perhaps the world needs Greyhound now, as they did back then. The story of a horse that loved people and the people that loved him back—an underdog story of an unwanted horse with the type of personality that could easily have been mishandled and ruined, but instead became the greatest trotter of all time. The story of an elderly owner who shared his tremendous fortune out of love and a genuine desire to see people happy and successful, expecting nothing in return. The story of an aged trainer-driver who learned, from earlier mistakes, of the importance of handling a horse with gentleness, patience, and respect. Perhaps that is the answer to why Greyhound, and why now: because right now, the world needs to be reminded of the power of compassion, gentleness, gratitude, generosity, respect, patience, and love.

With gratitude,
Cheryl L. Eriksen
Versailles, Kentucky, July 2024/April 2025

ACKNOWLEDGMENTS

A project like this can never be the work of a single person. The longer I worked on Greyhound and the deeper into my research I went, the clearer this became. I have met so many wonderful people through this project and have made some new friends as well. I would like to thank the following people who played a vital role in making this book a reality.

First, I must thank Richard Stone, whom I only just met a few months ago. He read my manuscript, offered some gentle direction, and then single-handedly spearheaded my fundraising campaign. He reached out to numerous people on my behalf, and without his efforts, it is doubtful this beautiful book would be in your hands today. There are not adequate words to show my gratitude, Richard. Thank you.

Several people gave freely of their time in helping me bring this book together. Alan Ackerman, Tom Charters, Neil Wingfield, and Richard Stone spent hours going over this manuscript, fact-checking and providing me with details about the history and interconnectedness of individuals and organizations that gave this story depth, breadth, and texture it otherwise would not have had. Dean Hoffman shared multiple stories with me about Doc Parshall, and shared his published articles about Greyhound, which were valuable resources. Neil Wingfield spoke with me about his father, sharing stories and information that helped me bring Jimmie to life on these pages. To all of you, I am forever grateful.

To Moira Fanning, who made a hugely generous donation from the Hambletonian Society a reality and provided the opportunity to launch this book at the 100th Hambletonian. You took a chance on me and I am deeply grateful. I cannot adequately express what your contribution means to this project. Thank you.

I'd like to thank the Harness Racing Museum and Hall of Fame in Goshen, New York, and specifically Executive Director Janet Terhune, Librarian Paul Wilder, and Collections Curator Rebecca Howard, who hosted me for eight days of research at their wonderful facility. Your assistance in navigating this massive collection of all things Greyhound is much appreciated and an experience I thoroughly enjoyed. Thank you especially to Rebecca for letting me see and handle Greyhound's blankets, shoes, guest book, and other special items. It helped me feel closer to him and also thrilled the horse-crazy kid in me, to be so close to my horse hero. Truly, thank you.

Gena Gallagher of the United States Trotting Association in Columbus, Ohio, gave hours of her time on multiple occasions (I made four trips to the USTA archives), fielding emails and making herself available to answer questions throughout this project. Gena provided the tools and space to research, scanned dozens of photos, and was an all-around awesome individual. Thank you, Gena.

Thank you also to Eric Krupa of the St. Charles Historical Society and Emma Rothenfluh of the St. Charles Public Library in Illinois. St. Charles was the first stop on my research trip. Emma and Eric got me off to a great start, providing research materials and information specific to St. Charles and Colonel Baker. Thank you to Eric for providing photos and video, and fielding tons of emails. I am so very grateful.

Thank you to my friend Laura Hicks, who provided me with tons of information from her vast collection of harness racing books. Her efforts and encouragement got me started on this journey, as did her accompanying me to my first harness races at the Red Mile.

A special thank-you to my new friend and fellow Greyhound lover Judith Berkshire-Jones. You helped me to connect with people I would not otherwise have met and you've been most encouraging and supportive. I'm so glad to have met you. Thank you.

To my dad, Robert Eriksen, my mom, Louise Bower, and my step-dad, Ron Bower—your love, support, encouragement and belief in me have kept me going through these lean times while I transition myself to this new dream. Not everyone has the love and support of their family. I count myself truly blessed to have it in spades. Thank you and I love you.

To my best friend (and the other half of my brain), Sarah. You have always believed in me, especially when I couldn't believe in myself. I'm so grateful to you and for you. I can't wait for our next big adventure. Thank you, my friend.

Finally I'd like to acknowledge the writers and reporters that shared Greyhound's life with their readers—people like John Hervey, Tom and George Gahagan (brothers), Jesse Shuff, Ken McCarr, Dwight Akers, June VanGundy, Maryjean Wall, and others who likely never knew in life just what their work would mean to someone like me decades later. The quality of writing in these old publications, the beautiful wordsmithing, the obvious love of the sport and appreciation of the horses themselves ... all contributed to my goal of writing about Greyhound and his people in a way that would bring them to life for the reader. If not for their quality work and thoughtfully written pieces, this manuscript would have much less color, texture, and life. Theirs is a lost art, and we have less because of it.

APPENDICES

Appendix 1

INDIANAPOLIS SPEED SALE 35

No. 36

GREYHOUND

From Sister of Peter the Brewer, 4, 2:02½.

In the Futurities.

Trotter. Grey gelding, foaled 1932. Bred and consigned by Henry H. Knight, Chicago, Ill. Registered Standard, A. T. R.

BY GUY ABBEY 68299.

Record, 2, 2:17½, 3, 2:06¾. Sire of Calumet Evelyn, p, 2, 2:07¾, Calumet Durham, 3, 2:09¾, Abnor G., 3, 2:10¼, Calumet Director, 3, 2:12¼, Calumet Dilly, p, 3, 2:12¾, Calumet Delphine, 3, 2:14, etc. Son of Guy Axworthy 37501, 4, 2:08¾, sire of Lee Axworthy 1:58¼, Guy McKinney, 4, 1:58¾, Mr. McElwyn 1:59¼, Arion Guy, 4, 1:59½, etc., and the dams of Protector, 3, 1:59½, The Marchioness, 3, 1:59¼, etc.; dam Abbacy, p, 2:04¼, dam of Calumet Brownie, p, 4, 2:01¾, etc., by The Abbe 44386, p, 2:04, trotting, 2:10½, a two-minute sire; grandam Regal McKinney, great brood mare by McKinney 8818, 2:11¼, sire of Sweet Marie 2:02, Coney, p, 2:02, and the dams of 4 in 2:00.

1st dam ELIZABETH, own sister to Peter the Brewer, 4, 2:02¼, **by PETER THE GREAT 28955, 4, 2:07¼,** sire of Miss Harris M., p, 1:58¼, Berry the Great, p, 2:00¼, Peter Stevens, p, 2:01½, Peter Nash, p, 2:01½, Mable Trask 2:01¾, Peter Look, p, 2:01¾, Peter Volo, 4, 2:02, The Great Volo 2:02¼, etc., and the dams of Margaret Dillon, p, 1:58¼, Tilly Brooke 1:59, Mr. McElwyn 1:59¼, Spencer, 3, 1:59¾, etc. Son of Pilot Medium 1579; dam Santos, dam of J. Malcolm Forbes, 4, 2:08, etc., by Grand Sentinel 865, 2:27¼.

2nd dam ZOMBREWER, p, 2:04¼, dam of Peter the Brewer 2:02½, Senator Brewer 2:05, Grey Brewer 2:05¼, Justice Brewer, p, 2:05½, Calumet Brewer, p, 3, 2:06½, Calumet Cream, 3, 2:08¾, Marjorie the Great, p, 2:09, t, 2:11, John Pershing, p, 2:09¼, etc., **by ZOMBRO, 28029, 2:11,** sire of Zomrect 2:03¾, Auto Zombro, p, 2:02½, etc., and dams of Peter the Brewer 2:02½, Hal Dee, p, 2:02¼, Bessie McKlyo, p, 2:01½, Guy Richard 2:02¾, Goldie Todd, p, 2:02¼, Berry the Great, p, 2:00¼, etc. Son of McKinney 8818, 2;11¼; dam Whisper, by Almont Lightning 1023.

3rd dam MARY BALES 2:26¼, dam of Zombrewer, p, 2:04¼, Wilkes Brewer 2:04½, Brownie Bales, p, 2:14¼, etc., **by MONTJOY 13003,** sire of Daisy J., p, 2:08½, Mary Bales 2:26¼, etc. Son of General Withers 1157; dam Alice Medium, by Happy Medium 400.

4th dam MOLLY J., dam of Daisy J., p, 2:08½, Mary Bales 2:26¼, etc., **by WALLER.** Son of Imp. Hurrah.

5th dam by a SON OF BOSTON.

6th dam by JOE GALES.

7th dam by PAUL JONES.

OWNER'S STATEMENT—This colt is eligible to the Hambletonian, American, National, Matron, Championship Stallion, The Horseman and Kentucky Futurity.

FUTURITY PROSPECTS

Attention is directed to the unusual number of young racing prospects named in this sale that are eligible to valuable Stakes and Futurities. Bidders should bear this advantage in mind, when seeking money winning chances on individuals offered at auction.

Catalog page from 1933 Indianapolis Speed Sale

Appendix 2
GREYHOUND'S RACE RECORD

AGE	YEAR	RESULTS BY RACE	RESULTS BY HEAT
2	1934	**9** (6-1-1-1)	**18** (12-2-1-2)
3	1935	**8** (8-0-0-0)	**20** (18-0-1-1)
4	1936	**6** (5-0-1-0)	**17** (15-2-0-0)
5	1937	**1** (1-0-0-0)	**5** (2-2-0-0)
6	1938	**5** (5-0-0-0)	**10** (10-0-0-0)
7	1939	**0** (0-0-0-0) *all starts were time trials or exhibitions*	
8	1940	**7** (7-0-0-0)	**15** (14-1-0-0)
Total Contests (races): 36 (32-1-2-1)			**Total Heats:** 82 (71-5-2-3)

Greyhound's winnings reported to be approximately $38,000 in purses. Some reports state between $52,000 and $55,000, but this number includes monies paid for exhibition trots and bonuses for record-breaking attempts.

Detailed Complete Record Including Time Trials

Reading the record: Horses are named in order of finish for the entire, multiple-heat race. Numbers behind each name represent how the horse finished in each heat. For example: 2-1 indicates the horse finished second in the first heat and first in the second heat. Times are listed for each heat, separated by a semicolon (;). Where available, quarter times are given prior to the final time, which appears in **bold**. An "ro" indicates the horse did not compete in the heat because it was a run-off to determine a winner between horses that had each won a heat. A "dr" indicates the horse was withdrawn.

WR—World Record
TR—Track Record
SR—State Record

―――――― 1934 ――――――

• **June 8—Ohio State Fairgrounds, Columbus, Ohio, 2yo Trot, Purse: $300***
Miss Evergreen 2-1
Greyhound 1-2
Calumet Farrona 3-2, Caharrus Boy 4-4, Lil Winess 5-5
2:17; 2:20 ½

*This race is inconsistently reported—sometimes as a two-heat contest with a $300 purse, other times as two single-heat one-mile dashes, each with a $150 purse. Overall results are the same in both accounts, but since some reports considered them individual events, Greyhound is sometimes said to have won his first race.

• **July 10—Ft. Miami Fairgrounds, Toledo, Ohio, Sherwood Trot, Purse $1,000**
Belvedere 1-1
Chica 2-4; Greyhound 4-2
M'Liss 7-3, Silver King 3-7, Miss Harris T. 5-5, Bookie Barnes 6-8, Senator Horn 8-6
:34 ½, 1:06 ½, 1:37 ½, **2:09**; :33, 1:04, 1:36, **2:09**

• **July 23—Thorncliffe Park, Toronto, Ontario, 2yo Trot, Purse $1,500**
Silver King 3-1-1
Belvedere 1-3-2
Mary Taylor 4-2-ro, Greyhound 2-7-ro, M'Liss 5-4-ro, Chica 7-5-ro, Miss Harris T. 6-6-ro
:32, 1:05, 1:40, **2:11**; :32 ¼, 1:05, 1:37 ½, **2:09**; :36 ½, 1:10 ¾, 1:42, **2:12 ½**

• **August 3—Rockingham Park, Salem, New Hampshire, 2yo Trot (single mile dash), Purse $400**
Greyhound 1
Salem 2, Mary Taylor 3, Countess Zabetta 4, Prince John 5, Zillah Hanover 6, Newton Hanover 7, Lema Noon 8
:35, 1:06 ¾, 1:41, **2:13 ¼**

• **August 14—Good Time Park, Goshen, New York, The Good Time, 2yo trot, Purse $1,800**
Greyhound 1-1
Lucre 2-5
Belvedere 6-2, Prince John 4-3, Salem 3-7, Mary Taylor 8-4, Baroness 5-6, Chica 7-8
:33 ½, 1:06, 1:37 ¼, **2:09 ½**; :31 ½, 1:03 ½, 1:36, **2:06 ¾**

• **August 22—Illinois State Fairgrounds, Springfield, Illinois, 2yo trot, Purse $1,627**
Greyhound 1-1

Lawrence Hanover 2-2
Prince John 3-4, Belvedere 5-3, Abbie Dodge 4-5
2:07 ¼; **2:06**

• **August 31—Syracuse New York, 2yo trot, Purse $1,000**
Greyhound 4-1-1
Prince John 1-3-2
Sliver King 7-2-ro, Lawrence Hanover 2-11-ro, Athlone Sally Boy 3-5-ro, Zillah Hanover 6-4-ro, Salem 5-6-ro, Lucre 10-7-ro, Miss Harris T. 8-8-ro, Baroness 9-10-ro, Twinkle 11-9-ro, Chica 12-12-ro
:31 ½, 1:04, 1:36, **2:07**; :33, 1:06, 1:36, **2:05 ½**; :34 ½, 1:07 ½, 1:40, **2:09**

• **September 5—Syracuse, NY, Horseman Futurity, 2yo trot, Purse $3,000**
Greyhound 1-1
Athlone Sally Boy 2-3; Prince John 3-2
Silver King 4-5, Flaxey Volo 6-4, Lema Noon 5-6
:32, 1:04, 1:36, **2:06**; :31, 1:03 ¼, 1:34, **2:04 ¾**
WR: fastest two-year-old gelding

• **October 3—KTBHA Track (Red Mile), Lexington, Kentucky, 2yo trot, Purse $2,000**
Greyhound 1-1
Belvedere 2-2
Prince John 3-3, Senator Horn 4-5, Zillah Hanover 6-4, Flaxey Volo 5-6
:33 ½, 1:05, 1:35 ¼, **2:06 ¾**; :34 ¼, 1:08, 1:40, **2:09**

—————————— 1935 ——————————

• **June 20—KTBHA Track (Red Mile), Lexington, Kentucky, 3yo trot, Purse $500**
Greyhound 1-1
Lawrence Hanover 2-2
Calumet Ferona 3-4, The Saint 5-3, Elizabeth Gaylworthy 4-5, Jeremiah 6-6
:34, 1:07 ½, 1:39 ¾, **2:09 ½**; :31, 1:04, 1:34 ¼, **2:04 ¼**

• **July 5—Ft. Miami Fairgrounds, Toledo, OH, Matron Stake, 3yo trot, Purse $4,105**
Greyhound 1-1-1
Lawrence Hanover 2-2-3
Tilly Tonka 3-6-2, Silver King 4-3-4, Calumet Finery 5-4-6, Alicea 6-5-5
:33, 1:04 ½, 1:36 ½, **2:06**; :33 ½, 1:05, 1:37, **2:06**; :32, 1:02 ½, 1:34, **2:03 ¼**

• **July 20—Thorncliffe Park, Toronto, Ont., 3yo trot, Purse $1,500**
Greyhound 4-1-1
Lawrence Hanover 1-3-3
Prince John 7-4-2, The Viscount 3-8-8, Pedro Tipton 9-6-4, Silver King 5-7-5, Volo Arion 6-5-7, Warwell Worthy 8-9-6, Tilly Tonka 2-2-dr
:32 ¼, 1:04 ½, 1:35, **2:06 ¼**; :31 ¼, 1:01 ½, 1:34, **2:02 ¼**; :31 ¼, 1:03 ¾, 1:36, **2:05 ¼**
TR: One Mile Trotting (2:02 ¼)

• **August 6—Rockingham Park, Salem, NH, Portland Express 3yo trot, Purse $600**
Greyhound 1-1-1
Pedro Tipton 2-2-2, Countess Zebetta 3-3-4, Miss Peter Belle 4-3-3, Salem 4-6-5, Patricia Hanover 5-5-6, Fez 7-7-7
:31 ¾, 1:04 ¾, 1:35 ¾, **2:05**; :33 ¾, 1:08, 1:41 ¼, **2:09 ¼**; :32 ½, 1:04 ½, 1:37 ½, **2:06 ¾**

• **August 14—Good Time Park, Goshen, NY, The Hambletonian Stake, Purse $33,321**
Greyhound 1-1
Warwell Worthy 7-2
Pedro Tipton 2-7, Lawrence Hanover 4-3, Tilly Tonka 3-9, Silver King 6-4, Volo Arion 5-5, Calumet Finery 9-6, Harper Hanover 8-8
:31 ¾, 1:02 ¾, 1:32 ¾, **2:02 ¼**; :30, :59 ¾, 1:31 ¾, **2:02 ¾**

• **August 21—Illinois State Fairgrounds, Springfield, IL, Illinois Review Futurity, Purse $1,610**
Greyhound 1-1
The Saint 2-2

Zilla Hanover 4-3, Arlington 3-4, Hope 6-5, Maudonna 5-6
:30 ¾, 1:03 ¾, 1:34 ¾, **2:05**; :30 ½, 1:01, 1:31, **2:00**
WR (2): fastest racing mile for a three-year-old trotter, and fastest mile trotted by a three-year-old gelding (2:00)
SR: only horse of any age to trot 2:00 that season

• **August 26—New York State Fairgrounds, Syracuse, NY, Championship Stallion Stake, Purse $8,070**
Greyhound 1-3-1
Lawrence Hanover 2-1-2
Silver King 5-2-3, Tilly Tonka 3-5-4, Warwell Worthy 4-6-5, Pedro Tipton 6-4-6
:30 ½, 1:02 ½, 1:33, **2:02 ¼**; 31 ¾, 1:03, 1:35, **2:04**; 30 ½, 1:01 ½, 1:31 ¾, **2:01 ½**

• **September 4—Indiana State Fairgrounds, Indianapolis, IN, Horseman Futurity, Purse $3,088.95**
Greyhound 1-1
Silver King 3-2
Pedro Tipton 2-4, Warwell Worthy 4-3
:31 ½, 1:04, 1:36 ½, **2:05**; :31 ½, 1:06, 1:36 ¾, **2:06**

—————————— 1936 ——————————

June 23—KTBHA Track (Red Mile), Lexington, KY, Exhibition Trot
Greyhound :31 ¼, 1:03, 1:32 ½, **2:01**

• **July 22—Historic Track (half-mile oval), Goshen, NY, FFA Trot, Purse $1,500**
Tara 3-2-1-1
Angel Child 1-3-3-2
Greyhound 2-1-2-dr, Silver King 4-4-4-ro
:31 ¼, 1:05 ¼, 1:38 ¼, **2:07**; :31, 1:02 ½, 1:36, **2:05**; :30 ¼, 1:01 ¾, 1:34 ¾, **2:05 ¼**

• **July 30—Old Orchard "Kite Track," Old Orchard Beach, Maine, Pine Tree Trot (1st Division), Purse $1,000**
Greyhound 1-1-1
Tara 2-2-2, Miss Peter Belle 4-3-3, Lu Barient 3-4-6, Calumet Durham 5-6-4, Raider 6-5-5, Silver King 7-dr
:30, 1:02, 1:33, **2:01**; :29 ¼, 1:02 ¾, 1:34 ½, **2:03 ½**; :30 ¾, 1:03 ¼, 1:34 ¼, **2:03**
WR: fastest mile trotted by a four-year-old gelding.
SR: Mile in 2:01 for trotter of any age.

• **August 13—Good Time Park, Goshen NY, Progressive Trot, (1st Division), Purse $1,500**
Greyhound 1-1-1
Tara 2-2-2
Angel Child 4-3-3, Calumet Evelyn 3-5-4, Raider 5-4-6, Hanover Peters 6-7-5, Warwell Worthy 7-6-7
:31, 1:02 ¼, 1:32 ¾, **2:01**; :30, 1:00 ¼, 1:31 ¼, **2:00 ¼**; :30, 1:00 ¼, 1:31, **2:00**
WR (3): fastest third heat (2:00), fastest total for three heats (6:01 ¼), and fastest mile trotted by a four-year-old gelding (2:00)

• **August 21—Illinois State Fairgrounds, Springfield, IL, FFA Trot, Purse $1,200**
Greyhound 1-1
Angel Child 2-2
:33, 1:04, 1:34, **2:02**; :29 ½, :59, :1:28 ½, **1:57 ¼**
WR (3): fastest trotting mile in racing conditions (1:57 ¼), fastest four-year-old trotting (1:57 ¼), fastest two-heat record (2:02, 1:57 ¼)

• **September 11—New York State Fairgrounds, Syracuse, NY, Empire State FFA Trot, Purse $4,000**
Greyhound 1-1-1
Calumet Evelyn 2-2-2
Tara 3-3-3, San Belini 4-4-4
:29 ¾, 1:01 ¼, 1:34, **2:02 ¼**; :29 ½, 1:02, 1:33, **2:01 ¾**; :31 ¼, 1:02 ¼, 1:32 ¾, **2:02**

• **September 25—Allentown Fairgrounds (half-mile oval), Allen-**

town, PA to beat 2:02 ¼ trotting
Greyhound :30 ½, 1:01 ½, 1:31 ½, **2:02**
WR: trotting mile on a half-mile track

- **October 1—KTHBA Track (Red Mile), Lexington, KY, The Transylvania FFA Trot, Purse $3,200**
  Greyhound 1-1-1
  Angel Child 2-2-3
  Tara 3-3-2, Miss Kate B 4-4-4
  :31 ½, 1:03 ½, 1:34, **2:02 ¾**; :29 ¾, 1:01 ½, 1:33, **2:01 ¼**; :32 ¾, 1:02, 1:31 ½, **2:00**

- **October 5—KTHBA Track (Red Mile), Lexington, KY, to beat 1:57 ¼ trotting**
  Greyhound :30 ½, :59 ½, 1:27 ½, **1:57 ¼**

- **October 14—KTHBA Track (Red Mile), Lexington, KY, to beat 1:57 ¼ trotting**
  Greyhound :29, :58, 1:27 ½, **1:57 ¼**

1937

- **July 16—Historic Track (half-mile oval) Goshen NY, to beat 2:02 ¾ trotting**
  Greyhound :29 ½, 1:00, 1:30 ½, **1:59 ¾**
  WR: fastest trotting mile on a half-mile track (also fastest mile at *either* gait on a half-mile track)

- **August 10—Good Time Park, Goshen, NY, to beat 1:59 ¾**
  Greyhound :30 ½, 1:01 ¼, 1:30, **1:58 ¼**
  TR: One Mile Trotting

- **August 20—Illinois State Fairgrounds, Springfield, IL, FFA Trot, Purse $1,805**
  Greyhound 1-1
  Angel Child 2-2
  Lee Hanover 3-3, Calumet Epson 5-4, Silver King 4-4
  :31 ¼, 1:01 ¾, 1:33, **2:01**; :30 ¼, 1:01, 1:31, **1:59 ¼**

- **September 14—Indiana State Fairgrounds, Indianapolis, IN to beat 1½ mile record 3:12 ½**
  Greyhound :31, 1:02, 1:32 ½, 2:03, 2:33, **3:02 ½**
  WR: 1½ miles trotting

- **September 22—KTHBA Track (Red Mile), Lexington, KY to lower his own record of 1:57 ¼**
  Greyhound :29 ¾, :58 ½, 1:27 ¾, **1:56 ¾**
  WR (2): one mile trotting (tied-1:56 ¾); fastest mile, five-year-old trotting (1:56 ¾)

- **September 29—KTHBA Track (Red Mile), Lexington, KY, to beat 1:56 ¾ trotting**
  Greyhound :29 ¼, :57 ½, 1:27 ½, **1:56**
  WR: one mile trotting (1:56)

1938

- **July 4—North Randall Track, Cleveland, OH, FFA Trot, Purse $3,275**
  Greyhound 1-1
  Rosalind 2-2
  Calumet Evelyn 3-3, Ed Lasater 4-4
  :30, 1:02, 1:33, **2:01**; :30 ¼, 1:02 ½, 1:34, **2:00 ¾**
  WR: fastest ¼ ever trotted (:26 ¾)

- **July 14—Historic Half Mile Track, Goshen, NY, Exhibition Mile**
  Greyhound :30 ½, 1:00 ¼, 1:31, **2:01**

- **July 29—Agawam Park, Agawam, MA, The American FFA Trot, Purse $3,100**
  Greyhound 1-1
  Rosalind 2-2
  Clever Hanover 3-3, Ed Lasater 5-4, Calumet Evelyn 4-5
  :31, 1:00 ½, 1:32 ½, **2:02 ¼**; :31 ¼, 1:04, 1:38, **2:05 ¼**

- **August 5—Agawam Park, Agawam, MA, FFA Trot, Purse $3,100**
  Greyhound 1-1
  Rosalind 2-2
  Ed Lasater 4-3, Clever Hanover 5-4, Calumet Evelyn 3-dr
  :30 ¾, 1:00, 1:31, **1:59 ½**; :30 ¼, 1:02 ¼, 1:32, **2:00 ¾**

- **August 9—Good Time Park, Goshen NY, FFA Trot, Purse $3,500**
  Greyhound 1-1
  Rosalind 2-2
  Ed Lasater 4-3, Brogan 3-4
  :30, 1:02, 1:33 ½, **2:02**; :30 ¼, 1:01 ½, 1:31 ¾, **1:59 ¼**

- **August 15—Illinois State Fairgrounds, Springfield, IL, Matron Stake All Age Trot, Purse $3,050**
  Greyhound 1-1
  Rosalind 2-2
  Ed Lasater 3-3
  :31, 1:02 ½, 1:33 ½, **2:02 ¼**; :31, 1:01 ½, 1:31 ¼, **1:59 ½**

- **August 30—New York State Fairgrounds, Syracuse, NY, Exhibition Trot**
  Greyhound :30 ½, 1:01, 1:30 ½, **1:59 ¼**

- **September 6—Indiana State Fairgrounds, Indianapolis, IN, to beat 2:00 ¾ trotting**
  Greyhound :30, :58 ¼, 1:27 ½, **1:56 ¾**
  TR: trotting one mile

- **September 23—KTHBA Track (Red Mile), Lexington, KY, to beat 1:56 trotting**
  Greyhound :28 ¾, :57 ½, 1:27, **1:56**

- **September 29—KTHBA Track (Red Mile), Lexington, KY, to beat 1:56 trotting**
  Greyhound :29 ¼, :58 ½, 1:26 ½, **1:55 ¼**
  WR: one mile trotting

- **October 4—KTHBA Track (Red Mile), Lexington, KY, to beat 1:55 ¼**
  Greyhound :28 ½, :56 ¾, 1:26, **1:55 ½**

1939

- **TR July 27—Old Orchard "Kite Track," Old Orchard Beach, ME, Exhibition trot, to beat 2:01**
  Greyhound :29, :59, 1:28, **1:57 ½**
  TR: one mile trotting

- **August 23—Wisconsin State Fairgrounds, Milwaukee, WI, Exhibition Trot – To beat state record 1:59 ¾** Greyhound :30 ½, 1:00, 1:29, **1:58**
  SR: one mile trotting

- **August 31—New York State Fairgrounds, Syracuse, NY, to beat 2:03 ¼ trotting (to pole)**
  Greyhound and Rosalind :31 ½, 1:01, 1:30 ½, **1:59**
  WR: one mile trotting, team to pole

- **September 5—Indianapolis State Fairgrounds, Indianapolis, IN, to beat 1:59 trotting (to pole)** Greyhound and Rosalind :31, 1:00 ½, 1:30, **1:58 ¼**
  WR: one mile trotting, team to pole

- **September 19—Indiana State Fairgrounds, Indianapolis, IN, to beat 4:10 ¼ trotting (two miles)**
  Greyhound :31, 1:02 ½, 1:33, 2:03, 2:33, 3:04 ¼, 3:35 ½, **4:06**
  WR: two miles trotting

- **September 26—KTHBA Track (Red Mile) Lexington, KY in double harness with running mate.** This is not mentioned in the official record so may not have been officially timed. There is however photographic evidence of this event.
  :34, 1:04 ¼, 1:33 ½, **2:00 ½**

1940

- **March 23—Aiken Mile Track, Aiken, South Carolina, Exhibition Trot**
  Greyhound **2:14 ½** (last quarter in :28 ½)

- **June 22—Indiana State Fairgrounds, Indianapolis, IN, Trotting Horse Club Trot (1st Division), Purse $2346.51**
  Greyhound 1-1
  Bagpiper 2-2
  Dale Hanover 3-4, Sister Mary 6-3, Clever Hanover 4-5, Ed Lasater 5-6
  :31 ¼, 1:02, 1:33, **2:02 ¾**; :32, 1:02 ¾, 1:34, **2:03 ¼**

- **July 9—Ft. Miami Fairgrounds, Toledo, OH, Trotting Club Trot (1st Division), Purse $2,641**
  Greyhound 1-1
  Dale Hanover 2-2
  Sister Mary 5-3, Bravo 3-5, Bagpiper 4-4, Clever Hanover 6-dr
  :32 ½, 1:01 ½, 1:32 ½, **2:01 ¼**; :33, 1:02 ½, 1:32 ¼, **2:01 ¼**

- **July 22—Narragansett Park, Pawtucket, RI, Trotting Club Trot, Purse $2,750**
  Greyhound 1-1
  Sister Mary 3-2
  Bagpiper 2-4, Bravo 5-3, Clever Hanover 4-5
  :32 ¾, 1:04, 1:36 ½, **2:05 ¾**; :33, 1:05, 1:35 ¾, **2:05**

- **July 29—Narragansett Park, Pawtucket, RI, Trotting Club Trot (1st Division), Purse $3,105.20**
  Greyhound 1-1
  Dale Hanover 2-2
  Sister Mary 3-3, Bravo 4-4
  :32 ½, 1:03 ½, 1:33, **2:03 ¼**; :31 ½, 1:02, 1:30, **2:01 ½**
  TR: one mile trotting (2:01 ½)

- **August 12—Good Time Park, Goshen, NY, Trotting Club Trot (1st Division), Purse $2,446.25**
  Greyhound 1-1
  Sister Mary 2-2
  Athlone Flaxey Guy 3-3, Bravo 5-4, Bagpiper 4-5
  :32 ½, 1:03, 1:33 ¾, **2:03 ½**; :31 ¾, 1:03, 1:34, **2:02 ½**

- **August 23—Illinois State Fairgrounds, Springfield, IL, FFA Trot, Purse $1,500**
  Greyhound 1-1
  Sister Mary 2-2
  Spentell 3-3
  :29 ¾, 1:00, 1:30, **1:59 ¼**; :31 ¼, 1:02 ½, 1:32 ½, **2:01 ½**

- **August 26—New York State Fairgrounds, Syracuse, NY, Trotting Club Trot (1st Division), Purse $1,733.75**
  Greyhound 2-1-1
  Peter Astra 1-2-6
  Bravo 6-6-2, Sister Mary 4-4-3, Dale Hanover 3-4-4, Calumet Dilworthy 5-5-5
  :30 ½, 1:00 ¼, 1:30 ½, **2:01 ½**; :32 ½, 1:03, 1:34 ½, **2:04 ½**; :32, 1:03, 1:34, **2:03**

- **September 11—Kentucky State Fairgrounds (half-mile oval), Louisville, KY, Exhibition Trot**
  Greyhound :30, 1:01, 1:30 ½, **2:00 ½**
  TR: one mile trotting

- **September 27—KTHBA Track (Red Mile), Lexington, KY, to beat 2:05¼ trotting (under saddle)**
  Greyhound :30 ½, 1:00 ¾, 1:31 ¾, **2:01 ¾**
  WR: one mile trotting, under saddle

Appendix 3

GREYHOUND'S WORLD RECORDS

Table reprinted from an article in *Harness Horse* (2/10/1965) showing a full account of Greyhound's world records and their status upon his death in February 1965.

WORLD RECORDS BY GREYHOUND

	Times	Broken by
2-Year-Old 1934		
Gelding in race	2:04¾	1950 Thunderation
Gelding in two-heat race	2:06-2:04¾	1950 Thunderation
3-Year-Old 1935		
Gelding in race	2:00	1953 Senator Frost
Gelding in two-heat race	2:02¼-2:02¾ .. 2:05-2:00	1950 Lord Steward
Gelding in three-heat race	2:06-2:06-2:03¼	Still stands
Gelding in three-heat divided race	202¼-2:04-2:01½*	Still stands
4-Year-Old 1936		
Gelding in race	1:57¼	Still stands
Trotter in race	1:57¼	1952 Star's Pride
Trotter on HMT	T2:02	1945 Titan Hanover
Gelding on HMT	T2:02	Still stands
Gelding in race	2:05	1941 Earl's Moody Guy
Trotter in three-heat race	2:01-2:01¼-2:00	Still stands
Gelding in three-heat race	(same)	Still stands
Gelding in two-heat race	2:02-1:57¼	1959 Senator Frost
Trotter in two-heat race	(same)	1941 Nibble Hanover
Trotter in second heat	1:57¼	1952 Star's Pride
5-Year-Old 1937		
Trotter on HMT	T1:59¾	1963 Matastar
Gelding on HMT	(same)	Still stands
Trotter, 1½ miles	T3:02½	Still stands
Trotter	T1:56	1938 Greyhound
Gelding trotter	(same)	1938 Greyhound
6-Year-Old 1938		
Trotter	T1:55¼	Still stands
Gelding trotter	(same)	Still stands
7-Year-Old 1939		
Trotter, team to pole (with Rosalind)	T1:58¼	Still stands
Trotter, 2-miles	T4:06	Still stands
8-Year-Old 1940		
Trotter, under saddle	T2:01¾	Still stands

* Greyhound won first and third heats.

Table reprinted from an article in *Harness Horse* (2/10/1965)

Records broken after that table was published in 1965 include:

- Fastest trotting mile: broken by Nevele Pride in 1969.
- Fastest gelding in a race (trotting): broken by Flirth in 1973.
- Fastest gelding trotter (any age): broken by I'm Impeccable in 1990.
- Under saddle record: broken by Preferential with Brooke Nickells in 1995.

I am certain that aside from the team to pole record, all others have fallen, though other than those noted above, I was unable to find exactly when and by whom the records were broken.

Appendix 4
GREYHOUND'S TWO-MINUTE MILES (TT = TIME TRIAL)

1. August 20, 1935, Springfield, IL 2:00

2. August 12, 1936, Goshen, NY 2:00

3. August 21, 1936, Springfield, IL .... 1:57 ¼

4. October 1, 1936, Lexington, KY 2:00

5. October 5, 1936, Lexington, KY .... 1:57 ¼ TT

6. October 15, 1936, Lexington, KY .... 1:57 ¼ TT

7. July 16, 1937, Goshen, NY .... 1:59 ¾ TT (half-mile track)

8. August 10, 1937, Goshen, NY .... 1:58 ¼ TT

9. August 20, 1937, Springfield, IL .... 1:59 ¼ TT

10. September 22, 1937, Lexington, KY .... 1:56 ¾ TT

11. September 29, 1937, Lexington, KY .... 1:56 TT

12. August 5, 1938, Agawam, MA .... 1:59 ½

13. August 9, 1938, Goshen, NY .... 1:59 ¼

14. August 15, 1938, Springfield, IL .... 1:59 ½

15. August 30, 1938, Syracuse, NY .... 1:59 ¼ TT

16. September 6, 1938, Indianapolis, IN .... 1:56 ¾ TT

17. September 23, 1938, Lexington, KY .... 1:56 TT

18. September 29, 1938, Lexington, KY .... 1:55 ¼ TT

19. October 4, 1938, Lexington, KY .... 1:55 ½ TT

20. July 27, 1939, Old Orchard, ME .... 1:57 ½ TT

21. August 23, 1939, Milwaukee, WI .... 1:58 TT

22. August 31, 1939, Syracuse, NY .... 1:59 TT (team)

23. September 5, 1939, Indianapolis, IN .... 1:58 ¼ TT (team)

24. October 7, 1939, Lexington, KY .... 1:56 ¾ TT

25. August 23, 1940, Springfield, IL .... 1:59 ¼

Appendix 5
Greyhound's Measurements

Length of Stride

It is difficult to be certain how long Greyhound's incredible stride was. Given the meticulous measurements taken by John Hervey (see below), it is surprising no attempt was made to measure the stride itself. Fans attempting to eyeball his stride claimed it to be over 30 feet. An article printed in the February 10, 1965 issue of Horseman and Fair World following Greyhound's death gave an account of a group of horsemen measuring his stride from hoofprints on the track after the horse made his record at Historic. They came up with 28 feet. In a 1975 interview, Jimmie told reporter Maryjean Wall that Doc Parshall measured Greyhound's stride at Lexington between heats on a freshly harrowed track.

"Sep brushed him real good and Doc went out and measured him at over thirty-two feet."

With no official measurement and the challenge of measuring a gait that can change length dramatically (a typical riding horse's trot stride is around four feet), it's hard to have a definitive answer, as the length of Greyhound's stride would have fluctuated with the conditions, the size of the track, and where on the track the stride was measured. For comparison, the galloping stride of Thoroughbred greats Man O' War (28 feet) and Secretariat (25 feet) give testament to just how unusual Greyhound was.

COMPARATIVE MEASUREMENTS OF UHLAN, PETER MANNING AND GREYHOUND

	Uhlan	Peter Manning	Greyhound
Height at withers	15.2¼	15.3⅛	16.1¼
Height at rump	15.1¾	15.2½	15.3⅝
Extreme length of body	15.3	15.2	15.1¼
Length of head, poll to tip of muzzle	25¼	26	23½
Length of neck	32¾	31	31
Girth at heart	69¾	69	70½
Girth at waist	69½	70	66⅜
Length of foreleg, body to ground	34	37	34⅜
Length of front cannon, knee to ankle	9	12	11
Around forearm at swell	20½	21½	17¾
Around front cannon midway	8	7⅞	7½
Length from point of knee to ground	18	19	19½
Length of hind leg, point of stifle to ground	40	40	42¾
Length from point of hock to ground	22	24	23½
Length from point of hip to point of hock	40	40	37⅞
Width of hips, point to point	22	24	18
Width of breast, point to point of shoulders	16½	14¾	13¾

Measurements originally appeared in "Comparing Three Champions." *Harness Horse*, December 16, 1936, p. 116

Appendix 5
Greyhound's Measurements

```
           MEASUREMENTS OF GREYHOUND, 4, 1:57¼
Height at withers ..................................   16.1¼
Height of croup ....................................   15.3⅝
Extreme length of body, point of breast to swell of quarter  15.1¼
Width of breast ....................................   13¾ in.
Length of head ....................................    23½
Circumference of muzzle ..........................    19⅞
Width between eyes ...............................    8⅞
Length of ear .....................................    5½
Around jowls .....................................    37
Around throat-latch ...............................    28¾
Length of neck ...................................    31
Girth around heart ................................    70½
Girth around waist ................................    66⅜
Width of hips, point to point .....................    18
Width of buttocks .................................    17⅝

Around gaskin ....................................    17
Around hock .....................................    16⅜
Width between fore-legs ..........................    3⅜
Around fore-arm, at swell ........................    17¾
Around front cannon .............................    7½
Around hind cannon .............................    8⅛
Length of fore leg, body to ground ...............    34⅜
Length of hind leg, body to ground ...............    42¾
Length of front cannon, center of knee to center of ankle ..  11
Length of front leg, back point of knee to ground ......  19½
Point of hip to point of hock .....................    37⅞
Point of stifle to point of hock ..................    24
Point of hock to ground ..........................    23½
Length of back ..................................    23¾
From coupling to tail ............................    16½
Height at setting-on of tail ......................    58¼
Length of shoulder ..............................    22¾
Length of body, belly line .......................    32⅛
Length of front pastern ..........................    4
Length of hind pastern ...........................    4⅛
Length of front foot .............................    5
Width of front foot ..............................    4¾
Length of hind foot ..............................    5⅛
Width of hind foot ...............................    4¾
```

Hervey's Greyhound Measurements (reprinted with permission of USTA *Harness Horse* Archive)

END NOTES

CHAPTER 1

Image: A portrait of Greyhound in his stall, most likely in his late teens (circa late 1940s, courtesy of the Harness Racing Museum & Hall of Fame, Goshen, NY; original photograph by Harold G. Strong).

Epigraph: Harrison, Jim, "King of Trotters is Gone," *Hoof Beats*, March 1965, 26. "The gray horse is gone …"

Putnam, Leone, personal notes, 1965. The bulk of this chapter is recreated from Leone's handwritten notes, which are stored in the archives at the Harness Racing Museum in Goshen, New York. She had notes about the weather, and that there was a private service, Doc Flanery cried, and guests were at the farm upon their return; she is also the source of information about the guest book, number of signatures, quotes from visitors, where they came from, and so on, and Dooley's concern about the public forgetting Greyhound.

1. **Flora, Earl, "The Unruffled Snow,"** *Hoof Beats*, **April 1965, p. 20.** Upon a visit to Flanery Farm in March 1965, Flora noted Christmas decorations still hanging and cards around, and info about the guest book and visitors.

2. **"Star's Pride Sets World Race Record of 1:57 ⅕,"** *Evening Sun* **(Hanover, PA), August 30, 1952, 8.**

3. **Putnam, Leone,** *Dooley and the Grey Ghost* **(Goshen, NY: Harness Racing Museum and Hall of Fame, 2018), 28.**

4. **Robertson, Orlo, "Honors Shared,"** *Cincinnati Enquirer*, **December 10, 1937, 19.** Greyhound is Algernon Daingerfield's choice for Horse of the Year in the *Horse and Horseman* poll. Selected over Seabiscuit and War Admiral.

5. **McCarr, Ken,** *The Kentucky Harness Horse* **(The University Press of Kentucky, 1978).** Quote: Greyhound was "by far the greatest horse before the public."

CHAPTER 2

Image: The foaling barn at Calumet Farm (1962, courtesy of the Keeneland Library Meador Collection); excerpts from a column appearing in the *Lexington Herald-Leader*, June 7, 1932.

Epigraph: Hervey, John, "Guy Abbey, Greyhound, and Calumet Evelyn," *Hoof Beats*, November 1935, 396. "Don't forget Guy Abbey …" Discussion about Guy Abbey, lameness and retirement.

1. **Auerbach, Ann Hagedorn,** *"Wild Ride: the rise and fall of Calumet Farm, Inc"* **(Holt McDougal, December 1995).** Discussion of William Monroe Wright's Standardbred operation as the original purpose of Calumet Farm, his son Warren Wright's takeover, and the uncertainty as the operation changed to Thoroughbreds.

2. **WEB, "Champion Colt Trotter, Fireglow, Died as Result of Stake Race Accident,"** *Philadelphia Inquirer*, **August 19, 1928, 45.** Details of the August 1928 accident at North Randall involving Guy Abbey. Walter Cox suspended one month, Fireglow dies from injuries (see note 3).

3. **"Fireglow Poisoned, Is Chemist Report,"** *New York Times*, **December 25, 1928, 34.** An unnamed expert chemist hired by owner W. H. Yane examined the horse's stomach and intestines and reported that Fireglow had been poisoned. Type of poison not mentioned. Fireglow noted as the heavy betting favorite in the Hambletonian, who had easily defeated his main competitors already that season.

4. **Hervey, John, "Guy Abbey, Greyhound, and Calumet Evelyn,"** *Hoof Beats*, **November 1935, 396.** Just a week after the accident at North Randall, Guy Abbey won the Horse Review Futurity at Goshen, New York, trotting the final quarter of the fourth heat in :29 ¾—amazing, as he was not quite sound. The next week in the Hambletonian, though quite lame, he trotted second against Spencer but was broken down, ending his racing career.

5. **Shuff, Jesse, "Trotting Horse Notes,"** *Lexington Herald-Leader*, **March 6, 1932, 7.** Shuff happened to see his friend Henry Knight (in Lexington, visiting family) on a visit to Calumet Farm days before Greyhound's birth. Together they looked at Knight's yearlings and broodmares, including Elizabeth.

6. **"Historic Almahurst Farm Will Be Sold to Settle Knight's Estate,"** *Lexington Herald*, **April 9, 1959, 1.** History of land given to Knight in the 1700s.

7. **"Almahurst Sets Unique Record in Double Role,"** *Lexington Herald-Leader*, **January 15, 1950, 84.** Dixie Knight bred Exterminator.

8. **Phelps, Frank Talmadge, "Man Has Plans, Will Travel On,"** *Lexington Herald*, **January 11, 1959, 103.** Henry's early adult life. Joe Knight buys Josephine Belle and breeds Nervolo Belle, dam of Peter Volo. Quote: "Father said I …"; quote: "I couldn't make any money …"

9. **Ibid.** Henry's early life and connection to Scott Hudson.

10. **"Scott Hudson Drove Four Winning Races,"** *Buffalo Review*, **July 26, 1902, 10.** Hudson drives four winners in one day, runs the card, and wins nearly $4,000.

11. **Danforth, Ed, "Scott Hudson and His Famous Blind Trotter,"** *Atlanta Journal*, **December 2, 1962, 227.** Background on Scott Hudson, mentor/uncle of Henry Knight.

12. **Phelps, Frank Talmadge, "Man Has Plans …" (see note 8).** "That's quite a story …"

13. **Ibid.** Henry, early adult life/jobs.

14. **Ibid.** "I couldn't make any money …"

15. **"Henry Knight Owns Three Great Stallions,"** *Lexington Herald*, **January 18, 1934, 18.** Overview of Knight's past. Guy Abbey, Mr. McElwyn, and Calumet Adam to stand at Almahurst.

16. **Gahagan, Tom, "Abbedale is Sold for $6000,"** *Indianapolis Star*, **May 30, 1930, 16.** Elizabeth sold to Henry Knight for $2,250, from the Candler dispersal.

END NOTES

17. Hervey, John, "About Greyhound," *Horse and Horseman*, December 1936, 24. Elizabeth was a natural pacer but Candler only liked trotters ...

18. Stoneridge, M. A., *Great Horses of Our Time* (Garden City, NY: Doubleday and Company, 1972), 269.

CHAPTER 3

Image: This 1934 ad shows Almahurst, located at the KTHBA Track in Lexington, and three of its best-known stallions (courtesy of the United States Trotting Association).

Epigraph: Hamilton, Pamela, *Lady Be Good: The Life and Times of Dorothy Hale* (PLH Media, LLC, 2021).

1. "Germany 1933 from Democracy to Dictatorship," Go In-depth, Anne Frank House, accessed April 18, 2024, https://www.annefrank.org/en/anne-frank/go-in-depth/germany-1933-democracy-dictatorship/.

2. "Franklin Delano Roosevelt Event Timeline," The American Presidency Project, University of California Santa Barbara, accessed April 18, 2024, https://www.presidency.ucsb.edu/documents/franklin-delano-roosevelt-event-timeline.

3. Auerbach, Ann Hagedorn, "*Wild Ride: the rise and fall of Calumet Farm, Inc*" (Holt McDougal, December 1995). Warren Wright, Sr. was determined to be a top breeder and racer of Thoroughbreds. Under his tenure, Calumet Farm experienced an astronomical rise to the top, producing multiple champions and Triple Crown winners until his death in 1950. The farm would continue to prosper into the 1970s, but would never surpass the greatness achieved by the Sr. Warren Wright.

4. Gahagan, George M, Hoof Beats (column), *Indianapolis Star*, December 16, 1933, 14. Knight established his Standardbred business and named it Almahurst. It is based out of the barns constructed for William Wright at the Kentucky Trotting Horse Breeders Track. Marvin Childs is the manager-trainer. Knight had considered Laurel, but decided he'd rather be close to his ancestral land.

5. "Almahurst Stable," *Hoof Beats*, Christmas 1933, 508-09. Knight purchased Guy Abbey from the Calumet dispersal.

6. Ibid. Henry Knight established Almahurst at the "top of the stretch" of the KTHBA Track (now the Red Mile) in a barn rented from Calumet.

7. "Dixie Knight Killed as He Begs for Life," *Kentucky Advocate* (Danville, Kentucky), August 2, 1934, 1.

8. "Illness Fatal to Jessamine County Leader," *Lexington Herald-Leader*, April 9, 1935, 1. Henry Knight's father, Grant Lee "Joe" Knight, died following a long illness.

9. "Around and About Almahurst," *Horseman and Fair World*, June 26, 1935, 293. The article shows images of new construction at the Knight family farm and one of Henry Knight's stallions outside the barn at the rented Calumet facility.

10. Shuff, Jesse, "Trotting Horse Notes," *Lexington Herald-Leader*, March 6, 1932, 7. Shuff saw Henry Knight and Elizabeth at Calumet Farm days before Greyhound was foaled.

CHAPTER 4

Image: Greyhound warming up at the KTHBA Track in Lexington (October 3, 1934, courtesy of the St. Charles Historical Society).

Epigraph: "News Views," *The Chicago Daily News* Pictorial Section, October 30, 1943, 5. Quote: "There were even some present at the time who didn't think he was worth $50." Col. Baker, 1943.

1. Shuff, Jesse, "Down in the Blue Grass Country," *Horseman and Fair World*, March 8, 1933, 73. On March 1, 15 yearlings are sent to Hunter C. Moody, colt starter. Greyhound is among the four owned by Knight.

2. Shuff, Jesse, "Down in the Bluegrass Country," *Horseman and Fair World*, May 10, 1933, 197. Moody turns out 14 yearlings; is reported to have had great luck breaking Thoroughbreds to harness, with many returning to the races as winners, including 1932 Kentucky Derby winner Burgoo King.

3. Hervey, John, "Greyhound and Other Geldings," 1935, 312. Hervey notes Greyhound's color and breeding likely contributed to his being gelded early.

4. Shuff, Jesse, "Around the Grand Circuit," *Lexington Herald*, August 22, 1935, 5. Knight gave Elizabeth to W. N. Reynolds.

5. Bower, Alex, "Can These Youngsters Follow In His Footsteps?" *Lexington Leader*, May 10, 1940, 6. Hunter Moody quote: "When a horse's mouth is properly balanced ..."

6. Shuff, Jesse, "With the Trotters," *Lexington Herald-Leader*, April 20, 1933, 6. Greyhound is the current star of Knight's yearlings with Moody. Notes Elizabeth is full sister to Peter the Brewer. He is the second fastest gray in Moody's stable of youngsters. Silver King, owned by E. J. Merkle, is the other, a gray colt by Mr. McElwyn.

7. Hervey, John, "Comparing Three Champions," *Harness Horse*, December 16, 1936, 116. The "trotting pitch," where the horse is higher behind than in front, is considered ideal for the trotter, or being even—but never being higher in front. Hambletonian and his world champion get were also built like this.

8. Shuff, *Horseman and Fair World*, May 10, 1933 (see note 2). Moody turns out yearlings.

9. Shuff, Jesse, "R. J. Reynolds Buys Tract Adjoining Trotting Oval," *Lexington Herald-Leader*, February 17, 1935, 6. Description of Calumet facility at KTHBA track.

10. Ibid. Notes Knight prepped and sold his yearlings from that facility in 1934.

11. Shuff, Jesse, "Down in the Bluegrass Country," *Horseman and Fair World*, October 25, 1933, 546. Marvin Childs is getting the Knight yearlings ready for the Indianapolis Speed Sale. Shuff notes Greyhound showed lots of speed in his early handling, which may have influenced Knight's purchase of his sire Guy Abbey earlier in the year.

12. Griffin, Gerald, "Greyhound's Brother Has Trotting Days Ahead," *Courier-Journal* (Louisville, Kentucky), June 24, 1939, 52. "Greyhound wasn't so impressive as a yearling according to Mr. Childs ..."

13. Shuff, *Horseman and Fair World*, October 25, 1933 (see note 11). Shuff notes Greyhound had a lot of early speed, and this may have influenced Knight's purchase of his sire Guy Abbey.

14. "Greyhound 3, 2:00," *Harness Horse*, December 18, 1935, 145. "You may not be strong for grey horses, but that bird sure can trot." Quote attributed to Knight, speaking to Baker.

15. Bower, *Lexington Leader*, May 10, 1940 (see note 5). Moody tells the story of how he and Dick McMahon convinced Baker to buy Greyhound. "That's where you're mistaken ..." Baker quote: "He doesn't move along fast enough ..."

16. Keller, Ed, "Still the King—Greyhound, Part 1," *Sunday Times* (Salisbury, MD), August 10, 1969, 40. Describes the moment Greyhound was sold.

CHAPTER 5

Image: Greyhound pulling an old-fashioned high-wheel sulky from the late 1800s (August 1938, courtesy of the Harness Racing Museum).

1. Kraft, Nicole, "100 Years in Harness" (Ohio: United States Trotting Association, 2008). Chapter epigraph and description of harness racing as "growing up" alongside America.

2. Dixon, Simon, "Horse Racing in Nineteenth-Century Russia," University College London, 12.

END NOTES

3. Ibid., 15.

4. Ibid., 28.

5. McCarr, Ken, *The Kentucky Harness Horse* (The University Press of Kentucky, 1978). "Some of the earliest contests …"

6. Akers, Dwight, "Drivers Up," (New York: G. P. Putnam's Sons, 1938), 5.

7. Ibid., 26.

8. Ibid.

9. Ibid. "On the foundation of his blood …"

10. Ibid., 28.

11. Ibid.

12. Ibid., 29. "Trotting as distinct from racing …"

13. Ibid., 30.

14. Ibid.

15. Ibid., 31.

16. Ibid., 27.

17. Sanders, Millard, *Two-minute Horses* (Cleveland, OH: Press of the Judson Company, 1922), 13.

18. Akers, Dwight, "Drivers Up" (see note 6), 35.

19. Ibid., 36.

20. Ibid., 37.

21. Ibid., 39.

22. Ibid., 44.

23. Ibid., 108.

24. Ibid., 32.

25. Ibid., 39.

26. Ibid., 50.

27. Ibid., 175.

28. Ibid., 176.

29. Ibid., 56.

30. Hervey, John, "A Pair of Shoes," *Harness Horse*, December 14, 1938, 125.

31. Akers, Dwight, "Drivers Up" (see note 6), 63.

32. Ibid., 229.

33. Ibid., 229.

34. Ibid., 230.

35. Harness Racing Museum tour guide. August 7, 2023.

36. Hervey, John, "Fortieth Anniversary," Harness Horse, September 1, 1943, 1277.

37. Akers, Dwight, "Drivers Up" (see note 6), 230.

38. McCarr, Ken, *The Kentucky Harness Horse* (see note 5), 69.

39. Akers, Dwight, "Drivers Up" (see note 6), 206.

40. Sanders, Millard, *Two-minute Horses* (see note 17), 14.

41. Akers, Dwight, "Drivers Up" (see note 6), 282.

CHAPTER 6

Image: Colonel E. J. Baker, in the gardens at Hotel Baker (circa 1940s, courtesy of the St. Charles Historical Society).

Epigraph: Gahagan, George M. "Baker's Return to Harness Racing is Welcomed." *Indianapolis Star* (Indiana), October 15, 1933, p. 18. "Few owners …"

1. Gahagan, George M, "Belgian Horseman buys Volo Dear; Selka Worthy Purchased by Italian," *Indianapolis Star*, November 8, 1933, 15. "Greyhound, a sensationally fast yearling gelding by Guy Abbey …" purchased by E. J. Baker for $900. Sales results for yearlings at the 1933 Indianapolis Speed Sale.

2. "Lawrence Hanover Is Sold to Chicagoan for $6800," *Evening Sun* (Hanover, Pennsylvania), November 29, 1933, 8. Information about Lawrence Hanover's pedigree and sale as yearling at Old Glory Sale.

3. "Housing 1929-1941," "Historic Events for Students: The Great Depression," *Encyclopedia.com*, accessed March 18, 2024, https://www.encyclopedia.com/education/news-and-education-magazines/housing-1929-1941

4. "Lawrence Hanover is Sold …" (see note 2).

5. Pearson, Ruth Seen, *Reflections of St. Charles* (St. Charles History Museum, 1976, 2019), 144.

6. Ibid.

7. Ibid., 145.

8. Ibid.

9. Ibid., 146.

10. Ibid.

11. Ibid., 147.

12. "St. Charles Benefactors—Baker Family," *Peterson-Anderson Family History*, Issue 80 (November 2019).

13. "Edward J. Baker Passes Away at Age 90," *St. Charles Chronicle*, January 21, 1959, 1.

14. "St. Charles Benefactors …" (see note 12).

15. "Gates' Millions to Widow and Son; Gifts to Friends," *Chicago Tribune*, August 31, 1911, 2.

16. Ibid., 1-2.

17. Ibid. Quote: "Mr. Gates always wanted Henry …"

18. Pearson, Ruth Seen, *Reflections of St. Charles* (see note 5), 149.

19. "Gates Heir Weds Nurse Sweetheart," *Inter Ocean* (Chicago), October 13, 1912, 1. Henry Baker's football injury leads to tuberculosis.

20. "Gates Fortune for Cure," *Belleville News-Democrat* (Illinois), March 5, 1913, 7. Dellora offers the Gates fortune, millions of dollars, to German doctor F. F. Friedman if he can cure Henry. Friedman claims

he is close to a cure for consumption, which later proves to be untrue.

21. **"St. Charles Child Heir to Millions,"** *True Republican* (Sycamore, Illinois), May 2, 1914, 4. Harriet Baker near collapse, condition serious.

22. **"Thousands at Baker Funeral,"** *Chicago Tribune*, May 4, 1914, 16.

23. Pearson, Ruth Seen, *Reflections of St. Charles* (see note 5), 152.

24. **"Edward J. Baker Passes Away …"** (see note 13).

25. Ibid.

26. Ibid.

27. **"Field Day at Crystal Brook Farm,"** *St. Charles Chronicle*, November 3, 1938, 1. Baker presents educational demonstrations for local farmers.

28. Colby, Lester B, **"St. Charles—the 'Fairy City,'"** *True Republican*, July 21, 1926, 6. Baker's contributions to the city. Quote as to why he donates so much to St. Charles and her people.

29. Ibid. "Why not?" Baker once said when asked …

30. **"St. Charles Benefactors …"** (see note 12).

31. Ibid.

32. Calkins, Ada C, **"The Baker Hotel to Open Saturday,"** *True Republican* (Sycamore, IL), May 30, 1928, 2. Description of Hotel Baker.

33. **"West Liberty Trainer to Race on Grand Circuit This Season,"** *Muscatine Journal* (Iowa), April 21, 1923, 6. Baker purchased a formidable string of harness horses in 1922 and turned them over to Kelly.

34. **"Trotting Gossip Heard at State Fair Race Camp,"** *Indianapolis News*, June 9, 1925, 25. Chet Kelly and Baker stable shipping to North Randall. Kelly has been ill and his son Harlan has been doing the work, but Chet is now back in the sulky.

35. **"Harness Racer Joins Throng,"** *Chicago Tribune*, January 17, 1926, 29. Reports that Baker has "sold out" of his harness racing establishment and is actively seeking a Thoroughbred racing stable.

36. **"Baker's Trotters to Go on Auction Block,"** *Star Press* (Indianapolis, Indiana), November 15, 1925, 11.

37. Rice, Grantland, **"Trotting Gossip,"** *Indianapolis News*, December 26, 1926, 13. Previous reports that Baker was getting out were rumors. He simply sold some stock and now is buying new stock for the upcoming season. All of his horses are with Palin now.

38. Gahagan, Will, Among the Equine Aristocrats (column), *Indianapolis Star*, June 19, 1927, 39. Palin has a new farm named after his horse, The Senator.

39. Hoofbeats (column), *Indianapolis Star*, February 27, 1929, 15. Palin was among the largest purchasers at an Indianapolis sale, stocking his farm with quality broodmares to be bred to The Senator. Baker also made many purchases.

40. Keller, Edwin T, **"Almost Hundred Races,"** *Cincinnati Enquirer*, February 9, 1930, 26. The Baker-Palin stable has won nearly 100 races in two years. Baker is the winningest owner, and Palin the winningest trainer in 1928 and 1929. As of February 1930, Palin has 35 head in training with a dozen Hambletonian contenders.

41. Gahagan, George M, **"Famous Hoosier Trotting Sire Acquired by Illinois Horseman at Local Sale,"** *Indianapolis Star*, November 13, 1931, 15. Baker goes $8,700 for The Senator at the Indianapolis Speed Sale.

42. Gahagan, Tom, **"E J Baker Getting Out of Racing, into Breeding of Harness Horses."** *Collyer's Eye and the Baseball World*, November 21, 1931, 3. Baker is selling his racing string and has purchased The Senator from Palin and his partners, as well as procuring some broodmares.

43. **"Johnson County Reinsman Attracts Attention of Grand Circuit Stable Owner,"** *Edinburgh Daily Courier* (Indiana), June 19, 1931, 1. Baker has a sixty-horse stable in three barns at Indianapolis fairgrounds.

44. Gahagan, George, **"Hoof Beats,"** *Indianapolis Star*, April 30, 1932, 23. Reports on records set by get of The Senator.

45. **"Hoof Beats,"** *Indianapolis Star*, October 5, 1932, 15. Baker announces dispersal of all stock at Senator Farm.

46. **"Horsemen Swarm at State Fairgrounds for Three-day Auction Sale of 260 Race Horses,"** *Indianapolis News*, November 14, 1932, 17. Baker and Palin sell all holdings—racing and breeding stock—at the Indianapolis Speed Sale, November 1932.

47. **"E.J. Baker herd brings $35,000 at auction sale,"** *Chicago Tribune*, December 1, 1932, 10. Baker sells off 172 Holstein Dairy cattle, a dispersal of the stock at his Silver Glen Farm. Average about $200 each.

48. Gahagan, George M, Hoof Beats (column), *Indianapolis Star*, November 19, 1932, 15. Quote: "It is too much to believe …" Baker leaving the sport following his dispersal at the November 1932 Indianapolis Speed Sale. **Author's Note:** This appears to be rumor based on speculation. I found no evidence Baker made such an announcement. However, he did take a step back from racing his stable in 1933, and from his role acting as secretary to the Indiana Board of Agriculture.

49. **"Trotters' Sale Prices Mount in Record Year,"** *Chicago Tribune*, October 10, 1933. The sales average for trotters is a third higher than expected. Lexington experiences a record-breaking year, with top prices ranging from $3,000 to $15,000.

50. Ibid. Harriman quote: "Such prices … make it look as if the harness sport never heard of the depression."

51. Ibid. Baker made his first return to racing, purchasing a yearling named Calumet Frolic for $2,100.

CHAPTER 7

Image: An undated portrait of Sep Palin (courtesy of the Harness Racing Museum & Hall of Fame, Goshen, NY).

Epigraph: "S. F. Palin Dies," *Hoof Beats*, November 1952, 8. "He had a keen mind …"

1. **"S. F. Palin Dies" (see above).** Palin quote: "Since I was so small, I had to climb …"

2. Ibid.

3. **"Greyhound, Now 17, Loafs; Palin Wins,"** *Rapid City Journal* (South Dakota), May 14, 1949, 10. Palin started as a groom for Billy Marvin.

4. **"William W. Marvin Dead; Was Famed as Horse Trainer,"** *Journal and Courier* (Lafayette, Indiana), May 17, 1941, 1. Palin tutored under Marvin.

5. **"Greyhound, Now 17 …"** (see note 3). Palin started training on his own in 1900.

6. Gahagan, Will, Horse Sense (column), *Indianapolis Star*, June 20, 1915, 21. Possibility is successful with Palin, winning 14 of 16 starts.

7. Gahagan, Will, **"Horse Sense: Palin Making Good."** *The Indianapolis Star*, November 22, 1914, 47. "A young Indiana teamster …" Talks about Sep Palin's 1914 season.

END NOTES

8. McGee, Wilson, "Grey Lucky to Sep Palin Famous Trotting Driver," *Orlando Sentinel*, **January 5, 1936, 8.** In 1913, Palin was a wholesale buyer and seller of draft horses.

9. Gahagan, Will, "Horse Sense: Palin Making Good" (see note 7). "A young Indiana teamster …"

10. **"Turfmen Expelled by Trotting Board,"** *Pittsburgh Post*, **May 7, 1914, 4.** Sep Palin is suspended by the National Trotting Association until he returns $511 in "unlawful winnings" by the horse Dan O, who was started out of class. Palin racing in the South in 1914—Alabama and Georgia.

11. **"Was it a Frame-Up?"** *Huntington Herald* (Indiana), **August 19, 1911, 8.** Details of "cheating scandal."

12. **"Driving Park at Columbus to be Razed,"** *Dayton Daily News* (Ohio), **December 29, 1925, 19.**

13. **"Green Pacer Goes Sensational Mile in Local Record Meeting,"** *Indianapolis News*, **June 15, 1918, 12.** Quote: "Esta G…Wiggles Around the Track …" Quote: "…the fastest piece of horse flesh …"

14. Gocher, W. H, Gossip of Light Harness Horses (column), *Lexington Herald-Leader*, **June 24, 1921, 12.** "No one has anything on Palin as a driver …"

15. **Ibid.**

16. Gahagan, Will, Among the Equine Aristocrats (column), *Indianapolis Star*, **September 11, 1921, 36.** Notes Palin's recent success with Galli Curci and that his previous trainer, Tommy Murphy, had some poor performances.

17. **"Hoosier Horseman to Celebrate Many Season's Victories Next Tuesday,"** *Indianapolis News*, **November 12, 1921, 14.** Palin among leading race winners of the year.

18. Gocher, W. H, "Murphy Again Leads Drivers On Grand Circuit," *Brooklyn Daily Eagle*, **October 19, 1924, 46.** Palin and White tied for second winningest drivers with 18 wins each.

19. Gahagan, Will, In the Harness World (column), *Indianapolis Star*, **December 20, 1925, 28.** "It is several years since Palin discarded …" Gahagan notes Palin has been sent horses other trainers had not been able to find success with.

CHAPTER 8

Image: Colonel Baker gives Greyhound a carrot. One of his Dalmatians, possibly Fibber, watches (circa 1936, Heitbrink Collection, courtesy of the Harness Racing Museum & Hall of Fame, Goshen, NY).

Epigraph: "Tom Gahagan Writes of His Visit to Hanover Shoe Farm," *Evening Sun* (Hanover, PA), November 22, 1933, 3. "Even with all the wealth …"

1. Simpson, Sr., John F, "The Theory of Shoeing and Balancing," in *Care and Training of the Trotter and Pacer*, by James C. Harrison (Columbus, Ohio: United States Trotting Association, 1968), 295-96.

2. Ibid., 300.

3. Ibid., 302.

4. Ibid., 346.

5. Ibid., 372.

6. Stoneridge, M. A, *Great Horses of Our Time* (Garden City, NY: Doubleday & Company, Inc, 1972), 269. Greyhound had a rather awkward and disjointed way of going.

7. Hervey, John, "The Story of Greyhound," *Horse and Horseman*, **February 1939, 26-7; 37-8.** 6-oz shoe in front, 4 oz behind.

8. Hinrichs, Art, "Shoeing the Champion," *Hoof Beats*, **January 1940, 14-15.** Hinrichs notes Greyhound never wore heavier than a 7-oz shoe, and wore a 5 ½-ounce shoe in front (a slight discrepancy from what Hervey said the year before).

9. **Author's Note:** I personally viewed and handled a full set and several single shoes of Greyhound's at the Harness Racing Museum in Goshen, and can attest they were quite simple. The fronts were plain, with a slight rounding at the toe on the left one. The right was slightly wider on the lateral side. The hinds were bar shoes with slightly squared toes and quarter clips. A second set of hind shoes had a small medial swedge at the toe. What is unknown is at what point in his career Greyhound wore these shoes. The hind shoes on display at the museum (donated from his years in retirement) had heel grabs.

10. Hinrichs, Art, "Shoeing the Champion" (see note 8), 15.

11. Baldwin, Ralph N, "Training the Two-Year-Old," in *Care and Training of the Trotter and Pacer*, by James C. Harrison, (Columbus, OH: United States Trotting Association, 1968), 156-62. Summary of early training for a two-year-old trotter.

12. Ibid., 182-83. The author used Baldwin's chart for working a northern-trained two-year-old to give the reader an idea of what Palin may have done with Greyhound. Times were adjusted to reflect the slower norms of the 1930s and what Greyhound was reported to have accomplished. When the chart was published (1968), conditions, specialized breeding, and other variables had produced overall faster horses.

13. Dancer, Stanley, "Training and Conditioning," in *Care and Training of the Trotter and Pacer*, by James C. Harrison (Columbus, OH: United States Trotting Association, 1968), 191. Regarding the importance of not pushing a young horse too fast too soon. "The worst thing you can do with a two-year-old is to get him tired and not finishing his mile strongly and willingly. A colt will learn a lot quicker when he's feeling good. For that reason, I never go all I can with a colt at any time."

14. Becker, Bob, "Plan Dredging Clean-Up for Fox River Bed," *Chicago Tribune*, **April 7, 1934, 24.**

15. **"Men and Women Join in River and Pool Work,"** *St. Charles Chronicle*, **June 29, 1933, 1.**

16. **"Edward J. Baker Passes Away at Age 90,"** *St. Charles Chronicle*, **January 21, 1959, 1.** Baker would sell a calf for $5.

17. **"Illinois Girl is National 4-H Champion,"** *Dixon Evening Telegraph* (Illinois), **February 23, 1932, 6.**

18. **"Facts on Union Cemetery May be of Interest,"** *St. Charles Chronicle*, **June 23, 1932, 1.**

19. **"Edward Baker Passes Away …"** (see note 16).

20. Wingfield, Neil, phone conversation, November 7, 2024.

21. Russell, Sanders, "Care of the Horse," in *Care and Training of the Trotter and Pacer*, by James C. Harrison (Columbus, OH: United States Trotting Association, 1968), 677-80. Information from this piece was used to reconstruct what Greyhound's early training routine *likely* looked like.

22. Gahagan, George M, "Horses in Training at State Fairgrounds Display Speed," *Indianapolis Star*, **May 10, 1934, 20.** Two-year-old trotter Greyhound steps a quarter in :31 at the end of a slow mile.

23. **Author's Note:** Palin working Greyhound, and the interactions between Palin and Hogan (including dialogue) and Hogan and Greyhound are a work of creative non-fiction, using reported facts and the author's personal observations of such interactions at the race track.

24. Lewis, Gary, "The Grey Ghost of Jimmy's Past," *Hoof Beats*, **December 1986, 64.** John Hogan was Greyhound's first groom.

END NOTES

25. Hoffman, Dean, in discussion with the author, September 29, 2023.

26. Reid, Jack, "Lord Jim and Bertha C. Hanover Are Now Co-Favorites," *Springfield News-Sun* (Ohio), April 29, 1934, 11. Reid notes Parshall had Lawrence Hanover go a mile in 2:26—four seconds faster than any other youngster in his stable.

27. "Lawrence Hanover is Showing Speed," *Evening Sun* (Hanover, PA), June 4, 1934, 8. Lawrence Hanover, looking like a star, worked a mile in 2:20 and then 2:15. Not likely to "disgrace his illustrious family."

28. Ibid.

29. Gahagan, George M, "Horses in Training at State Fairgrounds Display Speed," *Indianapolis Star*, May 10, 1934, 20. Two-year-old trotter Greyhound steps a quarter in :31 at the end of a slow mile.

30. Gahagan, George M, Hoof Beats (column), *Indianapolis Star*, May 5, 1934, 17. Greyhound works in 2:18.

31. Gahagan, George M, "Deal for Star Pacer Closed," *Indianapolis Star*, June 4, 1934, 14. Baker buys His Majesty.

32. Gahagan, George M, Hoof Beats (column), *Indianapolis Star*, June 7, 1934, 18. Lindy Volo, Senator Bedell, The Gem—all Baker horses under Palin for the Columbus meet.

33. Nason, Jerry, "Greyhound-Baker-Palin Best Hambletonian Bet," *Boston Globe*, August 7, 1935, 22. Palin quote: "He really loves horses. He comes into the stables and the horses make more of him than they ever do of me. And he knows every groom by first name. Darned if I do."

34. **Author's Note:** This section describing Baker viewing his horses in training, the interactions between Palin and his grooms, and Baker's notetaking and thoughts are constructed from the author's imagination based on reports of known facts for the purpose of telling the story. Baker's interactions in the barn are from a direct quote.

35. Keller, Edwin T, "Ohio Short Ship at Columbus," *Horseman and Fair World*, June 13, 1934, 284. Description of the Junior Trot at Columbus, June 8, 1934. Greyhound is the favorite going in.

36. Hailey, Foster, "Hurricane In Harness!" *New York Times Magazine*, July 2, 1939, 7-9. Dondarski Collection, Harness Racing Museum, Goshen, New York. Description of the start of a harness race.

37. **Author's Note:** The start of Greyhound's first race was recreated using known information and Hailey's description of the start of a harness race.

38. Keller, Edwin T, "Ohio Short Ship at Columbus" (see note 35). Greyhound's first race was recreated using Keller's facts and observations.

39. Trott, Frank G, "Sturbridge Harness Meet Opens at Cedar Lake Park," *Boston Globe*, June 18, 1934, 18. Lawrence Hanover works in 2:12 and 2:13.

40. Ibid. Tommy Berry likens Lawrence Hanover to Hanover's Bertha.

41. Reid, Jack, "Dayton Harness Meet to Open Wednesday with 2 Sessions," *Springfield News-Sun* (Ohio), July 1, 1934, 11. Lawrence Hanover contracts shipping fever, likely out for weeks.

42. "Silver King Beats Belvedere in Rainy Day Sweepstakes," *Dayton Daily News*, July 3, 1934, 16.

43. Gahagan, Tom, "Favorites Go Down at Toledo," *Horseman Fair and World*, July 18, 1934, 388. Information and observations from Gahagan's description of Sherwood Trot used to recreate the race.

44. Gahagan, Tom, "New Canadian Record at Toronto," *Horseman and Fair World*, August 1, 1934, 418. Description of two-year-old trot at Thorncliffe on July 23, 1934.

45. Associated Press, "Feature Event is Won By Silver King," *Star Press* (Indianapolis, IN), July 24, 1934, 8. Description of the July 23, 1934 Canadian National Trotting Stake at Thorncliffe Park, Toronto. Won by Silver King; Greyhound is fourth.

46. Gahagan, George M, Hoof Beats (column), *Indianapolis Star*, July 18, 1934, 12. Baker purchases The Auctioneer for $3,500. Undefeated in two starts.

47. "Auctioneer Takes $1000 Pace Purse," *Buffalo News*, August 11, 1934, 7. "Flashy roan comes down the stretch like a greyhound to snatch victory."

CHAPTER 9

Image: Greyhound at age 2, in Springfield, Illinois (August 22, 1934, courtesy of the Harness Racing Museum & Hall of Fame, Goshen, NY; original photograph by P. W. Moser).

Epigraph: Pines, Phil, "Greyhound—The Gray Ghost," *Off Track Magazine*, September 1995, 16. "Greyhound was a legend ..."

1. Hervey, John, "Comparing Three Champions," *Harness Horse*, December 16, 1936, 116-23. Trotting pitch. Comparison with Uhlan and Peter Manning.

2. Gahagan, Tom, "Ohio Colt Silver King is Winner at Rockingham Park," *Cincinnati Enquirer*, August 4, 1934, 13.

3. "Grand Circuit at Rockingham," *American Horse Breeder*, August 8, 1934, 251. Describes August 3 race at Rockingham. "...outraced Mary Taylor and Salem with something to spare."

4. **Author's Note:** The paragraph describing Hogan holding Greyhound prior to Palin's arrival is from the author's imagination, constructed from weather reports, assumed typical human behavior, and video clips of Greyhound being held and/or prepared for a race.

5. **Author's Note:** This video clip shows the action described here: https://youtu.be/43hqladtA60?si=I-KpICr2rVRxY0Sr

6. Associated Press, "Greyhound Wins Grand Circuit Feature Event," *Richmond Item*, August 15, 1934, 8. Race description for $1,800 Good Time Stake for two-year-old trotters at Good Time Park in Goshen, NY. Greyhound sets record for two-year-old mile.

7. Ibid.

8. Ibid.

9. "Summary: Good Time Consolation Two-Year-Old Trot," *Evening Sun* (Hanover, PA), August 18, 1934, 3, col. 3.

10. "Illinois State Fair Racing," *American Horse Breeder*, August 29, 1934, 275. Described August 22, 1934 junior division of the Illinois Review Futurity. Greyhound won, and could have trotted 2:05 if needed.

11. Associated Press, "Greyhound Sets Fast Time at Syracuse Track," *Richmond Item* (Indiana), September 1, 1934, 8. Description of the August 22 Two-year-old Stake for the Age at Syracuse.

12. Ibid. Second heat.

13. "Auction Betting," On the Other Hand (column), *Middletown Times Herald* (New York), July 23, 1936, 10.

14. Gahagan, Tom, "Two-Year-Old Harness Race Title Likely to be Decided at Lexington," *Collyer's Eye and the Baseball World*, September 29, 1934, 8. Describes Greyhound's win in the September 5 Horseman's futurity. "Greyhound is the standout junior of the season."

15. "Race Summaries: Second Race-Syracuse Hotel Stake and Fourth Race-Horseman Futurity," *Cincinnati Enquirer*, September 6, 1934, 15, col. 8.

END NOTES

16. "New Racing Record Set." *Urbana Daily Citizen* (Ohio), September 6, 1934, p. 8.

17. Gahagan, Tom, "Leading Trotting Stables on Way to Lexington," *Lexington Herald-Leader* (Kentucky), September 9, 1934, 20. A direct quote as to why Greyhound was not kept eligible could not be found; it may have been due to his poor season start. A list printed in the July 29, 1934 issue of the *Lexington Herald* shows Greyhound as still eligible. An ad in the March 16, 1932 *Horseman and Fair World* shows two-year-old payments were due May 1, 1934 and August 1, 1934. The speed of mail service has to be considered; it is likely the decision not to send the August 1 payment was made no later than mid-July. Greyhound's first win was August 3, and he did not lose again until 1936.

18. "Race Summaries: The Reading Fair Futurity," *Reading Times* (PA), September 12, 1934, 13, col. 1. Lawrence Hanover takes sixth and seventh.

19. "Futurity Candidates are Given Workouts," *Lexington Herald*, September 18, 1934, 18.

20. "Futurity for Juveniles Won by Silver King," *Lexington Herald*, September 25, 1934, 1, 9.

21. Ibid.

22. "All Feminine Fans Admitted for Free; Flashy Greyhound Slated to Race," *Lexington Herald*, October 3, 1934, 6.

23. Gahagan, George M, Hoof Beats (column), *Indianapolis Star*, September 22, 1934, 13. Greyhound to race in the two-year-old division of the Futurity on Monday. The brilliant son of Guy Abbey is at the top of his division. "The lanky gray has proved to be too much for his competition thus far."

24. Shuff, Jesse, Down in the Bluegrass Country (column), *Horseman and Fair World*, October 10, 1934, 610. Comments on weather during the trots. Larger crowds for the day of Greyhound's race.

25. Shuff, Jesse, "Greyhound, Ella Brewer Win Old Trotting Stakes," *Lexington Herald-Leader*, October 4, 1934, 10. Description of Greyhound's win in the October 3, 1934 Lexington Stake. "Greyhound never in serious trouble …"

26. Gahagan, Tom, "Grand Circuit Closes at Lexington," *Horseman and Fair World*, October 10, 1934, 608. Brief description of Lexington Stake. Greyhound did not "appear to be as sharp as he had in some of his previous races and was all out to beat the filly [Belvedere] in the first heat (2:06 ¾)."

27. Shuff, Jesse, "Greyhound, Ella Brewer …" (see note 25). Shuff noted the skip (bobble) as being in the first heat, but based on other accounts of the race, I believe this happened in the second heat.

28. Gahagan, Tom, "Grand Circuit Closes …" (see note 26).

29. Gahagan, Tom, "Hard Driving of Two-Year-Old Harness Horses is Breaking Them Down," *Cincinnati Enquirer*, September 30, 1934, 37. Description of Lawrence Hanover's near win in the Futurity at Lexington. Quote regarding hard racing of two-year-olds: "Such races are killing on …"

30. Bradburn, John, *Breeding and Developing the Trotter* (Boston: American Horse Breeder Publishing Company, 1906), 103.

31. Shuff, Jesse, "Horses Step Fast in Record Meeting," *Lexington Herald-Leader*, October 7, 1934, 9. Lawrence Hanover trots in 2:03 ¼.

32. Shuff, Jesse, "Lawrence Hanover Equals World Record for 2-yr. Old," *Lexington Herald-Leader*, October 12, 1934, 2.

33. "Protector," Trotting Notes (column), *Lexington Herald*, October 15, 1934, 5.

34. Reid, Jack, "Lawrence Hanover Picked to Win 1935 Hambletonian," *Springfield News-Sun*, October 21, 1934, 11.

35. "$20,000 Paid for Sire of Trotters," *Morning Call*, October 5, 1934, 35. Knight sells Guy Abbey at Tattersalls for $20,000.

36. "Leading Trotter May Train Here," *Indianapolis News*, February 27, 1935, 18. Baker is offered $20,000 for Greyhound towards the end of 1934.

37. Associated Press, "$3750 for Guy Abbey Colt Top Price at Sale," *Boston Globe*, September 24, 1934, 22.

38. Lewis, Gary, "The Grey Ghost of Jimmy's Past," *Hoof Beats*, December 1986, 64. John Hogan was Greyhound's groom at two; then Pete [Wilson] took over.

39. **Author's Note:** The surname of Greyhound's second groom could not be confirmed. The author's research found three different last names for Pete, and no second corroborating source for any of them. The name "Wilson" is used here as it was found in print in an article from 1935—the only reference from the era. Wilkins is the name recalled by Jimmie Wingfield in 1986, some fifty years after the fact. This may be a misremembering due to the similarity between "Wilson" and "Wilkins" and the fact that the groom of the much more recently famous "Speedy Crown" was named Pete Wilkins.

The final name was provided by former Executive Director of the Hambletonian Society and harness racing historian Tom Charters, who, in the mid-1990s, spoke to Richard D. Taylor, who was a groom for Sep Palin during the 1930s and 1940s and was well-regarded in the sport. Taylor recalled Pete's last name to be "Mir." When reviewing this book, Tom and I discussed this discrepancy at length. He checked with Taylor's daughter, who remembers the original conversation and confirmed Mir is the name her father (who passed in 2016) gave.

Many hours of research, including scouring old newspapers and census, military, birth, marriage, and death records did not yield a second reference to Pete's actual name or even a person I could suspect was Pete. Unfortunately, grooms are often unseen and easily forgotten in the world of racehorses, though they are the ones who know the horses best, and the job of training and racing could not be done without them. They live and travel with the horses, often having no home address, which unfortunately contributes to their lost history.

40. **Author's Note:** Using known facts and personal understanding of how a racehorse barn might operate, this paragraph and the next are constructed from the author's imagination.

CHAPTER 10

Image: Greyhound and Palin warming up for the Hambletonian (August 14, 1935, Hambletonian Society Collection, courtesy of the Harness Racing Museum & Hall of Fame, Goshen, NY).

Epigraph: Riddle, Max, "Greyhound Looms as Hambletonian Choice," *Richmond Item* (Indiana), August 11, 1935, 10. "All year owners and trainers …"

Author's Note: The paragraphs describing the fire are a work of creative non-fiction. The facts of what occurred are lifted from multiple reports of the event (see notes below). Dialogue is imagined but based on what was reported. Years later, the fire was mentioned in another piece. The second piece indicated there were many employees there that helped rescue the horses, with the writer indicating that "multiple boys" came up to tell him of that night. It is likely there were other grooms there from other barns, awakened by the commotion. Grooms often lived with or near their charges. Articles written the day following the fire only mention Charley and Andrew, along with neighbors and passing motorists. This is the way I've chosen to describe it here.

1. **"Four Horses Die in Blaze,"** *Indianapolis Times*, October 25, 1934, 1. Smoke awakened Andrew Smiley.

2. **Ibid.** Andrew woke Charley.

3. "Race Horses Perish in Fairground Fire," *Indianapolis News*, October 25, 1934, 3. "The runway between the stalls served as a flue …"

END NOTES

4. Gahagan, George M, "Harness Horses in Fire Affected by Smoke and Exposure," *Indianapolis Star*, October 26, 1934, 16. His Majesty balked and refused to move.

5. "Four Horses Die …" (see note 1). Andrew and Charley blindfolded the horses.

6. Finney, Jack, personal correspondence, December 7, 2023.

7. Ibid.

8. "Race Horses Perish …" (see note 3). Motorists and neighbors came to help or watch.

9. "Four Horses Die …" (see note 1). Horses were handed to bystanders.

10. "Race Horses Perish …" (see note 3). Charley collapsed after the horses were removed. Andrew has burns to hands and feet.

11. Ibid.

12. "Four Horses Die …" (see note 1). One horse panicked and escaped his handler, one hour to catch.

13. Ibid. Charley hospitalized with smoke inhalation. Andrew was treated for burns at the scene.

14. "Race Horses Perish …" (see note 3). Rain helped put out the fire. Names of four that died. Four others suffering from severe smoke inhalation.

15. Gahagan, George M, "Annual Speed Sale Starts Today," *The Indianapolis Star*, November 13, 1934, 14. The Auctioneer died from pneumonia developed from smoke inhalation after the fire.

16. Gahagan, George M, "Harness Horses in Fire …" (see note 4). Loss of feed and equipment.

17. Finney, Jack, personal correspondence (see note 6). Cause of fire never determined/reported.

18. Gahagan, George M, "Harness Horses in Fire …" (see note 4).

19. Trott, Frank G, "Today Linked Up with Racing: New Rich Futurity Proposed." *Boston Globe*, April 7, 1924. H. O. Reno comes up with the idea of the Hambletonian Stake.

20. Gahagan, Tom, "Two-Year-Old Harness Race Title Likely to be Decided at Lexington," *Collyer's Eye and the Baseball World*, September 29, 1934, 8. "Off-colored youngster …"

21. Shuff, Jesse, "Work Notes at the K.T.H.B.A. Track," Down in the Bluegrass Country (column), *Horseman and Fair World*, June 12, 1935, 270.

22. **Author's Note:** The conversation among the men in the track kitchen is a work of the author's imagination. The dialogue was created using known facts and comments of turf reporters attributed to the general public (see note 23).

23. Gahagan, George M, Hoof Beats (column), *Indianapolis Star*, January 19, 1935, 14. Lawrence Hanover 2:02, Greyhound 2:04 ¾, and Silver King 2:06 are pretty much early-year even-choice favorites for the Hambletonian. But the locals will argue that none can compete with Greyhound. None can close like he does in the last quarter. He outraced everyone as a two-year-old.

24. Wingfield, Neil, phone conversation, November 7, 2024.

25. Lewis, Gary, "The Grey Ghost of Jimmy's Past," *Hoof Beats*, December 1986, 64. How Jimmie came to work for Palin.

26. Gahagan, George M, Hoof Beats (column), *Indianapolis Star*, May 25, 1935, 15. Greyhound worked 2:13 and 2:18 in company (with The Gem).

27. Braucher, Bill, "Start Grand Circuit Cavalcade at Lexington June 15," *Times*, Hammond, Indiana, June 13, 1935, 46. Lawrence Hanover is Hambletonian favorite of some due to his world record (2:02), but he can be temperamental. Therefore, others prefer Greyhound, as he is training beautifully for Palin.

28. Shuff, Jesse, Down in the Bluegrass Country (column), June 12, 1935 (see note 21).

29. Shuff, Jesse, "Indianapolis Stable Arrives at Local Track," *Lexington Herald-Leader*, June 12, 1935, 8. Baker arrived at Lexington.

30. **Author's Note:** This paragraph is from the author's imagination, constructed using known facts.

31. **Author's Note:** This paragraph is from the author's imagination, constructed using known facts.

32. Gahagan, George M, "Local Speed Sale Highly Successful," *The Indianapolis Star*, November 18, 1934, 44. Mentions the previous month's fire. Gahagan admires and quotes Baker's philosophical response. "Oh, those fires will occur …"

33. "Edward J. Baker Passes Away at Age 90," *St. Charles Chronicle*, January 21, 1959, 1. Baker the animal lover, feeding strays, saving a pancake for Fibber.

34. Gahagan, Tom, "Between Showers at Lexington," *Horseman and Fair World*, June 26, 1935, 291. Details of the June 20 race at Lexington.

35. Gahagan, George M, Hoof Beats (column), *Indianapolis Star*, June 30, 1935, 11. "Probably the best trotting heat …"

36. Trott, Frank G, "Goshen and Lexington, KY, Have Meetings This Week," *Boston Globe*, June 17, 1935, 9. Belvedere is pulled from training for "eye troubles."

37. Harness Gossip (column), *Lexington Herald*, June 24, 1935, 8. Tilly Tonka's work times.

38. Kennedy, Maurice, "Sep Palin Wins with Greyhound," *Noblesville Ledger* (Indiana), July 6, 1935, 5. Sets a new record for three-year-old mile: 2:03 ¼. Greyhound is a fast closer, and came from behind in each heat to win at Toledo.

39. Hampson, Gene F, Thru Sportsland (column), *The Courier-News*, July 9, 1935, 14. Notes Greyhound's time in Matron Stakes was near to Lord Jim's time in winning last year's Hambletonian Stake. Most notable is that Greyhound trotted the last mile of the second heat in :59 ¾, and the final quarter in :28.

40. "Greyhound of Indianapolis Stable Now Favorite to Win $40,000 Hambletonian," *Indianapolis News*, July 19, 1935, 10. Prints a "well authenticated" rumor that a sportsman has declared he'd offer $25,000 for Greyhound.

41. The Weather (column), *Toronto Star*, July 19, 1935, 1. Toronto area weather report for Friday-Saturday, July 19-20, 1935.

42. Gahagan, Tom, "Canadians Hosts to Grand Circuit at Toronto," *The Horseman and Fair World*, July 24, 1935, 383. Summary and description of July 20, 1935 Toronto Globe Stake.

43. Shipman, Evan, In the Sulky (column), *The Nevada Morning Telegraph*, August 1935 clipping from Harness Horse Museum Archives. Greyhound dropped a heat at Toronto to Lawrence Hanover, his principal contender in the Hambletonian, but that was an accident. Palin, from over-confidence, "waited too long with him."

44. Gahagan, Tom, "Canadians Hosts …" (see note 42). Bettors quickly ran to lay bets on Lawrence Hanover for the second heat.

45. "Greyhound Wins Again," *Noblesville Ledger*, July 22, 1935, 5. Greyhound again establishes himself as leading three-year-old trotter

with a win in the Toronto Globe Stakes. Was 4th in the first heat, then won the other two easily. Set a new Canadian record in the second heat in 2:02 ¼. Last quarter in :28 ¼. Cardinal Prince also won for Palin.

46. Ibid. Details from Toronto Globe Stake.

CHAPTER 11

Image: A portrait of Greyhound and Sep Palin (courtesy of the United States Trotting Association), and a cartoon that appeared in *The Boston Globe*, August 10, 1937.

Epigraph: Runyon, Damon, "Upset is Likely in Hambletonian," *Buffalo News* (New York), August 13, 1935, 20. "There is no sporting scene …"

1. **Associated Press, "Eight Hambletonian Candidates to Race at Rockingham Today,"** *Burlington Daily News* **(Vermont), August 3, 1935, 7.** American Stake will have 8 Hambletonian contenders. Notably missing is Greyhound, who will run in a much cheaper race on the 6. Greyhound is considered the greatest three-year-old trotter in training.

2. **Clark, Johnny, "Lawrence Hanover Wins Stake at Rockingham Park,"** *Lexington Herald-Leader*, **August 4, 1935, 8.**

3. **"'Doc' Parshall Grooming Hopeful for Hambletonian,"** *Central New Jersey Home News*, **June 20, 1935, 18.** Doc Parshall's thoughts regarding the other hopefuls and about Lawrence Hanover's chances.

4. **Author's Note:** The paragraphs describing the race at Rockingham in Salem, NH, are a work of creative non-fiction. Facts regarding track condition, weather, attendance, and the nature of the race were pulled from Gahagan's August 14, 1935 article below (see note 5).

5. **Gahagan, Tom, "Great Meeting Closes at Rockingham Park,"** *Horseman and Fair World*, **August 14, 1935, 428.** Description of weather, crowds, track, and Greyhound's win at Rockingham on August 6, 1935.

6. **Moore, Walter, "Views of Rockingham Park,"** *Horseman and Fair World*, **August 14, 1935, 430.** Details of Lawrence Hanover's performance in the American and National Stakes (August 3 and 8, 1935). States the Hambletonian will be a race for second money.

7. **Nason, Jerry, "Greyhound-Baker-Palin Best Hambletonian Bet,"** *Boston Globe*, **August 7, 1935, 22.** Jerry Nason interview with Baker and Palin following Greyhound's win at Salem, August 6, 1935. Quotes from Palin about Greyhound and Baker. Quote from Baker about Greyhound's chances in the Hambletonian.

8. **Moore, Walter, "A Preview of the Hambletonian Stake,"** *Horseman and Fair World*, **August 7, 1935, 415.** "How can they beat a colt that can trot from fifth place …"

9. **Chapman, Ralph, "Greyhound Still Favorite to Win $40,000 Hambletonian,"** *The Record*, **August 13, 1935, 15.** Great description of the excitement building in Goshen prior to the big race.

10. **Hughes, Ed, "The Trotting Classic,"** *Brooklyn Daily Eagle*, **August 13, 1935, 8.** Columnist describes Hambletonian Week in Goshen.

11. **Cohen, Lou E, Sports Chats (column),** *Brooklyn Eagle* **(New York), August 14, 1935, 32.** Describes Hambletonian Day in Goshen, "when sleepy Goshen actually awakens." Notes some 400 horses will be in Goshen contesting a five-day race card worth $100,000. Interesting to note that the 400-horse figure was used repeatedly in 1930s accounts of race entries at Goshen Historic and at Good Time Park. The number may be more reflective of capacity at the two tracks, not actual head counts. It was noted that overflow from Good Time would be stabled at Historic—the two tracks were within walking distance of each other.

12. **Chapman, Ralph, "Greyhound Still Favorite …" (see note 9).**

13. **Ibid.**

14. **Author's Note:** Paragraph and dialogue are from the author's imagination. Dialogue is constructed from facts pulled from news reports and comments attributed to the general public. Description of clothing is consistent with the styles of the day.

15. **Gahagan, Tom, "Goshen's Grand Circuit Meeting,"** *Horseman and Fair World*, **August 21, 1935.** Description of Hambletonian win. Eli Crutch tent.

16. **Cameron, Stuart, "Greyhound is Standout of Decade in Trotting,"** *Times Union* **(Brooklyn, New York), August 15, 1935, 11.** Betting on the Hambletonian. Description of Hambletonian.

17. **Ibid.**

18. **McCarr, Ken, "The Trotter of the Century,"** *Hoof Beats*, **September 1971, 34.**

19. **Author's Note:** The description of Hambletonian is a work of creative non-fiction. The weather, track conditions, facts of the race, and positioning of the horses are pulled from Tom Gahagan's piece "Goshen's Grand Circuit Meeting" (see notes 15, 20). The start of the second heat is from Ken McCarr's "Trotter of the Century" (see note 18). The dialogue attributed to starter, Steve Phillips, is from the author's imagination.

20. **Gahagan, Tom, "Goshen's Grand Circuit Meeting" (see note 15).**

21. **Parker, Dan, "Greyhound is no Misnomer,"** *Waterbury Democrat* **(Connecticut), August 15, 1935, 13.** Greyhound nibbled the flower wreath.

22. **Author's Note:** There is a photograph depicting this moment (Palin's kiss) in the August 15, 1935 issue of the *Indianapolis Times*. This author tried for months to track down this image for use in this book and was unsuccessful.

23. **Gould, Alan, Sport Slants (column),** *Harrisburg Telegraph* **(Pennsylvania), August 20, 1935, 14.** Quotes from Sep Palin on Hambletonian win.

24. **McCarr, Ken, "The Trotter of the Century" (see note 18).** Details about Pete getting beer for him and Greyhound, and sharing with Pedro Tipton and his groom following the 1935 Hambletonian.

25. **Author's Note:** The description of the scene and exchange between Pete and his friend following the Hambletonian is a work of creative non-fiction. The facts (sharing a beer, giving some to the horses) used to create this portion of the story were taken from "The Trotter of the Century" article by Ken McCarr (see note 17).

26. **McCarr, Ken, "The Trotter of the Century" (see note 18).** Pete brought a flower to Pedro Tipton.

27. **Gahagan, Tom, "Trots Close at Good Time Park,"** *Cincinnati Enquirer*, **August 17, 1935, 13.** LaSalle horses transferred from Parshall to Henry Thomas.

28. **New York Central Time Tables, November 16, 1930, Form 1001, accessed December 13, 2024,** https://www.canadasouthern.com/caso/ptt/images/tt-1130.pdf. It is difficult to determine how long Greyhound spent on the train, but a look at this timetable shows nineteen hours from departure to arrival for a trip from Chicago to New York (approximately 800 miles).

29. **New York Central System Big Four Time Tables, July 15, 1936, accessed December 13, 2024,** https://www.canadasouthern.com/caso/ptt/images/tt-b4-0736.pdf. This timetable shows a trip from Indianapolis to Syracuse at twenty-six hours, with a train change at Cleveland.

30. **McCarr, Ken, "Transportation of Horses: Reminiscence of the Past,"** *Harness Horse*, **December 8, 1971, 8.**

31. **Ibid., 10.**

32. **Ibid.**

END NOTES

CHAPTER 12

Image: Greyhound (circa 1936, courtesy of the Hambletonian Society).

Epigraph: Gahagan, George M, "State Fair Racing is Decided Success," *Indianapolis Star,* September 8, 1935, 19. "Champions will come ..."

1. Moser, P. W., *The Story of Greyhound 1:55 ¼* (Harrisburg, PA: Harness Horse, 1940), 15.

2. Arbuckle, Woodruff, "Speed Barrage Features Springfield Grand Circuit Meet," *Horseman and Fair World,* August 28, 1935, 460.

3. Moser, P. W., *The Story of Greyhound 1:55 ¼* (see note 1). "Get that damn colt ..."

4. Ibid.

5. Harnessdom, "1935 Springfield State Fair Greyhound Sep Palin World Record," YouTube video, 2:47, July 24, 2017, https://www.youtube.com/watch?v=g9NwJb5BMfo

6. Arbuckle, Woodruff, "Speed Barrage Features ..." (see note 2). Greyhound shattered the world record for three-year-old trotting geldings, lowered the track record for trotters, came the last half of his record mile in :59, and won each heat with something to spare.

7. Stoneridge, M. A, *Great Horses of Our Time* (Garden City, NY: Doubleday & Company, Inc, 1972), 271. "On this occasion ..."

8. "Cardinal Prince Paces Heat in 1:59 ½," *Noblesville Ledger* (Indiana), August 22, 1935, 7. Palin is the first to drive two two-minute horses in the same day.

9. Leach, Brownie, "Sep Palin's 'Find,'" Down in Front (column), *Lexington Herald-Leader,* September 15, 1935, 8. Cardinal Prince information.

10. Gahagan, Tom, "Greyhound to Finish Campaign in Futurity at Lexington," *Cincinnati Enquirer,* September 1, 1935, 22. Description of the August 26 Stallion Stake at Syracuse. Quote: "The comeback staged ..."

11. Gahagan, Tom, "Great Speed Festival at New York State Fair," *Horseman and Fair World,* September 4, 1935, 476. Description of August 26, 1935 Stallion Stake at Syracuse. Greyhound wins 1-3-1, with Lawrence Hanover second, 2-1-2.

12. Ibid.

13. **Author's Note:** The paragraphs describing Greyhound's race at Syracuse are a work of creative non-fiction based on facts reported by Tom Gahagan in *The Cincinnati Enquirer* and *The Horseman and Fair World* (see notes 10 and 11). Concerns and actions attributed to Pete [Wilson] are from the author's imagination, based on knowledge of racehorse grooms and care of Standardbred racehorses.

14. Gahagan, Tom, "Great Speed Festival ..." (see note 11). "The comeback staged by Greyhound ..."

15. "Palin Horses Win First and Second," *Noblesville Ledger* (Indiana), September 4, 1935, 5. References Palin's successes with Greyhound and Cardinal Prince, muddy track issues (delaying Greyhound's race again), and some of the atmosphere of the 1935 Indiana state fair.

16. **Author's Note:** The two paragraphs about Wilson bringing Greyhound out for the crowd are created from the author's imagination, based on reports that Greyhound was brought before the crowds at Indianapolis and also observations of Greyhound's antics in such situations by people who knew him.

17. Lewis, Gary, "The Grey Ghost of Jimmy's Past," *Hoof Beats,* December 1986, 64. Greyhound's injury.

18. Ibid. Stiff but sound to race.

19. Gahagan, George M, "State Fair Racing is Decided Success," *Indianapolis Star,* September 8, 1935, 19. Gahagan describes Greyhound's impact on the attendance of the Indiana State Fair.

20. Gahagan, Tom, "Horseman Futurities Feature Indiana State Fair," *Horseman and Fair World,* September 11, 1935, 493. "The stand was packed, and every point of vantage was occupied." There was a brilliant exhibition of speed, however, as the last quarter of the first heat went in :28 ½.

21. Boxell, Paul, "Trot King Thrills Record Throng in 2-heat Victory," *Indianapolis Times,* September 5. 1935, 16. "The outstanding star of the afternoon, of course, was Greyhound." Greyhound "won as he pleased" in two straight heats.

22. **Author's Note:** The description of the second heat of the Horseman Futurity in Indianapolis is a work of creative non-fiction using facts as reported by Paul Boxell (see note 21).

23. Gahagan, George M, "State Fair Racing ..." (see note 19). Gahagan quotes about Greyhound's impact on people, how he brought them to the races, and so on.

24. Ibid. Quotes about Greyhound and how the people love him and love horses, and that is why they come to the races.

26. Fox Jr., W. F, "Greyhound, Pride of Palin, Displays much Horse Sense in Crowds, but has Fun at Home," *Indianapolis News,* September 5, 1935, 24. Following Horseman Futurity at Indianapolis. Mentions Pete Wilson and the injury to Greyhound. Writer "interviews" Greyhound.

27. McCarthy, Clem, At the Races (column), *Lexington Herald Leader,* October 15, 1937, 12. Baker is the only human allowed to give Greyhound sugar.

28. Gahagan, George M, "Palin Horses Off for Trots," *Indianapolis Star,* September 16, 1935, 17.

29. Leach, Brownie, Down in Front (column), *Lexington Herald-Leader,* September 11, 1935, 6.

30. Ibid. "... saved the race for Greyhound."

31. Ibid. "One of the grandest individuals..."

32. Leach, Brownie, Down in Front (column), *Lexington Herald-Leader,* September 19, 1935, 6, 8.

33. Ibid.

34. "Greyhound Withdrawn," *Indianapolis Star,* September 24, 1935, 15.

35. Sports in the Sun (column), *Evening Sun* (Hanover, Penn.), October 2, 1935, 3. Quotes from Gue.

36. Duffy, L.G, "Lexington Notes," *Horseman and Fair World,* October 2, 1935, 553. "... bruised himself to such an extent ..."

37. Sports in the Sun (column) (see note 35).

38. "Favorite Wins Rich Futurity," *Lexington Herald,* September 25, 1935, 6. "... given Greyhound the race of his life."

39. Ibid. Greyhound clearly lame.

40. Sports in the Sun (column) (see note 35).

41. Sports in the Sun (column), *Evening Sun* (Hanover, Penn.), September 30, 1035, 3. "... despite a leg injury ..." Lawrence Hanover lame after futurity.

42. Shuff, Jesse, "Harness Stars Seek Records," *Lexington Herald,* October 1, 1935, 7. Lawrence Hanover too lame to travel.

End Notes

43. Lewis, Gary, "The Grey Ghost of Jimmy's Past" (see note 17). Why "[Wilson]" left.

44. "Guy Abbey's Book Closed," *Horseman and Fair World*, November 13, 1935, 630.

45. "Amateur and Professional Champions of 1935," *Dispatch* (Moline, Illinois), December 31, 1935, 39.

CHAPTER 13

Image: Greyhound grazing (circa 1936, Hambletonian Society Collection, courtesy of the Harness Racing Museum & Hall of Fame, Goshen, NY).

Epigraph: Hervey, John, "Comparing Three Champions," *Harness Horse*, December 16, 1936, 116. "But a shadow has fallen …"

1. "Lexington, Kentucky—June 23," *Harness Horse*, July 1, 1936, 758. Palin quote: "… almost certain to go faster than …" Description of June 23 exhibition.

2. Gahagan, Tom, "Grand Circuit Racing Resumed at Goshen," *Horseman and Fair World*, July 29, 1936, 400.

3. Ibid.

4. **Author's Note:** The paragraphs describing the race are works of creative non-fiction using the facts and descriptions by Tom Gahagan (see note 2).

5. "Record Crowd Sees 1st Loss by Greyhound," *Middletown Times Herald* (New York), July 23, 1936, 1. Three wide, too much to overcome. Tara sets a new standard.

6. Associated Press, "Greyhound Loses Despite Fastest Heat," *Star-Gazette*, July 23, 1936, 21. Regarding Greyhound's being withdrawn from the fourth heat for the Times Herald FFA at Goshen: Palin did not wish to give GH such a severe test, as it was the colt's first start of the year.

7. "Record Crowd Sees 1st Loss …" (see note 5).

8. Harnessbred.com, "Racetracks Of The World – North America: United States Of America (Maine – Part Two: Closed Tracks)," https://harnessbred.com/racetracks-world-north-america-united-states-america-maine-part-two-closed-tracks/. Facts about Old Orchard Beach track.

9. Mason, Mrs C. P, "Old Orchard, Me.—July 30," *Harness Horse*, August 5, 1936, 860.

10. "Greyhound Sets New Mark at Old Orchard," *Bangor Daily News*, July 31, 1936, 48. Fought a neck-and-neck stretch duel in all three heats, and lowered the state record by ¼.

11. "Greyhound Thrills Crowd at Kite Track," *Biddeford-Saco Journal* (Maine), July 31, 1936, 8.

12. "Greyhound Sets New Mark …" (see note 10).

13. "Trio of Horses Lower Mark at Old Orchard," *Bangor Daily News*, August 1, 1936, 23. Cardinal Prince's new record.

14. "Woman Drives Trotter to Record Mile in 2:01 ¾," *Indianapolis News*, August 8, 1936, 4. Mrs. Gladys Harriman drives Greyhound to a record mile for a female driver.

15. *Harness Horse*, August 19, 1936, 912. "… four perfect trotters …"

16. "Amateur and Professional Champions of 1935," *Dispatch* (Moline, Illinois), December 31, 1935, 39.

17. *Harness Horse*, August 19, 1936 (see note 15).

18. Ibid.

19. Gahagan, Tom, "Grand Circuit at Good Time Park," *Horseman and Fair World*, August 19, 1936, 451.

20. Ibid.

21. *Harness Horse*, August 19, 1936 (see note 15).

22. Moser, P. W., "Springfield, Illinois—August 21," *Harness Horse*, August 26, 1936, 950.

23. Moser, P. W., *The Story of Greyhound 1:55 ¼* (Harrisburg, PA: Harness Horse, 1940), 20.

24. Moser, P. W., "Springfield, Illinois …" (see note 22).

25. **Author's Note:** This paragraph is a work of creative non-fiction using facts and observations from P.W. Moser's "Springfield, Illinois—August 21" (see note 22).

26. Moser, P. W., "Springfield, Illinois …" (see note 22).

27. Putnam, Leone, *Dooley and the Grey Ghost* (Goshen, NY: Harness Racing Museum and Hall of Fame, 2018), 28. Dooley sees Greyhound set a record at Springfield.

28. **Author's Note:** This paragraph is a work of creative non-fiction, crafted from the author's readings and observations from photos and film.

29. Henry, Marguerite, *Born to Trot* (New York: Rand McNally & Company, 1950).

30. Moser, P.W., *The Story of Greyhound 1:55 ¼* (see note 23).

31. "Harness Racing Rules Changed," *Call-Leader* (Elwood, Indiana), December 15, 1937, 6.

32. Associated Press, "Union of Harness Racing Bodies Appears Certain," *Wilmington News-Journal*, December 19, 1938, 6.

33. Creamer, Robert, "Harriman of Goshen," *Sports Illustrated*, July 9, 1962.

34. Harriman, E. Roland, *I Reminisce* (Garden City, NY: Doubleday & Company, 1975).

35. Gahagan, Tom, "The Syracuse Grand Circuit Meeting," *Horseman and Fair World*, September 16, 1936, 519.

36. "Grand Circuit Opens Today at Fair Grounds," *Reading Times* (Pennsylvania), September 14, 1936, 12.

37. Ibid. The first Grand Circuit meet in Pennsylvania in twenty years.

38. "Cardinal Prince Sets World Pace Mark Here," *Reading Times* (Pennsylvania), September 15, 1936, 14.

39. "Greyhound Sets New World Mark in Twice Circling Allentown Track," *The Morning Call* (Allentown, PA), September 26, 1936, 15.

40. Graham, Frank, "Setting the Pace," Mary Lou Dondarski Collection, Scrapbook 4, Harness Racing Museum, Goshen, New York.

41. "Greyhound Sets New World Mark …" (see note 39).

42. Ibid.

43. "Lexington, Kentucky—October 1," *Harness Horse*, October 7, 1936, 1104.

44. Ibid.

45. Ibid.

46. "Trotter Greyhound is Going After Manning's Mark," *Sacramento Bee*, December 26, 1936, 24. "He'll top it if he's sound …"

47. Hughes, Ed, "Peter Manning's Owner Lauds Greyhound," *Brooklyn Daily Eagle*, August 15, 1935, 18. "Well, I'll say this …"

48. Cameron, Stuart (United Press sports writer), "Hail Greyhound Greatest Trotter of Standard-bred," *Pomona Progress Bulletin* (California), August 15, 1935, 10. "He's the greatest trotter I've ever handled …"

CHAPTER 14

Image: Greyhound and Muscletone featured on the cover of *Harness Horse* (May 19, 1937, courtesy of the United States Trotting Association).

Epigraph: Roosevelt, Franklin D, "Fireside Chat 8," September 9, 1936. "No cracked earth …"

1. Hoyt, John C, "Drought of 1936," United States Department of the Interior, 1938, 7, accessed April 2, 2024, https://pubs.usgs.gov/wsp/0820/report.pdf

2. Ibid., plate 1.

3. Ibid., 8.

4. "The Dust Bowl," National Drought Mitigation Center, accessed September 20, 2023, https://drought.unl.edu/dustbowl/#Drought

5. Hoyt, John C, "Drought of 1936" (see note 1), 11.

6. "Heat Wave Toll Over 12,000 in 86 in Week," *Bulletin* (Bend, Oregon), July 25, 1936, 1.

7. Amadeo, Kimberly, "Great Depression Pictures," Thought Co., accessed April 2, 2024, https://www.thoughtco.com/photos-of-the-great-depression-4061803

8. "The Dust Bowl" (see note 4).

9. **Author's Note:** The source for this statement is the author's observation of the bound volumes of *Hoof Beats*, *Harness Horse*, and *Horseman and Fair World* in the USTA Archives. Harness racing enthusiast and history buff Alan Ackerman called me out on this, noting that "many longtime publications [met their end], such as *American Horse Breeder* (Boston), which ended its 40+ year run around 1935, the *American Sportsman* out of Cleveland, which ended its 40+ year run around the same time, the greatest harness horse publication of them all, the *Horse Review* out of Chicago, which ended its 40+ year run in 1932, and the *Trotter and Pacer*, also out of New York, which ended its 35+ year run in the early 1930s." Whether the publications (or loss of them) indicate popularity is secondary to the reports of increasing attendance, in my opinion. It is also possible that with an increasing globalization of information, made more readily accessible through radio and newswire, publications for specific regions became less necessary, with larger publications able to cover all areas.

10. "Adolf Hitler," History.com Editors, October 29, 2009, accessed April 24, 2024, https://www.history.com/topics/world-war-ii/adolf-hitler-1

11. Gahagan, Tom, "Greyhound and Rosalind may do Little Racing this Year," *Cincinnati Enquirer*, April 4, 1937, 48. No races for horses faster than 2:06 in 1937.

12. "Jesse Owens: American Hero," American Experience, PBS Learning Media, accessed April 24, 2024, https://ket.pbslearningmedia.org/resource/ush22-soc-ushowensohio/jesse-owens-american-hero/

13. "Horses of the Month," *Horse and Horseman*, August 1937, 25. "When about sixty years ago…"

14. Ibid., 45. "By the 1930s, the sport was powerfully organized … in Europe…"

15. "Russian Trotter Horses," Oklahoma State University, accessed April 2, 2024, https://breeds.okstate.edu/horses/russian-trotter-horses.html

16. "Horses of the Month" (see note 13).

17. Ibid., 46.

18. Ibid., 45.

19. Ibid., 46.

20. Ibid.

21. Clark, John H, "Match Races Between Greyhound and Muscletone in Prospect," *Lexington Herald-Leader*, May 14, 1937, 28.

22. Ibid.

23. "Russian Trotter Horses" (see note 15).

24. Clark, John H, "Match Races …" (see note 21). "We accept the challenge …"

CHAPTER 15

Image: Greyhound finishes his mile at the Historic Half Mile Track in Goshen, NY (July 16, 1937, courtesy of the Harness Racing Museum & Hall of Fame, Goshen, NY), and the Historic Half Mile Grand Circuit sign.

Epigraph: Hervey, John, "Greyhound's Mile Marks an Epoch," *Harness Horse*, July 21, 1937, 971. "But the old saying …"

1. Gahagan, Tom, "Greyhound and Rosalind may do Little Racing this Year," *Cincinnati Enquirer*, April 4, 1937, 48. Palin and White have agreed to not race their top trotters for purses of $1,500 or less. In 1937, there are no divisions offered for older horses that have gone faster than 2:06.

2. Hervey, John, "Greyhound's Mile Marks an Epoch," *Harness Horse*, July 21, 1937, 971. In 1903, Lou Dillion went the first sub two-minute mile. The same year, Cresceus set the record for a mile over a half-mile track in 2:09 ¼.

3. Moser, P. W., "Here and There," *Harness Horse*, July 21, 1937, 977. Describes track conditions and for Greyhound's July 16 record at Historic Half Mile Track.

4. Moore, Walter, "Goshen, New York at Historic Half-Mile—July 16," *Harness Horse*, July 21, 1937, 984. New Faber sulky, 28" tall weighing 26 pounds. Quote: Roy Miller, the starter, said, "I think that's the greatest mile I have ever seen." Quote: "…that big bold stride carrying him on with matchless power."

5. Moser, P.W, "Here and There" (see note 3). Palin's driving style for Greyhound's July 16 record at Historic Half Mile Track.

6. McCarr, Ken, "The Trotter of the Century," *Hoof Beats*, September 1971, 36. Went wide, long mile.

7. "Greyhound 1:56," *Harness Horse*, December 15, 1937, 182. Quote: "… he was trotting with machine-like precision …"

8. McCarr, Ken, "The Trotter of the Century" (see note 6). Rating back, chin tucked.

9. Moser, P.W, "Here and There" (see note 3). Palin's driving style.

10. Madden, William J, "Champion Slashes 26-year-old Mark," *The Record* (Hackensack, New Jersey), July 17, 1937, 15. Quote: "Mussolini might just as well recall …"

11. **Author's Note**: The description of the final loop of Greyhound's mile record at Historic is a work of creative non-fiction based on facts presented in the articles by Madden and Moser (see notes 3 and 6).

The dialogue is from the author's imagination.

12. Hervey, John, "Greyhound's Mile Marks ..." (see note 2). "The attainment of a mile in two minutes or better ..."

13. Gahagan, Tom, "The Grand Circuit at Goshen's Historic Track," *Horseman and Fair World,* **July 21, 1937, 416.** Greyhound beat Uhlan's record of 2:02 ¾ set over the same track in 1911 by three full seconds in 1:59 ¾ and lowered his own world record by two and one quarter seconds, set at Allentown earlier this year.

14. Madden, William J, "Champion Slashes 26-year-old Mark" (see note 10). Greyhound looks at the crowd.

15. Ibid. Palin quote: "He is the greatest trotter in the history of ..."

16. Author's Note: The closing paragraphs depicting Jimmie's interactions with Greyhound and the dog, Goshen, are a work of creative non-fiction. Dialogue is from the author's imagination.

CHAPTER 16

Image: Muscletone cartoon from the July 7, 1937 issue of *Harness Horse* (courtesy of the United States Trotting Association).

Epigraph: Madden, William J, "Champion Slashes 26-year-old Mark," *The Record* (Hackensack, New Jersey), July 17, 1937, 15. "Greyhound could probably lug a plow ..."

1. Williams, Joe, Joe Williams Says (column), *Minneapolis Journal,* **June 7, 1937, 21.**

2. Wallace, William N, "Joe Williams, 81, Sports Columnist," *New York Times,* **February 16, 1972, 43.**

3. "Williams, Joseph Peter 1889-1972," Contemporary Authors, *Encyclopedia.com,* **accessed March 18, 2024,** https://www.encyclopedia.com/arts/educational-magazines/williams-joseph-peter-1889-1972

4. Ibid.

5. Williams, Joe, "Mussolini Goes for Horses, Too; His Trotting Star May Invade America for Match Race," *Birmingham Post,* **June 14, 1937, 8.**

6. Madden, William J, "Champion Slashes 26-year-old Mark," *The Record* (Hackensack, New Jersey), **July 17, 1937, 15.** Muscletone "now on the high seas."

7. "Muscletone-Greyhound Match Status," *Horseman and Fair World,* **July 7, 1937, 358-A.**

8. Madden, William J, "Champion Slashes 26-year-old Mark" (see note 6).

9. "Greyhound-Muscletone Special is August 10, Day Before Hambletonian at Goshen Oval," *Cincinnati Enquirer,* **July 18, 1937, 23.**

10. Moore, Walter, "The Good Time Meeting," *Harness Horse,* **August 18, 1937, 1078.**

11. Ibid.

12. Ibid.

13. Clark, Al, The Sports Shop (column) *Harrisburg Telegraph,* **August 10, 1937, 16.** Clark interviews Tommy Murphy, Lawrence Sheppard, and Bowman A. Brown about Greyhound's attempt at lowering Peter Manning's record at Good Time Park. Quotes: "Do you think Greyhound will lower ..."; "Greyhound is no match for ..."; "Will Greyhound better Peter ..."; "Not today, son"; "Will Peter Manning lose his ..."; "Perhaps, but not today ..."; "But where and when ..."; "Not at Goshen ..."

14. Author's Note: The quotes from these three interviews were taken from the Al Clark piece (see note 13). The connecting actions are from the author's imagination.

15. Trott, Frank, G, "Day Not Right For Greyhound," *Boston Globe,* **August 11, 1937, 22.** Air hot and heavy with a stiff wind.

16. Clark, Al, The Sports Shop (column), *The Harrisburg Telegraph,* **August 11, 1937, 18.** "That track wasn't made for record breaking. It's triangular and has three turns. That first turn is bad, very bad, for any speed."

17. Moser, P. W., *The Story of Greyhound 1:55 ¼* (Harrisburg, PA: Harness Horse, 1940), **25.**

18. Gahagan, Tom, "Shirley Hanover Scores Upset in Hambletonian," *Horseman and Fair World,* **August 18, 1937, 484.** Description of Greyhound's mile at Good Time Park on August 10, 1937. On August 10, Greyhound set a new track record at Good Time Park, trotting a mile in 1:58 ¼ while attempting to beat Peter Manning's record of 1:56 ¾. He trotted the last half in :57, showing he has "all the speed that made him the sensation of the 1936 season." The largest non-Hambletonian crowd ever seen at Good Time Park assembled to see the attempt. Trotted the last quarter in :28 ¼.

19. Author's Note: The paragraphs describing Greyhound's August 10, 1937 mile at Good Time are a work of creative non-fiction using descriptions from Walter Moore's article "The Good Time Meeting" (see note 10) and Tom Gahagan's August 18 piece on Hambletonian Week (see note 18).

20. Clark, Al, The Sports Shop (column), August 11, 1937 (see note 16).

21. "Greyhound 1:56," *Harness Horse,* **December 15, 1937, 184.** Closed electrifying mile in :57.

22. Gahagan, Tom, "Shirley Hanover Scores Upset ..." (see note 18). The first time any horse negotiated the Good Time track in less than 2:00.

23. "Greyhound 1:56" (see note 21). "Due to an unusually high wind ..."

24. "Greyhound-Muscletone Special is August 10 ..." (see note 9).

25. Moore, Walter, "The Good Time Meeting" (see note 10). Maiani quote.

26. Robertson, Orlo, "12 Fast Ones to Race Today in Hambletonian," *Burlington Free Press* (Vermont), **August 11, 1937, 13.** Maiani quote.

27. Drysdale, R. A, "Greyhound is 1st in Fair's Feature Race," *Decatur Daily Review* (Illinois), **August 21, 1937, 3.** "... came around her like a streak ..."

28. Associated Press, "Springfield is Possible Site of Trot Race," *Decatur Daily Review,* **August 23, 1937, 7.** Muscletone and Greyhound connections met, and set an October date. Maiani said he will ship Muscletone following the August 29 race in Berlin.

29. Hervey, John, "Comment of the Week," *Harness Horse,* **October 6, 1937, 1274.** Quote: "Americans could not comprehend the way the horse was being managed ..." Quote: "The foreign news for months past has been ..." Hervey suggests Maiani waffling may be more about politics than sport. Muscletone went lame in Berlin.

30. "Eyes of the Trotting World Focus on Greyhound's Record Trial Friday," *Indianapolis News,* **September 9, 1937, 20.** Greyhound is reported as likely to go after Peter Manning's record on September 10. The match race with Muscletone is set for Springfield on October 8.

31. "Greyhound to Make Try for Mark at State Fair," *Vidette-Messenger of Porter County* (Indiana), **September 9, 1937, 6.** Greyhound slated to go against Angel Child's track record at Indianapolis. Some race trackers noted as saying with a fast track he could beat Peter Manning. $5,000 is offered by the fair's board.

32. "The Hotel Baker Stables," *Hoof Beats,* **January 1937, 506.**

33. Ibid. "Some of the well-informed horsemen expressed the opinion ..."

END NOTES

34. Ibid.

35. **Associated Press, "Greyhound-Muscletone Race Postponed," *Indianapolis News*, September 11, 1937, 4.** Maiani announces Muscletone is sick, and the match race postponed to 1938, with no date set.

36. **Moser, P. W., *The Story of Greyhound 1:55 ¼* (see note 17).**

37. **Hervey, John, "Comment of the Week" (see note 29).** "The foreign news for months …"

38. **Ibid.** Muscletone lame.

——————— CHAPTER 17 ———————

Image: Peter Manning, the world's fastest trotter, set his mile record of 1:56 ¾ on October 4, 1922 (courtesy of the United States Trotting Association).

Epigraphs: Clark, Al, The Sports Shop (column), *Harrisburg Telegraph*, August 10, 1937, 16. "Peter Manning Rules …" Hervey, John, "Comparing Three Champions," *Harness Horse*, December 16, 1936, 116-23. "We have every right to believe …"

1. **"Greyhound Breaks Mile and A Half World's Record," *The Lewiston Daily Sun*, September 15, 1937, 9.** Description of Greyhound's record-breaking mile and a half at Indianapolis September 14, 1937.

2. **United Press, "Greyhound Sets New Record in 1 ½ Mile," *Leader-Telegram* (Eau Claire, Wisconsin), September 15, 1937, 6.** Greyhound shattered the record for a mile and a half in an exhibition on August 14 at the state fairgrounds in Indianapolis. "The big grey gelding clipped 9 ¾ seconds from the old record set the week before by Rosalind last week at Syracuse," trotting the distance in 3:01 ½.

3. **"Greyhound Breaks Mile …" (see note 1).**

4. **Ibid.**

5. **Author's Note:** The paragraphs describing Greyhound's world record for a mile and a half are a work of creative non-fiction based on facts and descriptions from articles in the *Lewiston Daily Sun* and the *Leader-Telegram* (see notes 1 and 2). Dialogue is from the author's imagination.

6. **United Press, "Greyhound Sets New Record …" (see note 2).** "The big grey gelding clipped …"

7. **Bostwick, Mary E, "Greyhound Enquires 'How'm I doin?'" *Indianapolis Star*, September 15, 1937, 16.** Quote: "Greyhound just stood in his roomy stall and sort of …"

8. **Ibid.** "As he passed the grandstand giving a …"

9. **"Wind Too Strong for Speed Trial," *Indianapolis Star*, September 19, 1937, 21.**

10. **"Greyhound Ties World Mark of Peter Manning Set in '22," *Cincinnati Enquirer*, September 23, 1937, 13.**

11. **"Lexington—September 29," *Harness Horse*, October 6, 1937, 1299.**

12. **Ibid.** "C'mon, Greyhound!" "Drive him, Sep!"

13. **Ibid.** Palin gave Greyhound a little breather.

14. **Gahagan, Tom, "World Marks Lowered at Lexington," *Horseman and Fair World*, October 6, 1937, 615.** Describes Greyhound's world record mile at Lexington September 29, 1937. Two runners accompanied but didn't come close until the final quarter when they moved up to push the gray a little. Final quarter in :28 ½ (:29, :28 ¼, :30, :28 ½—1:56 flat).

15. **Author's Note:** The paragraphs describing Greyhound's world record at Lexington on September 29, 1937 are a work of creative non-fiction using facts and information from articles printed in the October 6, 1937 issues of *Horseman and World Fair* and *Harness Horse* (see notes 11 and 14).

16. **Shropshire, Laurence K, "Down in Front," *Lexington Herald-Leader*, September 30, 1937, 6.** Quotes from Baker and Palin regarding Greyhound's world record mark at Lexington. Description of the race and the crowds.

17. **Ibid.**

18. **Ibid.** "Ladies and gentlemen …" Baker quotes.

19. **Ibid.**

20. **Ibid.**

21. **"Lexington—September 29" (see note 11).** "He appeared visibly affected …"

22. **Shropshire, Laurence K, "Down in Front" (see note 16).** "Folks, it's a real pleasure …" Palin quotes.

23. **Ibid.** Knight takes Palin out.

24. **"Greyhound 1:56," *Harness Horse*, December 15, 1937, 182.** Quote: "The spectacle he presented, trotting through the …"

25. **Hervey, John, "Out of the Mail Bag," *Harness Horse*, October 27, 1937, 1363.** "It is indeed weird the effect he has on people …" Quotes from the letter of Miss Lena D. Paull.

26. **Shuff, Jesse, News of the Trotters (column), *Lexington Herald*, October 24, 1937, 12.**

——————— CHAPTER 18 ———————

Image: Greyhound flies around the track at Indianapolis during a workout with Sep Palin (June 30, 1937, courtesy of the Tim Bojarski Collection).

Epigraph: Hervey, John, *The American Trotter* (New York: Coward-McCann, Inc, 1947). "He seemed to gather and poise himself when he set sail …"

1. **"Greyhound, Famed Trotter Faces Biggest Test Friday," *Athol Daily News*, August 2, 1938, 5.** "This year it is evident there is a change in the trend of the sport …"

2. **Goodwin, Austin, Scanning Sports (column), *Evening Express* (Portland, Maine), July 31, 1939, 13.** "…see no beauty in anything …"

3. **Hervey, John, "New World's Champions," *Hoof Beats*, December 1937, 474.** Palin did not push Greyhound as a two- and three-year-old. Just fast enough to win. Quote: "I think we all owe a debt of thanks to …"

4. **Grayson, Harry (NEA Service), "Tobacco-Chewing Trotter was a 'Gift,'" *Cincinnati Post*, August 10, 1938, 12.**

5. **John Hervey [Salvatore, pseud.], "A Unique Compliment," *Harness Horse*, December 22, 1937.** Algernon Daingerfield casts his vote for Greyhound for Horse of the Year.

6. **Ibid.** "[To choose] between War Admiral and Seabiscuit, I would have to …"

7. **Ibid.** "Never before has any trotting …"

8. **Ackerman, Alan, email correspondence, September 16, 2024.** "Hervey was the greatest writer of harness racing ever, producing a weekly column for nearly 55 years. He was the editor of the *Horse Review*, and then wrote for *Hoof Beats* and *Harness Horse* until his death. When he wrote for the horse review, his nom de plume was Volunteer. He was so highly regarded that the Thoroughbred people had him write for them, too, which he did under the name of Salvator. In his final years, … Harriman paid him to write his magnum opus on harness racing, *The American Trotter*."

CHAPTER 19

Image: Champion trotting mare Rosalind at age three (1936, courtesy of the United States Trotting Association).

Epigraph: International News Service (INS), "Greyhound's Brilliance is Proved Again," *Lexington Herald-Leader*, July 5, 1938, 5. "Harness racing fans knew today without a doubt that Greyhound …"

1. Taylor, Samuel Walter (editor), **The Light Harness Horse (column)**, *Rider and Driver*, July 1938, 22. Quote: "Greyhound, world's champion trotter, after spending 1937 in exhibitions …"

2. Sports Chatter (column), *Athol Daily News* (Mass.), August 2, 1938, 5.

3. Henry, Marguerite. *Born to Trot* (New York: Rand McNally & Company, 1950).

4. **"North Randall Meeting,"** *Harness Horse*, July 13, 1938, 983. Greyhound heavily advertised. Largest crowd in a dozen years. Beautiful weather with a prevailing wind. "He put on a performance that thrilled the immense throng to the limit …" "Even the trainers … marveled at the rare ease …"

5. Gahagan, Tom, **"New Records at North Randall,"** *Horseman and Fair World*, July 13, 1938, 408. Description of July 4, 1938 FFA Trot at North Randall. Record crowd of over 10,000.

6. **Author's Note:** This description is creative non-fiction, based on first-person observations and typical American Independence Day clothing and costumes of the 1930s as seen in photographs.

7. Gahagan, Tom, "New Records …" (see note 5).

8. Ibid.

9. "North Randall Meeting," *Harness Horse* (see note 4).

10. Ibid.

11. Ibid.

12. Ibid.

13. Gahagan, Tom, "New Records …" (see note 5).

14. "North Randall Meeting," *Harness Horse* (see note 4). "He put on a performance …"

15. Hervey, John, **"Greyhound's Quarter in 26 ⅘,"** *Harness Horse*, July 13, 1938, 994-996. Trotting a quarter in :26 ⅘ is better understood when one considers that time is in league with the final quarter of a running race. Hervey cites a few examples of recent stakes races where the final quarter of a running race ranged from :26 ⅕ to :27 ⅗ seconds.

16. **Ibid.** Hervey also points out the significance of Greyhound's fastest quarter being at the end of his race, when the running horse generally gets slower from start to finish, and notes the benefit of the Thoroughbred's use of the chute.

17. Ibid. "Behind his speed is the carrying power …"

18. Keller, Edwin T, **"Highlights at Agawam,"** *Horseman and Fair World*, August 3, 1938, 459. Friday, July 29, 1938 saw some of the worst weather in Massachusetts, with the past three weeks a deluge. The horses had to face a stout wind all afternoon.

19. Gahagan, Tom, **"Agawam Opens Two-Week Meeting,"** *Horseman and Fair World*, August 3, 1938, 458. Description of American Stake on July 29, 1938. Weather, track at Agawam "rain proof," safe but slow.

20. Keller, Edwin T, "Highlights at Agawam" (see note 18).

21. **"Agawam, Mass.—July 29,"** *Harness Horse*, August 3, 1938, 1060. Describes American Stake FFA at Agawam July 29, 1938.

22. Ibid.

23. Gahagan, Tom, "Agawam Opens …" (see note 19).

24. "Agawam, Mass.—July 29" (see note 21).

25. Ibid.

26. **Author's Note:** The July 29, 1938 Agawam race description is a work of creative non-fiction using facts and descriptions from *Harness Horse* and *Horseman and Fair World* (see notes 18, 19, and 21).

27. **"Agawam, Mass.—August 5,"** *Harness Horse*, August 10, 1938, 1093-94. Description of August 5, 1938 National Stake. Injury to Calumet Evelyn.

28. Gahagan, Tom, **"Second Week at Agawam,"** *Horseman and Fair World*, August 10, 1938, 481. Description of Agawam, Mass National Stake FFA Trot. Trotted fastest mile of season on a notoriously slow track. Greyhound is a huge favorite—no mutuel betting was allowed on the result. Quote: "Rosalind trotted a good race but it was not good enough to make the gray trot to his limit."

29. "Agawam, Mass—August 5" (see note 27). "He trotted around them as if they were all novices …"

30. **"Good Time Park Mile Track, Goshen, N. Y.—August 9,"** *Harness Horse*, August 17, 1938, 1117. Description of the August 9, 1938 the FFA trot at Goshen, and Calumet Evelyn's injury the week before. May not return to racing. Henry Knight sponsored and presented the trophy.

31. **"Greyhound Vanquishes Rosalind to Capture $3500 Trotting Derby,"** *Middletown Times Herald*, August 10, 1938, 9. Describes the August 9, 1938 Trotting Derby at Good Time Park. Rosalind puts up a good fight in the first heat, just barely losing by a nose.

32. Ibid.

33. Ibid.

34. "Good Time Park Mile Track …" (see note 30).

35. Ibid.

36. St. Claire, Labert, **"Greyhound Coming Fast for Local Driver; Perils Dan Patch's 33-Year-Old Record,"** *The Indianapolis Star*, July 31, 1938, 17. Twenty-seven trotters in history have gone a mile in 2:00 (fifty-six pacers).

37. **"Official Roster of 2:05 Trotters & Pacers,"** *Hoof Beats*, April 1938, 123-28. Up-to-date list of two-minute horses.

38. **"Greyhound at Goshen,"** *Newsweek*, July 25, 1938, 20. "Unlike many pampered champions, Greyhound has no private van …"

39. Ibid. "Practically everyone who has visited the silvery-coated horse …" "The only time he forgets his good horse sense is when he sees a cigarette …"

40. **Trotting Notes (column),** *Lexington Herald-Leader*, November 3, 1940, 14. Jimmie mentions the tobacco gifted by Vice-Mayor Celeste of Toledo is nearly gone. Greyhound is not picky on brand.

41. **"Greyhound is First in Circuit Race at Fair,"** *Decatur Daily Review* (Illinois), August 16, 1938, 7. Description of the August 15, 1938 Matron Stake at Illinois State Fair. Mention of weather and wind conditions.

42. Moser, P.W, **"Illinois State Fair,"** *Harness Horse*, August 24, 1938, 1149. "… it was here he received the greatest ovation of his career …"

43. Ibid. "Baker has been bringing Greyhound to Illinois since he reached celebrity status…

End Notes

44. **Ibid.** "The crowd was made up of the home folks ..."

45. **Ibid.** Greyhound, facing a 30-mph headwind, marched the stretch quarter in :28 ¼.

46. **"Syracuse, New York (State Fair Grounds Mile Track),"** *Harness Horse*, **September 7, 1938, 1213.**

47. **Ibid.** Description of exhibition trot at Syracuse, August 30, 1938.

48. **Author's Note:** The paragraph describing Greyhound's mile at Syracuse is a work of creative non-fiction, using facts and observations from *Harness Horse* (see note 44).

49. **"Syracuse, New York ..."** Presentation of flower wreath.

50. **"Greyhound Fails to Break Record,"** *News and Observer* **(Raleigh, North Carolina), September 7, 1938, 8.** Greyhound goes 1:56 ¾ in an exhibition at Indianapolis on September 6—three-quarters of a second off his fastest mark, but still the fastest mile by any horse in 1938.

51. **St. Claire, Labert, "Greyhound Coming Fast for Local Driver; Perils Dan Patch's 33-Year-Old Record,"** *Indianapolis Star*, **July 31, 1938, 17.** Palin notes that humidity can slow down a horse's record by as much as one second. Interesting to note here that Dan Patch made much more money for his owner doing exhibitions, which in his day attracted more people, possibly due to his owner, M.W. Savage, being a master at promotion. Dan Patch made as much as $7,500 for a single appearance, according to St. Clair, getting as much as half the take at the gate.

52. **"Greyhound Trots Mile in 1:56 to Equal World's Mark Set Here Last Year,"** *Lexington Herald*, **September 24, 1938, 7.** Describes Greyhound's mile in 1:56 on September 23, 1938. Mentions the stiff wind hitting head-on in the upper turn. Palin's watch catches Greyhound in 1:55 ¾; Carlock, driving the prompter catches him in 1:55 4/5; and others catch him in just a hair under 1:56. But the time of 1:56 flat caught by the official timers stands.

53. **"Fastest Trotter Sold for a Song,"** *True Republican* **(Sycamore, Illinois), July 6, 1938, 5.** What Greyhound eats.

54. **"Trotting King in Search of New Honors,"** *Noblesville Ledger*, **April 17, 1939, 2.** Greyhound gets an orange every morning. Eats cigarettes and tobacco to control worms.

55. **Daughtry, Leo, interview clipping, Scrapbook 3, Mary Lou Dondarski Collection, Harness Racing Museum, Goshen, New York.** Description of Greyhound's work schedule.

56. **"Does Greyhound Take Off Shoes?"** *Sidney Daily News* **(Ohio), July 10, 1940, 8.**

57. **Graham, Frank, "Setting the Pace," Scrapbook 4, Mary Lou Dondarski Collection, Harness Racing Museum, Goshen, New York.** "That's just the way he is ..."

58. **Daughtry, Leo, "Silver Streak Munches Oats with New Relish After Trotting to Added Glory," Scrapbook 3, Mary Lou Dondarski Collection, Harness Racing Museum, Goshen, New York.** Goes for a walk in the evening to eat grass.

59. **Graham, Frank, "Setting the Pace" (see note 57).**

60. **Author's Note:** The questions and answers in this section were quoted directly from the sources in notes 52 through 58. The facial expressions, gestures, crowd reactions, and clothing descriptions are from the author's imagination and used here to tie these pieces together.

CHAPTER 20

Image: Greyhound, featured in the *Chicago Daily News* (October 1943, courtesy of the St. Charles Historical Society).

Epigraph: Wall, Maryjean, "Greyhound's Legacy Lives on 50 Years after Incredible Meet," *Lexington Herald-Leader*, September 27, 1988, 19, 24. "Old timers talk in fond ..."

1. **"Lexington—September 29,"** *Hoof Beats*, **October 5, 1938, 1345.** Description of the weather and of Greyhound's mile in 1:55 ¼.

2. **Ibid.**

3. **Ibid.** "... Herculean effort ..."

4. **Ibid.** "Drivers, prominent owners, and others hovered ..."

5. **Ibid.** Pulled up their collars.

6. **Ibid.** Scoring.

7. **Ibid.** "... he's rating all right ..."

8. **"Grey Ghost Beats Record for Trotting,"** *Lexington Herald-Leader*, **September 30, 1938, 11.** "Veteran horsemen who have witnessed many record miles were unanimous in pronouncing Greyhound's performance the greatest of all time."

9. **"Lexington—September 29,"** *Hoof Beats* **(see note 1).** Up to Greyhound's wheel.

10. **Ibid.** 1:26 ½, the fastest three-quarters ever trotted.

11. **Menke, Frank G, releases from "trotters and pacers" article, post-1946, Harness Racing Museum Collection.**

12. **"Lexington—September 29,"** *Hoof Beats* **(see note 1).** "... they cheered, yelled, shook hands..."

13. **Moser, P. W.,** *The Story of Greyhound 1:55 ¼* **(Harrisburg, PA: Harness Horse, 1940), 33.** "Men forgot the time ..."

14. **Fox Jr., W. F, "Greyhound, a Horse That's Fit for a Name That Fits,"** *The Indianapolis News*, **September 6, 1938, 18.** "Greyhound looked up ..."

15.

16. **Daughtry, Leo, "Silver Streak Munches Oats with New Relish After Trotting to Added Glory," Scrapbook 3, Mary Lou Dondarski Collection, Harness Racing Museum, Goshen, New York.** "We have to put a lock on the door ..."

17. **"Horse Sales End,"** *The Cincinnati Enquirer*, **September 30, 1938, 19.** Baker at Walnut Hall sale.

18. **Menke, Frank G, releases from "trotters and pacers" article (see note 11).** "The time of 1:55 ¼, which gave Greyhound a new world's record ..."

19. **Ibid.** At the ¾ pole, Greyhound's time was almost one second faster than Billy Direct.

20. **Moser, P. W.,** *The Story of Greyhound 1:55 ¼* **(see note 13).** About unpublicized attempts.

21. **"Grey Ghost Beats Record ..." (see note 8).**

22. **Hervey, John, "Greater Greyhound,"** *Harness Horse*, **September 13, 1939, 1291.** "But this I warrant you ..."

CHAPTER 21

Images: Top and below right, from a Houghton advertisement (circa 1938, courtesy of the United States Trotting Association). Below left, Greyhound yawning (circa 1940, courtesy of the Harness Racing Museum & Hall of Fame, Goshen, NY).

Epigraph: Hervey, John, "Greater Greyhound," *Harness Horse*, September 13, 1939, 1291. "He needs do nothing more ..."

END NOTES

1. Cleveland, Howard L, "Greyhound Pays No Heed to Noise of Racetracks …," *Lexington Herald*, October 1, 1936, 6. Trego was acquired from a dog track in Florida.

2. "Greyhound Doesn't Like 'Terbaccer'," *Hartford Daily Courant* (Connecticut), July 27, 1938, 11. Trego the greyhound has a track record in New York state.

3. **Author's Note:** There is film footage owned by the St. Charles Historical Society of Baker walking around the gardens of Hotel Baker, circa 1939, when he would have been around seventy. He is agile and moves easily, walking on paths, through the grass, and even along the rock edges of the ponds. He holds the cane but clearly doesn't rely on it.

4. Nason, Jerry, "Greyhound-Baker-Palin Best Hambletonian Bet," *Boston Globe*, August 7, 1935, 22. Sep Palin quote about Baker: "He really loves horses. He comes into the stables …" "And he knows every groom …"

5. Gahagan, Tom, "Chances Slim of Greyhound Meeting Rosalind This Year," *Cincinnati Enquirer*, March 5, 1939, 32. Gahagan reports on Rosalind and Greyhound at Seminole Park in Longwood, Florida.

6. **Ibid.** Mentions age restriction and purse drop of stakes the two raced in 1938.

7. **Ibid.** Not currently training for speed.

8. Mack, Gene, "Like Other Champs, Greyhound Is Stickler for Regular Habits," *Boston Globe*, July 29, 1937, 10. Quote: "A harness horse thrives on plenty of hard work. In this respect, he differs …" Wingfield describes Greyhound as a "good doer." "He's just as keen for his workouts as he is for his meals."

9. Hervey, John, "A Pair of Shoes," *Harness Horse*, December 14, 1938, 124. "Today, after five years of campaigning and a series of extreme miles, in and out …"

10. "Greyhound Will Try for Record at Daytona Beach," *Anderson Herald* (Indiana), March 17, 1939, 17. Palin plans to take Greyhound to Daytona Beach; if he likes the footing, he may go after a record mile on the straightaway.

11. "Trotting King in Search of New Honors," *Noblesville Ledger* (Indiana), April 17, 1939, 2. Palin believes Greyhound could trot 1:50 on a straightaway.

12. **Ibid.** Greyhound didn't like the waves.

13. Wall, Maryjean, "Greyhound's Legacy Lives on Fifty Years After Incredible Meet," *Lexington Herald-Leader*, September 27, 1988, 24. Hall of Fame trainer-driver Delvin Miller recalls a conversation with Jimmie Wingfield: "The day they trained him on the beach he said he just jogged [a mile] in [1]:56 or [1]:57, not trying to go fast. But then the weather got so bad that they never did get to go with him."

14. "Trotting King in Search of New Honors" (see note 11). Palin said he'd try again at Daytona after the Grand Circuit season.

15. **Ibid.** "Greyhound, the world's greatest trotting horse and holder of …" Greyhound arrives in Indianapolis from Florida in the first part of April. The article speculates about a match race between fastest pacer, Billy Direct, and fastest trotter, Greyhound.

16. Bogart, Walt, "Training a Great Race Horse," Scrapbook 4, Mary Lou Dondarski Collection, Harness Racing Museum, Goshen, New York.

17. Graham, Frank, "Setting the Pace," Scrapbook 4, Mary Lou Dondarski Collection, Harness Racing Museum, Goshen, New York. Jimmie's thoughts on his job and his life with horses.

18. "Fastest Trotter and Pacer to Compete," *Rider and Driver*, April 1939, 19. Suggests that the trainer-driver of Billy Direct 1:55, Vic Flemming, is open to discussing a series of match races between the two fastest harness horses in the world. No note on whether Baker or Palin is interested.

19. **Author's Note:** The paragraphs describing Jimmie jogging Greyhound and thinking about various articles are from the author's imagination. The articles referenced are real, as are Jimmie's thoughts about working with horses. *Jimmie's thoughts about the match race are speculation on the part of the author, and assigned to him only to move the story along.*

CHAPTER 22

Image: Greyhound's letter to *Hoof Beats* editor Dick Case, and Greyhound with Baker, Knight, Palin, and Wingfield at Red Gate (August 1939, courtesy of the United States Trotting Association).

Epigraphs: "Greyhound 1:55 ¼ The Incomparable," *Harness Horse*, December 13, 1939, 112. "Greyhound accomplishes …" "Old Orchard, Me.—July 27," *Harness Horse*, August 2, 1939, 1063. "He is the horse which never …"

1. "Old Orchard, Me.—July 27," *Harness Horse*, August 2, 1939, 1063. Description of the July 27 exhibition trot at Old Orchard, Maine. "… bursting into the homestretch … Greyhound marching off space as though propelled by steam, electric power, or some force other than muscular energy."

2. **Ibid.**

3. **Ibid.** Jimmie brought the prompter up to Greyhound's sulky wheel for the last quarter, and with no prompting from Palin, Greyhound finished his mile in 1:57 ½.

4. Gahagan, Tom, "Old Orchard Closes Great Meeting," *Horseman and Fair World*, August 2, 1939. Greyhound smashes the track record (2:01) he set there three years ago. Trotted the quarter in :29, the half in :59, three-quarters in 1:28 with a final record-smashing time of 1:57 ½—a record for the track and also for New England.

5. Goodwin, Austin, Scanning Sports (column), *Evening Express* (Portland, Maine), July 31, 1939, 13.

6. **Ibid.** "With a long and powerful stride …"

7. **Ibid.** Palin interview with radio commentator.

8. Greyhound to Dick Case c/o *Hoof Beats*, letter, August 20, 1939. 1,500 guests came to Red Gate to see Greyhound and other celebrity horses such as Rosalind, Winnipeg, Her Ladyship, Peter Astra, Cardinal Prince, and more.

9. "E. J. Baker's Two-Minute Horses," *Harness Horse*, December 16, 1936, 125. "At all times pleasant and courteous …"

10. "Greyhound Trots Exhibition in 1:58," *Evening Sun* (Hanover, Pennsylvania), August 24, 1939, 8. Greyhound's August 23 exhibition mile at Milwaukee.

11. **Ibid.** Mentions Rosalind's win in the FFA trot.

12. "Seen at Syracuse," *Hoof Beats*, October 29, 1939, 8. Description of Greyhound and Rosalind's attempt at lowering the record for team to pole at Syracuse August 31, 1939. Sky overcast.

13. **Ibid.** Crowd asked not to applaud.

14. **Ibid.** "… working like a docile …"

15. **Ibid.** Palin took the first turn slowly.

16. Associated Press, "Two Horses Break Mark at Syracuse," *Democrat and Chronicle* (Rochester, New York), September 1, 1939, 30. Lowered the existing mark set in 1912 by over four seconds. 1:59 vs 2:03 ¼. Covered the last half mile in a remarkable :58. Peter Astra wins the $7,500 Governor's Cup at the same meet.

END NOTES

17. Hervey, John, "A Team Mile in 1:59," *Harness Horse*, September 6, 1939, 1252-53. "Those fortunate enough to be present ..."

18. Associated Press, "Greyhound, Rosalind Seek New Track Mark," *La Crosse Tribune* (Wisconsin), September 3, 1939, 9. Reports Palin signed a contract promising $2,000 if he staged another team-to-pole record attempt at the Indiana state fairgrounds, with a $500 bonus if they succeed.

19. Gahagan, George M, "Greyhound and Rosalind Break World's Record at State Fair," *Indianapolis Star*, September 6, 1939, 16. "But mere breezes ..." Description of Greyhound and Rosalind's team-to-pole mile, lowering their record to 1:58 ¼ at the Indiana State Fair. Final quarter in :28 ¼.

20. Putnam, Leone, *Dooley and the Grey Ghost* (Goshen, NY: Harness Racing Museum and Hall of Fame, 2018), 41.

21. Putnam, Dooley, voice recording, Heitbrink Collection, Harness Racing Museum, Goshen, New York.

22. "Greyhound Steals Show with Fifteenth World Record," *Indianapolis News*, September 20, 1939, 16. Greyhound sets the two-mile world record of 4:06, beating Peter Manning's record of 4:10 ¼.

23. Associated Press, "Four Top Harness Racing," *Herald and Review* (Decatur, Illinois), December 26, 1939, 14. Greyhound is to only race in exhibitions. The top horses of 1939 are Billy Direct, Greyhound, Peter Astra, and Dean Hanover.

24. "Greyhound 1:55 ¼ The Incomparable," *Harness Horse*, December 13, 1939, 112. "Just when you think ..."

25. Author's Note: The conversation among the patrons in the bar is from the author's imagination. As with other such conversations in this book, the quotes are taken from facts and information printed in sports columns by Tom Gahagan (*Cincinnati Enquirer*, April 7, 1940). In other words, the men are repeating what they read.

26. Associated Press, "Four Top Harness Racing" (see note 23). Peter Astra tops the list.

CHAPTER 23

Image: Art of Greyhound, from "Sport Slants" by Pap (*Bennington Banner*, August 9, 1940).

Epigraph: "Trotting and Pacing News from Harness Racing Circles," *Morning Call* (Paterson, New Jersey), August 7, 1940, 18. "They say that youth must be served ..."

1. Gahagan, Tom, "Greyhound's Name on Eligible List for Six Events," *Cincinnati Enquirer*, April 7, 1940, 34. Gahagan reports on the creation of a series of stakes to lure Greyhound out of retirement, and mentions the champion is on the list of entries for six of them.

2. "E. Roland Harriman Dies at his Arden Home," *Horseman and Fair World*, February 22, 1978, 14.

3. "Trotting Greats Thrill Railbirds on Aiken Track," *The State* (Columbia, S.C.), February 10, 1940, 7. Wintering in Aiken for the first time, at a new facility. Palin arrived in early February. Twenty-one trotters are in the stable.

4. Fennell, Abe, "2500 People See Aiken Racing Meet," *The State* (Columbia, South Carolina), March 24, 1940, 11. Description of Aiken exhibition mile.

5. "A Fast Mile by Greyhound at Fairgrounds," *Noblesville Ledger* (Indiana), April 26, 1940, 2. "Fine fettle."

6. Murphy, Merritt, Along the Trotting Trail (column), *Noblesville Ledger* (Indiana), June 1, 1940, 2. Greyhound trots a mile in 2:03, the last half 1:00 flat, for the fastest reported training mile of the season so far.

7. Shropshire, Larry, Down in Front (column), *Lexington Herald*, June 9, 1940, 8. Parshall says only Spentell and Greyhound can match strides with Peter Astra.

8. "Will Use New Barrier System to Start Fair Races Here," *Morning Call*, September 6, 1939, 14. Describes the new McNamara barrier starting system.

9. Reid, Jack, "Spectators Favor Overhead Barrier for Racing Starts," *Dayton Daily News*, November 12, 1939, 41. Palin and other reinsmen oppose the new barrier system.

10. Gahagan, George M, "Greyhound Scores Straight-Heat Victory," *Indianapolis Star*, June 23, 1940, 37. Describes American Trotting Club Trot, June 22, 1940. Comment on slower speeds possibly being due to placement of the McNamara barrier.

11. Shuff, Jesse, "1940 Good Year for Trotters," *Lexington Herald-Leader*, January 12, 1941, 75. Comments on mandatory use of McNamara barrier.

12. "Gray Ghost Defeats Fast Field at The Fairgrounds," *Noblesville Ledger*, June 24, 1940, 2. Describes the American Trotting Club Stake, June 22, 1940.

13. Ibid. Sister Mary passes Greyhound and takes the lead.

14. **Author's Note:** The paragraphs describing Greyhound's race on June 22, 1940, are works of creative non-fiction, drawing from facts and information provided in articles in *The Indianapolis Star* and *The Noblesville Ledger* (see notes 10 and 12).

15. "Parshall Suspended by Trots Official," *Cincinnati Post*, June 21, 1940, 23. Doc Parshall is suspended for insubordination at the Marion meet.

16. "Toledo, Ohio Grand Circuit," *Harness Horse*, July 17, 1940. An unusually large crowd is on hand to see Greyhound at Ft. Miami.

17. Ibid. Won heat with a new speed record for the season.

18. Ibid. Clever Hanover is withdrawn after a bad showing.

19. Ibid. Greyhound rambled home in the second heat in 2:01 ¼ with Palin reining him in.

20. Trott, Frank G, "Greyhound Wins Easily," *Boston Globe*, July 23, 1940, 6. Description of Greyhound's July 22, 1940 win at Narragansett. Photo banner reads: "Same old story, Greyhound first, the rest..."

21. "Trotter Takes Race in Two Heat Victory Over Field of Stars," *Evening Sun* (Hanover, Penn.), July 26, 1940, 8. Peter Astra comes fourth in the Goldsmith Maid Trot.

22. "Greyhound Wins at Narragansett," *Bangor Daily News*, July 30, 1940, 14. Describes Greyhound's heat wins at Narragansett, Trotting Horse Club Stake, Pawtucket, Rhode Island, July 29, 1940, and that he set a new track record (2:01 ½). Palin kept him under restraint for the first heat. In the second, he let him have his head a little, and Greyhound opened a large gap between him and his nearest competitor.

23. "Pawtucket, R.I," *Harness Horse*, August 7, 1940. Description of second heat of July 29, Pawtucket, Rhode Island, Trotting Horse Club Stake at Narragansett Park.

24. "Trotting and Pacing News from Harness Racing Circles," *Morning Call*, August 7, 1940, 18. Palin and Parshall are both confident their horse can defeat the other.

25. "Astra Eligible in Two Races," *Middleton Times Herald* (New York), August 10, 1940, 2. Peter Astra is listed as a possible entrant in the Stake against Greyhound or the Trotting Derby at Goshen.

26. Ibid. Peter Astra will have to "go a lot faster than he has been going" to win.

27. **"Eight-year-old Greyhound Wins Race,"** *Star-Gazette* **(Elmira, New York), August 13, 1940, 23.** Betting is closed to Greyhound and stablemate Sister Mary. Largest opening day crowd in the history of Good Time Park.

28. **"Record First-Day Crowd Cheers Greyhound to Final Victory at Goshen,"** *Middletown Times Herald*, **August 13, 1940, 1.** Stumbled first heat.

29. **Ibid., 9.** Sister Mary and Athlone Flaxey Guy hung with Greyhound.

30. **Ibid., 1.** The crowd cheered every time he passed the grandstand; "… scores flocked about …"

31. **"Greyhound Like a Ghost Only He's Something Real,"** *Middletown Times Herald* **(New York), August 13, 1940, 9.** Mentions James Cagney's appearance. Photographed with Greyhound. "The son of Guy Abbey has the popularity …"

32. **"Springfield, Illinois—August 23,"** *Harness Horse*, **August 28, 1940, 1271-72.** Greyhound trotted the first mile of the season in two minutes or better.

33. **Ibid.** A walkover for Greyhound. Largest crowd to ever attend races at Springfield.

34. Lewis, Gary, **"The Grey Ghost of Jimmy's Past."** *Hoof Beats*, December 1986, 64.

CHAPTER 24

Image: A candid shot of Jimmie and Greyhound (circa 1939, Hambletonian Society Collection, courtesy of the Harness Racing Museum & Hall of Fame, Goshen, NY).

Epigraph: Moser, P. W., *The Story of Greyhound 1:55 ¼* (Harrisburg, PA: Harness Horse, 1940). "It is not possible …"

1. Lewis, Gary, **"The Grey Ghost of Jimmy's Past,"** *Hoof Beats*, December 1986, 64. Palin pacing, and Greyhound's long trip and jogging miles after his arrival at Syracuse.

2. **"Syracuse, New York,"** *Harness Horse*, **September 4, 1940, 1305.** Description of August 26, 1940 race at Syracuse. Greyhound shunted well back of the field. Palin pulled him out and took him around the field, going the half in an unverified :57 ½.

3. **Ibid.** Palin tapped Greyhound at the 7/8 mark but he did not respond. Baker was not present to state future plans regarding racing another season.

4. Associated Press, **"Greyhound Loses First Heat this Year,"** *St. Louis Post-Dispatch*, **August 26, 1940, 11.** Description of the first heat of the August 26, 1940 race at Syracuse, where Peter Astra edged Greyhound by a nostril.

5. **"Syracuse, New York,"** *Harness Horse* **(see note 2).** Palin quote: "Greyhound raced at Springfield, Illinois, last Friday shipped 1,000 miles to Syracuse, and did not get to the state fair track until Sunday afternoon. He's just a little groggy, that's all."

6. **"Greyhound Wins Last Race but Loses First Heat,"** *Noblesville Ledger*, **August 27, 1940, 2.** Description of the August 26, 1940 race at Syracuse. Palin drove him "lovingly."

7. Gill, Wesley, **"Greyhound Wins Race After Losing Heat for First Time in Four Years,"** *Middletown Times Herald* **(New York), August 27, 1940, 9.** Description of the August 26, 1940 race at Syracuse.

8. **"Syracuse, New York,"** *Harness Horse* **(see note 2).** Palin "high lined," asking for more speed, Greyhound delivered …

9. **Ibid.** Palin accepts the trophy from the Fair Queen. Baker is not present due to illness.

Author's Note: This chapter is a work of creative non-fiction, using facts and information gleaned from articles in *The St. Louis Post-Dispatch* (8/26/40), *The Noblesville Ledger* (8/27/40), *The Middletown Times Herald* (8/27/40), and *Harness Horse* (9/4/40) (see notes 2, 4, 6, and 7).

CHAPTER 25

Image: Jimmie stands with Greyhound next to Uhlan's world record marker at the Historic Half Mile Track in Goshen, New York (circa 1938, courtesy of the United States Trotting Association).

Epigraph: Stoneridge, M. A, *Great Horses of Our Time* (Garden City, NY: Doubleday & Company, Inc, 1972).

1. **Author's Note:** This interaction between Jimmie and Greyhound is from the author's imagination, based on the knowledge that Greyhound was first saddled at Louisville (see note 7).

2. **"Harness Horses are Back,"** *Owensboro Messenger* **(Kentucky), September 11, 1940, 4.** Grand Circuit Harness racing returns to the Kentucky State Fair after over-15-year hiatus.

3. **"Top Horses Lined Up for Fair Races,"** *Courier-Journal* **(Louisville), September 5, 1940, 18.** Greyhound to arrive in Louisville on September 8.

4. **"Giant Trotter Lands Victory,"** *Lexington Herald-Leader*, **September 11, 1940, 6.** Greyhound leads a parade of two-minute performers between races at the Kentucky State Fair in Louisville.

5. **"Louisville—September 11,"** *Harness Horse*, **September 18, 1940, 1386.** Exhibition over the half-mile oval at Louisville. Poor footing; cuppy, slow track. Air chilly enough for sweaters. Attracted a new record crowd, who cheered loudly when Palin let Greyhound out a notch for the final quarter in :30. Watched by Dr. Parshall and Vic Flemming, who felt, given the conditions, Greyhound's effort was on par with his sub-two-minute mile at historic track.

6. **Ibid.**

7. Dunn, Neville, **"Greyhound May Try for Record Under Saddle,"** *Lexington Herald*, **September 17, 1940, 7.** Greyhound preparing for possible under saddle record at Lexington. First ride was at Louisville when "walked around the state fair ring with Wingfield on his back." Parade of Greyhound and family planned during the trots.

8. Wall, Maryjean, **"Trotters with Saddles Not New Experience at the Red Mile,"** *Lexington Herald*, **June 17, 1976, 38.** Jimmie walked Greyhound an eighth of a mile before asking for a trot.

9. Wall, Maryjean, **"The Gray Ghost Remembered,"** *Lexington Herald*, **January 29, 1975, 16.** "When I started posting …"

10. Dunn, Neville, **"Greyhound May Try …"** (see note 7). Jimmie continued under saddle work with Greyhound at Lexington.

11. Wall, Maryjean, **"The Gray Ghost Remembered"** (see note 9). Frances rode Greyhound only once before the record ride.

12. Shuff, Jesse, **"Parade of Greys Set for Today,"** *Lexington Herald*, **September 26, 1940, 8.**

13. **"Lexington—September 27,"** *Harness Horse*, **October 2, 1940, 1458.** In front of an extremely enthusiastic crowd. Palin drove the prompter.

14. **Ibid.** Greyhound trotted like a machine into the stretch; the crowd's enthusiasm flowed onto the track in the form of whoops and hollers, cheering and shouts of encouragement. Baker was not in attendance.

15. Gahagan, Tom, **"Trot Record Made,"** *Cincinnati Enquirer*, **September 28, 1940, 15.** Greyhound sets a record for one mile under saddle and beats the previous record set by Hollyrood Boris. Sister Mary wins Transylvania.

CHAPTER 26

Image: A cartoon drawn by Jimmie's mother Mary Wingfield, on the occasion of Greyhound's retirement (1941, courtesy of the Wingfield family).

END NOTES

Epigraph: George H. Sweetnam, *Hoof Beats*, January 1942, 49 (excerpt from poem).

1. Associated Press, "Greyhound Trots his Last Race – This Year," *Chippewa Herald-Telegram* (Chippewa Falls, Wis.), August 27, 1940, 7. Palin quotes: "Yep, it's his last race—this season." "He'll race again next year—if there are any races for him."

2. Murphy, Merritt, Along the Trotting Trail (column), *Noblesville Ledger*, October 9, 1940, 2. Announces complete dispersal of all Baker's racing stock at the November Indianapolis Speed Sale.

3. Ibid. Baker has been ill for most of the year, spending much of that time in the hospital.

4. "Mrs. E. J. Baker of St. Charles is Dead at 73," *Chicago Tribune*, July 2, 1940, 16. Harriet Baker's obituary. Mentions Mr. Baker is hospitalized in Geneva following a recent surgery.

5. Putnam, Leone, *Dooley and the Grey Ghost* (Goshen, NY: Harness Racing Museum and Hall of Fame, 2018), 47. Baker fired Palin.

6. Burgess, Dale, "Baker Sells all his Harness Horses but One—Greyhound," *Palladium-Item* (Richmond, Indiana), December 13, 1940, 12. Palin has driven fifty-eight two-minute miles. Indicates Palin not expecting Greyhound to retire.

7. Gahagan, Tom, "Former Frances Dodge, Auto Heiress, Pays Top Price for Yearling Trotter," *Collyer's Eye and the Baseball World*, November 23, 1940, 7. Frances Dodge Johnson purchases Grey Fox for $6,100 from Henry Knight, and Sister Mary for $2,300 from Colonel Baker.

8. "Greyhound Returns to Pass Winter in Aiken," *Aiken Standard* (South Carolina), January 3, 1941, 8. Greyhound moved with the Palin stable to Aiken, South Carolina, December 21, 1940. Details a reporter's visit with the Wingfield and Palin horses, and Greyhound, at the Aiken Mile Track.

9. Burgess, Dale, "Baker Sells all …" (see note 6). "If Greyhound trains as well as …"

10. Murphy, Merritt, Along the Trotting Trail (column), *Noblesville Ledger* (Indiana), January 24, 1941, 2. Palin and his wife are leaving for Aiken, South Carolina. Jimmie Wingfield, Greyhound, and the Palin stable are already there.

11. Dickerson, C. G, "Trots Regain Prestige," *Lexington Herald-Leader*, January 12, 1941, 74. Stats according to USTA: Harness racing was conducted in 42 states in 1939 and 1940. Small tracks alone were responsible for $1.5 million in prize money. Roosevelt Raceway saw $1.2 million handled over the course of a 27-day meet in 1940.

12. Reid, Jack, "Champ 1940 Pacer Being Trained on Trot," *Springfield News-Sun* (Ohio), January 12, 1941, 11. Stats: As of January 1941, 32 horses have trotted miles of two minutes or better; 108 total miles have been trotted in two minutes or better, and 25 of these were trotted by Greyhound.

13. "Greyhound Returns to Pass Winter …" (see note 8). Jimmie says Greyhound is unlikely to race again, but will do exhibitions.

14. Breitz, Eddie, "Trotter Greyhound Declared Lame and Through as Racer," *Evening Star* (Washington, D. C.), June 13, 1941, 48.

15. Breitz, Eddie, "Greyhound not Lame," *Des Moines Tribune*, June 16, 1941, 13.

16. "Stalls Filled at OO Track," *Sun-Journal*, (Lewiston, Maine) July 12, 1941, 8. Greyhound is at Old Orchard, traveling with the racing stable, and is in "light training" but it "is doubtful if he ever starts again."

17. Harness Notes (column), *Hartford Courant* (Connecticut), July 13, 1941, 36. Greyhound has worked in 2:30.

18. Taylor, Ken, "1941 Trot Record at Fair," *Courier-Journal*, September 10, 1941, 18. Greyhound is to do an exhibition each afternoon this week at the fair.

19. "Half-Miler Takes Pacing Stakes," *Cincinnati Enquirer*, September 11, 1941, 23. Greyhound is presented at the Kentucky State Fair.

20. The Jog Cart (column), *Lexington Herald-Leader*, September 30, 1941, 7. Palin reports Greyhound is going well after "leg trouble" in the spring, and has been a mile in 2:20. His future plans are indefinite—maybe the exhibition circuit.

21. "The Champ—To Race No More," *Lexington Herald-Leader*, October 17, 1941, 6. Greyhound's retirement is announced; the champ is vanned from Indianapolis to Red Gate Farm in St. Charles, Illinois.

22. Ibid. Quotes from Jimmie Wingfield.

23. Gahagan, Tom, "E. J. Baker Back in Trot Game." *Cincinnati Enquirer*, November 2, 1941, 35. Baker bought two yearlings at Lexington and then went $1,900 for a pacing yearling called Noble Hal.

24. Harness Notes (column), *Collyer's Eye and the Baseball World*, November 29, 1941, 7. Baker has two yearlings in training with Harry Fitzpatrick.

25. "King's Counsel, Pacing Colt, Sold for $20,000 at Du Quoin State Fair," *Perry County Advocate* (Pickneyville, Illinois), September 9, 1943, 1.

26. Shuff, Jesse, Trotters and Pacers (column), *Lexington Herald*, October 5, 1946, 5. Baker sells King's Counsel to Gainesway.

27. Miles Michelson, "Kings Counsel Standardbred," n.d., accessed April 12, 2024, https://www.allbreedpedigree.com/kings+counsel5

28. Murphy, Merritt, "Greyhound is Retired," *Harness Horse*, October 22, 1941, 1532. Palin and Wingfield are both noted as having become quite attached to the intelligent horse. Lists Greyhound's 18 world records.

29. The Jog Cart (column), *Lexington Herald-Leader* (see note 20). "Too much horse to turn out…"

30. "The Champ—To Race No More" (see note 21). Jimmie tells reporters Greyhound is 16.1 ½ and weighs 1,200 lbs.

31. Putnam, Leone, *Dooley and the Grey Ghost* (Goshen, NY: Harness Racing Museum and Hall of Fame, 2018), 53. Greyhound is spooked by a rabbit. Baker sends him to Flanery.

32. Ibid. Greyhound sent to Flanery.

CHAPTER 27

Image: Dooley and Greyhound at the opening of Maywood Park (June 6, 1946, courtesy of the United States Trotting Association).

Epigraph: VanGundy, June, "Calling on Greyhound," *Hoof Beats*, January 1942, 41.

1. Putnam, Leone, *Dooley and the Grey Ghost* (Goshen, NY: Harness Racing Museum and Hall of Fame, 2018), 5. Dooley gets his name.

2. Ibid., 1. Working for Dunk Harris.

3. Ibid., 9. Brown County fairgrounds.

4. Ibid. Dooley talking with dad Hatch.

5. Ibid., 10. Relocate to Mason City, Illinois.

6. Ibid., 13. Emma Lou born.

7. Ibid. Flanery calls Dooley.

END NOTES

8. **Bower, Alex, The Side Show (column),** *Lexington Herald-Leader***, July 20, 1940, 6.** Details about Senator Crawford—purchase, ownership, show record, and retirement.

9. **Ibid.**

10. **Putnam, Leone,** *Dooley and the Grey Ghost* **(see note 1), 13.**

11. **Putnam, Dooley, voice recording, Heitbrink Collection, Harness Racing Museum.**

12. **VanGundy, June, "Calling on Greyhound,"** *Hoof Beats***, January 1942, 41.**

13. **Ibid.** "I wasn't doing so much …"

14. **Ibid.** "… stall manners of a six-month-old puppy …"

15. **Putnam, Leone,** *Dooley and the Grey Ghost* **(see note 1), 128.** Greyhound didn't like the other horses.

16. **Putnam, Dooley, voice recording (see note 11).**

17. **Putnam, Leone,** *Dooley and the Grey Ghost* **(see note 1), 53.** "I just hope he likes me …"

18. **Pearson, Ruth Seen,** *Reflections of St. Charles* **(St. Charles History Museum, 1976, 2019), 157.**

19. **Murphy, Merritt, Along the Trotting Trail (column),** *Noblesville Ledger* **(Indiana), January 24, 1941, 2.** Jimmie Wingfield in Aiken with Greyhound and the Palin stable.

20. **Putnam, Leone,** *Dooley and the Grey Ghost* **(see note 1), 53.** …Eagle eyes.

21. **Ibid.** "Like he can see …"

22. **Putnam, Leone,** *Dooley and the Grey Ghost* **(see note 1), 56.**

23. **Ibid.**

24. **Ibid.**

25. **Ibid., 56-7.**

26. **Ibid., 93.**

27. **Ibid., 57.**

28. **Ibid.**

CHAPTER 28

Image: Greyhound feeling fresh with Doc Flanery at Hollywood Park (1947, courtesy of the Harness Racing Museum & Hall of Fame, Goshen, NY).

Epigraph: Aston, Joe, By Joe Aston (column), *Cincinnati Post* (Ohio), October 3, 1945, 14. "The old harness men …"

1. **"Greyhound is Rescued from Farm Blaze,"** *Daily Chronicle* **(De Kalb, Illinois), February 20, 1942, 1.**

2. **"Flannery Home Blazes but Greyhound Safe,"** *Lexington Herald-Leader***, February 19, 1942, 9.** The Flanery home at Highland View Farm, 15 miles west of Elgin, burns on February 18, 1942. Neighbors created a bucket brigade and assisted two small fire departments in wetting the barn to prevent the fire from spreading, thus saving the horses, including Greyhound.

3. **Putnam, Leone,** *Dooley and the Grey Ghost* **(Goshen, NY: Harness Racing Museum and Hall of Fame, 2018), 66.**

4. **Ibid.**

5. **Cronin, Ned, untitled sports column,** *Daily News* **(Los Angeles), April 2, 1947, 35.** Baker has shipped Greyhound across the country at his own expense since his retirement.

6. **Arbuckle, W. J, "Greyhound's Day at Baker's Acres,"** *Harness Horse***, October 27, 1943, 1536.** Description of decorations, guests were "wined and dined …"

7. **Ibid.** Even Senator Crawford made an appearance.

8. **Putnam, Leone,** *Dooley and the Grey Ghost* **(see note 3), 72.**

9. **Ibid., 73.**

10. **Ibid., 93.**

11. **United Press, "Four Stakes Races Top Harness Meet Card,"** *Santa Barbara News-Press***, April 15, 1946, 10.**

12. **Hebert, Bob, "Longshots Score at Hollywood Park,"** *Daily News***, April 10, 1947, 12.** Greyhound and Flanery do a trot exhibition after the third race on $50k trot and $50k pace day.

13. **United Press, "Four Stakes Races …" (see note 11).** Greyhound receives a standing ovation during an exhibition trot at Santa Anita.

14. **Menke, Frank G, "Trotters and Pacers,"** *Evening Sun***, July 19, 1948, 8.** "He was always a superb …" "Greyhound would take to …"

15. **Cronin, Ned, untitled sports column (see note 5).** Baker has a 15-horse stable at Hollywood Park.

16. **Putnam, Leone,** *Dooley and the Grey Ghost* **(see note 3), 105.** A Hollywood camera crew follows Greyhound and Dooley. "We didn't know …"

17. **Ibid., 100.**

18. **Putnam, Dooley, voice recording.** Dooley talks about Greyhound's blankets and why he wore them.

19. **Author's Note:** The playful interaction between Dooley and Greyhound described here is from the author's imagination, but is based on observations of Greyhound on film and in pictures interacting with others.

20. **Putnam, Leone,** *Dooley and the Grey Ghost* **(see note 3), 107.** Baker dispersal auction.

21. **Ibid., 108.** Bakers Acres sold.

22. **Reinert, Judy, "Hambletonian Winner was Colonel Baker's Baby,"** *Kane County Chronicle* **(Geneva, Illinois), August 5, 1998, C1, 5.** Baker, not used to hearing "no," offered to build Greyhound a stall.

23. **Author's Note:** The scene and the dialogue between Doc and Baker are from the author's imagination, based on information found in the *Kane County Chronicle* (see note 22).

CHAPTER 29

Image: Greyhound at age 30, in the snow (1962, courtesy of the Harness Racing Museum & Hall of Fame, Goshen, NY).

Epigraph: Hervey, John, *The American Trotter* (New York: Coward-McCann, Inc, 1947). "A more fitting finale …"

1. **Putnam, Leone,** *Dooley and the Grey Ghost* **(Goshen, NY: Harness Racing Museum and Hall of Fame, 2018), 113.** Greyhound's housewarming party, held on October 11, 1949.

2. **Putnam, Leone, personal notes, Heitbrink Collection, Harness Racing Museum and Hall of Fame, Goshen, New York.** Stall has multiple means of escape.

END NOTES

3. **Ibid.** Description of lounge.

4. **Putnam, Leone,** *Dooley and the Grey Ghost* **(see note 1), 111.** Greyhound was the only horse with an apartment attached to his barn instead of the other way around.

5. **Flora, Earl, "The Unruffled Snow,"** *Hoof Beats*, **April 1965, 20.** "He would never roll on the ground, with just one exception," Dooley related. "He dearly loved snow and would go wild when turned loose on a day like this. He'd romp and roll until you wondered where he was getting the strength to get up."

6. **Putnam, Leone,** *Dooley and the Grey Ghost* **(see note 1), 121.** July 1, 1954 at Sportsman's Park.

7. **Stanley Bergstein to Vernor "Dooley" Putnam, letter, July 2, 1954, Heitbrink Collection, Harness Racing Museum and Hall of Fame, Goshen, New York.**

8. **Putnam, Leone,** *Dooley and the Grey Ghost* **(see note 1), 121.** Greyhound's final appearance in harness was at the Illinois State Fair, 1954.

9. **Putnam, Leone, personal notes (see note 2).** Greyhound's final time hooked to a cart was 1956.

10. **Putnam, Leone,** *Dooley and the Grey Ghost* **(see note 1), 121.** Greyhound was provided for in Baker's will.

11. **Ibid., 110.** "I'll never have to worry …"

12. **Putnam, Leone, personal notes (see note 2).** 1958, Baker's last visit with Greyhound.

13. **"Colonel Baker Mourned by Trotting Sport,"** *Hoof Beats*, **March 1959.** Reprint of Lawlis quote: "Churches, city hall, and municipal …"

14. **Beckwith, B. K,** *Step and Go Together: The World of Horses and Horsemanship* **(New York: A. S. Barnes and Company, 1967), 147.** A young man from Holland told Leone he came to see the Statue of Liberty, the Grand Canyon, and Greyhound.

15. **Charlo Maurer, letter, 1965, Heitbrink Collection, Harness Racing Museum and Hall of Fame, Goshen, New York.**

16. **Putnam, Leone,** *Dooley and the Grey Ghost* **(see note 1), 118.** Greyhound wipes his nose on the glass.

17. **Putnam, Leone, personal notes (see note 2).** The "vacuum game."

18. **Putnam, Leone,** *Dooley and the Grey Ghost* **(see note 1), 128.** Final appearances.

19. **Ibid.** "… like he can see right through me."

20. **Mrs. C M Bonner, letter, 1964, Heitbrink Collection, Harness Racing Museum and Hall of Fame, Goshen, New York.**

21. **Marianne Weyker, letter, 1964, Heitbrink Collection, Harness Racing Museum and Hall of Fame, Goshen, New York.**

22. **Art Morris, letter, 1964, Heitbrink Collection, Harness Racing Museum and Hall of Fame, Goshen, New York.**

23. **Kathy Fletcher, undated letter, Heitbrink Collection, Harness Racing Museum and Hall of Fame, Goshen, New York.**

EPILOGUE

Image: Greyhound says hello to a puppy, somewhere during his travels in retirement (circa late 1940s, courtesy of the Hambletonian Society).

Epigraph: Wall, Maryjean, "Greyhound Greatest Hero," *Lexington Herald*, June 13, 1975, 85. "If there is anything …"

1. **Putnam, Leone,** *Dooley and the Grey Ghost* **(Goshen, NY: Harness Racing Museum and Hall of Fame, 2018).**

2. **Ibid.** Dr. Foley came, Greyhound clamoring for attention.

3. **Ibid.** Description of the night, heard a nicker.

4. **Reinert, Judy, "Hambletonian Winner was Colonel Baker's Baby,"** *Kane County Chronicle* **(Geneva, Illinois), August 5, 1998, C1, 5.** Busloads to visit his grave, and press from all over, even Europe.

5. **"S. F. Palin Dies,"** *Hoof Beats*, **November 1952, 8-9.**

6. **Wall, Maryjean, "The Gray Ghost Remembered,"** *Lexington Herald*, **January 29, 1975, 16.** "I remember him …"

7. **Don Daniels to Mary Lou Dondarski, email, May 22, 2010, Dondarski Collection, Harness Racing Museum, Goshen, NY.**

8. **"James K. Wingfield (obituary),"** *Horseman and Fair World*, **June 10, 1987.**

9. **Blount, Rachel, "Harness Horseman Wingfield Dies,"** *Atlanta Journal*, **June 10, 1987, 63.** Sanders quote: "He was a gentleman's gentleman …"

10. **"Henry Knight Succumbs After a Two-Week Illness,"** *Lexington Herald-Leader*, **March 8, 1959, 1.**

11. **Phelps, Frank Talmadge, "Man Has Plans, Will Travel On,"** *Lexington Herald*, **January 11, 1959, 103.**

12. **Ibid.**

13. **Ibid.**

14. **"Henry Knight Succumbs …" (see note 10).**

15. **Lucander, Karel Bond,** *Riding on the Edge: Frances Dodge and Dodge Stables*, **(Rochester, MI: Meadow Brook Press, 2017).**

16. **Ibid.**

17. **"Dellora A. Norris," biography,** www.norrisculturalarts.com

18. **Guyer, Kathy, "Crown Jewel Adorned,"** *Kane County Chronicle* **(Geneva, Illinois), November 22, 1997, 1, 6.**

19. **"History of a Great Horse Preserved,"** *Chronicle* **(Goshen, New York), May 23, 2014, 30.**

20. **Ibid.**

BIBLIOGRAPHY

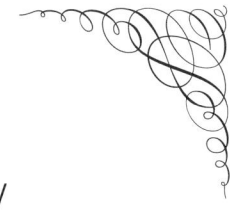

A

Aiken Standard (SC). "Greyhound Returns to Pass Winter in Aiken." January 3, 1941.

Akers, Dwight. *Drivers Up*. New York: G. P. Putnam's Sons, 1938.

Amadeo, Kimberly. "Great Depression Pictures." Thought Co. Accessed April 2, 2024. https://www.thoughtco.com/photos-of-the-great-depression-4061803.

American Horse Breeder. "Grand Circuit at Rockingham." August 8, 1934.

American Horse Breeder. "Illinois State Fair Racing." August 29, 1934.

Anderson Herald (IN). "Greyhound Will Try for Record at Daytona Beach." March 17, 1939.

Arbuckle, W. J. "Greyhound's Day at Baker's Acres." *Harness Horse*, October 27, 1943.

Arbuckle, Woodruff. "Speed Barrage Features Springfield Grand Circuit Meet." *Horseman and Fair World*. August 28, 1935.

Associated Press. "$3750 for Guy Abbey Colt Top Price at Sale." *Boston Globe*, September 24, 1934.

Associated Press. "Eight Hambletonian Candidates to Race at Rockingham Today." *Burlington Daily News* (Vermont), August 3, 1935.

Associated Press. "Feature Event is Won By Silver King." *Star Press* (Indianapolis, Indiana), July 24, 1934.

Associated Press. "Famed Horseman Palin Dies at 74; Drove at Kite Track." *Portland Press Herald* (Maine), October 4, 1952.

Associated Press. "Four Top Harness Racing." *Herald and Review* (Decatur, Illinois), December 26, 1939.

Associated Press. "Greyhound Loses Despite Fastest Heat." *Star-Gazette*, July 23, 1936.

Associated Press. "Greyhound Loses First Heat this Year." *St. Louis Post-Dispatch*, August 26, 1940.

Associated Press. "Greyhound-Muscletone Race Postponed." *Indianapolis News*, September 11, 1937.

Associated Press. "Greyhound, Rosalind Seek New Track Mark." *La Crosse Tribune* (WI), September 3, 1939.

Associated Press. "Greyhound Sets Fast Time at Syracuse Track." *Richmond Item*, September 1, 1934.

Associated Press. "Greyhound Trots his Last Race – This Year." *Chippewa Herald-Telegram* (Chippewa Falls, WI), August 27, 1940.

Associated Press. "Greyhound Wins Grand Circuit Feature Event." *Richmond Item*, August 15, 1934.

Associated Press. "Springfield is Possible Site of Trot Race." *Decatur Daily Review*, August 23, 1937.

Associated Press. "Two Horses Break Mark at Syracuse." *Democrat and Chronicle* (Rochester, NY), September 1, 1939.

Associated Press. "Union of Harness Racing Bodies Appears Certain." *Wilmington News-Journal*, December 19, 1938.

Aston, Joe. By Joe Aston (column). *Cincinnati Post* (Ohio), October 3, 1945.

Athol Daily News (MA). "Greyhound, Famed Trotter Faces Biggest Test Friday." August 2, 1938.

Athol Daily News (MA). Sports Chatter (column). August 2, 1938.

Atlanta Journal. "Harness Horseman Wingfield Dies." June 10, 1987.

Auerbach, Ann Hagedorn. *"Wild Ride: the rise and fall of Calumet Farm, Inc."* Holt McDougal, December 1995.

B

Baldwin, Ralph N, "Training the Two-Year-Old," in *Care and Training of the Trotter and Pacer*, ed. James C. Harrison (Columbus, Ohio: The United States Trotting Association, 1968), 156-62.

Bangor Daily News (ME). "Greyhound Sets New Mark at Old Orchard." July 31, 1936.

Bangor Daily News (ME). "Greyhound Wins at Narragansett." July 30, 1940.

Bangor Daily News (ME). "Trio of Horses Lower Mark at Old Orchard." August 1, 1936.

Baxter Bulletin (Mountain Home, AR). "Verner L. Putnam (obituary)." November 29, 1979.

Becker, Bob. "Plan Dredging Clean-Up for Fox River Bed." *Chicago Tribune*, April 7, 1934.

Beckwith, B. K. *Step and Go Together: The World of Horses and Horsemanship*. New York: A. S. Barnes and Company, 1967.

Belleville News-Democrat (IL). "Gates Fortune for Cure." March 5, 1913.

Biddeford-Saco Journal (ME). "Greyhound Thrills Crowd at Kite Track." July 31, 1936.

Blount, Rachel. "Harness Horseman Wingfield Dies." *Atlanta Journal*, June 10, 1987.

BIBLIOGRAPHY

Bogart, Walt. "Training a Great Race Horse." Scrapbook 4, Mary Lou Dondarski Collection, Harness Racing Museum, Goshen, New York.

Bostwick, Mary E. "Greyhound Enquires 'How'm I doin?'" *Indianapolis Star*, September 15, 1937.

Bower, Alex. "Can These Youngsters Follow In His Footsteps?" *Lexington Leader*, May 10, 1940.

Bower, Alex. The Side Show (column). *Lexington Herald-Leader*, July 20, 1940.

Boxell, Paul. "Trot King Thrills Record Throng in 2-heat Victory." *Indianapolis Times*, September 5, 1935.

Bradburn, John. *Breeding and Developing the Trotter*. Boston: American Horse Breeder Publishing Company, 1906.

Braucher, Bill. "Start Grand Circuit Cavalcade at Lexington June 15." *Times* (Hammond, IN), June 13, 1935.

Breitz, Eddie. "Greyhound not Lame." *Des Moines Tribune*, June 16, 1941.

Breitz, Eddie. "Trotter Greyhound Declared Lame and Through as Racer." *Evening Star* (Washington, DC), June 13, 1941.

Buffalo News (NY). "Auctioneer Takes $1000 Pace Purse." August 11, 1934.

Buffalo Review (NY). "Scott Hudson Drove Four Winning Races." July 26, 1902.

Bulletin (Bend, OR). "Heat Wave Toll Over 12,000 in 86 in Week." July 25, 1936.

Burgess, Dale. "Baker Sells all his Harness Horses but One—Greyhound." *Palladium-Item* (Richmond, IN), December 13, 1940.

──────── C ────────

Calkins, Ada C. "The Baker Hotel to Open Saturday." *True Republican* (Sycamore, IL), May 30, 1928.

Call-Leader (Elwood, IN). "Harness Racing Rules Changed." December 15, 1937.

Cameron, Stuart. "Greyhound is Standout of Decade in Trotting." *Times Union* (Brooklyn, NY), August 15, 1935.

Cameron, Stuart. "Hail Greyhound Greatest Trotter of Standard-bred." *Pomona Progress Bulletin* (CA), August 15, 1935.

Case, Dick. "Memories of Men and Magical Miles." *Hoof Beats*, May 1984.

"Castleton Farm: A Rich and Storied History." Informational pamphlet.

Central New Jersey Home News. "'Doc' Parshall Grooming Hopeful for Hambletonian." June 20, 1935.

Chapman, Ralph. "Greyhound Still Favorite to Win $40,000 Hambletonian." *Record* (Hackensack, New Jersey), August 13, 1935.

Chicago Daily News. "News Views." Pictorial Section, October 30, 1943.

Chicago Tribune. "E.J. Baker herd brings $35,000 at auction sale." December 1, 1932.

Chicago Tribune. "Gates' Millions to Widow and Son; Gifts to Friends." August 31, 1911.

Chicago Tribune. "Harness Racer Joins Throng." January 17, 1926.

Chicago Tribune. "Mrs. E. J. Baker of St. Charles is Dead at 73." July 2, 1940.

Chicago Tribune. "Thousands at Baker Funeral." May 4, 1914.

Chicago Tribune. "Trotters' Sale Prices Mount in Record Year." October 10, 1933.

Cincinnati Enquirer. "Greyhound-Muscletone Special is August 10, Day Before Hambletonian at Goshen Oval." July 18, 1937.

Cincinnati Enquirer. "Greyhound Ties World Mark of Peter Manning Set in '22." September 23, 1937.

Cincinnati Enquirer. "Half-Miler Takes Pacing Stakes." September 11, 1941.

Cincinnati Enquirer. "Horse Sales End." September 30, 1938.

Cincinnati Enquirer. "Race Summaries: Second Race-Syracuse Hotel Stake and Fourth Race-Horseman Futurity." September 6, 1934.

Cincinnati Post. "Parshall Suspended by Trots Official." June 21, 1940.

Clark, Al. The Sports Shop (column). *Harrisburg Telegraph*, August 10, 1937.

Clark, Al. The Sports Shop (column). *Harrisburg Telegraph*, August 11, 1937.

Clark, John H. "Match Races Between Greyhound and Muscletone in Prospect." *Lexington Herald-Leader*, May 14, 1937.

Clark, Johnny. "Lawrence Hanover Wins Stake at Rockingham Park." *Lexington Herald-Leader*, August 4, 1935.

Cleveland, Howard L. "Greyhound Pays No Heed to Noise of Racetracks ..." *Lexington Herald*, October 1, 1936.

Cohen, Lou E. Sports Chats (column). *Brooklyn Eagle* (NY), August 14, 1935.

Colby, Lester B. "St. Charles—the 'Fairy City.'" *True Republican* (Sycamore, IL), July 21, 1926.

Collyer's Eye and the Baseball World. Harness Notes (column). November 29, 1941.

Courier-Journal (Louisville, KY). "Top Horses Lined Up for Fair Races." September 5, 1940.

Cronin, Ned. Untitled sports column. *Daily News* (Los Angeles), April 2, 1947.

──────── D ────────

Daily Chronicle (DeKalb, IL). "Greyhound is Rescued from Farm Blaze." February 20, 1942.

Daily Chronicle (DeKalb, IL). "R.C. Doc Flanery (obituary)." November 2, 1974.

Dancer, Stanley, "Training and Conditioning," in *Care and Training of the Trotter and Pacer*, ed. James C. Harrison (Columbus, Ohio: The United States Trotting Association, 1968), 191.

Danforth, Ed. "Scott Hudson and His Famous Blind Trotter." *Atlanta Journal*, December 2, 1962.

Daughtry, Leo. Interview clipping. Scrapbook 3, Mary Lou Dondarski Collection, Harness Racing Museum, Goshen, New York.

BIBLIOGRAPHY

Daughtry, Leo. "Silver Streak Munches Oats with New Relish After Trotting to Added Glory." Scrapbook 3, Mary Lou Dondarski Collection, Harness Racing Museum, Goshen, New York.

Dayton Daily News (OH). "Driving Park at Columbus to be Razed." December 29, 1925.

Dayton Daily News (OH). "Silver King Beats Belvedere in Rainy Day Sweepstakes." July 3, 1934.

Decatur Daily Review (IL). "Greyhound is First in Circuit Race at Fair." August 16, 1938.

Des Moines Register (IA). "Leone Putnam (obituary)." December 28, 1995.

Dickerson, C. G. "Trots Regain Prestige." *Lexington Herald-Leader*, January 12, 1941.

Dispatch (Moline, IL). "Amateur and Professional Champions of 1935." December 31, 1935.

Dixon Evening Telegraph (IL). "Illinois Girl is National 4-H Champion." February 23, 1932.

Dixon, Simon. "Horse Racing in Nineteenth-Century Russia," University College London. Accessed April 2, 2024. https://discovery.ucl.ac.uk/id/eprint/10110997/3/Dixon_SEER%20SUBMITTED%20VERSION%20Horse-Racing%20in%20Nineteenth-Century%20Russia.pdf.

Drysdale, R. A. "Greyhound is 1st in Fair's Feature Race." *Decatur Daily Review* (Illinois), August 21, 1937.

Duffy, L.G. "Lexington Notes." *Horseman and Fair World*, October 2, 1935.

Dunn, Neville. "Greyhound May try for Record Under Saddle." *Lexington Herald*, September 17, 1940.

E

Edinburgh Daily Courier (IN). "Johnson County Reinsman Attracts Attention of Grand Circuit Stable Owner." June 19, 1931.

Evening Sun (Hanover, PA). "Lawrence Hanover is Showing Speed." June 4, 1934.

Evening Sun (Hanover, PA). "Lawrence Hanover Is Sold to Chicagoan for $6800." November 29, 1933.

Evening Sun (Hanover, PA). Sports in the Sun (column). October 2, 1935.

Evening Sun (Hanover, PA). Sports in the Sun (column). September 30, 1935.

Evening Sun (Hanover, PA). "Star's Pride Sets World Race Record of 1:57 ⅕." August 30, 1952.

Evening Sun (Hanover, PA). "Summary: Good Time Consolation Two-Year-Old Trot." August 18, 1934.

Evening Sun (Hanover, PA). "Trotter Takes Race in Two Heat Victory Over Field of Stars." July 26, 1940.

Evening Sun (Hanover, PA). "Trotters and Pacers." October 4, 1952.

F

Fennell, Abe. "2500 People See Aiken Racing Meet." *The State* (Columbia, South Carolina), March 24, 1940.

Finney, Jack, in correspondence with the author, December 7, 2023.

Flora, Earl. "The Unruffled Snow." *Hoof Beats*, April 1965.

Fox Jr., W. F. "Greyhound, Pride of Palin, Displays much Horse Sense in Crowds, but has Fun at Home." *Indianapolis News*, September 5, 1935.

Fox Jr., W. F. "Greyhound, a Horse That's Fit for a Name That Fits." *Indianapolis News*, September 6, 1938.

"Franklin Delano Roosevelt Event Timeline." The American Presidency Project, University of California Santa Barbara. Accessed April 18, 2024. https://www.presidency.ucsb.edu/documents/franklin-delano-roosevelt-event-timeline.

G

Gage, Fred. "Trotters Getting Riders Up." *Sun-Journal* (Lewiston, Maine), August 4, 1995.

Gahagan, George M. "Annual Speed Sale Starts Today." *Indianapolis Star*, November 13, 1934.

Gahagan, George M. "Baker's Return to Harness Racing is Welcomed." *Indianapolis Star*, October 15, 1933.

Gahagan, George M. "Belgian Horseman buys Volo Dear; Selka Worthy Purchased by Italian." *Indianapolis Star*, November 8, 1933.

Gahagan, George M. "Deal for Star Pacer Closed." *Indianapolis Star*, June 4, 1934.

Gahagan, George M. "Famous Hoosier Trotting Sire Acquired by Illinois Horseman at Local Sale." *Indianapolis Star*, November 13, 1931.

Gahagan, George M. "Greyhound and Rosalind Break World's Record at State Fair." *Indianapolis Star*, September 6, 1939.

Gahagan, George M. "Greyhound Scores Straight-Heat Victory." *Indianapolis Star*, June 23, 1940.

Gahagan, George M. "Harness Horses in Fire Affected by Smoke and Exposure." *Indianapolis Star*, October 26, 1934.

Gahagan, George M. Hoof Beats (column). *Indianapolis Star*, April 30, 1932.

Gahagan, George M. Hoof Beats (column). *Indianapolis Star*, December 16, 1933.

Gahagan, George M. Hoof Beats (column). *Indianapolis Star*, January 19, 1935.

Gahagan, George M. Hoof Beats (column). *Indianapolis Star*, July 18, 1934.

Gahagan, George M. Hoof Beats (column). *Indianapolis Star*, June 30, 1935.

Gahagan, George M. Hoof Beats (column). *Indianapolis Star*, June 7, 1934.

Gahagan, George M. Hoof Beats (column). *Indianapolis Star*, May 25, 1935.

Gahagan, George M. Hoof Beats (column). *Indianapolis Star*, May 5, 1934.

Gahagan, George M. Hoof Beats (column). *Indianapolis Star*, November 19, 1932.

BIBLIOGRAPHY

Gahagan, George M. Hoof Beats (column). *Indianapolis Star*, September 22, 1934.

Gahagan, George M. "Horses in Training at State Fairgrounds Display Speed." *Indianapolis Star*, May 10, 1934..

Gahagan, George M. "Local Speed Sale Highly Successful." *The Indianapolis Star*, November 18, 1934.

Gahagan, George M. "Palin Horses Off for Trots." *Indianapolis Star*, September 16, 1935.

Gahagan, George M. "State Fair Racing is Decided Success." *Indianapolis Star*, September 8, 1935.

Gahagan, Tom. "Abbedale is Sold for $6000." *Indianapolis Star*, May 30, 1930.

Gahagan, Tom. "Agawam Opens Two-Week Meeting." *Horseman and Fair World*, August 3, 1938.

Gahagan, Tom. "Between Showers at Lexington." *Horseman and Fair World*, June 26, 1935.

Gahagan, Tom. "Canadians Hosts to Grand Circuit at Toronto." *Horseman and Fair World*, July 24, 1935.

Gahagan, Tom. "Chances Slim of Greyhound Meeting Rosalind This Year." *Cincinnati Enquirer*, March 5, 1939.

Gahagan, Tom. "E. J. Baker Back in Trot Game." *Cincinnati Enquirer*, November 2, 1941.

Gahagan, Tom. "E J Baker Getting Out of Racing, into Breeding of Harness Horses." *Collyer's Eye and the Baseball World*, November 21, 1931.

Gahagan, Tom. "Favorites Go Down at Toledo." *Horseman Fair and World*, July 18, 1934.

Gahagan, Tom. "Former Frances Dodge, Auto Heiress, Pays Top Price for Yearling Trotter." *Collyer's Eye and the Baseball World*, November 23, 1940.

Gahagan, Tom. "Goshen's Grand Circuit Meeting." *Horseman and Fair World*, August 21, 1935.

Gahagan, Tom. "Grand Circuit at Good Time Park." *Horseman and Fair World*, August 19, 1936.

Gahagan, Tom. "Grand Circuit Closes at Lexington." *Horseman and Fair World*, October 10, 1934.

Gahagan, Tom. "Grand Circuit Racing Resumed at Goshen." *Horseman and Fair World*, July 29, 1936.

Gahagan, Tom. "Great Meeting Closes at Rockingham Park." *Horseman and Fair World*, August 14, 1935.

Gahagan, Tom. "Great Speed Festival at New York State Fair. *Horseman and Fair World*, September 4, 1935.

Gahagan, Tom. "Greyhound and Rosalind may do Little Racing this Year." *Cincinnati Enquirer*, April 4, 1937.

Gahagan, Tom. "Greyhound to Finish Campaign in Futurity at Lexington." *Cincinnati Enquirer*, September 1, 1935.

Gahagan, Tom. "Greyhound's Name on Eligible List for Six Events." *Cincinnati Enquirer*, April 7, 1940.

Gahagan, Tom. "Hard Driving of Two-Year-Old Harness Horses is Breaking them Down." *Cincinnati Enquirer*, September 30, 1934.

Gahagan, Tom. "Horseman Futurities Feature Indiana State Fair." *Horseman and Fair World*, September 11, 1935.

Gahagan, Tom. "Leading Trotting Stables on Way to Lexington." *Lexington Herald-Leader* (Kentucky), September 9, 1934.

Gahagan, Tom. "New Canadian Record at Toronto." *Horseman and Fair World*, August 1, 1934.

Gahagan, Tom. "New Records at North Randall." *Horseman and Fair World*, July 13, 1938.

Gahagan, Tom. "Ohio Colt Silver King is Winner at Rockingham Park." *Cincinnati Enquirer*, August 4, 1934.

Gahagan, Tom. "Old Orchard Closes Great Meeting." *Horseman and Fair World*, August 2, 1939.

Gahagan, Tom. "Second Week at Agawam." *Horseman and Fair World*, August 10, 1938.

Gahagan, Tom. "Shirley Hanover Scores Upset in Hambletonian." *Horseman and Fair World*, August 18, 1937.

Gahagan, Tom. "The Grand Circuit at Goshen's Historic Track." *Horseman and Fair World*, July 21, 1937.

Gahagan, Tom. "The Syracuse Grand Circuit Meeting." *Horseman and Fair World*, September 16, 1936.

Gahagan, Tom."Tom Gahagan Writes of His Visit to Hanover Shoe Farm." *Evening Sun* (Hanover, PA), November 22, 1933.

Gahagan, Tom. "Trot Record Made." *Cincinnati Enquirer*, September 28, 1940.

Gahagan, Tom. "Trots Close at Good Time Park." *Cincinnati Enquirer*, August 17, 1935.

Gahagan, Tom. "Two-Year-Old Harness Race Title Likely to be Decided at Lexington." *Collyer's Eye and the Baseball World*, September 29, 1934.

Gahagan, Tom. "World Marks Lowered at Lexington." *Horseman and Fair World*, October 6, 1937.

Gahagan, Will. Among the Equine Aristocrats (column), *Indianapolis Star*, June 19, 1927.

Gahagan, Will. Among the Equine Aristocrats (column). *Indianapolis Star*, September 11, 1921.

Gahagan, Will. Horse Sense (column), *Indianapolis Star*, June 20, 1915.

Gahagan, Will. "Horse Sense: Palin Making Good." *Indianapolis Star*, November 22, 1914.

Gahagan, Will. In the Harness World (column). *Indianapolis Star*, December 20, 1925.

Gallagher, Gena. Personal conversations. June 2023

"Germany 1933 from Democracy to Dictatorship." Go In-depth. Anne Frank House. Accessed April 18, 2024. https://www.annefrank.org/en/anne-frank/go-in-depth/germany-1933-democracy-dictatorship/

Gill, Wesley. "Greyhound Wins Race After Losing Heat for First Time in Four Years." *Middletown Times Herald* (New York), August 27, 1940.

Gocher, W. H. Gossip of Light Harness Horses (column), *Lexington Herald-Leader*, June 24, 1921.

BIBLIOGRAPHY

Gocher, W. H. "Murphy Again Leads Drivers On Grand Circuit," *Brooklyn Daily Eagle*, October 19, 1924.

Goodwin, Austin. Scanning Sports (column). *Evening Express* (Portland, Maine), July 31, 1939.

Gould, Alan. Sport Slants (column), *Harrisburg Telegraph* (Pennsylvania), August 20, 1935.

Graham, Frank. "Setting the Pace." Scrapbook 4, Mary Lou Dondarski Collection, Harness Racing Museum, Goshen, New York.

Grayson, Harry (NEA Service). "Tabacco-Chewing Trotter was a 'Gift.'" *Cincinnati Post* (Ohio), August 10, 1938.

Greyhound to Dick Case, c/o *Hoof Beats*. Letter. August 20, 1939.

Griffin, Gerald. "Greyhound's Brother Has Trotting Days Ahead." *Courier-Journal* (Louisville, Kentucky), June 24, 1939.

H

Hailey, Foster. "Hurricane In Harness!" *New York Times Magazine*, July 2, 1939. Mary Lou Dondarski Collection, Harness Racing Museum.

Hampson, Gene F. Thru Sportsland. *Courier-News* (Bridgewater, New Jersey), July 9, 1935.

Harnessdom. "1935 Springfield State Fair Greyhound Sep Palin World Record." YouTube video, 2:47. July 24, 2017. https://www.youtube.com/watch?v=g9NwJb5BMfo

Harness Horse. August 19, 1936.

Harness Horse. "Agawam, Mass.—August 5." August 10, 1938.

Harness Horse. "Agawam, Mass.—July 29." August 3, 1938.

Harness Horse. "E. J. Baker's Two-Minute Horses." December 16, 1936.

Harness Horse. "Good Time Park Mile Track, Goshen, N. Y.—August 9." August 17, 1938.

Harness Horse. "Greyhound 1:55 ¼ The Incomparable." December 13, 1939.

Harness Horse. "Greyhound 1:56." December 15, 1937.

Harness Horse. "Greyhound 3, 2:00." December 18, 1935.

Harness Horse. "Lexington, Kentucky—June 23." July 1, 1936.

Harness Horse. "Lexington, Kentucky—October 1." October 7, 1936.

Harness Horse. "Lexington—September 27." October 2, 1940.

Harness Horse. "Lexington—September 29." October 6, 1937.

Harness Horse. "Louisville—September 11." September 18, 1940.

Harness Horse. "North Randall Meeting." July 13, 1938.

Harness Horse. "Old Orchard, Me.—July 27." August 2, 1939.

Harness Horse. "Pawtucket, R.I." August 7, 1940.

Harness Horse. "Springfield, Illinois—August 23." August 28, 1940.

Harness Horse. "Syracuse, New York." September 4, 1940.

Harness Horse. "Syracuse, New York (State Fair Grounds Mile Track)." September 7, 1938.

Harness Horse. "Toledo, Ohio Grand Circuit." July 17, 1940.

Harness Racing Museum tour guide, tour presentation at Harness Racing Museum, Goshen, NY, August 7, 2023.

Harnessbred.com. "Racetracks Of The World – North America: United States Of America (Maine – Part Two : Closed Tracks)." Harnessbred—Driving the Future of Harness Racing, September 6, 2022. https://harnessbred.com/racetracks-world-north-america-united-states-america-maine-part-two-closed-tracks/.

Harriman, E. Roland. *I Reminisce*. Garden City, NY: Doubleday & Company, 1975.

Harrison, Jim. "King of Trotters is Gone." *Hoof Beats*, March 1965.

Hartford Courant (CT). "Greyhound Doesn't Like 'Terbaccer'." July 27, 1938.

Hartford Courant (CT). Harness Notes (column). July 13, 1941.

Hebert, Bob. "Longshots Score at Hollywood Park." *Daily News* (Los Angeles), April 10, 1947.

Henry, Marguerite. *Born to Trot*. New York: Rand McNally & Company, 1950.

Hervey, John. "About Greyhound." *Horse and Horseman*, December 1936.

Hervey, John. *The American Trotter*. New York: Coward-McCann, Inc, 1947.

Hervey, John. "Comment of the Week." *Harness Horse*, October 6, 1937.

Hervey, John. "Comparing Three Champions." *Harness Horse*, December 16, 1936.

Hervey, John. "Fortieth Anniversary," *Harness Horse*, September 1, 1943.

Hervey, John. "Greater Greyhound." *Harness Horse*, September 13, 1939.

Hervey, John. "Greyhound and Other Geldings." 1935.

Hervey, John. "Greyhound's Mile Marks an Epoch." *Harness Horse*, July 21, 1937.

Hervey, John. "Greyhound's Quarter in 26 ⚑." *Harness Horse*, July 13, 1938.

Hervey, John. "Guy Abbey, Greyhound, and Calumet Evelyn." *Hoof Beats*, November 1935.

Hervey, John. "New World's Champions." *Hoof Beats*, December 1937.

Hervey, John. "Out of the Mail Bag." *Harness Horse*, October 27, 1937.

Hervey, John. "A Pair of Shoes." *Harness Horse*, December 14, 1938.

Hervey, John. "The Story of Greyhound." *Horse and Horseman*, February 1939.

Hervey, John. "A Team Mile in 1:59." *Harness Horse*, September 6, 1939.

Hervey, John [Salvatore, pseud.]. "A Unique Compliment." *Harness Horse*, December 22, 1937.

Hinrichs, Art. "Shoeing the Champion." *Hoof Beats*, January 1940.

History.com. "Adolf Hitler." October 29, 2009. Accessed April 24, 2024. https://www.history.com/topics/world-war-ii/adolf-hitler-1

Hoffman, Dean, in discussion with the author, September 29, 2023.

Hoof Beats. "Almahurst Stable." Christmas 1933.

Hoof Beats. "Colonel Baker Mourned by Trotting Sport." March 1959.

Hoof Beats. "The Hotel Baker Stables." January 1937.

Hoof Beats. "Lexington—September 29." October 5, 1938.

Hoof Beats. "Official Roster of 2:05 Trotters & Pacers." April 1938.

Hoof Beats. "S. F. Palin Dies." November 1952.

Hoof Beats. "Seen at Syracuse." October 29, 1939.

Horse and Horseman. "Horses of the Month." August 1937.

Horseman and Fair World. "Around and About Almahurst." June 26, 1935.

Horseman and Fair World. "E. Roland Harriman Dies at his Arden Home." February 22, 1978.

Horseman and Fair World. "Guy Abbey's Book Closed." November 13, 1935.

Horseman and Fair World. "James K. Wingfield." June 10, 1987.

Horseman and Fair World. Kentucky Futurity Nomination Fees announcement. March 16, 1932.

"Housing 1929-1941." "Historic Events for Students: The Great Depression." Encyclopedia.com. Accessed March 18, 2024. https://www.encyclopedia.com/education/news-and-education-magazines/housing-1929-1941

Hoyt, John C. "Drought of 1936." United States Department of the Interior, 1938. Accessed April 2, 2024. https://pubs.usgs.gov/wsp/0820/report.pdf

Hughes, Ed. "Peter Manning's Owner Lauds Greyhound." Brooklyn Daily Eagle, August 15, 1935.

Hughes, Ed. "The Trotting Classic." Brooklyn Daily Eagle, August 13, 1935.

Huntington Herald (IN). "Was it a Frame-Up?" August 19, 1911.

I

Indianapolis News. "Eyes of the Trotting World Focus on Greyhound's Record Trial Friday." September 9, 1937.

Indianapolis News. "Green Pace Goes Sensational Mile in Local Record Meeting." June 15, 1918.

Indianapolis News. "Greyhound of Indianapolis Stable Now Favorite to Win $40,000 Hambletonian." July 19, 1935.

Indianapolis News. "Greyhound Steals Show with Fifteenth World Record." September 20, 1939.

Indianapolis News. "Hoosier Horseman to Celebrate Many Season's Victories Next Tuesday." November 12, 1921.

Indianapolis News. "Horsemen Swarm at State Fairgrounds for Three-day Auction Sale of 260 Race Horses." November 14, 1932.

Indianapolis News. "Leading Trotter May Train Here." February 27, 1935.

Indianapolis News. "Race Horses Perish in Fairground Fire." October 25, 1934.

Indianapolis News. "Trotting Gossip Heard at State Fair Race Camp." June 9, 1925.

Indianapolis News. "Woman Drives Trotter to Record Mile in 2:01 ¾." August 8, 1936.

Indianapolis Star. "Greyhound Withdrawn." September 24, 1935.

Indianapolis Star. Hoof Beats (column). February 27, 1929.

Indianapolis Star. Hoof Beats (column). October 5, 1932.

Indianapolis Star. "Wind Too Strong for Speed Trial." September 19, 1937.

Indianapolis Times. "Four Horses Die in Blaze." October 25, 1934.

Inter Ocean (Chicago, IL). "Gates Heir Weds Nurse Sweetheart." October 13, 1912.

International News Service (INS). "Greyhound's Brilliance is Proved Again." Lexington Herald-Leader, July 5, 1938.

J

"Jesse Owens: American Hero." American Experience. PBS Learning Media. Accessed April 24, 2024. https://ket.pbslearningmedia.org/resource/ush22-soc-ushowensohio/jesse-owens-american-hero/

Journal and Courier (Lafayette, IN). "Sep Palin, Ace Driver, Is Dead." October 4, 1952.

Journal and Courier (Lafayette, IN). "William W. Marvin Dead; Was Famed as Horse Trainer." May 17, 1941.

K

Keller, Ed. "Still the King—Greyhound, Part 1." Sunday Times (Salisbury, Maryland), August 10, 1969.

Keller, Edwin T. "Almost Hundred Races." Cincinnati Enquirer, February 9, 1930.

Keller, Edwin T. "Highlights at Agawam." Horseman and Fair World, August 3, 1938.

Keller, Edwin T. "Ohio Short Ship at Columbus." Horseman and Fair World, June 13, 1934.

Kennedy, Maurice. "Sep Palin Wins with Greyhound." Noblesville Ledger (Indiana), July 6, 1935.

Kentucky Advocate (Danville, KY). "Dixie Knight Killed as He Begs for Life." August 2, 1934.

Kraft, Nicole. 100 Years in Harness. Ohio: United States Trotting Association, 2008.

L

Leach, Brownie. Down in Front (column). Lexington Herald-Leader, September 11, 1935.

Leach, Brownie. "Sep Palin's 'Find.'" Down in Front, Lexington Herald-Leader, September 15, 1935.

Leach, Brownie. Down in Front (column). Lexington Herald-Leader, September 19, 1935.

BIBLIOGRAPHY

Lewis, Gary. "The Grey Ghost of Jimmy's Past." *Hoof Beats*, December 1986.

Lewiston Daily Sun. "Greyhound Breaks Mile and A Half World's Record." September 15, 1937.

Lexington Herald. "All Feminine Fans Admitted for Free; Flashy Greyhound Slated to Race." October 3, 1934.

Lexington Herald. "Favorite Wins Rich Futurity." September 25, 1935.

Lexington Herald. "Futurity Candidates are Given Workouts." September 18, 1934.

Lexington Herald. "Futurity for Juveniles Won by Silver King." September 25, 1934.

Lexington Herald. "Greyhound Trots Mile in 1:56 to Equal World's Mark Set Here Last Year." September 24, 1938.

Lexington Herald. Harness Gossip (column). June 24, 1935.

Lexington Herald. "Henry Knight Owns Three Great Stallions." January 18, 1934.

Lexington Herald. "Historic Almahurst Farm Will Be Sold to Settle Knight's Estate." April 9, 1959.

Lexington Herald. "Protector." Trotting Notes (column). October 15, 1934.

Lexington Herald-Leader. "Almahurst Sets Unique Record in Double Role." January 15, 1950.

Lexington Herald-Leader. "Castleton Buys Bret Hanover for $2 Million." August 26, 1966.

Lexington Herald-Leader. "The Champ—To Race No More." October 17, 1941.

Lexington Herald-Leader. "Flannery Home Blazes but Greyhound Safe." February 19, 1942.

Lexington Herald-Leader. "Giant Trotter Lands Victory." September 11, 1940.

Lexington Herald-Leader. "Grey Ghost Beats Record for Trotting." September 30, 1938.

Lexington Herald-Leader. "Henry Knight Succumbs After a Two-Week Illness." March 8, 1959.

Lexington Herald-Leader. "Illness Fatal to Jessamine County Leader." April 9, 1935.

Lexington Herald-Leader. The Jog Cart (column). September 30, 1941.

Lexington Herald-Leader. Trotting Notes (column). November 3, 1940.

Lucander, Karel Bond. *Riding on the Edge: Frances Dodge and Dodge Stables*. Rochester, MI: Meadow Brook Press, 2017.

M

Mack, Gene. "Like Other Champs, Greyhound Is Stickler for Regular Habits." *Boston Globe*, July 29, 1937.

Madden, William J. "Champion Slashes 26-year-old Mark." *Record* (Hackensack, New Jersey), July 17, 1937.

Mason, Mrs. C. P. "Old Orchard, Me.—July 30." *Harness Horse*, August 5, 1936.

McCarr, Ken. "The Immortals: Septer F. Palin and Walter T. Candler." *Hoof Beats*, February 1977.

McCarr, Ken. *The Kentucky Harness Horse*. The University Press of Kentucky, 1978.

McCarr, Ken. "Transportation of Horses: Reminiscence of the Past." *Harness Horse*, December 8, 1971.

McCarr, Ken. "The Trotter of the Century." *Hoof Beats*, September 1971.

McCarthy, Clem. At the Races (column). *Lexington Herald Leader*, October 15, 1937.

McGee, Wilson. "Grey Lucky to Sep Palin Famous Trotting Driver." *Orlando Sentinel* (Florida), January 5, 1936.

Menke, Frank G. Releases from "trotters and pacers" article. Post-1946. Harness Racing Museum Collection.

Menke, Frank G. "Trotters and Pacers." *Evening Sun* (Hanover, Penn.), July 19, 1948.

Michelson, Miles. "Kings Counsel Standardbred," n.d. Accessed April 12, 2024. https://www.allbreedpedigree.com/kings+counsel5

Middletown Times Herald (NY). "Astra Eligible in Two Races." August 10, 1940.

Middletown Times Herald (NY). "Auction Betting." On the Other Hand (column). July 23, 1936.

Middletown Times Herald (NY). "Greyhound Like a Ghost Only He's Something Real." August 13, 1940.

Middletown Times Herald (NY). "Greyhound Vanquishes Rosalind to Capture $3500 Trotting Derby." August 10, 1938.

Middletown Times Herald (NY). "Record Crowd Sees 1st Loss by Greyhound." July 23, 1936.

Middletown Times Herald (NY). "Record First-Day Crowd Cheers Greyhound to Final Victory at Goshen." August 13, 1940.

Moore, Walter. "A Preview of the Hambletonian Stake." *Horseman and Fair World*, August 7, 1935.

Moore, Walter. "Goshen, New York at Historic Half-Mile—July 16." *Harness Horse*, July 21, 1937.

Moore, Walter. "The Good Time Meeting." *Harness Horse*, August 18, 1937.

Moore, Walter. "Views of Rockingham Park." *Horseman and Fair World*, August 14, 1935.

Morning Call (Allentown, PA). "$20,000 Paid for Sire of Trotters." October 5, 1934.

Morning Call (Allentown, PA). "Greyhound Sets New World Mark in Twice Circling Allentown Track." September 26, 1936.

Morning Call (Allentown, PA). "Will Use New Barrier System to Start Fair Races Here." September 6, 1939.

Morning Call (Paterson, NJ). "Trotting and Pacing News from Harness Racing Circles." August 7, 1940.

Moser, P.W. "Illinois State Fair." *Harness Horse*, August 24, 1938.

Moser, P.W. Here and There (column). *Harness Horse*, July 21, 1937.

Moser, P.W. "Springfield, Illinois—August 21." *Harness Horse*, August 26, 1936.

Moser, P.W. *The Story of Greyhound 1:55 ¼*. Harrisburg, PA: Harness Horse, 1940.

Murphy, Merritt. Along the Trotting Trail (column). *Noblesville Ledger* (Indiana), January 24, 1941.

Murphy, Merritt. Along the Trotting Trail (column). *Noblesville Ledger* (Indiana), June 1, 1940.

Murphy, Merritt. Along the Trotting Trail (column), *Noblesville Ledger* (Indiana), October 9, 1940.

Murphy, Merritt. "Greyhound is Retired." *Harness Horse*, October 22, 1941.

Muscatine Journal (IA). "West Liberty Trainer to Race on Grand Circuit This Season." April 21, 1923.

N

Nashville Banner (TN). "Kentucky State Fair Opens Today." September 8, 1941.

Nason, Jerry. "Greyhound-Baker-Palin Best Hambletonian Bet." *Boston Globe*, August 7, 1935.

Nevills, Joe. "Kentucky Farm Time Capsule: Before it Belonged to Kitten's Joy, Almahurst Raised Exterminator." Paulick Report. November 7, 2018. Accessed May 6, 2024. https://paulickreport.com/nl-art-1/kentucky-farm-time-capsule-before-it-belonged-to-kittens-joy-almahurst-raised-exterminator

New York Central System Big Four Time Tables, July 15, 1936. Accessed December 13, 2024. https://www.canadasouthern.com/caso/ptt/images/tt-b4-0736.pdf

New York Central Time Tables, November 16, 1930, Form 1001. Accessed December 13, 2024. https://www.canadasouthern.com/caso/ptt/images/tt-1130.pdf

New York Times. "Fireglow Poisoned, Is Chemist Report." December 25, 1928.

News and Observer (Raleigh, NC). "Greyhound Fails to Break Record." September 7, 1938.

Newsweek. "Greyhound at Goshen." July 25, 1938.

Noblesville Ledger (IN). "Cardinal Prince Paces Heat in 1:59 ½." August 22, 1935.

Noblesville Ledger (IN). "A Fast Mile by Greyhound at Fairgrounds." April 26, 1940.

Noblesville Ledger (IN). "Gray Ghost Defeats Fast Field at The Fairgrounds." June 24, 1940.

Noblesville Ledger (IN). "Greyhound Wins Again." July 22, 1935.

Noblesville Ledger (IN). "Greyhound Wins Last Race but Loses First Heat." August 27, 1940.

Noblesville Ledger (IN). "Only Greyhound Left in the Palin-Baker Stable." December 28, 1940.

Noblesville Ledger (IN). "Palin Horses Win First and Second." September 4, 1935.

Noblesville Ledger (IN). "Trotting King in Search of New Honors." April 17, 1939.

O

Owensboro Messenger (KY). "Harness Horses are Back." September 11, 1940.

P

Parker, Dan. "Greyhound is no Misnomer." *Waterbury Democrat* (Connecticut), August 15, 1935.

Pearson, Ruth Seen. *Reflections of St. Charles*. St. Charles History Museum, 1976, 2019.

Perry County Advocate (Pickneyville, IL). "King's Counsel, Pacing Colt, Sold for $20,000 at Du Quoin State Fair." September 9, 1943.

Phelps, Frank Talmadge. "Man Has Plans, Will Travel On." *Lexington Herald*, January 11, 1959.

Pines, Phil. "Greyhound—The Gray Ghost." *Off Track Magazine*, September 1995.

Pines, Philip A. *The Complete Book of Harness Racing*. New York: Arco Publishing Inc., 1982.

Pittsburgh Post (PA). "Turfmen Expelled by Trotting Board." May 7, 1914.

Putnam, Leone. *Dooley and the Grey Ghost*. Goshen, NY: Harness Racing Museum and Hall of Fame, 2018.

Putnam, Leone. Personal notes. 1965. Heitbrink Collection, Harness Racing Museum and Hall of Fame, Goshen, New York.

R

Rapid City Journal (SD). "Greyhound, Now 17, Loafs; Palin Wins." May 14, 1949.

Reading Times (PA). "Cardinal Prince Sets World Pace Mark Here." September 15, 1936.

Reading Times (PA). "Grand Circuit Opens Today at Fair Grounds." September 14, 1936.

Reading Times (PA). "Race Summaries: The Reading Fair Futurity." September 12, 1934.

Reid, Jack. "Champ 1940 Pacer Being Trained on Trot." *Springfield News-Sun* (Ohio), January 12, 1941.

Reid, Jack. "Dayton Harness Meet to Open Wednesday with 2 Sessions." *Springfield News-Sun* (Ohio), July 1, 1934.

Reid, Jack. "Lawrence Hanover Picked to Win 1935 Hambletonian." *Springfield News-Sun*, October 21, 1934.

Reid, Jack. "Lord Jim and Bertha C. Hanover Are Now Co-Favorites." *Springfield News-Sun* (Ohio), April 29, 1934.

Reid, Jack. "Spectators Favor Overhead Barrier for Racing Starts." *Dayton Daily News* (Ohio), November 12, 1939.

Reinert, Judy, "Hambletonian Winner was Colonel Baker's Baby," *Kane County Chronicle* (Geneva, Illinois), August 5, 1998.

Rice, Grantland. Trotting Gossip. *Indianapolis News*, December 26, 1926.

Riddle, Max. "Greyhound Looms as Hambletonian Choice." *Richmond Item* (Indiana), August 11, 1935.

Rider and Driver. "Fastest Trotter and Pacer to Compete." April 1939.

Bibliography

Robertson, Orlo. "12 Fast Ones to Race Today in Hambletonian," *Burlington Free Press* (Vermont), August 11, 1937.

Robertson, Orlo. "Honors Shared." *Cincinnati Enquirer,* December 10, 1937.

Roosevelt, Franklin D. "Fireside Chat 8." September 9, 1936.

Runyon, Damon. "Upset is Likely in Hambletonian." *Buffalo News* (New York), August 13, 1935.

"Russian Trotter Horses." Oklahoma State University. Accessed April 2, 2024. https://breeds.okstate.edu/horses/russian-trotter-horses.html

Russell, Sanders, "Care of the Horse," in *Care and Training of the Trotter and Pacer*, ed. James C. Harrison (Columbus, Ohio: The United States Trotting Association, 1968), 677-80.

S

Sacramento Bee (CA). "Trotter Greyhound is Going After Manning's Mark." December 26, 1936.

Sanders, Millard. *Two-minute Horses.* Cleveland, OH: Press of the Judson Company, 1922.

Shipman, Evan. "In the Sulky." *The Nevada Morning Telegraph*, August 1935.

Shuff, Jesse. "1940 Good Year for Trotters." *Lexington Herald-Leader*, January 12, 1941.

Shuff, Jesse. Around the Grand Circuit (column), *Lexington Herald*, August 22, 1935.

Shuff, Jesse. Down in the Bluegrass Country (column). *Horseman and Fair World*, June 12, 1935.

Shuff, Jesse. Down in the Bluegrass Country (column). *Horseman and Fair World*, March 8, 1933.

Shuff, Jesse. Down in the Bluegrass Country (column). *Horseman and Fair World*, May 10, 1933.

Shuff, Jesse. Down in the Bluegrass Country (column). *Horseman and Fair World*, October 10, 1934.

Shuff, Jesse. Down in the Bluegrass Country (column). *Horseman and Fair World*, October 25, 1933.

Shuff, Jesse. "Work Notes at the K.T.H.B.A. Track." Down in the Bluegrass Country (column). *Horseman and Fair World*, June 12, 1935.

Shuff, Jesse. "Greyhound, Ella Brewer Win Old Trotting Stakes." *Lexington Herald-Leader*, October 4, 1934.

Shuff, Jesse. "Harness Stars Seek Records." *Lexington Herald*, October 1, 1935.

Shuff, Jesse. "Horses Step Fast in Record Meeting." *Lexington Herald-Leader*, October 7, 1934.

Shuff, Jesse. "Indianapolis Stable Arrives at Local Track." *Lexington Herald-Leader*, June 12, 1935.

Shuff, Jesse. "Lawrence Hanover Equals World Record for 2-yr. Old." *Lexington Herald-Leader*, October 12, 1934.

Shuff, Jesse. News of the Trotters (column), *Lexington Herald*, October 24, 1937.

Shuff, Jesse. "Parade of Greys Set for Today." *Lexington Herald*, September 26, 1940.

Shuff, Jesse. "R. J. Reynolds Buys Tract Adjoining Trotting Oval," *Lexington Herald-Leader*, February 17, 1935.

Shuff, Jesse. Trotting Horse Notes. *Lexington Herald-Leader*, March 6, 1932.

Shuff, Jesse. Trotters and Pacers (column). *Lexington Herald*, October 5, 1946.

Shuff, Jesse. With the Trotters (column). *Lexington Herald-Leader*, April 20, 1933.

Shropshire, Laurence K. Down in Front (column). *Lexington Herald*, June 9, 1940.

Shropshire, Laurence K. Down in Front (column). *Lexington Herald-Leader*, September 30, 1937.

Sidney Daily News (OH). "Does Greyhound Take Off Shoes?" July 10, 1940.

Simpson, Sr., John F, "The Theory of Shoeing and Balancing," in *Care and Training of the Trotter and Pacer*, ed. James C. Harrison (Columbus, OH: United States Trotting Association, 1968), 292-372.

"St. Charles Benefactors—Baker Family," *Peterson-Anderson Family History*, Issue 80 (Nov. 2019). Accessed March 22, 2023. https://static1.squarespace.com/static/563bdb42e4b010211207bf71/t/5f08f37f60bdf331331508fe/1594422176937/FHN_MultiIssue_79to87_FamilyHistory_StC_Benefactors.pdf

St. Charles Chronicle (IL). "Edward J. Baker Passes Away at Age 90." January 21, 1959.

St. Charles Chronicle (IL). "Facts on Union Cemetery May be of Interest." June 23, 1932.

St. Charles Chronicle (IL). "Field Day at Crystal Brook Farm." November 3, 1938.

St. Charles Chronicle (IL). "Men and Women Join in River and Pool Work." June 29, 1933.

St. Charles Chronicle (IL). "Party to Honor Col. Baker and Famous Greyhound." September 29, 1949.

St. Claire, Labert. "Greyhound Coming Fast for Local Driver; Perils Dan Patch's 33-Year-Old Record." *Indianapolis Star*, July 31, 1938.

Stanley F. Bergstein to Vernor "Dooley" Putnam, letter, July 2, 1954. Heitbrink Collection, Harness Racing Museum and Hall of Fame, Goshen, New York.

Star Press (Indianapolis, IN)."Baker's Trotters to Go on Auction Block." November 15, 1925.

Star-Gazette (Elmira, NY). "Eight-year-old Greyhound Wins Race." August 13, 1940.

State (Columbia, SC). "Trotting Greats Thrill Railbirds on Aiken Track." February 10, 1940.

Stoneridge, M. A. *Great Horses of Our Time*. Garden City, NY: Doubleday & Company, Inc, 1972.

Sun-Journal (Lewiston, ME). "Stalls Filled at OO Track." July 12, 1941.

Sweetnam, George H. Untitled poem. *Hoof Beats*, January 1942, 49.

BIBLIOGRAPHY

T

Talbot, Gayle. "Greyhound, Ruler of Trotting World, Having Easy Life." *Muncie Evening Press* (Indiana), February 8, 1939.

Taylor, Ken. "1941 Trot Record at Fair." *Courier-Journal* (Louisville, Kentucky), September 10, 1941.

Taylor, Samuel Walter (editor). The Light Harness Horse (column), *Rider and Driver*, July 1938.

"The Dust Bowl." National Drought Mitigation Center. Accessed September 20, 2023. https://drought.unl.edu/dustbowl/#Drought

Toronto Star (Ontario, Canada). Weather report. July 19, 1935.

Trott, Frank G. "Day Not Right For Greyhound," *Boston Globe*, August 11, 1937.

Trott, Frank G. "Goshen and Lexington, KY, Have Meetings This Week." *Boston Globe*, June 17, 1935.

Trott, Frank G. "Greyhound Wins Easily." *Boston Globe*, July 23, 1940.

Trott, Frank G. "Sturbridge Harness Meet Opens at Cedar Lake Park." *Boston Globe*, June 18, 1934.

Trott, Frank G. "Today Linked Up with Racing: New Rich Futurity Proposed." *Boston Globe*, April 7, 1924.

True Republican (Sycamore, IL). "Fastest Trotter Sold for a Song." July 6, 1938.

U

United Press. "Four Stakes Races Top Harness Meet Card." *Santa Barbara News-Press* (CA), April 15, 1946.

United Press. "Greyhound Sets New Record in 1 ½ Mile." *Leader-Telegram* (Eau Claire, WI), September 15, 1937.

Urbana Daily Citizen (OH). "New Racing Record Set." September 6, 1934.

V

VanGundy, June. "Calling on Greyhound." *Hoof Beats*, January 1942.

Vidette-Messenger of Porter County (IN). "Greyhound to Make Try for Mark at State Fair." September 9, 1937.

W

Wall, Maryjean. "Greyhound Greatest Hero." *Lexington Herald*, June 13, 1975.

Wall, Maryjean. "Greyhound's Legacy Lives on 50 Years after Incredible Meet." *Lexington Herald-Leader*, September 27, 1988.

Wall, Maryjean. "The Gray Ghost Remembered." *Lexington Herald*, January 29, 1975.

Wall, Maryjean. "Trotters with Saddles Not New Experience at the Red Mile." *Lexington Herald*, June 17, 1976.

Wallace, William N. "Joe Williams, 81, Sports Columnist." *New York Times*, February 16, 1972.

WEB. "Champion Colt Trotter, Fireglow, Died as Result of Stake Race Accident." *Philadelphia Inquirer*, August 19, 1928.

White, Tom. "500 Catalogued for Three-Session Tattersalls Sale," *Lexington Herald-Leader*, December 4, 1966.

White, Tom (ed.). *The Red Mile: A Century of Speed 1875-1975; The Tradition Continues 1976-2003*. Lexington, KY: Lexington Trots Breeders Association, 2003.

Williams, Joe. Joe Williams Says (column). *Minneapolis Journal*, June 7, 1937.

Williams, Joe. "Mussolini Goes for Horses, Too; His Trotting Star May Invade America for Match Race." *Birmingham Post* (Alabama), June 14, 1937.

"Williams, Joseph Peter 1889-1972." *Contemporary Authors*. Encyclopedia.com. Accessed March 18, 2024. https://www.encyclopedia.com/arts/educational-magazines/williams-joseph-peter-1889-1972

Wingfield, Neil, in discussion with the author, November 7, 2024.

Wingfield, Neil, text messages to the author, October-December 2024.

Wrensch, Frank A. *Harness Horse Racing*. New York: D. Van Nostrand Co., 1948.

INDEX

Bold numbers followed by **p** reference the numbered photographs in the photo insert.

A

Akers, Dwight, 28–29, 30–31, 32, 34
Alicea (horse), 87
Almahurst Farm, **4p**, 10, 17–18, 257
American Standardbred, 29–35. *See also* Harness racing
American Trotting Association, 122, 122n
American Trotting Register, 122
Angel Child (horse), **28p**, 116–117, 118–120, 124–125, 144, 145
Arbuckle, W. J., 235
Athlone Flaxey Guy (horse), 199–200
Athlone Sally Boy (horse), 74

B

Bagpiper (horse), 195, 196–197, 199–200
Baker, Dellora (sister), 39–41
Baker, Edward John "E. J."
    as ambassador of harness racing, 123, 187
    as animal lover, 86, 179–180
    background, 38–41
    Baker-Palin stable, 42–45, 47, 217. *See also* Cardinal Prince; Greyhound; The Master
    death of, 244
    generosity of, 41–42, 58–59, 123, 244–245
    Greyhound memorabilia, **119p, 136–137p**
    Greyhound purchased by, 24–25, 45
    Greyhound's parties hosted by, **96p**, 186–187, 234–235
    on Greyhound's personality, 236
    Greyhound's race season (1934), 61–62
    Greyhound's race season (1935), **15–16p, 18p, 27p**, 93–94, 98, 109
    Greyhound's race season (1936), **32p**, 115–116, 119
    Greyhound's race season (1937), **40p, 62p**, 140, 141, 144–145, 152–153
    Greyhound's race season (1938), **51p**, 167, 168, 176
    Greyhound's race season (1939), **75p**
    Greyhound's race season (1940), **80p**
    Greyhound's retirement and burial managed by, 4, **101p, 110p, 121–122p**, 227, 228–229, 233–238, 244
    health issues, 206, 217, 237, 243–244
    Hervey's praise for, 157–158
    as honorary colonel, 123
    inheritance, 41
    post-Baker-Palin stable dispersal, **99p**, 221, 236–237
    St. Charles's benefactor, **2–3p, 7–10p, 129p**
Baker, Harriet, **2p**, 40, 41, 217, 258
Baker, Henry Rockwell (son), 40–41, 258
Baker, Lavern (sister), 40

Baker-Palin stable, 42–45, 47, 217. *See also* Cardinal Prince; Greyhound; The Master
Bakers Acres, **99p**, 233–238
Belvedere (horse), 64, 65–66, 70, 72, 73, 74, 75, 87
Bergstein, Stanley, 243
Berry, Tommy, 64, 65, **65p**
Beveridge, Frances, 228
Billy Direct (horse), 176, 182, 191
Bobby Belwin (horse), 84
Bogart, Walt, 181
Bonner, C M, 246
Born to Trot (Henry), 245
Bostwick, Mary E., 150
Bravo (horse), 198, 199–200, 204–205
Brejc, Nancy, 258–259
Brogan (horse), 166
Brown, Bowman A., 142
Burnett, Don, **107p**

C

Cagney, James, **78p**, 200
Caharrus Boy (horse), 63–64
Calumet Dilworthy (horse), 204
Calumet Evelyn (horse), **64p**, 77, 117–118, 119, 122–123, 162, 163, 164–165
Calumet Farm
    Greyhound's birthplace, **3p**, 7–10, 12–13, 18
    harness horse breeding at, 211
    transition to thoroughbred farm, 16–17, 45
Calumet Ferona (horse), 63–64
Calumet Finery (horse), 87
Campbell, Charley, 78, 81–83
Canadian National Trotting Stakes, 65
Candler, Walter, 12
Cane, W. H., **15p**, 95
Cardinal Prince (horse), **27–28p**, 104–105, 107, 118, 121, 123, 150, 186
Carlock, Roscoe, 175
Carlson, Nina, 40
Carr, Ralph, **94p**
Case, Dick, 186
Caton, Will, 97
Chica (horse), 65
Childs, Marvin, 23, 24
Clark, Al, 142
Clever Hanover (horse), 162, 165–166, 197
Cline, Fred, 50, 51
Cooke, Jim, 252, 257

Index

Cooke, Lori, 257
Countess Zabetta (horse), 93
Cox, Walter, 9

D

Daingerfield, Algernon, 5, 158–159
Dale Hanover (horse), 195, 196, 198, 204
Dan O. (horse), 49
Dan Patch (horse), 154, 176, 182
Dean Hanover (horse), 191
Depression era, 15–16, 35, 43–45, 58, 127–129, 234, 253
Dickerson, Will, 110
Djer Kiss (horse), 83
Dooley and the Grey Ghost (unpublished manuscript), 255
Duffy, L.G., 111
"Dust Bowl," 127–128

E

Eastman, Everett, 243–244
Eclipse (horse), 30–31
Ed Lasater (horse), **65p**, 118, 121, 162, 163, 165–166, 167, 195, 196
Egan, Fred, 64, 65, 74–75, 87, 89
Eisenhower, Dwight, 243
Eli Crutch, 96
Elizabeth (horse), **6p**, 7–10, 12, 22, 77, **81p**, 211, 235–236, 257
Erskine, Spec, 103–104, 153
Esta G. (horse), 50
Eugenia Volo (horse), 83
Ewing, Jack, 226

F

Fibber (dog), **70p**, 86, 136n, 187
Fiesta Belle (horse), 49
Finn, Alessandro, 130, 141, 143–145
Fitzpatrick, Harry, 221
Flanery, R. C. "Doc," 4, **91p**, **94–97p**, **107p**, 221, 222, 226–229, 233–234, 236–238, 243, 255–256
Flanery Farm, 4–5, **122–123p**, 238, 241–248, 251–252, 255, 258–259
Flanery Stables, **131p**, 228, 229–231, 233
Flemming, Vic, 163, 210
Fletcher, Kathy, 246–247
Fox, W.F., Jr., 176

G

Gahagan, George M., 44, 61, 75, 84, 85, 87, 109, 189, 195
Gahagan, Tom, 43, 74, 75, 76, 84, 86–87, 106, 108, 117, 221
Gahagan, Will, 48, 51
Galli Curci (horse), 51
Gates, Charles, 40
Gates, Dellora, 39–41
Gates, John Warne, 39–40
Gleason, Irving W., 125
Glidden, Joseph, 39
Gocher, W. H., 50
Goodwin, Austin, 186
Goshen (dog), **70p**, 136, 136n, 154, 187
Gray, as "unlucky" color, 8, 21–22
Great Depression, 15–16, 35, 43–45, 58, 127–129, 234, 253
Grey Fox (horse), **6p**, 22, 211, 218
Greyhound (horse). *See also* Greyhound photos
  Baker's purchase of, 23–25

barn fires, 81–83, 233
birth of, 7–10, 12
daily feeding and work schedule, 169–170
death and burial of, 3–4, 251–252
early life as yearling, 12–13, 21–24
early training, 21–24, 55–58, 158
fan letters, 4–5, 245, 246–248
first defeat since 1934, 117
first win, 70
grooms. *See* Hogan, John; Putnam, Verner "Dooley"; Wilson, Pete; Wingfield, Jimmie
as "horse of the people," 109–110
Horse of the Year votes, 157–159
impact and legacy of, 100, 173–177, 219–221, 252
mascot for, **70p**, 136, 136n, 154, 187
Muscletone match race, 130–131, 139–146
naming of, 12
nicknames, 98, 100
Palin's confidence in, 70, 115–116, 125, 136, 153, 186, 204, 206
parties in honor of, 186–187, 234–235, 243
personality and presence, 104, 107, 109–110, 150, 167–168, 176, 197, 197n, 228–229, 230–231, 236–237, 245–246
physical features, 69–70, 133
race driver other than Palin, 118
race earnings and winnings (lifetime), 252–253
race season (1934), 59–66, 70–78, 70n, 84
race season (1935), 85–89, 92–94, 103–112
race season (1935)–as Hambletonian contender, 84–85, 87–89, 91–94
race season (1935)–Hambletonian Stake, 94–100
race season (1936), 115–125
race season (1937), 129–131, 133–136, 139–146, 149–154
race season (1938), 161–170, 173–177
race season (1939), 180–182, 185–191
race season comeback (1940), 193–201, 203–206, 209–212
racing against time–team-to-pole with Rosalind, 187–189, 190
racing against time–under-saddle, 210–212, 218
records (overview), 4–5, 189–190
records (1935), 104
records (1936), 117–118, 119, 120–121, 124, 125, 228–231
records (1937), 135–136, 141, 143, 150, 151, 152, 157–158
records (1938), 166, 175–176
records (1939), 180–181, 187–190
records (1940), 189, 194, 209–212
retirement announcement and appearances, 4, 190, 217–222, 228–231, 233–238, 243, 246
retirement film, 236–237
retirement stall and lounge, 238, 241–242, 258–259
retirement turnout, 242–243
Greyhound photos
  Baker and, **101p**
  birthday celebrations, **106–107p**, **113p**
  death and burial of, **109p**, **117p**, **120–121p**
  fan mail, **106p**
  memorabilia, **119p**, **135–137p**
  race season (1934), **12–13p**
  race season (1935), **14–27p**
  race season (1936), **28–31p**, **46p**, **59p**, **66p**
  race season (1937), **33–40p**, **41–44p**, **60–63p**, **68p**
  race season (1938), **45p**, **47–58p**, **64–65p**, **67–68p**
  race season (1939), **69–74p**, **75p**, **79–80p**, **88–89p**, **92–93p**
  race season (1940), **82–87p**
  retirement appearances, **95–98p**, **115–116p**, **124p**, **134p**
  retirement at Flanery Farm, **122–123p**
  retirement at Flanery Stables, **131p**
  retirement stall and lounge, **100–102p**, **102p**, **111–113p**, **127–128p**, **130p**
  retirement turnout, **118p**, **125–126p**, **132p**
  retirement with Dooley, **103–108p**
  under saddle, **83p**, **86p**

INDEX

sleigh ride, **76p**
Gue, Gurney C., 111
Guy Abbey (horse), **3p**, 8–9, 12, 17, 22, 23, 75, 77, 87, 112, 117–118, 211, 257
Guy Axworthy (horse), 9

H

Hambletonian 10 (horse), 23, 29
Hambletonian Stake
    Hambletonian Week in Goshen, 95
    historical context, 74, 83–84
    race contenders (1935), 84–85, 87–89, 91–94
    race day (1935), 94–100
    race day (1936), 118, 128
    race day (1937), 162
    race day (1939), **77p**
Hampson, Gene F., 87
Hanover's Bertha (horse), 64, 76
Hanover Shoe Farm, 38, 100, 142, 189
Hardy Hoover (horse), 254
Harness racing
    cheating and, 49–50
    competition classification, 121–122
    in Europe, 144–145
    foreign horse buyers, 129–131, 130n. See also Muscletone
    Grand Circuit, 42–43, 45, 49–50. See also Hambletonian Stake
    gray as "unlucky" color, 8, 21–22
    growth of, 45, 128–130, 161, 219–221, 252–253
    historical context, 27–35, 28n
    horse sales during Depression, 45
    organizations, 31, 32, 45, 122, 122n, 140, 161, 193, 193n, 253–254
    road racing, 28, 28n
    starting system evolution, 63, 97, 195–196, 219, 253
    sulkies evolution, 32–33
    Thoroughbred racing comparison, 32
    trotters and pacers, 23, 27–34, 56–57
Harness Racing Museum & Hall of Fame, 70n, 95n, **119p**, **128p**, 247, 255, 258, 259
Harper Hanover (horse), 96–97
Harriman, E. Roland, 45, 118, 122n, 161, 193, 193n
Harriman, Gladys, 118
Harris, Dunk, 225–226
Hatch, Dad, 226
Heitbrink, Emma Lou (Putnam), 255
Henrichs, Art, 57
Henry, Marguerite, 245
Henry Rockwell Baker Community Center, **1–2p**, **7p**, 41, 258
Her Ladyship (horse), 186
Hervey, John
    Greyhound fan letters printed by, 154
    on Greyhound-Rosalind team-to-pole record, 188
    on Greyhound's speed, 164, 177
    on Greyhound's training and management, 157–158, 180
    on harness racing turns, 164n
    on Horse of the Year voting, 158
    on mile record, 135–136
    on Muscletone challenge, 140, 145, 146
    on thoroughbred racing, 32, 158, 163
Highland Scott (horse), 118
His Majesty (horse), 62, 82, 85
Hitler, Adolf, 15–16, 128–129, 146
Hogan, John, 59–60, 71
Hollyrood Boris (horse), 210, 212
Homicide Hunter (horse), 252
Horine, Alma, 11
Hotel Baker, **7–10p**, 42, **129p**, **137p**, 244, 258
Hotel Baker Stable. See Baker, Edward John "E. J."; Greyhound; Palin, Septer Faith "Sep"

Hubley, John, 226
Hudson, Scott, 11
Hughes, Ed, 95

I

Indianapolis Speed Sales, 16, 23, 24, 37, 44, 45, 217
Irwin, E. E., 144, 145

J

Johnson, Frances Dodge, **83p**, 210–212, 218, 256
Josephine Knight (horse), 11

K

Kelley, Chet, 42–43, 218
Kenney, E. J., 38
King's Counsel (horse), 221
Knight, Dixie, 10–11, 17
Knight, Grant Lee "Joe," 11, 17, 38
Knight, Henry H.
    Almahurst Farm established by, 17–18, 23
    celebrating Greyhound, **75p**, 153, 186, 187
    death of, 256
    early life, 11–12
    Elizabth repurchased by, 257
    family history, 10–11
    foal crop (1933), 16, 17, 21–23
    Greyhound's breeder, **5–6p**, 10, 12, 18, **80p**
    horse sales by, 24–25, 38, 77, 218
    horses raced by, 88
    KTHBA track run by, 75
    legacy of, 256
Knight, William, 10–11

L

Labrador (horse), 244
Lady Suffolk (horse), 31, 32
Lafoon, Ruby, 123
LaSalle Stable, 38, 60–61, 100
Lawlis, Woodford, 245
Lawrence, John, 31
Lawrence Hanover (horse)
    breeding and confirmation, 37–38, 60, 64
    as Hambletonian contender, 84–85, 87, 91–92, 93, 94
    Hambletonian Stake (1935), 95–100
    Old Glory Sale price, 35–36, 37
    race season (1934), 64, 72–73, 74–77, 84
    race season (1935), 85–89, 91, 93, 105–106, 110–112
    temperament, 61, 85
Leach, Brownie, 110
Lee Hanover (horse), **63p**
Lewis Forrest (horse), 188
Lindy Volo (horse), 62
Long Key (horse), 199
Lou Dillon (horse), 34, 134
Lucre (horse), 71

M

Mack, Gene, 180
Madden, William J., 136
Maiani, Giovanni, **40p**, 130–131, 139–141, 143–146
Marvin, Billy, 48

INDEX

Mary Taylor (horse), 65, 70, 71–72
Maurer, Charlo, 245
McCarthy, Clem, 118
McMahon, Dick, 9, 24
McMahon, Mr., 10
McNamara starting system, 195–196, 219
Menke, Frank G., 176, 236
Messenger (horse), 28–29, 31
Miller, Delvin, 181
Miller, Roy, 136
Miss Almadale (horse), 83
Miss Bertha Dillon (horse), 38
Miss Evergreen (horse), 63–64
Miss Greyhound (horse), 211
Miss Kate B (horse), 124–125
M'Liss (horse), 65
Moody, Hunter, 21–23, 24–25, 56
Moore, Walter, 93, 94
Morgans, 31
Morris, Art, 246
Moser, P. W., 120, 146, 167, 176
Mr. McElwyn (horse), 88
Murphy, Merrit, 194
Murphy, Thomas, 153
Murphy, Tommy, 51, 142
Muscletone (horse), 130–131, 139–141, 143–146
Mussolini, Benito, 128, 139–140, 141, 146

N

Nancy Hanks (horse), 33
Narragansett trotter, 31
Nason, Jerry, 93–94
Nathalie Grey (horse), 211
National Trotting Association, 49, 122, 122n
Nervolo Belle (horse), 11
Nevele Pride (horse), 252
New York Trotting Club, 30–31
Nibble Hanover (horse), 199, 235
Noble Hal (horse), 221
Norris, Dellora Angell, **15p**, **20p**, 41, 257–258

O

Old Glory Sales, 37–38, 43
Owens, Jesse, 129

P

Palin, Septer Faith "Sep"
  background, 34, 47–50
  on Baker's personal qualities, 179–180
  barn fire, 83
  death of, 254
  "early" success of, 51
  Greyhound's purchase, 24–25, 38
  Greyhound's racing career and, 43–45, 47, 55–58. *See also* Greyhound
  on Greyhound's retirement, 221
  on Greyhound's speed (1934), 70
  on Greyhound's speed (1936), 94, 115–116, 125
  on Greyhound's speed (1937), 136, 153
  on Greyhound's speed (1939), 186
  on Greyhound's speed (1940), 204, 206
  on Hambletonian contenders (1935), 94
  Hervey's praise for, 157–158
  legacy of, 253–254
  money won by (1935), 112
  Muscletone telegram and meetings, 140–141, 143–145
  other horses raced by, 104–105, 107
  at parties celebrating Greyhound, 187
  photos, **15p**, **19–27p**, **40p**, **62p**, **68p**, **76p**, **90p**
  post-Baker-Palin stable dispersal, 218–220
  racing other horses, 45, 66, 103–104, 121
  records set by, 112
  training methods, 48, 50–51, 57, 210–212, 218
  veterinary care by, 108
Parshall, Daryl, 72–73
Parshall, Hugh "Doc"
  on Greyhound's speed (1940), 210
  on Hambletonian contenders (1935), 91–92
  Hambletonian winner, **77p**
  Lawrence Hanover transferred from, 100
  license suspension, 197
  Muscletone's trainer, 130
  training and driving Lawrence Hanover, 60–61, 64, 72–73, 74–77
  training and driving Peter Atra, 194–195, 197–199, 204–206
  training and driving Prince John, 71
Paull, Lena D., 154
Pedro Tipton (horse), **24p**, 89, 92–93, 96–97, 99, 108
Peter Astra (horse), 186, 190–191, 193–195, 197–199, 200–201, 204–206, 235–236
Peter Manning (horse), 69, 94, 104, 115–116, 120, 123, 149–154, 189
Peter the Brewer (horse), 64
Peter the Great (horse), 9, 11, 12
Peter Volo (horse), 11, 35, 38, 88, 193
Philips, Steve, 97
Possibility (horse), 48
Prince John (horse), 70, 71–73, 74–75, 88–89, 92
Probst (horse), 146
Putnam, Emma Lou, 189, 226, 228, 244, 255
Putnam, Leone, 3–4, **115p**, 226, 228, 229n, 242, 245–246, 252, 255, 256
Putnam, Verner "Dooley"
  attending Greyhound's races, 120–121, 189, 229, 229n, 248
  background, 225–226, 228
  death of, 255
  as Greyhound's groom, 229–231, 235–238, 242–248, 255
  on Greyhound's presence, 234, 248
  losing Greyhound, 3–5, 251–252
  photos with Greyhound, **95–96p**, **103–109p**, **115p**, **118p**, **127p**, **130–132p**, **134p**

R

Red Gate Farm, 4, **121p**, 186–187, 218, 220–222, 228–229, 238, 244, 252, 257
Reid, Jack, 64, 77
Reno, H. O., 83
Reynolds, W. N., 22, 119, 257
Rockwell, Harriet, 40–41
Roosevelt, Franklin D., 16
Rosalind (horse), **64–65p**, **71p**, **79p**, 118, 121, 128, 150, 161–168, 180, 186, 187–189, 245
Russell, Sanders, 85
Russell, Walter, 255

S

Salem (horse), 70, 71
San Bellini (horse), 122–123
Seabiscuit (horse), 158
Sedgwick, Gordyne, 206
Senator Bedell (horse), 62, 83
Senator Crawford (horse), **94p**, 221, 222, 227, 235, 238

Index

Senator Farm, 43
Sheppard, Lawrence, 142
Shipman, Evan, 88
Shuff, Jesse, 10, 18, 22, 23, 75, 84, 85, 154, 196
Silver King (horse)
    as yearling, 22
    race season (1934), 64, 65–66, 70, 72, 73, 74–75
    race season (1935), 91, 105–106, 108–109
    race season (1935), as Hambletonian contender, 84, 85, 87, 94
    race season (1935), Hambletonian Stake, 95–100
    race season (1936), 116
    race season (1937), **63p**, 144
Simpson, Johnny, 56–57
Sir Henry (horse), 30–31
Sister Mary (horse), 195, 196, 197, 198, 199–200, 204–205, 218
Smiley, Andrew, 78, 81–83
Spencer (horse), 87
Spentell (horse), 195
Spud Hanover (horse), 199
Standardbreds, 29–35. *See also* Harness racing
Stanley Dancer (horse), 252
Star Pointer (horse), 34
Star's Pride, 5
St. Charles (IL)
    Baker's dedication to, **1–2p**, **7–10p**, 41–42, 58, **129p**, **137p**, 244–245, 257–258
    Baker's hometown, 38–39, 40, 123
    Red Gate Farm, 4, **121p**, 186–187, 218, 220–222, 228–229, 238, 244, 252, 257
Stephen A. Palin (horse), 48

T

Tara (horse), **28p**, 116–118, 119, 122–123, 124–125, 129
Taylor, A. A., 119–120
Terhune, Janet, 259
Texas Oil Company, 39
The Auctioneer (horse), 66, 76, 83
The Gem (horse), 62, 83
"The Mare" (horse), 124
The Master (horse), 86, 118
The Saint (horse), 86, 87, 103–104
The Senator (horse), 43, 44, 129
The Viscount (horse), 88
Thomas, Henry, 100, 105–106, 110–111
Thoroughbreds and Thoroughbred racing, 27–33, 34, 49–50
Tilly Tonka (horse), **24p**, 87–89, 91, 92, 94, 95–100, 106
Topgallant (horse), 30–31
Trego (dog), **70p**, 179, 187
Trott, Frank G., 64, 197–198
Trotting Club of America, 140
Trotting Horse Club, 45, 161, 193
Trotting Horse Registry, 31, 32

U

Uhlan (horse), 69, 115, 136, 188
Una Signal (horse), 70
United States Trotting Association (USTA), 122, 122n, 193n, 253–254

United Trotting Association, 122

V

VanGundy, June, 228–229
Van Lennep, Frances Dodge Johnson, 256
Volo Arion (horse), 88
Volo Song (horse), 244

W

Walker, Ken, 258
Wallace, John H., 31–32
Walnut Hall, 77, 257
War Admiral (horse), 158
Warwell Worthy (horse), 89, 97–99, 108–109
Weyker, Marianne, 246
Whippet (horse), 211
White, Ben, 51, **65p**, 118, 121, 134, 161–162, 163, 165, 180, 187
White, Gibson, 118, 121, 162, 245
Williams, Joe, 139–140
Wilson, H. C., 254
Wilson, Pete, **16p**, 78, 86, 98, 99, 100, 105, 106, 107–108, 109, 112
Wingfield, Jimmie
    background, 85, 112
    death of, 255
    driving horses, **73p**, **86p**, 158
    on Grehound's feed and work schedule, 169–170
    on Greyhound's retirement, 220–221
    legacy of, 254–255
    military service of, 254
    post-Baker-Palin stable dispersal, 219, 220
    race season (1936), **46p**, **59p**, 121, 124
    race season (1937), **44p**, **60–61p**, 136, 153, 154
    race season (1938), **48–50p**, **52p**, 174, 176
    race season (1939), 180–181, 185–186
    race season (1940), **85–86p**, **89p**, 194, 201, 203, 204–205, 209–211
    at Red Gate Farm party, **70p**, **75p**, 187
    visiting Greyhound in retirement, 254
Wingfield, Neil, 136n, 254–255
Winnipeg (horse), 123, 186, 244
World War II, 15–16, 128–129, 139–140, 141, 146, 253, 254
Wright, Warren, 7, 16–17
Wright, William Monroe, 7, 8, 9, 12, 211

Y

Yankee Maid (horse), 235, 257
Yount, Pansy, 227

Z

Zigler, Bud, **107p**
Zillah Hanover (horse), 74
Zombrewer (horse), 12, 211, 246

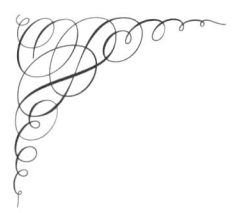 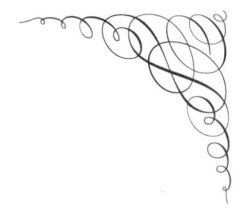

— *in memoriam* —

BOEDY

FEBRUARY 7, 2010 – JUNE 16, 2025

Research assistant, writing buddy, best friend. Boedy and I logged thousands of travel miles together, going as far east as New York, as far west as Montana, as far north as Minnesota, and as far south as South Carolina and Georgia in our nearly 15 years together. His last big trip was to New York and New Jersey, helping me bring Greyhound to life. Thousands of hours in the foaling barn, napping at my feet as I wrote, hiking trails together, or just hanging out—I'm grateful for every single moment. Thank you, my dear, sweet friend. I love you forever.

Cheryl

thank you